# NORTHWARD BOUND

# NORTHWARD BOUND

# BOUND

## THE

## MEXICAN

## IMMIGRANT

## EXPERIENCE IN

## BALLAD

## AND

## SONG

## María Herrera-Sobek

Indiana University Press       Bloomington and Indianapolis

The paper used in this publication meets the minimum requirements of American National Standard for Information Sciences—Permanence of Paper for Printed Library Materials, ANSI Z39.48-1984.

Manufactured in the United States of America

**Library of Congress Cataloging-in-Publication Data**

Herrera-Sobek, María.
Northward bound : the Mexican immigrant experience in ballad and song / María Herrera-Sobek.
p.    cm.
Includes bibliographical references and index.
ISBN 0-253-32737-7
1. Mexican Americans—Music—History and criticism. 2. Folk songs, Spanish—United States—History and criticism. 3. Folk music—United States—History and criticism. 4. Folk music—Mexico—History and criticism.    I. Title.
ML3558.H47  1993
782.42162'6872073—dc20          92-22209
1  2  3  4  5  97  96  95  94  93

*To my brothers*
*José Luis Herrera*
*Patrick Lee Herrera*
*and to my son*
*Erik Jason Sobek*

Wherever you go, you shall go singing.

Huitzilopochtli

Out of poverty, poetry; out of suffering, song.

Mexican proverb

# Contents

x    Contents

# Preface

In 1976 I introduced a course at the University of California, Irvine, entitled "Folklore of the Southwest." In preparation for this course, as I researched the various topics I planned to lecture on, I uncovered a number of folk songs that spoke of the Mexican immigrant experience. Since at that time I was also working on my first book, *The Bracero Experience: Elitelore versus Folklore* (1979), I incorporated the sixteen immigrant songs I had collected for my Spanish class into that volume. From that point on, I became more and more fascinated with the immigrant's perspective, as delineated through folk songs, regarding the historical process of immigration. I recognized that the Mexican immigrant experience remained very much alive and that songs continued to expound upon this experience. Many such songs were being written and sung during this period; my original collection eventually mushroomed to more than 150 folk songs. This collection of Mexican immigrant songs and the analysis of them form the principal contents of this study.

The collecting and researching of Mexican immigrant songs was undertaken in various museums and libraries in both Mexico and the United States. In 1979 I spent the summer in Mexico City working in the archives of the Biblioteca Nacional de México, the Biblioteca de la Ciudad de México, and the Anthropology Museum. I also canvassed during those summer months the many flea markets, bookstalls, bookstores, and record shops in Mexico City. Similar work was done in southern California, Baja California (Tijuana and Ensenada), the Colorado River and Sonora–Yuma area in Arizona, and the Phoenix area. I also obtained documents from various universities through the interlibrary loan office at the UCI library. From all these sources I was able to examine more than 5,000 texts of *corridos* (ballads) and *canciones* (songs) and culled those with immigrant content.

The present work is divided into two parts with thirteen chapters and an introduction and epilogue. The introduction gives the theoretical framework employed in the analysis of the songs, the central thesis posited in this work, and a brief historical overview of both Mexican immigration in the United States and the corrido, or Mexican ballad.

Since a principal point of this study is that Mexican immigrants have been quite cognizant of their role in history, I have endeavored to present the songs in chronological order. I take as my point of departure the year 1848, the date the Treaty of Guadalupe Hidalgo was signed and Mexico lost half its northern territory (what is known today as the American Southwest) to the United States. Part one (chapters 1–6) covers the first period of Mexican immigration, 1848–1964, and part two (chapters 7–13) the contemporary period, after 1964.

Chapters 1 and 2 look at the opening of the Southwest and comment on the two important areas of activity for Mexican immigrants in the second half of the nineteenth century immortalized in corridos: the cattle drive and work and travel on the railroad. Chapter 3 zeroes in on the 1910–1920 era of revolution and war, while chapter 4 discusses the establishment of *colonias*, or Mexican *barrios* (neighborhoods), in large cities in the United States as well as the emergence of the acculturated Mexican American, or *pocho*, in the 1920s. Chapter 5 considers the immigrants' deportation experience during the Great Depression (1929–1939), and chapter 6 centers on the *bracero* (worker) experience (1942–1964).

Part two begins with a chapter on César Chávez, the Farm Workers' Union, and songs of protest (chapter 7). I consider Chávez's movement to be the most important factor in the renaissance of the corrido in the second half of the twentieth century. Since songs with Mexican immigrant content proliferated during the 1970 and 1980 decades, I was forced to take a different strategy in organizing the numerous songs collected for the contemporary period. Instead of ordering the songs in a sequential manner I decided to present them according to the several themes highlighted in the lyrics: border-crossing strategies, racial tension, political issues, love, acculturation, and death (chapters 8–13). Finally, the epilogue comments on the current status of Mexican immigrants songs and their continued production.

The bibliography has three sections: books and articles that served as references for this study, major corrido collections, and a list of songs about the immigrant experience. The song list gives publication data and information about who wrote and who (if anyone) recorded the version presented. For some lyrics, the source is cited parenthetically at the end of the Spanish version. For those lyrics whose source is not cited in the text, details will be found in the song list. Asterisks after a few words in the lyrics denote nonstandard Spanish; these usages are explained in notes at the end of the lyrics.

A shorter version of chapter 8 was published as "Mica, Migra, and Coyotes: Contemporary Issues in Mexican Immigrant Corridos and Canciones," in *Creative Ethnicity: Symbols and Strategies of Contemporary Ethnic Life* (Logan: Utah State University Press, 1991), 87–104. A section of chapter 10 was published in "Mexican Immigration and Petroleum: A Folklorist's Perspective," *New Scholar* 9 (1984): 99–110. A shorter section of chapter 12 was published in "The Acculturation Process of the Chicana in the *Corrido*," *De Colores Journal* 6 (1982): 7–16 and in the *Proceedings of the Pacific Coast Council of Latin American Studies* 9 (1982): 25–34.

I have two principal goals in publishing this study. First, I want to present the songs and their variants virtually in their entirety so that scholars may use them in future research on Mexican immigration to the United States. (Only some stanzas that are repeated have been dropped.) More important, I want to demonstrate that Mexican immigrants are conscious of their position as actors on the stage of American history. By sheer force, will power, and creativity, Mexican immigrants have imprinted themselves on the pages of history and have left us (and indeed are leaving us) their own perceptions, impressions, and subjective feelings about this historical process. Mexican immigrants insist on recording their (and our) history through the main medium at their disposal: the folk song. Other immigrant groups have also left a corpus of immigrant songs. But the Mexican immigrants' corpus covers the widest span of time (nearly a century and a half), and through the songs' lyrics, Mexican immigrants have been able to articulate their own personal viewpoints on a wide panorama of American history. They have left an invaluable record in song that is not only highly interesting but also fairly accurate, as I have endeavored to show by correlating the data in the lyrics with more orthodox historical documents.

# Acknowledgments

I owe a great debt of gratitude to funding sources at the University of California, Irvine, which made this project possible: UCI's Summer Research and Travel Committee; Professor Jaime Rodríguez, Director, Mexico/Chicano Focus Research Program; Professor Eloy Rodríguez, Director, International Chicano Studies Program; the Humanities Research and Travel Committee; Professor Spencer Olin, Director, Focus Research Program for Orange County Studies; Professor Mark Baldassare, Director, Center for Orange County Studies; and Professor Juliet MacCannell, former Director, Women's Studies, and present Director of Focus Research Project on Gender Studies and on Woman and the Image. In addition I gratefully acknowledge funding from the UCI Chicano/Latino Program SCR 43 Grant.

Many hours were spent typing and undertaking research for this manuscript. I want to thank several students for their help in typing the various drafts and for their aid in library research: Cynthia Norte, Bertha Lemús, Sonia Ibarra, Juan Bernal, David Becerra, Jennifer Windburn, Noé Chávez, Esther Soto, Sylm Tieu, and María González. My sincere thanks to past and present Spanish Department secretaries: Geneva López, Tina Metevier, Celia Bernal, and Julie Foraker. A word of appreciation is due to my sister Rosa Herrera and my brother José Luis Herrera for assisting me in locating some of the Mexican immigrant songs included in this volume.

I also want to express my thanks to photographers Herlinda Cansino, Daniel A. Ituarte, and Roberto Córdova. I thank the Huntington Library at San Marino, California, for their permission to publish some of the photographs included in chapter 1.

I warmly thank my son, Erik Jason, and my husband, Joseph, for their love and patience while I worked on this project.

I gratefully thank the following publishers and individuals for permission to reproduce some of the ballads and songs quoted in this book. Every effort was made to locate all possible copyright holders. I apologize for any unintentional omission and will be happy to insert appropriate acknowledgment in any subsequent edition of this book.

EMI Music Publishing for "Al cruzar la frontera," by Eladio J. Velarde and "Desde el México de afuera," by José Vaca Flores.

The University of Illinois Press and Professor Américo Paredes for "Kiansis I," "Kiansis II," "La Pensilvania," "Desde Mexico he venido," "Los mexicanos que hablan inglés," "From a Border Zarzuela," and "Mucho me gusta mi novia."

BMG Edim, S.A. de C.V. for "Corrido al Chicano," by Juan Zaizar Torres; "De bracero a petrolero," by Melesio Díaz Chaídez; "De sangre mexicana," by Francisco Trujillo Cornejo; "El Pocho," by Nicolás González Franco; and "La descriminación," by Juan Manuel Leobardo Pérez Sánchez.

EDIMUSA, S.A. de C.V. for "Lamento de un bracero," by Francisco Camacho Garza; "De las tres que vienen ahi," by Antonio Aguilar Barraza, © Brambila Musical México, S.A. de C.V.; "Fronteras del Rio Bravo," by Benjamin Sánchez Mota, © Brambila Musical Méxicano S.A. de C.V.; "Juan Mojao," by Eulalio Gonález (Piporro), © Acapulco Music, S. A. de C.V.

Discos Cronos for "El mojado fracasado," by Salomón Valenzuela Torres.

Paulino Musical for "El vagón de la muerte," by Paulino Vargas Jiménez.

Alfa Music for "La patera" ("Juana la Patera"), by Magdaleno Oliva Molina.

Ediciones Musicales Rimo, S.A. de C.V. for "Los alambrados," by Marco Antonio Solís.

Dover Publications, Inc. for "El renegado," "El Padre del Charro Vargas," "Los Betabeleros," "Vida, Proceso, y Muerte de Aurelio Pompa," "El ferrocarril," "Los inmigrantes," "La de la nagua azul," and "Los paños colorados," published in Manuel Gamio, *Mexican Immigration to the United States: A Study of Human Migration and Adjustment*, 1971.

Peer Music for "Corrido de Joaquín Murieta," by Felipe Valdes Leal, © 1964 by Promotora Hispano Americana de Música, S.A. All rights administered by Peer International Corporation. International copyright secured. All rights reserved. Used by permission. "La amnistía," by Alfredo Maldonado Gutiérrez, © 1977 by Peer International Corporation. International copyright secured. All rights reserved. Used by permission. "Los mandados," by Jorge Lerma, © 1978 by Peer International Corporation. International copyright secured. All rights reserved. Used by permission. "Los que cruzaron" by Victor Cordero, © 1954 by Promotora Hispano Americana de Música, S.A. Copyright renewed. All rights administered by Peer International Corporation. International copyright secured. All rights reserved. Used by permission.

Texas Folklore Society for the corridos found in Paul S. Taylor's article "Songs of Mexican Migration" in *Puro Mexicano*, Publications of the Texas Folklore Society No. XII, 1935. The corridos include: "Canción del interior," "Corrido de la emigración," "Corrido de Texas," "Los deportados," "Despedida de un norteño," "Efectos de la crisis," "Platica entre dos rancheros," and "De las tres que vienen ai."

Mr. Armando Vallejo, director la casa de la Raza Cultural Arts (Santa Barbara, Calif.), for "El corrido del campesino," by José Luis Carrera; "El corrido del chicano mexicano," by Ramón Fajardo; "El corrido del Rancho Sespe," by Don Jesús Toledo; "El mojado," by M. Unzueta; "Tanto tienes, tanto vales," by Pablo Botello; and "Yo soy mexicano señores," by Juan Manuel Valdovinos.

Inez Cardozo-Freeman, "Corrido de los desarraigados," by Arnulfo Castillo.

Guillermo Hernández for "Radios y Chicanos 1 and 2," "Ramón Delgado," "El rancho donde yo nací," and "En estos tiempos modernos," published in *Canciones de la Raza: Songs of the Chicano Experience.* Berkeley, Calif.: El Fuego de Aztlán, 1978.

The Center for the Study of Comparative Folklore and Mythology at the University of California, Los Angeles, for the corridos: "Corrido de César Chávez," by Lalo Guerrero and "El corrido de César Chávez," "Corrido de la causa, "El corrido del ilegal," and "El corrido de la marcha a Modesto," all by Francisco García and Pablo and Juanita Saludado.

# Introduction

Humans are historical animals. The ability to recall dates, events, images is innate in the human being. It was inevitable, therefore, that eventually a means of recording these images, verbal structures, impressions, and so forth would be developed. Since the imagination is not restricted to one set of vectors but is free to explore various methods of recording phenomena, many devices have been invented and in fact are constantly invented. One of the oldest forms of recording historical events is oral poetry: epic, saga, romance, ballad. It is in this tradition that the Mexican immigrant folk song anchors its historical roots.

The great number of songs depicting the Mexican immigrant experience affords an excellent opportunity to analyze a particular historical phenomenon from a different perspective, the subjective viewpoint of the immigrant and of other persons who identify and are closely associated with that experience. In this study I posit that the immigrant consciously has willed himself or herself into the pages of history in spite of not having the publishing establishment at his or her disposal. This he or she has done through the medium of song and music. It is my contention that ballads *(corridos)* and songs *(canciones)* dealing with the Mexican immigrant experience share one salient characteristic: insistence on the subject, the I, as the most important protagonist in the ballad. The majority of these ballads and songs are structured with a subject as the narrator of the historical event.

## Historical Background

The Treaty of Guadalupe Hidalgo, signed after the United States–Mexican War in 1848, set the international boundary between the United States and Mexico at the Rio Grande, or Río Bravo. This did not mean, however, that the constant crossing between the two countries would cease. On the contrary, the political slicing of the area produced a stream of people that is still much in evidence today. The human migration across the international boundary has fluctuated both in intensity and direction. An effective barometer of the political, economic, and social situation of the two nations, this stream of men and women has changed directions from north to south, from south to north, in an unending flow. At the end of the war of 1848, Mexican citizens residing in what is now known as the American Southwest were granted the right to move to the Mexican side. A good number, not wishing to live under Anglo domination and culture, picked up their belongings and left. Others, seeking a new life, moved across to the new U.S. territory. It was thus that Mexican immigration to the United States began.

The Mexican-origin population residing in the United States today therefore traces its antecedents to two sources: to those Mexican citizens who colonized the Southwest and were here before the Mexican-American War and who chose to remain after Mexico's defeat, and to continued Mexican immigration into the United States after 1848. Great waves of Mexican immigrants, for example, came during President Porfirio Díaz's regime (1880–1910). This was in part due to the dire economic and political conditions existing in Mexico at the time and the job opportunities offered in the United States as a result of the opening of the Southwest. A second great wave of Mexican nationals entered the United States during the Mexican Revolution (1910–1917). The bloody civil war that erupted in Mexico during this period impelled great numbers of middle-class as well as working-class and *campesino* (farm worker) citizens to emigrate to the United States in search of more peaceful conditions in which to raise their children and commence a new life. It was during this period that the *barrios* in the metropolitan areas of the United States began to experience tremendous growth as a result of the incoming refugees. East Los Angeles is a prime example of the type of Mexican-American neighborhood that began to take shape and personality during this period (see Camarillo 1979, Romo 1979, Griswold del Castillo 1979).

It was also during this period that the United States became embroiled in World War I. Mexican labor was particularly needed and encouraged in these critical war years. Under the auspices of the first *bracero* program, Mexican workers responded to the call, arriving in large numbers (see Galarza 1964). As is to be expected, the drive to recruit Mexican workers not only encouraged those able to obtain legal contracts but also stimulated those unable to enter "legally" to cross the border "undocumented" (Samora 1971:33–40).

The so-called Mexican problem began to emerge after World War I as a result of the postwar economic recession and the perception that Mexicans were taking jobs away from U.S. citizens. By the middle of the 1920s strong anti-Mexican sentiment began to be evident. Congress drafted and approved various immigration laws which, in effect, restricted Mexican immigration (Reisler 1976:198–226). When the Great Depression descended in the 1930s, sentiment against the Chicano population had increased to such an extent that large numbers of Mexican nationals and U.S. citizens of Mexican descent were "repatriated" and deported to Mexico without major public protest (see Hoffman 1976 and Carreras de Velasco 1974).

In the early 1940s, with the threat of a second world war looming on the horizon and Latin America increasingly becoming an important element in world affairs, President Franklin Delano Roosevelt instituted a good neighbor policy and began to make a series of friendly advances to the Latin American nations. In 1942, with the United States embroiled in World War II, once more the U.S. government perceived a need for Mexican labor to harvest the nation's agricultural fields and to work in the country's railroads. An agreement was signed on August 4, 1942, by Mexico and the United States to import Mexican workers under what came to be known as the bracero program (see Galarza 1964 and Craig 1971).

The intense efforts to recruit Mexican labor that took place during the 1940s stimulated a totally unexpected response. Millions of Mexican laborers who could not obtain legal contracts crossed the border "illegally" and went to work for U.S. farmers, who welcomed them with open arms, albeit with low wages. By the middle of the 1950s the flow of undocumented Mexican labor into the Southwest was such that the United States felt compelled to institute Operation Wetback to stem the flow. The term *wetback* gained currency at this point because of the exceedingly high number of immigrants who crossed the Rio Grande by swimming it and thus were literally soaking wet when they reached the banks on the U.S. side. The term was disparaging and vividly shows the hostility and low regard the general U.S. population had for these hardworking men and women. The Mexican press used the more neutral term *espaldas mojadas,* which was a literal translation from the English but did not carry the hostility and implications of racial superiority which the term *wetback* denoted. But many Mexicans and Chicanos used the term *mojado* (wetback), which also carried a connotation of disparagement and opprobium as well as feelings of superiority toward the "lowly" Mexican immigrant worker. In California the term *alambrado* (wire fence) arose because Mexican nationals cut holes in the fences constructed along the California-Mexico border. Other terms, such as *norteños* (northerners), *ilegales* (illegals), *enganchados* (contracted workers), *reenganchados* (recontracted workers), *braceros* (manual laborers, from *brazo,* arm), and *indocumentados* (undocumented workers), have also been used at one time or another.

In the 1960s César Chávez achieved prominence as a leader championing the rights of the campesino. He began to organize farmers in California under the banner of the United Farm Workers Union. At this time the United States was embroiled in military combat in Vietnam. Mexican immigration in the 1960s did not make the headlines as it previously had, although the flow of Mexican nationals continued.

In the 1970s, after the Vietnam conflict was settled, the cry against Mexican immigration began to be heard once more. Since then, various proposals and bills have come before Congress to stop Mexican immigration. On May 5, 1987, the Immigration Reform and Control Act of 1986 (popularly known as the amnesty program) took effect. This new law sought to legalize undocumented workers who had lived in the United States continuously for the preceding five years. The legalization process continued for one year. However, even that law was surrounded by heated debate and controversy. No one single piece of legislation on immigration has pleased the majority of people in the United States.

Mexican immigration continued unabated through the 1980s. Economic problems experienced by Mexico, including devaluation of the peso, perhaps increased the flow. But no reliable count is available, since Mexicans continue to cross the border one way or another, as they have done since the seventeenth and eighteenth centuries when they first colonized the Southwest.

All of the historical periods of Mexican immigration are duly recorded in Mexican corridos and canciones. The lyrics presented in this volume are the historical record which Mexican workers or those identifying with their experience have written and left to posterity. In these lyrics one detects the varied emotions of men and women who leave their country for a foreign land. The spectrum of emotions—joy, sadness, homesickness, regret, happiness, love, anger, hostility, hate, surprise, astonishment, hurt, disbelief, eagerness, optimism, pride, and humiliation—is wide and vivid. Through these lyrics we come to know the immigrant as a multidimensional, true-to-life individual, not a stereotypical, abstract entity. We increase our understanding both of the forces that compel men and women to leave their homes, their children, and their beloved land and of the feelings that accompany these drastic actions. And we learn of the contributions these immigrants have made and are making to the development and well-being of the United States. Their involvement in every major undertaking in the opening of the Southwest—the cattle industry, agriculture, railroads, construction, the steel industry, and many, many other areas of endeavor—is faithfully recorded.

## Selection Criteria

Mexican immigrant ballads and songs selected for this study are those that specifically state in their lyrics one or more of the following points: the immigrant is coming from Mexico to the United States; he or she came from Mexico and is now working or residing in the United States; the protagonist or secondary characters are referred to as illegal aliens, enganchados or reenganchados, alambristas, mojados, indocumentados or *sin documentos* (without green cards or legal documents), braceros, espaldas mojadas, or mexicanos. Also included are variants of versions which definitely mention in their lyrics that the protagonists are from Mexico and are emigrating to the United States.

## The Corrido

The trajectory of the corrido from Spanish *romance* (ballad) to its present form has been a topic of concern to scholars. Most experts are in accord in tracing the roots of these songs to the romances brought from Spain during the Conquest in the musical repertoire of the soldiers. Bernal Díaz del Castillo, for example, cites several romances in his monumental *Historia de la conquista de la Nueva España* (1632). But controversy arises when we try to pinpoint the geographic center of the renaissance of this genre in the nineteenth century. Vicente T. Mendoza and Merle T. Simmons trace a direct line of descent and evolution of these folk songs from the Spanish romances in Mexico proper, while the Mexican-American folklore scholar Américo Paredes makes a strong case for a hiatus of corrido production during the seventeenth and eighteenth centuries and a renaissance in the Lower Rio Grande Valley in Texas in the mid–nineteenth century.[1]

Paredes's theory is particularly strong, since many corridos began to surface in the 1850s in south Texas. These early ballads depicted cultural conflict between the encroaching Anglos who took possession of the Mexican territory in 1848 after the Mexican-American War and the Mexican folk who had been living there since the early 1700s. The exploits of Texas-Mexican folk heroes began to be sung in the lyrics of these early corridos. The "Corrido de Gregorio Cortez" became its maximum expression. According to Paredes (1978), the paradigmatic form of the Lower Rio Grande corrido captured the Mexican imagination and was soon used in the structuring of Mexican songs depicting the early guerrilla rebels who fought against the despotic Porfirio Díaz regime in 1880–1910.

When the Mexican Revolution erupted in 1910, the *pueblo* (people) found in the corrido a most appropriate musical form to express the historical events that were unfolding before their eyes. Thus what is considered by scholars the most creative period in corrido production—and indeed, what has become known as the golden age of the corrido—crystallized in 1910–1917. It is during this period that we encounter such classics as "Corrido de la toma de Zacatecas," "Corrido de la muerte de Emiliano Zapata," "Carabina 30–30," "Corrido de la muerte de Pancho Villa," and many others depicting this tumultuous era (see Campos 1962).

Mexico again experienced a tremendous outpouring of corrido production during the Cristero Civil War (1927–1929). A peasant rebellion against the reforms newly institutionalized by the Mexican government that were leveled at the Catholic Church produced numerous corridos depicting the various battles and eulogizing the many heroes who fought in the uprising (see Bonfil 1970).

Corrido production continued during the 1940s and 1950s. But it was not until the 1960s, during César Chávez's drive to organize a farm workers' union, that the genre's form again seemed an appropriate vehicle with which the workers could express their grievances and discontent. A new explosion of corrido texts ensued.

In the 1970s and 1980s corridos continued to surface. Many of these contemporary ballads are primarily concerned with the experiences of undocumented workers. The genre has proved to be a hardy offshoot of the romance and continues to thrive in the present decade.

Although this study is more concerned with historical than with structural analysis, the reader should be aware that the formal structure of the corrido is one of the principal factors that have guaranteed its popularity and longevity. The rhyme scheme is extremely flexible. For example, a four-line strophe may have an ABAC, ABCB, ABBA, or ABBC rhyme scheme. The number of lines in each strophe is likewise variable, although the four-line strope seems to be the most popular.

An in-depth study undertaken by Armand Duvalier on the structure of these ballads yielded six primary formulas and eight secondary ones (see Castañeda 1943:18–19). The primary formulas are:

1. Initial call from the corridista to his or her public
2. Place, date, and name of the protagonist
3. Formula preceding the protagonist's arguments
4. Message
5. Protagonist's farewell
6. Corridista's farewell

The eight secondary formulas are:

1. Reiterated phrase or phrases admonishing the audience not to forget a particular event
2. Exclamation or reflection the corridista makes regarding the events narrated
3. Biographical data and other information pertaining to the protagonist
4. Summary and synthesis of the main theme expressed in the corrido
5. An invitation from the corridista to buy the corrido (that is, the broadside containing the ballad)
6. The ending of the first corrido and an invitation to stay and listen to the second part of the song or to a new ballad
7. Name of the author of the folk song
8. Beginning of the second part of the corrido just sung or beginning of the singing of another corrido analogous to the previous one

Of course, all of these formulas do not occur in each and every song. The Mexican corrido is denominated as such when it exhibits one or more.

## The Canción

The term *canción* is equivalent to the English word *song* and is used to designate any musical composition that has words in it. Vicente T. Mendoza traces its roots to the medieval troubadours and jongleurs of Europe. Basically the canción differs from the corrido in that the latter is characterized by its narrative content. That is to say, most corridos tell a story. The canción, on the other hand, tends to be more sentimental and lyrical (as opposed to epic), leaning toward topics of love and loss of love (see Mendoza 1982).

Since both corridos and canciones incorporate the theme of immigration, I include both genres in this study. The corrido was the preferred mode of expression in the nineteenth and early twentieth centuries for Mexican immigrant songs, while the canción seems to be gaining in popularity in the second half of the twentieth century for this same theme.

# PART ONE
## 1848–1964

# Cowboys and Outlaws

> Cowboys were cattle herders. They were products of two cultures, the Anglo-Saxon from the eastern slopes of the Appalachians, who ran a few cows along the slopes and up valleys, and the Spanish-Mexican Indian of the American Southwest, who ranged his cattle over thousands of semiarid square miles, paying little attention to his herd except for twice-a-year round-ups. These two cultures converged in Texas where they blended into that unique American, the western cowboy.
>
> Charles Zurhorst, *The First Cowboys and Those Who Followed* (1973:9)

*One* History belongs to the conqueror. The vanquished disappear in a sea of half-truths, distortions, and misconceptions. Frequently the defeated serve only as a footnote to those who savor the thrill of victory and reap the hosannas of history. As in other areas of human endeavor the winner-takes-all syndrome prevails, not only on the battlefield but in the cultural and social domains. Such is the story of the well-known cultural artifact which is the cowboy—that archetypal embodiment of what has been imprinted in the popular mind as quintessentially American.

The wholehearted acceptance by the American public of the cowboy as representative of what is wholesome and archetypically American has not extended to a general knowledge or acceptance of the cowboy's origins. The Mexican and Texas *vaqueros* who happen to be the cultural ancestors of the Anglo-American cowboy are hardly acknowledged in textbooks discussing cowboy lore and cowboy history. Mexicans have been all but obliterated from historical texts in the United States except for a line or two commenting on this people's contributions to the American Southwest. It is indeed ironic that politicians of the stature of Mirabeau Buonapart Lamar, who succeeded Sam Houston as president of the Texas Republic, should utter this "definition" of the cowboy: "Rustlers of longhorns who hated all things Mexican" (Zurhorst 1973:12). The truth is that most of the things the cowboy was wearing, using, and even speaking were Mexican. Any serious discussion of the cowboy must include the fact that the cowboy of the American Southwest is a direct cultural descendant of the Mexican vaquero. This chapter discusses the role of the Mexican immigrant as a cowboy and later as a rebel guerrilla fighter as exemplified in ballads about Joaquín Murieta (also spelled Murrieta) and from the perspective of the immigrant himself as he reflexively comments on his role in history through the lyrics of songs.

## The Mexican Vaquero

The Mexican vaquero was a standard entity in many of the great Mexican *haciendas* (large landed estates), particularly in central and northern Mexico. The Texas longhorn, a staple indispensable to the cowboy, arrived with the *conquistadores,* who in their search for gold and fabulous empires trekked across the North American continent in small expeditions. These expeditions failed to discover a second Aztec empire but nevertheless dotted the landscape with the cattle and horses they left behind. The conquistadores often died en route to the mythical golden empire or stumbled back to Mexico City half dead and emptyhanded. But the cattle and horses that remained in the Southwest found the climate and terrain particularly hospitable, and with the passage of time they multiplied many times over.

Not all of the Spanish expeditions were hunting gold. Spanish settlers began to populate all of Mexico and the American Southwest. The area around the tip of what is now Texas was colonized in 1749 by Don José de Escandón. Settlements thrived along the fertile lands bordering the Rio Grande. It is estimated that by 1835 the inhabitants numbered 15,000 while the livestock was nearing three million in the Rio Grande Nueces area (Paredes 1978:9).

Needless to say, the people involved in this incipient cattle industry knew how to work horses and cattle. Horses, cattle, and cowboys formed a basic triad. Mexicans in central and northern Mexico had a strong tradition of working with cattle inherited from the Spaniards. The people of Nuevo Santander likewise shared in this tradition and were later to pass it on to the Anglo-American settlers.

The Lower Rio Grande border was not the only area where cattle, horses, and men mingled and nourished a strong vaquero tradition. The New Mexican landscape was equally noted for its sheep and cattle industry, and songs regarding these activities there abound; "El vaquero" (see Campa 1946:219) and "El Revillón" (ibid.:111–112) detail the dangers and perils of cattle and sheep raising.

In California and other western states another tradition closely related to that of the cowboy developed: the buckaroo. Etymologically the term *buckaroo* derives directly from *vaquero,* and according to Arnold Rojas in his *Lore of the California Vaquero* (1958), the cowboy and the buckaroo share many similarities. There are also important differences between the two traditions: the manner of dress, the style and manner of working the cattle, the manner of saddling the horse (single-rig center fire for the buckaroo, double-rig rim fire for the cowboy). Both, however, trace their ancestry to the Mexicans, since it was the Mexicans who were inhabiting the Southwest when the Anglo-Americans began their incursions.

Some scholars believe that the first contact between Mexicans and the early European settlers in Texas was not characterized by violence or conflict.[1] These scholars posit that initial contact was marked by accommodation and goodwill, the Anglos benefiting greatly from the experience and skill of the original Mexican settlers. Animosity between the two groups eventually emerged when the desire for land and cattle by the ever-growing Anglo population pushing from the east could only be satisfied by expropriation, intimidation, and outright theft.

> After 1848 the Nueces–Rio Grande area—the northern half of the former province of Nuevos Santander—became part of the United States. A foreign Civil War type of carpetbagger moved into the territory to make his fortune, using the Texas legend as his excuse for preying on the newly created Americans of Mexican descent. The Mexican's cattle were killed or stolen. The Mexican was forced to sell his land; and if he did not, his widow usually did after her husband was "executed" for alleged cattle rustling. Thus did the great Texas ranches and the American cattle industry begin. (Paredes 1978:134)

Obliteration of the Mexican from U.S. history began to take place at this juncture. A systematic decimation of the physical presence of Mexicans characterized these early years. The large number of Mexican settlers and continued immigration from Mexico did not allow the extermination of this ethnic group as was done with Native Americans in most parts of the United States. But studied neglect and black legend had the ultimate effect of transforming the Mexican-American population into an invisible minority, a people existing in the United States without being formally acknowledged in history books, mass media, government, public institutions, or socioeconomic structure. It was as if this people had never existed, had not contributed to the development and enrichment of this great country. Only recently, spearheaded by Mexican Americans themselves, has a reevaluation, a revision, of U.S. history and the role of Mexican-American citizens come into being.

Because the vanquished Mexican-American population in the 1850s and thereafter did not have access to established means of communication such as presses and publishing houses, much of the history of these people has been lost. However, there existed within the culture a rich oral tradition. It is within the confines of this splendid oral tradition that the historian can uncover a vast body of information detailing the daily life of the Mexican in the nineteenth and twentieth centuries. Corridos and canciones form a significant corpus of folk songs that provide a glimpse into a long-gone era as well as insights into the experiences of Mexican Americans and their self-perceptions in regard to the encroaching European-American population.

## The Cattle Drive

One of the earliest corridos, "Kiansis I," substantiates the involvement of Mexicans in the cattle industry after the U.S. takeover in the second half of the nineteenth century. A second version, "Kiansis II," speaks of Mexicans in the cattle industry in the twentieth century.

The cattle drive to Kansas is the main theme of these corridos. The trail drive remains in the American consciousness as the embodiment of the opening and settlement of the West. In literature, in folklore, and of course in the most popularizing agents of all, movies and television, the cattle drive and the cowboys who accompanied the cattle epitomize the practical, rugged individualism, the don't-fence-me-in spirit, of the open West and of freedom-loving people. The cattle drivers therefore have been impregnated with large doses of myth and fantasy.

In *The American Cowboy: The Myth and the Reality*, Joe B. Frantz and Julian Ernest Choate, Jr., describe the organization of the trail drive:

> Like any giant undertaking, a trail drive didn't just happen, but in a lesser way required the kind of organization, not to mention imagination coupled with devotion to detail, that goes into staging a military operation. In the spring, the prospective driver, who might be a rancher ranging thousands of acres or just some buyer starting on a shoestring without a square foot of land of his own, would begin to gather a quota of steers. If he were purchasing, he would probably make a round of ranches, buying and obtaining agreements to have the cattle delivered to a certain place where the herd would be made up. The cattle would be bought at so much a head, with a same price being paid for each, regardless of age or conditions or weight, most weights being "guessed off" in those days. When the cattle had been received at the agreed-on point, they would be run through a chute and road branded to show a change of ownership and thereby to prevent misunderstanding up in the trail. (Frantz and Choate 1955:35–36)

The driver hired the trail bosses, or *caporales*, as they are called in Spanish. The trail boss was an extremely important component of the trail drive, for he was in charge of men, cattle, and other gear, which could conceivably represent an investment in the hundreds of thousands of dollars (ibid., 36). Frantz and Choate note that cowboys working for the trail boss were in their late or early twenties. The cowboy's two essential skills were riding a horse and handling wild cattle.

The trails from Texas to Abilene and Dodge City were two of the most important trails. They have been engraved forever in the American imagination through countless works of fiction and songs. Frantz and Choate emphatically state that

> without the Chisholm Trail, without the Western Trail, the American cowboy might never have emerged as a hero of fiction, folklore and balladry. If the place

setting of the cowboy can be narrowed to two locales, those locales belong to the trails from Texas and to the little frontier towns lined across that gritty ironing board known as Kansas. The trail gave the cowboy the stature of a heroic frontiers-man; the cowtown at the end of the trail gave him a bad reputation which in the long run brought him as much fame and appreciation as his more heroic qualities. The trail, the town, and the cowboy are inseparable. (47)

As the Kianais corridos state, the Mexican cowboy formed an integral part of these cattle drives. Américo Paredes, in *A Texas-Mexican Cancionero: Folksongs of the Lower Border* (1976), describes the singing style of the Kiansis corridos: "'Kiansis I' is sung in a slow, reflective tempo, most often by one singer alone and frequently without guitar accompaniment. The rhythm is not the usual one-two-three strum used for the corrido. It is more of a three-one-two-three-one rhythm similar to the colombiana or yucateca strums. 'Kiansis II' has a straight corrido rhythm. It is more often sung by two voices, with guitar accompaniment. It is a canción de grito, the type you would expect to hear at cantinas as well as at ranchos" (53–55).

## Kiansis I

Cuando salimos *pa'** Kiansis
con una grande partida,
¡ah, qué camino tan largo
no contaba con mi vida!

Nos decía el caporal,
como queriendo llorar
—allá va la novillada
no me la dejen pasar.—

¡Ah, qué caballo tan bueno!
todo se le iba en correr.
¡y, ah, qué fuerte aguacerazo!
no contaba yo en volver.

Unos pedían cigarro,
otros pedían que comer,
y el caporal nos decía:
—Sea por Dios, que hemos de hacer—

En el charco de Palomas
se cortó un novillo bragado,
y el caporal lo lazó
en su caballo melado.

## Kansas I

When we left for Kansas
With a great herd of cattle,
Ah, what a long trail it was!
I was not sure I would survive.

The *caporal* would tell us,
As if he was going to cry,
"Watch out for that bunch of steers
Don't let them get past you."

Ah, what a good horse I had!
He did nothing but gallop.
And, ah, what violent cloudbursts!
I was not sure I would come back.

Some of us asked for cigarettes,
Others wanted something to eat;
And the *caporal* would tell us,
"So be it, it can't be helped."

By the pond at Palomas
A vicious steer left the herd,
And the *caporal* lassoed it
On his honey-colored horse.

Avísenle al caporal
que un vaquero se mató,
en las trancas del corral
nomás la cuera dejó.

Go tell the *caporal*
That a vaquero has been killed;
All he left was his leather jacket
Hanging on the rails of the corral.

Llegamos al Río Salado
y nos tiramos *al nado,***
decía un americano:
—Estos hombres ya se
ahogaron.—

We got to the Salado River,
And we swam our horses across;
An American was saying,
"Those men are as good as drowned."

Pues qué pensaría ese hombre
que venimos a *esp'rimentar,****
si somos del Río Grande,
de los buenos pa' nadar.

I wonder what the man thought,
That we came to learn, perhaps;
Why, we're from the Rio Grande,
Where the good swimmers are from.

Y le dimos vista a Kiansis,
y nos dice el caporal:
—*Ora***** sí somos de vida,
ya vamos a hacer corral.—

And then Kansas came in sight,
And the *caporal* tells us,
"We have finally made it,
We'll soon have them in the corral."

Y de vuelta en San Antonio
compramos buenos sombreros,
y aquí se acaban cantando
versos de los aventureros.

Back again in San Antonio,
We all bought ourselves good hats,
And this is the end of the singing
Of the stanzas about the trail drivers.

(Paredes 1976:53–54)
*pa' = *para*
**al nado = *a nadar* (to swim)
***esp'rimentar = *exprimentar* (to experiment)
****ora = *ahora* (now)

Paredes informs us that "Kiansis I" is

> the oldest Border *corrido* that has come down in complete form. . . .[It] records
> the novelty of the first cattle drives to Kansas in the late 1860's and early
> 1870's. Nicanor Torres, one of those from whom I have collected the ballad . . .,
> was five years old when the Kansas Trail opened in 1867. Some of his cousins
> and his older brothers made the trip to Kansas. Hilario Cisneros, born in 1867,
> also gave me the ballad. He learned it from one of the men who made the trip.
> From their accounts it seems definite that "El Corrido de Kiansis" was being
> sung in the Brownsville-Matamoros area by 1870. (141)

The historical authenticity of the event narrated in the corrido is confirmed by
factual data found in archives about the Kansas Trail and by eyewitness
accounts recorded by Paredes.

"Kiansis II" has interesting variations: the girl left behind and the father who just lost a son. As can be expected, the men going off on the long cattle drives worried about their women, who might or might not be faithful. It is interesting to note the philosophical advice offered by the seasoned foreman: "No tengas cuidado, es sola; / que la mujer que es honrada / aunque viva entre la bola." The mother who has just lost a son provides the image of the waiting woman whose husband, son, or lover leaves and never returns. Later corridos reiterate this theme of the waiting kinfolk, particularly the mother or girl-friend.

## Kiansis II

Cuando salimos pa' Kiansis
con una grande corrida,
gritaba mi caporal:
—Les encargo a mi querida.—

Contesta otro caporal:
—No tengas cuidado, es sola;
que la mujer que es honrada
aunque viva entre la bola.—

Quinientos novillos eran,
todos grandes y livianos,
y entre treinta americanos
no los podían embalar.

Llegan cinco mexicanos,
todos bien enchivarrados,
y en menos de un cuarto de hora
los tenían encerrados.

Esos cinco mexicanos
al momento los echaron,
y los treinta americanos
se quedaron azorados.

Los novillos eran bravos,
no se podían soportar
gritaba un americano:
—Que se baje el caporal.—

Pero el caporal no quiso
y un vaquero se arrojó;
a que lo matara el toro,
nomás a eso se bajó.

## Kansas II

When we left for Kansas
On a big cattle drive,
My *caporal* shouted,
"Take good care of my beloved."

Another *caporal* replied,
"Have no fear, she has no other loves.
For if a woman is virtuous,
No matter if she lives among men."

Five hundred steers there were,
All big and quick;
Thirty American cowboys
Could not keep them bunched
together

Then five Mexicans arrived,
All of them wearing good chaps;
And in less than a quarter-hour,
They had the steers penned up.

Those five Mexicans
Penned up the steers in a moment
And the thirty Americans
Were left staring in amazement.

The steers were vicious,
It was very hard to hold them;
An American shouted,
"Let the *caporal* go into the corral."

But the *caporal* refused,
And a vaquero took the dare;
He got himself killed by the bull,
That's all he managed to do.

| | |
|---|---|
| La mujer de Alberto Flores | The wife of Alberto Flores |
| le pregunta al caporal: | Asks of the *caporal*, |
| —Deme usted razón de mi hijo, | "Give me word of my son, |
| que no le he visto llegar.— | I have not seen him arrive." |
| | |
| —Señora, yo le diría, | "Lady, I would tell you, |
| pero se pone a llorar; | But I know that you will cry; |
| lo mató un toro frontino | He was killed by a bull with a blazed face |
| en las trancas de un corral.— | Against the rails of a corral." |
| | |
| Ya con ésta me despido | Now with this I say farewell, |
| por el amor de mi querida, | By my sweetheart's love; |
| ya le canté a mis amigos | I have now sung for my friends |
| los versos de la corrida. | The stanzas about the cattle drive. |

(Paredes 1976:55)

In a third variant, the tragedy of the gored young man is emphasized.

| Corrido de Kansas | Ballad of Kansas |
|---|---|
| Cuando salimos pa' Kansas | When we left for Kansas |
| Con una grande partida, | With a large party, |
| Nos decía el caporal: | The foreman said to us: |
| —No cuento yo con mi vida.— | "I can't guarantee my own life." |
| | |
| Quinientos novillos eran | There were five hundred steers |
| Pero todos muy livianos, | And they were all very wild, |
| No los podíamos reparar | We could not keep them herded |
| Siendo treinta mexicanos. | Being only thirty Mexicans. |
| | |
| Cuando llegamos a Kansas | When we arrived in Kansas |
| Un torito se peló, | A young steer took off. |
| Fue a tajarle un mozo joven | A young boy went to cut him off |
| Y el caballo se voltió. | And his horse fell down. |
| | |
| Cuando dimos visto a Kansas | When we came in sight of Kansas |
| Se vió un fuerte aguacero, | There was a heavy rainshower, |
| No los podíamos reparar | We could not keep them herded |
| Ni formar un tiroteo. | Nor get a shooting started. |
| | |
| Cuando dimos visto a Kansas | When we came in sight of Kansas |
| Era puritito correr, | It was nothing but run, run, run, |
| Eran los caminos largos, | The roads were long, |
| Y pensaba yo en volver. | And I thought about turning back. |

La madre de un aventurero
Le pregunta al caporal:
—Oiga, deme razón de mi hijo,
Que no le he visto llegar.—

The mother of a driver
Asks the foreman:
"Listen, give me news of my son,
As I have not seen him arrive."

—Señora, le voy a decir
Pero no se vaya a llorar,
A su hijo lo mató un novillo
En la puerta de un corral.

"Lady, I will tell you
But don't start to cry,
A steer killed your son
On the gate of a corral.

Treinta pesos alcanzó
Pero todo limitado,
Y trescientos puse yo
Pa' haberlo sepultado.

"Thirty pesos were left over
But it was all claimed for,
And I put in three hundred
To have him buried.

Todos los aventureros
Lo fueron a acompañar
Con sus sombreros en las manos,
A verlo sepultar.—

"All the drivers
Went to accompany him,
With their hats in their hands,
To see him buried."

(Boatright 1946)

## The Outlaw

The outlaw, a staple of western movies, was a principal character in the ongoing drama of the settlement of the West. The Mexican population had its share of outlaws, often referred to as *bandidos,* or bandits. However, while most Anglo-American literature refers to Mexican outlaws as bandits, Chicano historians and more sensitive and knowledgeable Anglo scholars view many of them as rebels, precursors of modern-day Chicano militants. They are perceived as persons making early attempts at resistance and rebellion against what these recalcitrant men felt was an unjust system. Many of these nineteenth-century rebels were not regarded by the Mexican population as criminal elements but were categorized as heroes fighting for their rights and the rights of other Mexicans who were being crushed by Anglo domination.

The U.S.-Mexican War of 1848 produced conditions which were conducive to the germination and proliferation of individuals who refused to accept second-class citizenship and bow to the trampling of their human rights. Eric Hobsbawn, who studied the phenomenon of social banditry, posits that the rise of banditry "may reflect the disruption of an entire society, the rise of a new class and social structure, the resistance of entire communities or peoples against the destruction of its way of life" (1981:23).

In his provocative *Bandits* (1981), Hobsbawn distinguishes between bandit and social bandit. The former is "anyone belonging to a group of men who attack and rob with violence" (11). To the latter belong those "peasant outlaws whom the lord and state regard as criminals but who remain within peasant society, and are considered by their people as heroes, as champions, avengers, fighters for justice, perhaps even leaders of liberation, and in any case as men to be admired, helped and supported" (17). Furthermore, "social banditry of this kind is one of the most universal social phenomena known to history, and one of the most amazingly uniform." Examples may be found in such diverse places as China, Peru, Sicily, Ukraine, Indonesia, Europe, the Arab countries, South and East Asia, and Australia (8). Peasant societies are more likely to produce bandits. More specifically, "social banditry is universally found, wherever societies are based on agriculture (including pastoral economies), and consist of peasants and landless labourers ruled, oppressed and exploited by someone else—lords, towns, governments, lawyers, or even banks" (19–20). Banditry tends to manifest itself in "human societies which lie between the evolutionary phase of tribal and kinship organization and modern capitalist and industrial society, but including the phases of disintegrating kinship society and transition to agrarian capitalism" (18). It is frequently common that where raiding and fending between social units existed, these tended to "pass into social banditry whether in the form of resistance to the rich, to foreign conquerors or oppressors, or to other forces destroying the traditional order of things" (19).

The social conditions delineated by Hobsbawn existed during the major part of the nineteenth century in the American Southwest. Mexico, after its wars of independence (1810–1821), found it difficult to govern its northern territories. Texas became independent from the Mexican nation in 1836. By 1848, after the disastrous war with the States, Mexico had lost half its territory. The changes concomitant with this political restructuring became evident with the rise in power of the new Anglo settlers and colonizers and the consequent oppression of the Mexican population. It was inevitable that these conditions would give rise to many men and women who would challenge this new hegemony and rise up in defiance, men and women who would be "unwilling to accept the meek and passive social role of the subject peasant; the stiffnecked and recalcitrant, the individual rebels. Men who made themselves respected" (Hobsbawn 1981:35); or, as Américo Paredes puts it, men willing to defend their rights "con su pistola en la mano [with their pistol in their hand]" (Paredes 1978). These were men who, perceiving social injustice and having no recourse to legal channels or the law, took matters into their own hands and resorted to outlawry and violence to demonstrate that their rights could not be easily trampled. They were men willing to stand up and fight for their rights and the rights of others.

Such a man was Joaquín Murieta, who, according to the corrido "Joaquín Murieta," was a Mexican immigrant from Hermosillo, Sonora. Murieta came north seeking work in California during the Gold Rush of 1848. To better understand the legend of Joaquín Murieta, a brief glimpse into the era that produced him is in order.

The change in governments after the war proved disastrous to the Mexican population residing in California. As the Anglo settlers moved westward, strong racial animosity surfaced between the two populations. Anglo Americans perceived the Mexican as an inferior creature, a subhuman not worthy of U.S. citizenship. The discovery of gold in 1848 and the expertise of the Mexicans and other Latin Americans competing in the mining of the precious metal contributed to even more hostility and hatred on the part of the Anglo-American miners toward the Latinos.

Leonard Pitt, in his perceptive *Decline of the Californios: A Social History of the Spanish-Speaking Californians, 1846–1890* (1966), describes the beatings and lynchings that exploded after the discovery of gold. A general climate of fear and intimidation prevailed. The Californio, the original discoverer and settler of California, was soon forced to carry a pass "signed by the army's secretary of state, which certified him a bona fide citizen deserving of every right and privilege, of every lawful aid and protection" (51–52).

The danger from Yankee animosity did not stop the hardy Mexican miners from searching for gold. Large contingents from Mexico, especially from the northern state of Sonora where Joaquín was supposedly born, made their way into the High Sierras of California. Pitt comments that

> Sonorans gravitated mainly toward the San Joaquín River tributaries, called the "southern mines" or "dry diggings," especially near a spot named in their honor, Sonora. Here they introduced Yankees to many of the rudimentary mining techniques that typified the early gold rush era. Sonorans somehow could probe the top soil with knives and bring up nuggets, or work the *batea* (pan) to great advantage. Where water was scarce and quartz plentiful, as in the southern mines, they had the endurance to sit for hours and winnow dirt in their serapes, sometimes using their own gargantuan breath if the wind died down. They could also improvise the arastra [sic] (mill), consisting of a mule harnessed to a long spoke treading in a circle and grinding ore under a heavy, flat boulder. Others eventually caught on to those techniques and machines and later surpassed them, but the Sonoras' sixth sense for finding gold and their willingness to endure physical hardship gave them great advantage. Talent made them conspicuously "lucky"—and, therefore, subject to attack by jealous Yankees. (54–55)

And attack they did. The Anglo's desire to eradicate the Mexican presence from the mining scene and indeed from California provoked a systematic harassment of all Hispanic-looking people. Floggings, killings, lynchings, jailings, evictions from mines and lands without compensation, and other atrocities were inflicted on Latinos.

The violence against Mexicanos, Californios, and other Hispanics sprang not just from rednecks and the dregs of society; it was perpetrated by supposedly respectable citizens. Pitt declares that "in truth, a great deal of antiforeigner agitation originated from the most reputable new citizens—

army officers, lawyers, merchants, clergy, and public officials. It is a fact that the first organized and officially sanctioned outburst against Spanish Americans came from three hundred 'white-collar' Yankees" (55).

With the majority of new citizens harboring ill feelings toward Hispanics, it was easy to begin enacting laws that heavily discriminated against them. The most infamous of these laws which seriously harmed the economic interests of Hispanics and exacerbated race relations was the foreign miners' tax passed in 1850 by the California legislature. The law required all "foreigners" involved in mining to buy a monthly mining permit at $20 per month. Mexicans protested vehemently, but to no avail. Pitt describes the increase in tension produced by the implementation of the new tax law:

> An impressive array of 4,000 "aliens"—mostly Mexicans—congregated on outskirts of Sonora on Sunday, May 19, to consider proper action against the law, which was to take effect the next day. To the collector's face the delegation flatly declared that the foreign-born might pay $3 or even $5 monthly, but not $20—a token sum for protection against rowdies, but not an entire fortune nonetheless. . . . Local officials prohibited merchants from selling supplies to any foreign miners and spread an alarm to nearby camps to call up reinforcements for the forthcoming "war" at the county seat. (61)

One hundred and fifty war veterans responded, and soon "one trooper recalls seeing 'men, women and children—all packed up and moving, bag and baggage. Tents were being pulled down, houses and hovels gutted of their contents; mules, horses and jackasses were being hastily packed, while crowds were already in full retreat' " (62).

After these events a number of atrocities began to surface. Both whites and Latinos were murdered, and racial tensions continued to rise. This led to a proposal to

> cleanse the hillside thoroughly of every Spanish American with the least tinge of "evil." The present emergency demanded that "all Mexicans should suffer for a few." The "better element" of Yankee in the southern mines who normally recoiled from drastic measures, now feared that their territory was fast acquiring the reputation of a bandit refuge, which was bad for business, and felt impelled to join the broadside attack. Outshouting one dissenting voice, a large public meeting in Sonora (Calif.) voted to force all foreigners to deposit their arms with Americans and apply for permits of good conduct. All Latin Americans except "respectable characters," were given fifteen days in which to depart. The Mormon Gulch Veterans set to work enforcing these dicta with gusto. (63)

The extremely hostile climate surrounding the mining camps prompted thousands of Mexican and Latin American miners to leave their claims and return to their country of origin or to other parts of California.

Joseph Henry Jackson, in his introduction to Yellow Bird's *Joaquín Murieta* (Ridge 1986), provides an insight into the time, telling of the damage caused by the tax law to Hispanics and the hostile climate it created.

> The law provided what amounts to a confiscatory tax; it stipulated that if they wished to dig for gold, "foreigners" must buy a license which must be renewed, with another fee, each thirty days. It provided further that if the "foreign" miner refused or neglected to renew his license each month, the sheriff should summon a "posse of American citizens" and drive him off. If this occurred, all further mining by such a "foreigner" should be punishable by a heavy fine and imprisonment. As the historian, Hittell, noted, it was an outrageous and oppressive law, rendered even more outrageous by the fact that the tax collectors were to be appointed at the pleasure of the governor, their wages to be retained by them out of the taxes they collected. A more efficient way could scarcely have been devised to encourage persecution of the "foreigners" and corruption of every sort. (xv–xvi)

Jackson concludes that this hostile environment led many Hispanics to commit unlawful acts:

> At first the "foreign" miners tried to fight the law. . . . But the end was inevitable. With Americans flooding the mines as fast as overland caravans and ships could bring them, with every kind of non-Mexican—Germans, French, even men from Australia's convict settlements—defined by consent as "American," the Latin-Americans had no chance. Many went home; there was a large-scale exodus from the mines that year, chiefly of Chileans and Peruvians. Thousands stayed, however, mostly the Mexican-Californians whose homes, after all, were in the state. It was hardly surprising that a good many of these should take to outlawry when it was made so plain to them that they could not look for fair treatment from the *gringo*. Nor is it surprising that such outlaws were aided covertly by sympathetic countrymen. (xi)

The many native Californians, having nowhere to go, were forced to suffer the continued indignities visited upon them by the rowdy, unscrupulous, Spanish-hating sector of the non-Hispanic population. Historians report an "inordinately high number of Mexicans whipped, vanished, or hanged from 1849 to 1860," and the San Francisco *Daily Alta California* reported in 1854 that "it was almost a by-word in our midst, that none but Mexicans could be convicted of a capital offense" (Pitt 1966:70).

Mexicans and other Latin Americans could find no respite from this constant persecution in the state's judicial courts. The pervasive racism and hatred toward the "greasers" dictated harsh treatment in and out of the courts. "Greasers" had public opinion ranged against them from the outset: "To shoot these Greasers ain't the best way," one lyncher is quoted as saying. "Give 'em a fair trial, and rope 'em up with all the majesty of the law. That's the cure" (ibid.:71).

Racial violence and hatred of the Mexican during the Gold Rush culminated in the lynching of a *mexicana*, Juanita of Downieville, in 1851. Juanita, accused of stabbing an Anglo, was summarily "tried" and executed by a lynch mob. Writes Pitt:

> Because Juanita was the only woman lynched in the mines, and one of the few in all frontier history, her case has remained symbolic to this day. Josiah Royce marks it as a nadir of California history, an instance of the depravity *not* of Mexicans, but of "respectable" Americans. Joseph Henry Jackson, after closely studying crime and punishment in the mines, observes that for the "Honest Miner," Juanita's hanging marked the end of innocence: it inaugurated a five-year era in which he either committed crimes or meted out punishment with particular fury and sadism. (74)

This then was the ambiance that gave birth to the legend of Joaquín Murieta, the archetypal social bandit from California. Hobsbawn (1981:20) classifies social bandits into three categories: noble robber, or Robin Hood; resistance fighter, or guerrilla; and avenger. He further details the noble robber's primary characteristics:

(1) The noble robber begins his career of outlawry not by crime, but as the victim of injustice, or through being persecuted by the authorities for some act which they, but not the custom of his people, consider as criminal.
(2) He "rights the wrongs."
(3) He "takes from the rich to give to the poor."
(4) He "never kills but in self-defense or just revenge."
(5) If he survives, he returns to his people as an honourable citizen and member of the community. Indeed, he never actually leaves the community.
(6) He is admired, helped and supported by his people.
(7) He dies invariably and only through treason, since no decent member of the community would help the authorities against him.
(8) He is—at least in theory—invisible and invulnerable.
(9) He is not the enemy of the king or emperor, who is the fount of justice, but only of the local gentry, clergy or other oppressors. (42–43)

The figure of Joaquín Murieta and the legend associated with him perfectly fits Hobsbawn's description of the social bandit. The corrido "Joaquín Murieta" depicts the life and exploits of this early Californio.

### Joaquín Murieta

Yo no soy americano
pero comprendo el inglés.
Yo lo aprendí con mi hermano
al derecho y al revés
A cualquier americano
lo hago temblar a mis pies.

### Joaquín Murieta

I am not an American
But I do understand English.
I learned it with my brother
Forward and backward
And any American
I make tremble at my feet.

Cuando apenas era un niño
huérfano a mi me dejaron.
Nadie me hizo ni un cariño,
a mi hermano lo mataron,
Y a mi esposa Carmelita,
cobardes la asesinaron.

When I was barely a child
I was left an orphan.
No one gave me any love,
They killed my brother,
And my wife Carmelita,
The cowards assassinated her.

Yo me vine de Hermosillo
en busca de oro y riqueza.
Al indio pobre y sencillo
lo defendí con fiereza
Y a buen precio los sherifes
pagaban por me cabeza.

I came from Hermosillo
In search of gold and riches.
The Indian poor and simple
I defended with fierceness
And a good price the sheriffs
Would pay for my head.

A los ricos avarientos,
yo les quité su dinero.
Con los humildes y pobres
yo me quité mi sombrero.
Ay, que leyes tan injustas
fué llamarme bandolero.

From the greedy rich,
I took away their money.
With the humble and poor
I took off my hat.
Oh, what unjust laws
To call me a highwayman.

A Murieta no le gusta
lo que hace no es desmentir.
Vengo a vengar a mi esposa,
y lo vuelvo a repetir,
Carmelita tan hermosa,
como la hicieron sufrir.

Murieta does not like
To be falsely accused.
I come to avenge my wife,
And again I repeat it,
Carmelita so lovely
How they made her suffer.

Por cantinas me metí,
castigando americanos.
"Tú serás el capitán
que mataste a mi hermano.
Lo agarraste indefenso,
orgulloso americano."

Through bars I went
Punishing Americans.
"You must be the captain
Who killed my brother.
You grabbed him defenseless,
You stuck-up American."

Mi carrera comenzó
por una escena terrible.
Cuando llegué a setecientos
ya mi nombre era temible.
Cuando llegué a mil doscientos
ya mi nombre era terrible.

My career began
Because of a terrible scene.
When I got to seven hundred (killed)
Then my name was dreaded.
When I got to twelve hundred
Then my name was terrible.

Yo soy aquel que domina
hasta leones africanos.
Por eso salgo al camino
a matar americanos.
Ya no es otro mi destino
¡Pon cuidado, parroquianos!

I am the one who dominates
Even African lions.
That's why I go out on the road
To kill Americans.
Now my destiny is no other,
Watch out, you people!

Las pistolas y las dagas
son juguetes para mi.
Balazos y puñaladas,
carcajadas para mi.
Ahora con medios cortados
ya se asustan por aquí.

No soy chileno ni extraño
en este suelo que piso.
De México es California,
porque Díos así lo quiso,
y en mi sarape cosida
traigo mi fe de bautismo.

Qué bonito es California
con sus calles alineadas,
donde paseaba Murieta
con su tropa bien formada,
con su pistola repleta,
y su montura plateada.

Me he paseado en California
por el año del cincuenta,
Con mi montura plateada,
y mi pistola repleta,
Yo soy ese mexicano
de nombre Joaquín Murieta.

Pistols and daggers
Are playthings for me.
Bullets and stabbings
Big laughs for me.
With their means cut off
They're afraid around here.

I'm neither a Chilean nor a stranger
On this soil which I tread.
From Mexico is California
Because God wanted it that way,
And in my stitched serape,
I carry my baptismal certificate.

How pretty is California
With her well-laid-out streets,
Where Murieta passed by
With his troops,
With his loaded pistol,
And his silver-plated saddle.

I've had a good time in California
Through the year of '50
With my silver-plated saddle
And my pistol loaded
I am that Mexican
By the name of Joaquín Murieta.

(Sonnichsen 1975:5)

The figure of Joaquín Murieta looms large against the climate of racial prejudice and violence in California society of the 1850s. The legend surrounding this bandido took hold of the imagination, and soon a book appeared narrating this exploits. Historical fact, legend, and myth are intermingled in the story. Some historians deny he existed at all; others believe he did live but that his life was blown totally out of proportion. Jackson believes the legend arose out of a need for a folk hero.

The fictionalized account of Joaquín's "career" as a social bandit appeared at the right time and in the right place: John Rollin Ridge's *Life and Adventures of Joaquín Murieta, the Celebrated California Bandit,* published in San Francisco in 1854. Ridge, a half-Cherokee called Yellow Bird who was working as a journalist for a San Francisco newspaper, became acquainted with the various reports on Joaquín's exploits and recognized the intrinsic appeal of such a legendary character. As Jackson writes in his introduction to the 1986 edition of Yellow Bird's tale,

Joaquín Murieta, the California bandido.

California's folk hero, then, if there was to be one at all, had to be something other than a symbolic enlargement of the patiently grubbing, ragged, homesick, and fever-ridden "honest miner."

There had long been such another figure embedded in folk memory. He was the hero who sprang spontaneously to life whenever and wherever some people had and others had nothing. He was, in every land, the man who took from the rich and gave to the poor. He was, in fact, the Dashing Outlaw in whose person all might find recklessly displayed their own hidden defiances, their private longings to be something both worse and better than they had it in them to be. In California, in the fifties, no such hero existed, but that did not matter. Ridge obligingly fashioned one in the image men have always liked for their folk heroes—that of the romantic Bandit—lent him a name, gave substance, and fixed him forever in print. (Ridge 1986:xx)

Margaret Williams, in her study of "Murrieta," provides a summary of the highlights of Joaquín's life:

In 1848 Murrieta went to California to seek his brother, Carlos; but as he did not find him, he returned to Sonora. Two years later he returned to San Francisco with his wife, Rosita. Within a year his claim at Saw Mill flat on the Stanislaus River, had been seized, and his wife killed; and his brother had been accused of stealing a mule, and despite the effort of [the] marshal, constable of Murphy's Diggings, to prevent the outrage, he was hanged, and Joaquín was whipped as an accomplice in the stealing. Toward the end of the year 1850 the outlaw career of Joaquín Murrieta began. (Williams 1935:5)

The confusion of facts is a result of the many works of fiction that surfaced. Some of these works shamelessly plagiarized Ridge's version, while others took the core information and elaborated on the legend. Four years after Ridge published his supposed biography of Murieta, a dramatic play written by Charles E. B. Howe appeared, entitled *Joaquín Murieta de Castillo, the Celebrated California Bandit* (1858). A copy can be found in the Huntington Library in San Marino, California. This play too was published in San Francisco.

Ridge's fictionalized account of Joaquín's adventures and misadventures did not immediately become a best-seller. However, in 1859 a reworked version appeared in ten issues of the *California Police Gazette*, retitled *The Life of Joaquín Murieta, Brigand Chief of California*, and this serialized text later appeared in paperbound book form (Ridge:xxxiii). This pirated version was responsible for the introduction of Joaquín's wife as "Carmela" instead of "Rosita," as the Ridge version had originally penned it. Furthermore, Carmela is raped and killed, and a second mistress, "Clarina," is introduced. Francis P. Farquhar, in notes accompanying a republication of the *Police Gazette* version, states that a perusal of the numerous books of which Joaquín Murieta is the hero indicates that there are two principal versions of the story, distinguished by the name of the heroine. In one she is Rosita; in the other she is Carmela, or Carmen, supplanted later by Clarina, or Clarita. The significance of this distinction is that there were two "lives" of Murieta which gained currency not long after the bandit's death. All subsequent Murieta narratives, with the exception of Burns' recent book, appear to be derived from one or the other of these versions. (1932:3)

After the publication of the 1859 version, the popularity of the work exploded, reaching into the far corners of Spain and France and traveling back to the Americas to Chile, where it appeared as *El caballero chileno*, supposedly written by a "Professor" Acigar. (There is a controversy over whether Joaquín was Chilean or Mexican. Pablo Neruda, the Chilean poet, wrote a play based on Joaquín's life [see Neruda 1972]. The corrido, of course, emphatically states that he is Mexican.)

The literary reworking of the Joaquín legend continued in the late nineteenth century and was still much alive in the first half of the twentieth century.[2] Jackson informs us that the final stroke of authenticity was supplied by the highly respected historians Hubert Howe Bancroft and Theodore Hittell.

Both took their Murieta from Ridge's fiction. Bancroft used the Ridge "Third Edition" straight, added some even more fanciful dialog and a few quotations from newspaper accounts. . . . Hittell, writing more carefully, admitted that the sources on Murieta were "to a great extent unreliable," but nevertheless quoted Ridge as his authority, with exact page references to the "Third Edition." (Ridge 1986:xxxviii)

Joaquín appealed particularly to the Mexican people because he represented them in their outrage. He was a metaphor for all the frustrations, humiliations, vexations, and injured pride they had received at the hands of the Anglos.

The first stanza of the corrido immediately posits a man in conflict with Anglo society, an "outsider" as perceived by Anglos and as internalized by the protagonist himself: "I am not an American" which can be more appropriately translated "I am not an Anglo." The qualifier "but I do understand English"—signifies "I understand their society, their way of thinking, and *they* don't scare *me; I* scare *them. I* speak their lingo, which is violence." The stanza that follows narrates the tragic events that propelled the protagonist into the violent world of the social bandit: Joaquín's wife and brother were murdered.

These two heinous deeds provide the motive for vengeance. The protagonist will henceforth perceive himself as an avenger of his wife's death and

# Beadle's Dime New York Library

COPYRIGHTED IN 1881, BY BEADLE & ADAMS.

ENTERED AT THE POST OFFICE AT NEW YORK, N. Y., AT SECOND CLASS MAIL RATES.

Vol. XIII.   Published Every Week.   *Beadle & Adams, Publishers,* 98 WILLIAM STREET, N. Y., December 21, 1881.   Ten Cents a Copy. $5.00 a Year.   No. 165

# JOAQUIN, THE TERRIBLE.

### The True History of the Three Bitter Blows that Changed an Honest Man to a Merciless Demon.

## BY JOSEPH E. BADGER, JR.,

AUTHOR OF "EQUINOX TOM," "SOL SCOTT," "ALABAMA JOE," "JACK RABBIT," "CAPTAIN COOL-BLADE," "PACIFIC PETE," ETC., ETC.

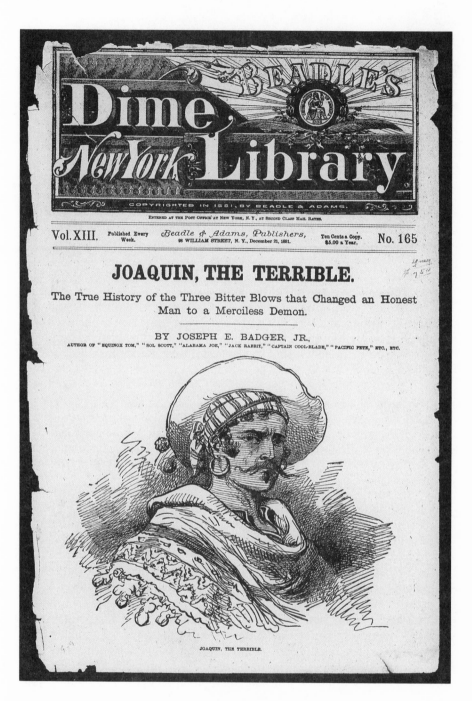

JOAQUIN, THE TERRIBLE.

Installments of the Joaquín Murieta romance.
Courtesy of the Huntington Library.

COPYRIGHTED IN 1882, BY BEADLE & ADAMS.

ENTERED AT THE POST OFFICE AT NEW YORK, N. Y., AT SECOND CLASS MAIL RATES.

Vol. XVI. Published Every Week. *Beadle & Adams, Publishers,* 98 WILLIAM STREET, N. Y., August 30, 1882. Ten Cents a Copy. $5.00 a Year. No. 201

# THE PIRATE OF THE PLACERS; or, JOAQUIN'S DEATH-HUNT.

## BY JOSEPH E. BADGER, JR.,

AUTHOR OF "EQUINOX TOM," "SOL SCOTT," "ALABAMA JOE," "JACK RABBIT," "CAPTAIN COOL-BLADE," "PACIFIC PETE," "OLD '49," "THREE-FINGERED JACK," "THE LONG-HAIRED PARDS," "JOAQUIN THE SADDLE KING," ETC., ETC.

"BEHOLD THE WORK OF JOAQUIN MURIETA! FIRST BLOW, BUT NOT THE LAST!"

honor (she was also raped) and of his brother's defenseless and brutal killing. Ridge renders two key episodes in the life of Joaquín that converted him into an outlaw seeking revenge:

> A band of these lawless men [Americans], having the brute power to do as they pleased, visited Joaquín's house and peremptorily bade him leave his claim, as they would allow no Mexicans to work in that region. Upon his remonstrating against such outrageous conduct, they struck him violently over the face, and, being physically superior, compelled him to swallow his wrath. Not content with this, they tied him hand and foot and ravished his mistress before his eyes. They left him but the soul of the young man was from that moment darkened. (10)

Even though Joaquín tried to get on with his life as best he could after the first episode, a second outrage transpired shortly thereafter:

> He [Joaquín] had gone a short distance from Murphy's Diggings to see a half-brother. The animal [i.e., the horse he was riding] proved to have been stolen, and being recognized by a number of individuals in town, an excitement was raised on the subject. Joaquín suddenly found himself surrounded by a furious mob and charged with the crime of theft. He told them how it happened that he was riding the horse and in what manner his half-brother had come in possession of it. They listened to no explanation, but bound him to a tree, and publicly disgraced him with the lash. They then proceeded to the house of his half-brother and hung him without judge or jury. It was then that the character of Joaquín changed, suddenly and irrevocably. Wanton cruelty and the tyranny of prejudice had reached their climax. His soul swelled beyond its former boundaries, and the barriers of honor, rocked into atoms by the strong passion which shook his heart like an earthquake, crumbled around him. Then it was that he declared to a friend that he would live henceforth for revenge and that his path should be marked with blood. Fearfully did he keep his promise. . . . (12–13)

Ridge's version does not have Rosita die after being ravished. However, in Howe's dramatic play *Joaquín Murieta de Castillo*, Joaquín's wife, Belloro, succumbs from the ordeal and the young husband swears revenge.

> *Joaquín.* Revenge—deep revenge! 'Twill help to cure the sorrow of my soul, and I will have it. (Kneels at the grave.) Oh, by the sainted soul, dear wife, by every spot hallowed to mortality, I swear I will revenge thee! With thy body has gone down into the grave all that is good on earth of me! Revenge, with its unholy light, takes possession of my soul! Oh, thou furies of the eternal shades, aid me, that I may wreak a vengeance on mankind that will make devils laugh. Hecate, embitter my soul! I will not believe in celestial heat; and my soul and body will I give to thee, oh hell, when my vengeance is complete! (Howe 1858:29)

The corrido's third stanza delineates the birthplace of the hero and the reasons for migrating north: gold and riches (the American dream). The protagonist furthermore presents himself as a resistance fighter on the side of the downtrodden: "Al indio pobre y sencillo / lo defendí con fiereza." And the fourth stanza amplifies his role as a noble robber, or Robin Hood, who takes from the rich and gives to the poor.

These first four stanzas, then, define the hero in terms of those three major categories posited by Hobsbawn: the social bandit as noble robber, resistance fighter, and avenger. Walter Noble Burns, in *The Robin Hood of El Dorado* (1932), concurs with the corrido's view of Joaquín vis-à-vis his Robin Hood status:

> The strength of his outlaw organization, the audacity and the rapidity of its movements, and the success of its operations, gave the young leader in their [the Mexicans'] eyes the prestige of a military hero. They called him El Patrio and looked upon him, not as a bandit, but as a leader of revolt against American domination, engaged in righteous war against the injustice and oppression of the Yankee invaders. Murrieta undoubtedly had some such exalted idea of his status and, with complacent egotism, viewed himself as an insurrectionist actuated by motives of patriotism and destined to be the liberator of his people." (34)

Indeed, Murieta, according to various accounts, was admired and esteemed by many and was even considered a gentleman. Williams (1935:5–10) cites many anecdotes that have been recorded with regard to Joaquín's generosity and gentleness toward the opposite sex. According to Williams, Ernest Klette's novel *The Crimson Trail of Joaquín Murrieta* "is based on the bandit's gratitude to a man who had saved his life." Supposedly this was James E. Hunt, a soldier who came to California during the Mexican war and whose memoirs, which include a Joaquín anecdote, are in the California State Library in Sacramento.

Murieta's military prowess is highly extolled by Bancroft. The California historian goes so far as to compare him to a Mexican Napoleon:

> In the Canyons of California, he was what Napoleon was in the cities of Europe; and it is but fair to say that he has visibly displayed a high order of genius. Joaquín would have been no more out of place commanding at Toulon, than Napoleon would have been scouring the Salinas plains. . . . (Bancroft 1888:645–646).

Others, however, view him less kindly. Historian Theodore H. Hittell, in his *History of California* (1897), asserts that "it is not unlikely that the anti-foreign persecution . . . made him much worse than he would otherwise have been, [but] it is not at all probable . . . that he was ever anything but a vicious and abandoned character" (vol. 3:713).

Joaquín the resistance fighter protests against the unjust laws of the land and against the negative reputation he has acquired, for in the credo of Mexican-American rebels, it was a man's right to defend "su derecho, con su pistola en la mano" (Paredes 1978). There is lively speculation about whether Joaquín actually planned to raise an army, take over California, and return it to its former Mexican status (Williams 1935:19–35). Regarding Murieta's ulterior motives for his outlaw activities, Bancroft offers these comments:

> Murrieta had higher aims than revenge and pillage. His continous conflicts with the military and civil authorities, . . . would, in any other country in America have been dignified with the term revolution. . . . It is easy to see that he regarded himself rather as a champion of his country than as an outlaw. (645–646)

Williams points out the similarity of statements by Bancroft and Horace Bell. Bell, in *Reminiscenses of a Ranger, or Early Times in Southern California* (1881), wrote:

> No one will deny the assertion that Joaquín in his organizations, his successful ramifications of his various bands, his eluding capture, the secret intelligence conveyed from points remote from each other, manifested a degree of executive ability and genius that well fitted him for a more honorable position than that of chief of a band of robbers. In any country in America except the United States, the bold defiance of the power of the government, a half year's successful resistance, a continouous conflict with the military and civil authorities and the armed populace, . . . the operations of Joaquín Murietta would have been dignified by the title of revolution, and the leader with that of a rebel chief. For there is little doubt in the writer's mind that Joaquín's aims were higher than that of mere revenge and pillage. Educated in a school of revolution in his own country, where the line of demarcation between rebel and robber, pillager, and patriot was dimly defined, it is easy to perceive that Joaquín felt himself to be more the champion of his countrymen than an outlaw and an enemy to the human race. (107–108, as quoted in Williams 1935:21)

In several of the fictional accounts, including the *Police Gazette* version and Howe's play, Joaquín is portrayed as a revolutionary, a guerrilla fighter. In Howe's work there is a scene explicitly detailing Joaquín's revolutionary plans to redress the wrongs done to Mexico and the Mexicans.

> *Joaquín:* Our organization will be two thousand men when all is completed, and they are in Mexico, Lower California, and in this State. So, you see that I have not been idle. With the money you had when I joined you, and that I have taken since, we have money in abundance. I found twenty thousand dollars in the saddle-bags of one, fifteen thousand with another, and all is deposited in a safe place; and now I intend to send one hundred thousand dollars to Mexico, and then equip fifteen hundred men, and sweep this State from Mokelumne Hill to the Colorado. I intend also to kill the Americans by wholesale, burn their

villages and ranches, and run off all their property so fast that they will not be able to collect an opposing force, and that will finish our work, and my revenge will be completed. And then, my brother, we will be paid, too, for some of the wrongs of poor Mexico. (33)

Although many of the accounts are fictitious, nevertheless they demonstrate, as Williams perceptively points out, that many people viewed Joaquín as "a wronged man, a champion of defeated Mexico" (23).

Robert J. Rosenbaum, in *Mexicano Resistance in the Southwest: The Sacred Right of Self-Preservation* (1986), includes Joaquín Murieta in a chapter called "Social Bandits and Community Upheavals."

> The point about Joaquín Murieta is not whether he existed but the fact that Anglos and *californios* alike thought that he did. Overt hostility between conqueror and conquered was at a high during the early fifties. *Californios* struck out in many ways against the tangible manifestations of Anglo control, and Joaquín focused their anger and resentment. Anglos knew of this hostility, and their eagerness to believe in a criminal mastermind indicates the depth of their fear.

Whatever Joaquín's ultimate plans for the state of California, his career continues its inexorable path of violence and vengeance. He seeks those responsible for killing his wife and brother and encounters them in each Anglo face in the local bars. The carnage left in Joaquín's path increases in logarithmic proportions:

Cuando llegué a setecientos
ya mi nombre era temible.
Cuando llegué a mil doscientos
ya mi nombre era terrible.

Hobsbawn attempts to construct a rationale for the exhibition of such extreme violence on the part of the social bandit.

> Two possible reasons can be accepted, but are not sufficient to account for the role of ultra-violence. The first is that, in the words of the Turkish author Yashar Kemal, "brigands live by love and fear. When they inspire only love, it is a weakness. When they inspire only fear, they are hated and have no supporters." In other words, even the best of bandits must demonstrate that he can be "terrible." The second is that cruelty is inseparable from vengeance, and vengeance is an entirely legitimate activity for the noblest of bandits. To make the oppressor pay for the humiliation inflicted on the victim in his own coin is impossible; for the oppressor acts within a framework of accepted wealth, power and social superiority which the victim cannot use, unless there has been a social revolution which unseats the mightly as a class and elevates the humble. (1981:63)

The social bandit further becomes invincible: "domina hasta leones africanos." He vanquishes man and beast; he is all-powerful, invincible, often invisible. Nothing can stop him—all weapons (pistols and daggers) are ineffective against him. He becomes a terror sent from heaven to avenge the weak against the rich (Mexican against Anglo), and even the hero himself cannot control the situation—it is his destiny to continue the fight until all who commit injustices are punished. So beware: "Ya no es otro mi destino / ¡Pon cuidado, parroquianos!"

The tenth stanza underlines Joaquín's right to be in California and insists that those forces that try to exile or expel him from this land are unjustified to do so, for California belonged to Mexico in previous years. In addition, he dispels any doubts about his national origin, stating in no uncertain terms that he is not a Chilean nor a stranger in this California land but one who belongs here by birthright and God's will.

The eleventh stanza constructs a visual panorama of the man on horseback with his "troop" parading along the streets of California towns. It is a personification of the handsome hero, a matinee-idol figure, sitting tall on his shimmering, silvery saddle, his pistol glistening in the sunlight. The last two lines reaffirm the existence of the hero through his nationality (Mexican) and his name.

Historical records gleaned from newspaper accounts and legislative acts confirm the existence of a Joaquín or, more precisely, various Joaquíns: Muriata, Carillo, Ocomorenia, Valenzuela, Boteller, and Murieti Botello (Pitt 1996:79). Right after the foreign miners' tax was enacted, various episodes of violence, of highway robberies, cattle rustling, and murders, began to take place around Calaveras County. All of these criminal activities were attributed to "Joaquín," and immediately thereafter any atrocious crime was linked to "Joaquín" and his band. He was supposedly spotted throughout the state; often witnesses swore they had seen him at opposite ends of the state. Pitt chronicles the series of events that instigated the Joaquín scare:

> At Big Bar on the Consumnes, six Chinese were killed and robbed of $1,000, and the same amount was taken from other Chinese a short time later; a mail rider was assaulted; the body of a Chinese sprawled in the road, a short distance away lay a mortally wounded American; now a solid camp of Chinese, now a stagecoach, now a lone teamster suffered. The bandidos evidently operated by a rule of thumb: steal everything valuable, leave no witnesses and never stop to fight. (78)

As Joaquín's notoriety increased, so did the fear and anger of the Anglo population. Soon pressure was brought to bear on the state legislature. The *Placer Times and Transcript* reported on May 5, 1853:

> In the Senate, May 4: Mr. Wade presented a petition from the citizens of Mariposa, praying for the organization of a company, to be called California

Rangers, whose duty it shall be to traverse the state, for the purpose of arresting Joaquín and other robbers, and protecting the citizens. Referred to Committee on Military Affairs. (Quoted in Williams 1935:2)

And on May 11, 1853, this note followed:

In the Assembly: Mr. Herbert offered a bill providing that Capt. Love be authorized to raise a company of mounted Rangers for the purpose of capturing the robber Joaquín and exterminating his band was referred to a Select Committee. (Ibid.)

Strong opposition arose from a minority contingent headed by Chairman J. M. Covarrubias. The objections were officially submitted in a report of the Committee on Military Affairs.

Mr. Speaker:
Your Committee on Military Affairs, to which was recommitted Assembly Joint Resolution "requiring the comptroller of State to draw his warrants for five thousand dollars in favor of any person or persons arresting or capturing the robber Joaquín, dead or alive," has considered the same, and a minority beg leave to report: That a desire to prevent the perpetration of outrages and crimes, and to insure the safety of our people in remote and unprotected portions of the State from aggression, as well as the glaring nature and boldness of the atrocities ascribed to this individual, and the failure of all attempts hitherto to capture him, induced them unanimously at first to recommend the adoption of the resolution.
On more mature deliberation, however, it has occurred to a minority of your committee, that the principle involved in offering such reward is not justifiable in equity, nor would it be a safe and effectual mode of remedying the evil which we suffer. To set a price upon the head of any individual who has not been examined and convicted by due process of law, is to proceed upon an assumption of his guilt. The minority of your committee does not think that floating rumor and mere statements of newspapers shall be taken as conclusive evidence either of the commission of crime or of the guilt of one accused. On the contrary, they are confident that the accounts given are somewhat erroneous. Unless the said Joaquín be endowed with supernatural qualities, he could not have been seen at the same time in several places, widely separated from each other. The offer of such reward would be likely to stimulate cupidity, to magnify fancied resemblance, and dozens of heads similar in some respects to that of Joaquín might be presented for identification.
The magnitude of the reward might tempt unscrupulous and unprincipled men to palm off by purchased evidence, the head of another for that of Joaquín, and thus defraud the State Treasury. Besides, the danger of mistaking the identity of individuals in this country is very common. [An example of mistaken identification is offered.]
It may not be improper here to remark, that there are citizens of this state, descendants of ancient and honorable families, who bear the name of Joaquín

Carrillo, the name by which the individual is known for whose capture this reward is proposed to be offered. The minority of your committee will allude to two who are well known to them. One is a very respectable citizen of the County of Sonoma, and the other is the District Judge of the Second Judicial District, who enjoys a distinguished reputation and discharges his high and delicate duties with the integrity befitting an honorable and renowned magistrate.

For the reasons set forth, the minority of the committee recommend that the whole matter be indefinitely postponed.

J. M. Covarrubias,
Chairman

In spite of this articulate opposition, a special force was authorized (twenty to twenty-five rangers for a period of three months) to hunt down "Joaquín." The state governor followed suit and offered $1,000 reward money for the capture of "Joaquín." Captain Harry S. Love was appointed to head this special force (Pitt 1966:79).

On July 25, 1853, just before the three months stipulated for the capture of Joaquín was about to expire, Captain Love appeared with what was purportedly the head of Joaquín. Love and his outfit had come upon a group of Mexicans, a battle followed, and most of the Mexicans were killed. Capt. Love had severed the head of one and cut off the hand of another ("Three-Fingered Jack"), then proceeded to put both head and hand in a jar filled with alcohol, and thereupon based his claim for the reward money. The legislature happily granted Captain Love $5,000, and the head of "Joaquín" became an object of curiosity, exhibited in a world tour (ibid.:82).

A controversy arose as to whether the man who was killed and whose head had been severed was in fact the "celebrated bandit." The corrido does not document Joaquín's death. In this it departs from the typical corrido structure and from numerous extant corridos in which the corrido's hero actually dies. In fact, death is what makes the heroes heroic. The "Corrido de Benito Canales" and corridos on Emiliano Zapata's and Pancho Villa's death are examples. It is therefore rather strange that Murieta's corrido does not end with his death. Perhaps it was because numerous people, including Joaquín's friends, swore that the pickled head was not Murieta's but was that of Joaquín Valenzuela. *Alta California* at the end of August 1853 derisively and at the same time bitterly intimates that the people of California have been the victims of a scam:

It affords some amusement to our citizens, the reading of the various accounts of the capture and decapitation of the "notorious Joaquín Murieta." The humbug is so transparent that it is surprising any sensible person can be imposed upon by the various statements of the affair which have appeared in the prints. The act of the Legislature authorizing the raising of a company "to capture the *five* Joaquíns, to wit, Joaquín Carillo, Joaquín Murieta, Joaquín

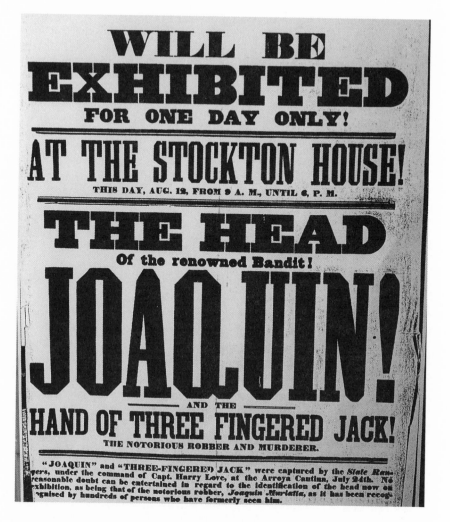

Poster advertising exhibition of the head of "Joaquín."
Courtesy of the Huntington Library.

Valenzuela, etc. etc." was in itself a farce, and these names were inserted in order to kill the bill. Does a Legislature soberly and seriously outlaw five men, without previous conviction, and whose name not one member in ten had ever even heard mentioned? Joaquín Murieta is undoubtedly a very great scoundrel, though the old saying that "the devil is not as black as he is painted" will apply to him as well as to the gentleman below. At the time of the murder of General Bean, at the Mission San Gabriel, Joaquín Murieta was strongly suspected of the crime, and efforts were made to arrest him, but he managed to escape; and since then every murder and robbery in the country has been attributed to

Joaquín. Sometimes it is Joaquín Carillo that has committed all these crimes; and then it is Joaquín Murieta, and then Joaquín something else, but always Joaquín. . . .

A few weeks ago a party of native Californians and sonorians started for the Tulare valley, for the express and avowed purpose of running mustangs. Three of the party have since returned, and report that they were attacked by a party of Americans, and the balance of their party, four in number, had been killed; that Joaquín Valenzuela, one of them, was killed as he was endeavoring to escape, and that his head was cut off by his captors as a trophy. It is too well known that Joaquín Murieta is not the person killed in Rancho Pass. The head recently exhibited in Stockton bears no resemblance to that individual, and this is positively asserted by those who have seen the real Murieta and the spurious head. All the accounts wind up by recommending the continuance of Love's company in service. All right. The term of service was about expiring, and although I will not say that interested parties have gotten up this Joaquín expedition, yet such expeditions can generally by traced to have an origin with a few speculators. (Quoted in Williams 1935:4)

There is a possibility, of course, that the corrido was written before Joaquín Murieta was assassinated. Most corridos are written soon after the newsworthy events take place. There is a controversy regarding when the Joaquín Murieta corrido came into being. Some date the corrido to the 1930s. The version cited here was in fact recorded in the 1930s. However, it was no doubt in existence before that time.

The corrido has similarities with the fictionalized accounts published after the 1850s. For example, the corrido's second strophe states:

Cuando apenas era un niño
huérfano a mi me dejaron.
Nadie me hizo ni un cariño

In Howe's *Joaquín Murieta*, Joaquín, in a soliloquy uttered as he walks about in his cell in a monastery, laments his fate as an orphan:

*Joaquín:* Oh, how gloomy these walls have become. They are hateful to my sight; for their darksome shadow finds a reflection in my thoughts, and makes me sick at heart. What is there to cure this despondency? What thought, of all I have read, will aid to dispel these fancies of a home and a mother? I never knew what it was to have maternal care; yet how precious is the very sound of such a name as mother; and when connected with the name of home, oh how much more dear it sounds! There's a charm in the words that thrills through me as if they were electricity. Mother and Home! From all that I have heard of them, I have learned to long for their existence; yet I know them only by name. The blessed of this world are those who have a mother, to counsel with and guide them, and the roof-tree to shelter them in hours as dark as mine. Mother and Home! I never tire repeating them. (10–11)

There are several other points of convergence between the fictional works and the corrido: the name Joaquín Murieta, nationality (Mexican), hatred for the Anglo, orphaned as a child, brother killed, wife tortured and murdered, Joaquín a miner, Joaquín as a Robin Hood figure, prize on Joaquín's head, gallant and charming, vengeance as the primary motive, Joaquín punishes the guilty, is indomitable, invincible, fearless, conscious of his conquered status as a Mexican, and he has troops.

The corrido therefore serves as another document that can be added to the great puzzle that was the dashing Robin Hood figure of Joaquín Murieta. Both as a historical figure and as a mythic legendary figure, he represents the turmoil and hostility that existed between Mexicans and Anglos in California during the Gold Rush era and the period of colonization. History, legend, and myth have converged to stimulate the powers of the creative imagination and to provide a mythic figure with which to ponder the deeds of men who populated the nineteenth-century West.

# Working and Traveling on the Railroad

*Two* Corridos and canciones with railroad themes can be classified in two major categories: those that tell of the experiences of Mexican immigrants working on the railroad and those that mention the train as the mode of transportation the immigrants used in their travels to, from, and across the United States.

### Working on the Railroad

A comprehensive history of the thousands of Mexicans who participated in the building and maintenance of railroads in the United States has yet to appear. Some history books, such as Robert Edgar Riegel's *Story of the Western Railroads from 1852 through the Reign of the Giants* (1926), fail to mention Mexican labor participation in the construction of railroads. Careful research, however, demonstrates that from the very beginning of railroad building in the Southwest, Mexican nationals as well as Mexican Americans participated in construction crews, in maintenance crews, and as section hands. Such major concerns as the Southern Pacific and Santa Fe railroads used Mexican workers in the 1880s; these crew members played a significant role in the completion of the various lines crisscrossing the Southwest (Kirstein 1977:2).

Mexican involvement in railroad construction increased in the last decade of the nineteenth century. The continued iron-fisted rule of dictator Porfirio Díaz produced rampant poverty in Mexico. The peonage system in the huge haciendas provided no means for upward mobility and, as a matter of fact, condemned the majority of the Mexican population to slavelike conditions. Many a peon, mistreated by his *patrón* (boss) or the many henchmen working for the patrón, sought to escape this oppressive environment. Since the hacienda system was the prevailing form of farming during the nineteenth century in Mexico and since the *hacendados* (hacienda owners) were frequently related to each other either through marriage or by blood, the peon could not escape to another estate. The system afforded no means of relief from this exploitative situation. Often a recalcitrant peon was brought back to his *patrón* by a neighboring hacienda owner who did not approve of peons leaving their patrones. And frequently after a peon was returned to his hacienda he was summarily executed. The only possible form of escape from these intolerable conditions was to emigrate north to the United States.

According to folk-song lyrics, conditions in the Mexican nation during the Porfiriato regime served as a significant "push" factor in propelling Mexicans to leave their homeland. These conditions precipitated the flow of humanity streaming northward in search of a better life, and what at first was a trickle turned into a swift current in the twentieth century. On the other hand, the "pull" factor in the Mexican immigration equation was the increasing demand for unskilled workers, particularly by growers and railroad companies. The contribution Mexican immigrants made in the development of the transportation networks of the United States cannot be overestimated. The Santa Fe and Southern Pacific railroads in particular benefited from Mexican labor in the last two decades of the nineteenth century, and Mexican worker involvement in the construction of the tracks did not stop but continued in the ensuing years (see Reisler 1976 and Jones 1945).

The first decade of the twentieth century experienced a tremendous increase in Mexican labor for railroads. As Chinese immigration (and later Japanese as well) continued to be restricted both by popular demand and by Congress, Mexican workers continued to supplant the hardworking Chinese work gangs. In 1909 the Dillingham Commission, which was researching the immigrant population in the United States, found that "for the past several years Mexicans had done most of the railroad construction work in Southern California, Arizona, New Mexico, and Nevada (Reisler 1976:3). The U.S. Bureau of Labor Statistics also reported that in 1909 "nine western railroads employed about 6,000 Mexicans in their 'maintenance of way' departments" (3). More than 70 percent of these workers had lived in the United States fewer than five years, and 98 percent were aliens (17–18).[1] They constituted 17 percent of the total maintenance force on these nine lines. Indeed, the Mexican workers were establishing for themselves an enviable reputation as hardworking, peace-loving, and dependable persons.

In part, of course, it was the lower wages paid to Mexicans that made them so attractive. The *Annual Report of the Commission-General of Immigration* published by the U.S. Department of Commerce and Labor in 1911, perhaps unaware of the racist connotations therein, reported that

> Mexican labor met an economic condition demanding laborers who could stand the heat and other discomforts of that particular section. The peon makes a satisfactory track hand, for the reasons that he is docile, ignorant, and nonclannish to an extent which makes it possible that one or more men shall quit or be discharged and others remain at work: more he is willing to work for a low wage. (Quoted in Reisler 1976:4)

Indeed, the differential in wages was the significant factor contributing to the general attractive nature of Mexican labor. The Southern Pacific Railroad was paying Greeks $1.60 per day and Japanese $1.45, while the Mexican worker earned only $1.25 (4).[2]

When the prospective railroad worker sings of the *enganche*—literally, the "hook"—he is referring to practices of recruiting agencies that went into Mexico and actively solicited Mexicans to work for railroad companies in the United States. It was during the first decade of the twentieth century that employment agencies recruiting Mexicans on a large scale started to proliferate. These agencies were large and

> efficiently organized enterprises with headquarters in El Paso, the most important point of entry for Mexicans. Their personnel met penniless aliens at the border, provided them with provisions, and transported them to railroad lines in need of labor. A few of the larger agencies did not charge the worker a placement fee. This was true of the Holmes Supply Company and the Manning Company, which secured workers for the Santa Fe and the Southern Pacific Railroads, respectively. These two concerns recruited labor in return for the exclusive privilege of furnishing the workers with food, clothing and other necessities. (Reisler 1976:8)

These agencies functioned as restaurateurs and furnished supplies to the track workers, who paid dearly for their services. The agencies, on the other hand, profited handsomely from these enterprises. One agency, "which placed about 13,000 Mexicans annually, charged a total of $6.00 per man for its employment and supply services, while incurring a maintenance expense of only $1.00 per person. It thus earned a net profit of $65,000 for the year" (9).[3]

The lucrative nature of the business stimulated the growth of these recruiting agencies, and with their proliferation came instances of exploitation and fraud. The significant expansion of contracting agencies brought eager and unscrupulous agents who stopped at nothing in their efforts to entice Mexican immigrant workers into the United States. Reisler states that "agents traveled to the interior of Mexico to spread the news of high American wages. In some cases they apparently hired workers within Mexico and arranged their rail passage to the border" (9).[4] The Mexican worker in this manner was indeed "hooked" like a fish into coming to the United States by promises of easy wealth to be made. The contractors were called *enganchistas* ("those of the hook"), and "to go on a contract" was to go on an enganche.

No doubt the image of the United States as the land of milk and honey began to take root with the vivid descriptions the overenthusiastic enganchistas made to prospective workers, or *enganchados*. The myth that money could be swept off the streets in "el Norte" (the USA) took hold in the Mexican imagination and has persisted to the present day. The glowing descriptions of the United States offered by enganchista agents to open-mouthed, eager workers were so effective that in 1911 the commissioner-general was compelled to make a statement regarding "undue stimulation of Mexican immigration by labor agents" (Reisler 1976:10). The railroad companies were the principal concerns that set up recruiting agencies in Mexico.

The railroad companies who secured Mexican workers through contracting agencies or otherwise frequently lost them, however, to farms, for these employers, in an effort to keep workers, paid slightly higher wages. The railroads were forced to continually replenish their supply of workers by importing more and more Mexican nationals. It is estimated that in 1900 there were 103,393 Mexican-born persons in the United States; by 1910 the number had climbed to 221,915, and by 1920 it had reached 486,418.

The strife and disruption caused by the Mexican Revolution (1910–1917) propelled hundreds of thousands of Mexican nationals to leave their homeland during the second decade of the twentieth century. The United States, a nation that prided itself on being a nation of immigrants, began to be concerned and apprehensive about overpopulation, particularly in regard to the darker-skinned immigrants who were streaming in. The Immigration Act of February 5, 1917, sought to curtail this flow of human migration. Among its various provisions were an $8.00-per-head poll tax and a literacy test. This law of course affected the Mexican immigrants, since many were from the peasant class and possessed neither the necessary funds nor the required literacy. Mexico at the beginning of the century had an illiteracy rate as high as 85–90 percent. The Immigration Act of 1971 threatened to put a substantial brake on Mexican immigration.

This state of affairs did not last long, however. The United States entered World War I in April 1917, and a strong need for Mexican workers was immediately perceived by farmers, railroad companies, and other industries. The 1917 act had provisions for flexibility in its implementation, and pressure by various concerns was building. Secretary of Labor William B. Wilson on May 23, 1917, declared Mexican agricultural workers exempt from "all tests imposed by the Immigration Act of 1917" (Cardoso 1979:18). This exemption was extended to railroad track workers in July 1918. This waiver, initiated at the specific request of agricultural and railroad concerns as well as other industrial sectors, lasted until March 1, 1921. Under the waiver, it is estimated, as many as 250,000 braceros entered the United States legally between 1918 and 1920 (19).

The wartime boom and prosperity came to a standstill after the war. By 1922 the United States found itself in the throes of a recession. A decline in Mexican immigrant workers ensued. Luckily this postwar recession lasted only a short period; by 1923 the U.S. economy was again experiencing healthy growth.

The wartime experience of using Mexican workers had left a positive impression on employers, and when the economy began to rebound, there arose a clamor from the industrial, railroad, and farming sectors in the United States to import more Mexican workers to meet their needs. The call did not go unanswered; it is reported that by March 1923, 1,000 Mexican immigrants were arriving daily in the border town of Juárez. Many of these workers found their way to various railroad companies operating in the Southwest and Midwest. It was in the 1920s that Mexican nationals became the predominant labor force working on the railroads. Reports show that 32,000 to 40,000 Mexicans were working for the Southern Pacific; Union Pacific; Western Pacific; Atchison, Topeka, and Santa Fe; Colorado and Southern; and Denver and Rio Grande Southern. This number constituted 75 percent of the total labor force working on track maintenance for these railroads (Reisler 1976).

The Great Depression of the 1930s stymied Mexican immigration into the United States. As a result of deportation efforts, Mexican migration out of the United States was actually greater than the inward flow. This period will be the central subject of chapter 5, for it is an important period in Mexican migratory movements, one that is thematized in many corridos. There is, however, very little material on the theme of Mexican labor on the railroads during this traumatic era. Suffice it to say that scholars are in agreement that Mexican workers, both in agriculture and on the railroads, were not completely eliminated but continued to thrive, even though the general climate in the United States was extremely hostile to Mexican workers. Farming concerns and railroad enterprises maintained their need for Mexican workers even during the years of the Great Depression.

The decrease in Mexican migration to the United States did not last long. Devastation due to acts of war in Europe stimulated economic conditions in the United States in the late 1930s. Possible U.S. participation in these events led to a fear of a massive labor shortage in farm fields as well as in industry.

The threat of war brought on the Selective Service and Training Act to recruit young men into the military. It also reduced the farm population by an estimated 280,000 from April 1, 1940, to January 1, 1942 (Kirstein 1977:12). But the armed services' vigorous recruitment of young men was not the sole factor in farm personnel reduction. Contributing to the abandonment of agricultural work were the various defense industries that cropped up as a result first of the threat and then of actual U.S. entry into World War II. On June 5, 1941, the *New York Times* reported that "323,900 additional workers will be needed by the shipbuilding industry, 408,400 by aircraft, 291,600 by machine tools and ordinance and 384,400 by other defense industries. . . . It is estimated . . . 227,500 unskilled workers will be needed" (quoted in ibid.: 13). As a result of the obvious labor shortage, a new call for Mexican labor began to be articulated at the highest levels of U.S. government.

Mexican government officials were understandably reluctant to initiate a mass migration program after the mass deportations of Mexicans during the 1930s. However, the Japanese attack on Pearl Harbor and the formal U.S.

declaration of war produced a change in governmental agencies vis-à-vis Mexican labor. Various U.S. agencies began to investigate the feasibility of importing Mexican labor: the War Manpower Commission, the Department of Agriculture, the Department of State, the Department of Labor, the Department of Justice, and the Office of the Coordinator of Inter-American Affairs. These agencies found a great need for Mexican labor, and in June 1942 a request was made to Mexico (13).

Requests for labor again emanated principally from two sources: agriculture and the railroad companies. As early as 1941 the Southern Pacific in San Francisco "had requested permission from the Immigration and Naturalization Service to bring in Mexican workers for temporary maintenance of way work" (Jones 1945:26). These requests were firmly opposed by organized labor. However, the lack of a stable labor supply, as perceived by the railroad companies, became more and more acute as U.S. involvement in the war effort continued. The pressure on the War Manpower Commission from the powerful railroad companies eventually began to produce the results railroad concerns wanted. On April 29, 1943, duly authorized representatives of the U.S. government together with authorized representatives from the Mexican government reached an agreement covering the recruiting of nonagricultural workers in Mexico. The War Manpower Commission was the agency responsible for the smooth working of the program. It in turn appointed the Railroad Retirement Board to carry out the recruitment and placement aspects of the program. Among the Railroad Retirement Board's duties were assisting in processing the paperwork required; negotiating with contracting railroads as to need for workers, provisions for transportation, and provisions for housing; disseminating information to workers regarding contracts, wage rates, housing, medical care, and other pertinent information; and compiling accurate records on workers, i.e., deaths, illnesses, departures. In the initial stages of the program the recruitment process took place in the National Stadium in Mexico City; in April 1944 it was transferred to San Luis Potosí, then to Queretaro. The number of workers contracted was 20,000 in June 1943. By March 1944 the quota had reached 40,000, and a few months later (July 1944) it topped 50,000 (28).

The process of recruiting the workers involved the concerted effort of various agencies. Recruitment for railroad workers was basically the same as for agricultural workers. Representatives from the Immigration Service, the U.S. Health Service, the Railroad Retirement Board, and the Mexican government filed a request with the Mexican governor of a state. Upon approval by the governor of the state, local authorities authorized the number of men recruited. Eligible Mexican men were screened, given a preliminary examination, and sent to the recruiting center for further processing. Few were turned down.

The contracts issued to the workers involved the two governments or their duly authorized representatives (the chairman of the War Manpower Commission for the U.S.) and each individual bracero. These contracting documents were written in Spanish and English. Several guarantees and privileges for the workers were stipulated in each contract. For the railroad workers, for example, each carrier provided free transportation to and from Mexico. The bracero hired for railroad work was to be exclusively employed in this capacity. He was to work the "same number of hours per week as other workers engaged in similar occupations" (Jones 1945:31). The Mexican worker was

> guaranteed a minimum of 75 percent of full time employment in each pay period and at least 90 percent of full time employment during the period for which contracted. This guarantee does not apply, however, if the worker is unable or unwilling to work and is offered employment. Workers who are unable to work receive no compensation and are subject to the same charge as other workers for their board unless they are hospitalized at other than their own expense. Time lost through sickness or injury can be counted towards meeting the guarantee if employment is available. The worker is to be paid, however, a regular hourly rate for each hour that the Employer fails to offer him an opportunity to work as required by the contract. (31)

The Mexican railroad track worker proved so valuable that on October 2, 1943, the War Manpower Commission requested to the Board of Immigration Appeals the transfer of railroad track workers to other areas of railroad employment: shops, stores, mechanical duties, roundhouse, blacksmith, bridge repair, building maintenance, station, terminal and storehouse duties, assistant foremen, and machine operators. In addition, workers were requested for maintenance of equipment and stores and for maintenance of way and structures and transportation groups (33).

There was a possibility of contract renewal for the worker, and a specific grievance machinery was set up to deal with complaints from the workers. In practice, however, the Mexican consuls and labor inspectors were the agents most used by braceros who had complaints or unsatisfactory conditions (35). There were various problems related to this issue. The Mexican labor inspectors (total of ten) had vast territories to cover, and visits to the camps were infrequent. In addition,

> the workers often do not know to whom they should direct their inquiries or complaints. The Mexican consulates are the only places which most of them know about where they can go for information and these are often far distant. The employment offices are often for the most part only open during regular working hours and are usually located at some distance, so that it is necessary for workers to lose a day's work to even make an inquiry in person. Very few of the personnel of these officers, except where a large resident Spanish speaking population exists, understands Spanish, so that efforts at interpretation or at giving information are often ineffective. (35)

In spite of various problems associated with the labor program, Mexican nationals kept coming to the United States. Statistics plainly point out the importance of Mexican railroad workers during the 1940s war effort.

Up to December 31, 1944, a total of 80,273 Mexican Nationals had been recruited and 80,137 had been delivered to employers for railroad work. On that date 32,978 were available for work within the United States and up to that time 47,159 worker's contracts had expired: 26,208 contracts had been renewed; and 25,257 workers had terminated their contracts before the termination of their employment period. The Immigration Service had reported the repatriation of 43,694. (39–40).

Over half the workers were employed by two main carriers—the Atchison, Topeka, and Santa Fe and the Southern Pacific railroads. Mexican nationals worked in various parts of the United States. States with heavy bracero concentrations included Montana, Washington, Oregon, California, Nevada, and Arizona. However, Mexican railroad workers were also found in New York City, Cleveland, Chicago, Dallas, and Kansas City (40).

Several Mexican songs deal principally with Mexicans working on the railroads during the latter half of the nineteenth century and the first half of the twentieth century. After that time, few corridos or canciones specifically mention men coming to work on the railroad tracks. This does not mean that Mexican involvement in the building and maintenance of railroads ceased. Both documented and undocumented workers continued to work on the railroads. However, after midcentury the songs for some reason ceased to depict the travails of working on the railroad and concentrated more on the adventures and misadventures of working in the agricultural fields of the United States.

The folk song "Los reenganchados a Kansas" details the trip of Mexican workers who crossed "illegally" *(de contrabando);* their destination: Kansas City. Awe is expressed regarding the speed of the huge machine—the train. A strong sense of pride in being Mexican is expressed. The Mexican work gang is entreated to join the Union (the USA), but the men refuse, stating: "Lo que es la unión no entramos; / Esta no es nuestra bandera; / Porque somos mexicanos." Evidently the Mexican workers confused the term *union* (*sindicato* in Spanish) with *unión,* i.e., the United States, *la unión americana.*

## Los reenganchados a Kansas

Un día tres de septiembre,
Ay, ¡qué día tan señalado!
Que salimos de Laredo
Para Kansas reenganchados.

## The Kansas Contractees

One day the third of September,
Oh, what an unusual day!
We left Laredo
Signed up for Kansas.

Cuando salimos de Laredo
Me encomendé al Santo Fuerte,
Porque iba de contrabando
Por ese lado del puente.

Uno de mis compañeros
Gritaba muy afanado:
—Ya nos vamos reenganchados
A trabajar al contado.—

Corre, corre, maquinita,
Por esa línea del Quiri,
Anda a llevar este enganche
Al estado de Kansas City.

Salimos de San Antonio
Con dirección a Laguna,
Le pregunté al reenganchista
Que si íbamos para Oklahoma.

Respondió el reenganchista:
—Calle, amigo, no suspire,
Pasaremos de Oklahoma
Derechito a Kansas City.—

Ese tren a Kansas City
Es un tren muy volador,
Corre cien millas por hora
Y no le dan todo el vapor.

Yo les digo a mis amigos:
—El que no lo quiera creer,

Que monte en el Santa Fe,
A ver a donde está al amanecer.—

Al llegar a Kansas City
Nos queríamos regresar,
Porque nos dieron el ancho
con las veras de alinear.

Decían los americanos
con muchísimo valor:
—Júntense a los mexicanos
Para meterlos en la unión.—

Nosotros le respondimos:
—Lo que es la unión no entramos,

When we left Laredo
I committed myself to the strong saint,
Because I was traveling illegally
On that side of the bridge.

One of my companions
Shouted very excitedly:
"Now we are going under contract
To work for cash."

Run, run, little machine,
Along that Katy line,
Carry this party of laborers
To the state of Kansas City.

We left San Antonio
In the direction of Laguna,
I asked the contractor
If we were going through Oklahoma.

The contractor replied:
"Quiet, friend, don't sigh,
We shall pass through Oklahoma
Right straight to Kansas City."

That train to Kansas City
Is a flying train,
It travels one hundred miles per hour
And they don't give it all the steam.

I say to my friends:
"Let him who doesn't want to believe
      it
Get aboard the Sante Fe
Just to see where he will be by morn-
      ing."

On arriving at Kansas City
We wanted to return,
Because they gave us a raw deal
With the aligning bars.

The Americans said
With a great deal of bravery:
"Round up the Mexicans
So as to put them in the union."

We replied to them:
"We will not join this thing called
      union,

| | |
|---|---|
| Esta no es nuestra bandera. | This is not our flag |
| Porque somos mexicanos. | Because we are Mexicans. |
| | |
| Si no siguen molestando | "If you continue to bother us |
| Nos vamos a regresar | We will go back |
| Para el estado de Tejas | To the state of Texas |
| Donde hay en que trabajar.— | Where there is work." |
| | |
| Agarramos un volante, | We got in a flier (gang). |
| Trabajamos noche y día, | We worked night and day, |
| Nomás deban de comer | All they gave us to eat |
| Solo purita sandía. | Was plain watermelon. |
| | |
| Vuela, vuela, palomita, | Fly, fly, little dove, |
| Párate en ese manzano, | Light on that apple tree. |
| Estos versos son compuestos | These verses are composed |
| A todos los mexicanos. | For all the Mexicans. |
| | |
| Ya con ésta me despido | Now with this (verse) I bid farewell |
| Por la flor del granado, | With the flower of the pomegranate, |
| Aquí se acaba cantando | Here one stops singing |
| Los versos de los reenganchados. | The verses about the contractees. |

(McNeil 1946:11)

Two additional variants appear: "Los inmigrantes" in Manuel Gamio's *Mexican Immigration to the United States* (1971), and "Versos de los enganchados" in Frank Goodwyn's collection "Versos populares de los Tejanos de habla española" (1944). "Los inmigrantes" situates the point of departure in El Paso, Texas, and the point of destination in Louisiana. However, verses identical to variant one appear in different stanzas. The arduous work of railroad building is described. Many regret having come.

| **Los inmigrantes**<br>**(Los enganchados)** | **The Immigrants**<br>**("The Hooked Ones")** |
|---|---|
| El 28 de Febrero, | On the 28th day of February, |
| Aquel día tan señalado, | That important day |
| Cuando salimos de El Paso | When we left El Paso, |
| Nos sacaron reenganchados. | They took us out as contract labor. |
| | |
| Cuando salimos de El Paso | When we left El Paso |
| A las dos de la mañana, | At two in the morning, |
| Le pregunté al reenganchista, | I asked the boss contractor |
| Si vamos para Louisiana. | If we were going to Louisiana. |
| | |
| Llegamos a la laguna | We arrived at Laguna |
| Sin esperanza ninguna | Without any hope. |

Le pregunté al reenganchista
Si vamos para "Oclajuma."

I asked the boss
If we were going to Oklahoma.

Por esas líneas del Kiri
Pasa un tren muy volador
Corre cien millas por hora
Y no le dan todo el vapor.

Along the line of the Katy
There goes a very fast train.
It runs a hundred miles an hour
And then they don't give it all the
    steam.

Y el que no lo quiera creer

And he who doesn't want to believe
    it,

No más que venga a montar
No más que monte de noche
Lo verá donde va a dar.

Just let him get on board.
Just let him get on board at night;
He will see where he gets to.

Llegamos el día primero
Y al segundo a trabajar
Con los picos en las manos
Nos pusimos a trampar.

We arrived on the first day
And on the second began to work.
With our picks in our hands
We set out tramping.

Unos descargaban rieles
Otros descargaban "tallas"
Y otros de los compañeros
Echaban de mil malhayas.

Some unloaded rails
And others unloaded ties,
And others of my companions
Threw out thousands of curses.

Los que sabían el trabajo
Iban recorriedo el "llaqui"
Martilleros y paleros
Echándole tierra al "traque."

Those who knew the work
Went repairing the jack
With sledgehammers and shovels,
Throwing earth up the track.

Ocho "varas" alineadas
Nos seguíamos disgustados
A los gritos y las señas
Nos quedamos paraos.*
Mas valiera estar en Kansas
Que nos mantenga el gobierno.

Eight crowbars lined up,
We followed disgusted;
To shouts and signs
We remained indifferent.
It would be better to be in Kansas
Where the government would main-
    tain us.

Decía Jesús el Coyote
Como queriendo llorar
Valía más estar en Juárez
Aunque sea sin trabajar.

Said Jesús the Coyote,
As if he wanted to weep,
It would be better to be in Juárez
Even if we were without work.

Estos versos son compuestos
Por un pobre mexicano
Pa' ponerlos al corriente
Del sistema americano.

These verses were composed
By a poor Mexican
To spread the word about
The American system.

(Gamio 1971:84–86)
*paraos = parados (standing up)

"Versos de los enganchados" reiterates the hardships involved in railroad construction. Notice the Hispanicized English words: Katy, "Keri"; tramp, "trampar"; jack, "Yaque"; track, "traque," etc. This corrido seems to be a shorter version of "Los inmigrantes." The second and third strophes, present in "Los inmigrantes," are missing.

## Versos de los enganchados

El veinte y ocho de Febrero
¡Ah, que día tan señalado!
Cuando salimos de El Paso,
nos sacaron reenganchados.

Por esas líneas del Keri
pasa un tren muy volador,
corre cien millas por hora
y no le dan todo el vapor.

Y el que no lo quiera creer,
no más que venga a montar,
no más que monte de noche,
lo verá donde va a dar.

Llegamos el día primero,
y al segundo, a trabajar.
Con los picos en las manos,
nos pusimos a trampar.

Unos descargaban rieles;
otros descargaban tallas
y otros de los compañeros
echaban de mil malhayas.

Los que sabían el trabajo
iban recorriendo el yaque.
Martilleros y paleros
echaban tierra al traque.

Ocho varas alineadas
nos seguíamos disgustados
A los gritos y las señas
nos quedábamos parados.

Decía José Morelos
como queriendo llorar:
—Valía más estar en Juárez,
aunque sea sin trabajar.—

## Verses of the Hooked Ones

On the twenty-eighth of February
That very important date
When we left El Paso,
They took us out as contract laborers.

Along the line of the Katy
There goes a very fast train,
It runs a hundred miles an hour
And then they don't give it all the
    steam.

And he who doesn't want to believe it
Just let him get on board
Just let him get on board at night
He will see where he gets to.

We arrived on the first day
And on the second began to work.
With our picks in our hands,
We set out tramping.

Some unloaded rails
And others unloaded ties
And many of my companions
Spit out thousands of curses.

Those who knew the work
Went repairing the jack
With sledgehammers and shovels,
Throwing earth up the track.

Eight crossbars lined up
We followed disgusted;
To the shouts and signs
We remained indifferent.

Said José Morelos
As if he wanted to weep:
"It would be better to be in Juárez,
Even if we were without work."

| Estos versos son compuestos | These verses were composed |
|---|---|
| por un pobre mexicano | By a poor Mexican, |
| pa ponerlos al corriente | To spread the word about |
| del sistema americano. | The American system. |

(Goodwyn 1944:415–435)

The corrido "De 'El traque' o de 'El lavaplatos' " introduces the element of humor and self-satire. The immigrant worker begins to see his experience in the United States and the hardships encountered in a humorous light. Expecting to go to Hollywood to become a big movie star, he ends up working in a railroad gang, later picking tomatoes and hoeing beets. He seems to enjoy the traveling and lists the many states in which he has traveled.

## De "El traque" o de "El lavaplatos"

Soñé yo en mi juventud ser una estrella de cine
y un día de tantos me viene a visitar jolibud (Hollywood).

Un día, muy desesperado de tanta revolución,
me pasé para este lado sin pagar la inmigración.

    ¡Qué vacilada! ¡Què vacilada!
Me pasé sin pagar nada.

Al llegar a la Estación me tropecé con un cuate
y me hizo la invitación de trabajar en "El Traque."

Yo, "El Traque," me suponía que sería algún almacén;
y era componer la vía por donde camina el tren.

¡Ay, qué mi cuate! ¡Ay, qué mi cuate!
¡Cómo me llevas pa' "El Traque"!

Cuando me enfadé de "El Traque" me volvió a invitar aquel
a la pizca del tomate y a desahijar betabel.

Allí gané indulgencias caminando de rodillas,
haciéndoles reverencias tres o cuatro y cinco millas.

¡Ah, qué trabajo tan mal pagado
Por andar arrodillado!

Mi cuate, que no era maje, él siguió dándole guerra
y al completar su pasaje se regresó pa' su tierra.

Y yo hice cualquier bicoca y me fui pa' Sacramento;
cuando no quedó ni zoca, tuve que entrarle al cemento.

¡Ay, qué tormento! ¡Ay, qué tormento!
es el mentado cemento.

Echéle tierra y arena a la máquina batidora a
cincuenta centavos hora hasta que el pito no suena.

Recorrí pueblos y villas, todo aquello es un primor:
pasé por San Luis Misuri y llegué a Nueva York.

A Ditroi, Michiga fui, ciudad de los automóviles:
visité sus maquinarias, ¡ay, qué bonito, señores!

Me pasé al Polo Norte, vi sus grandes pesquerías:
vi las focas y gaviotas que yo no las conocía.

Me pasé a California vi sus grandes naranjales,
y vi sus grandes plantíos de grandes jitomatales.

Bonito Estado de Texas por su grande agricultura
pues tiene mucho plantíos. Todo es una hermosura.

Los gringuitos me decían:—Te gusta lo que aquí ves
Era de los mexicanos y ahora de nosotros es.

Adiós, los americanos, también las americanas.
quédense, adiós, ya me voy; voy a ver mis mexicanas.

¡Bonito Estados Unidos, que no me quedó ni duda!
Me vine de por allá por el amor de mi Julia.


## About "The Railroad Worker" or "The Dishwasher"

I dreamed in my youth of being a movie star,
And one fine day I came to visit Hollywood.

One day, desperate from all the revolutions,
I crossed to the USA without paying the immigration:

What a joke, what a joke!
I crossed without paying a cent!

Upon reaching the station, I came upon a "brother⁻
And he invited me to work for the "Traque."

I thought "El Traque" was a fancy department store,
But it was fixing the rails where the trains run.

What a "brother"! What a "brother"!
How you took me to the railroad tracks!

When I got tired of "El Traque" he invited me again
To pick tomatoes and to hoe beets.

There I earned indulgences crawling on my knees,
Bowing down for three, four, and five miles.

What poorly paid work
For working on one's knees!

My friend, who was no dummy, he stuck to it,
And when he had his fare he returned home to Mexico.

I worked for almost nothing and left for Sacramento.
When I had nothing left I had to work on the cement.

What a horrible torment! What a horrible torment!
That so-called cement.

Pour some dirt and sand into the cement mixer.
Fifty cents an hour all day 'til the whistle blows.

I traveled through towns and cities, and all is such beauty.
I went through St. Louis, Missouri, and arrived at New York.

I went to Detroit, Michigan, the city of the automobile.
I visited the assembly lines, how beautiful it was!

I went on to the North Pole; I saw all its great fisheries.
I saw all the seals and swallows, which I have never seen.

I traveled on to California and saw all its orange groves
And all the huge tomato farms.

The beautiful state of Texas with its huge agricultural farms
Has many crops; all is very beautiful.

The gringuitos would ask me, "Do you like what you see?"
It used to belong to the Mexicans, now it is all ours.

Good-bye, American men, good-bye, American girls.
I take my leave, good-bye, I am going to see my Mexican girls.

The United States is beautiful, there is no doubt about that.
I had to return home, because of my love for Julia.

(Herrera-Sobek 1979:90–91)

## Traveling by Train

Porfirio Díaz's single-minded vision of an industrialized, "European" Mexico did establish a railroad system, which by 1910 boasted various linkages from Mexico City and other important cities in the central part of Mexico to the northern provinces and most significantly to the United States.

Diaz's cadre of *científicos* (scientists), impregnated with the French philosophy of positivism, exhibited an unshakable belief in progress through science and technology. This predisposition to industrialize Mexico facilitated the promotional activities of European and North American entrepreneurs who were eager to exploit the rich raw materials found in Mexico. To facilitate the process, great railroad networks were built between 1880 and 1910. The railroads penetrated into those regions rich in mineral and oil resources. Generous concessions were granted to foreign investors to promote incoming capital. Thus Mexico's railroad system was born out of the necessity to transport the mineral and petroleum products and other raw materials to Europe and the United States.

A side effect, which some historians view as the most important contribution the railroad system offered Mexico in the late nineteenth and early twentieth centuries, was the impulse it gave to internal migration. Huge numbers of peasants could be rapidly transported, at low cost, from their home villages and ranches to the new centers of industrial and agricultural production.

Undoubtedly the new railroad network did bring profound social changes to Mexico. The relative ease of traveling by train as opposed to other systems such as stagecoach stimulated in the villagers a desire to visit relatives, to travel to those faraway cities they had only heard of; it made it possible to leave the village behind in pursuit of better wages, of a better life. Travelers reaching the small towns and villages brought news and stories of other lands, of other ways of viewing the world; and as returned emigrants came back for a visit, they too encouraged relatives and friends to leave the confines of their village and seek a better life.

The changes in travel brought about by the Mexican railroad system are seen by contrasting figures cited for travelers in 1887–1892 with those for 1910. In the earlier period, travelers totaled 393,371 by stagecoach, 1,509,297 by horseback, and 4,113,267 by foot. In 1910, 15,821,921 passengers traveled by train.

Several corridos detail the traveling experiences of Mexican men and women going to the United States and using the train as a mode of transportation. The image of the train became a standard motif of early twentieth-century immigrant ballads, serving two major functions—one visual-aural, the other psychological—in the artistic elaboration of the songs.

First, the train image provided a dynamic visual construct that moved rapidly through the landscape of Mexico. As the train moved on its designated trajectory in the song, it served as a focus for other sensory stimuli. There was the "vapor," or steam, serving as a secondary image to the primary one of the moving object (the train). The "vapor" too "traveled" upward and eventually was lost in a faraway horizon, having dissipated in the vast infinitude of space. The train in an analogous manner disappeared behind a mountain or in the unending Chihuahua desert as it left the village. There was also the sensory stimuli of the whistle. The train rushed into the small towns and cities of Mexico accompanied by a loud, piercing whistle. This warning sound communicated to the waiting passengers that it was time to depart. The train's departure again called for the whistle at full blast. Long after the train had been lost to sight its whistle could still be heard echoing in the vast expanse of the horizon. Of course, since the train was the major form of transportation in the first quarter of the twentieth century, the train stations were a major focus of activity. The train stations were a moveable feast of visual experience: there were the throngs of people crowded excitedly near or around the train, where many of the anxious, happy relatives greeting incoming passengers; worried mothers and children seeing their husbands or fathers off to an unknown area or country; vendors hawking their food; excited children crying—all this contributed to the general visual-aural imagery complex associated with the train.

A second important factor associated with the train motif is the psychological response this particular machine had on both the passenger and the people left behind. The train moved slowly at first as it inched away from the station and the town. This provided the passenger with precious additional minutes to say good-bye. As the train slowly rolled away, passengers poked their heads out the windows for a last, lingering look or handshake. Once the train left town, it picked up speed and for the passenger of those days it seemed to be literally flying through the Mexican terrain. The excitement was of course intense, and it is expressed in the lyrics of the songs.

The train, however, is viewed with suspicion in the corrido "El ferrocarril," for it literally swallows up young men in the dark of the night, never to be seen again.

| El ferrocarril | The Railroad |
|---|---|
| La máquina pasajera | The fleeting engine |
| no puede hacer cosa buena | Can't do anything good |
| porque "oscurece" en su case | Because at dusk it is at home |
| y amanece en tierra ajena. | And at dawn in a strange country. |
| | |
| ¡Ay! ¡que dolor! | Oh! What sadness! |
| Tendrían los mexicanos | The Mexicans will have to see |
| al ver el ferrocarril | The railroad train |
| que traen los americanos. | That the Americans bring. |

| | |
|---|---|
| La máquina chiquitita | The very littlest engine |
| es la que ha quedado aquí | Is the one that has been left here, |
| y la quieren llegar | And they expect it to go |
| hasta San Luis Potosí. | As far as San Luis Potosí. |
| | |
| Oigan y oigan | Listen, listen, |
| el ferrocarril bramar. | To the train puffing; |
| el que lleva a los hombres | The train which carries men away |
| y nunca los vuelve a traer. | And never brings them back again. |

(Gamio 1971:92–93)

But from the point of view of many young men, the train is an exciting means of escape from their villages. The excitement and the emotional high are evident in the lyrics of "De 'La maquinita' o de 'El emigrante,' " collected by Vicente T. Mendoza (1964:383).

## De "La maquinita" o de "El emigrante"

¡Corre, corre, maquinita; corre por esa ladera
parece que voy llegando a orillas de la frontera.
¡Adiós, parientes y hermanos! ¡Adiós, todos mis amigos!
¡Quédense, adiós, ya me voy a los Estados Unidos!
Salí de San Luis Potosí con rumbo de Aguascalientes.
¡Adiós, todos mis amigos! ¡Adiós todos mis parientes!
Al pasar por Zacatecas vi todos sus minerales,
que desde el tren se devisan chorreadores de metales.
Al pasar por el Torreón me dijo una chimolera:
—Mañana sale el enganche, ¿qué dice, señor, me lleva?
—No, señora, no la llevo, porque tengo a quien llevar.
Y hasta lloraba la ingrata que no se quería quedar.
Pasé por Gómez Palacio, vi el Río del Tlahualilo,
(que) riega los algodonales de San Pedro y de El Higo.
Desde ahí se devisa Parras de la Fuente,
donde hacen muy buen vino y también muy buen aguardiente.
De Parras pasé a Chihuahua hasta que llegué a Juárez,
y al día siguiente salí a visitar sus ramales.
Trabajé en el "Traque," me dieron mi provisión;
desde allí me *juí** bajando Estación por Estación.

*jui = *fui* (went)

## About "The Little Machine" or "The Immigrant"

Run, run, little machine, run through those farms!
It feels like we are getting nearer the border.
Good-bye, relatives and brothers, good-bye, my friends!

I take my leave, good-bye, I'm going to the United States!
I left San Luis Potosí, headed toward Aguascalientes.
Good-bye, my friends, good-bye, my relatives!
While passing through Zacatecas, I saw all its mineral richness.
You can see even from the train the glitter of metal everywhere.
While passing through Torreón, a young "chick" told me,
"Tomorrow the enlisted crew leaves; will you take me with you?"
"No, my dear lady. I cannot take you, because I have someone else already."
And the poor girl cried and cried for she did not want to stay behind.
We passed through Gómez Palacio; I saw the Tlahualilo River,
Whose waters irrigate the cotton fields of San Pedro and El Higo.
From there you can see Parras de La Fuente,
Where good wine is made and good firewater.
From Parras we passed through Chihuahua and then we arrived at Juárez.
And the next day I went to visit the local sights.
I worked on the railroad line; they gave me groceries.
From there on I stopped at every station.

Much is written about the male Mexican immigrant; most studies have
concentrated on men who crossed the border legally or illegally. However,
women have always been a part of that large exodus of human beings who
have sought to make the United States their home. Five variants of one
corrido focus on the relationship between the male immigrant and his girl.

The first variant, "De las tres que vienen ai," dramatizes an exchange
between an eager young man cajoling his girl to "stop your corn-grinding"
and "let us go to the United States." The two embark on their northward
journey, and the song further narrates how time was spent to make the
journey a pleasant one. Again the train is the preferred mode of transportation. This corrido, although devoting its theme to traveling back to the United
States with the girl, obliquely makes a protest in the seventh and eighth
quatrains. In the seventh, the immigrant requests not to be sent to Texas or
Oklahoma because "they hate those who drink"—the reference is to their
being dry states. In the eighth, the traveler pokes fun at his fellow travelers
who, while busy talking, are relieved of their luggage by an enterprising thief.

## De las tres que vienen ai [ahi]

¿De las tres que vienen ai
cual te gusta, valedor?
Esa del vestido rojo
me parece la mejor.

Vente, deja de moler,
ya no muelas nixtamal.
Vamonos pa' Estados Unidos,
que allá iremos a gozar.

## Of the Three Approaching Girls

"Of the three that are coming,
Which one do you like, partner?"
"That one in the red dress
Seems to be the best."

"Come on, stop your corn-grinding;
Don't grind corn any more.
Let's go to the United States,
For we shall enjoy ourselves there."

| | |
|---|---|
| Chatita, ai viene el tren; | "Sweetheart, here comes the train; |
| óyelo que *silvos** da. | Listen to the whistling it does. |
| No más un favor te pido, | One favor of you I ask, |
| que no llores por allá. | Don't cry while we are away." |
| | |
| Querido ya voy cansada, | "Dear, I am already tired, |
| y apenas aquí es Torreón, | And we are only in Torreón; |
| para no sentir casancio, | So that I shall not feel fatigued, |
| cántame una canción. | Sing me a song." |
| | |
| Qué canción tan rebonita, | "Oh, what a pretty song, |
| que jamás la había oído yo, | I had never heard it before. |
| cántame otra más bonita, | Sing me another one that's prettier, |
| y después te canto yo. | And then I shall sing to you." |
| | |
| Yo le dije al reenganchista, | "I told the contractor, |
| yo le dije que volvía, | I told him that I would return, |
| pero que no venía solo, | But that I wouldn't return alone, |
| que hora *traiba*** compañía. | That now I had someone with me. |
| | |
| No me mandes para Tejas, | "Do not send me to Texas, |
| ni al Estado de Oklahoma, | Nor the state of Oklahoma; |
| son puntos muy desgraciados, | They are awful places |
| que aborrecen al que toma. | That make it hard for one who drinks. |
| | |
| Todos vienen platicando | "Everyone is talking |
| que pasaron por San Luis | About passing through St. Louis, |
| y al llegar a San Antonio, | And how on arriving at San Antonio, |
| les robaron el veliz. | Their suitcase was stolen." |
| | |
| Ya con esta me despido, | With this I take my leave |
| con apretón de manos, | With a hearty handshake. |
| estos versos son compuestos | These verses are composed |
| por los nobles Mexicanos. | By the proud Mexicans. |

(Taylor 1969:221–245)
*silvos = *silbidos* (whistle)
**traiba = *traía* (brought)

The variant "La de la nagua azul" contains some identical strophes. An interesting point is brought up at the end of this song. The singer warns the immigrants not to bring their beautiful women to California because there are many dandies there who will take them away.

| **La de la nagua azul** | **She of the Blue Skirt** |
|---|---|
| De las dos que vienan *ai** | Of the two who are coming there |
| Cual te gusta, valedor, | Which one do you like, friend? |

Esa de la *nagua*** azul.
Me parece la mejor.

¿Qué dices chata, nos vamos

Pa' los Estados Unidos
Donde gozan las mujeres
Al lado de sus maridos?

Si me quieren sé querer,
Si me olvidan sé olvidar,

Como lo quieran hacer,
Para mi todo es igual.

¿Qué dice mi reenganchista,
No le dije que volvía?
Mándame pa' donde quiera
Que ya traigo compañía.

Si me quieren, etc.

Pues, muchacho mexicano
yo sí te sabré decir
De los reengaches que hay,
¿Para dónde quieres ir?

No me manden para Kansas,
Ni tampoco pa' Oclajuma
Son estados desgraciados
Que aborrecen al que fuma.

Si fueres pa' California
No lleves mujer bonita
Porque allí hay muchas panteras***
y cualquiera te la quita.

She of the blue skirt
Seems the best to me.

What do you say, pugnose; shall we go

To the United States
Where women have a good time
Living with their husbands?

If you love me, I know how to love;
If you forget me, I know how to forget.

Whatever you want to do,
It's all the same to me.

What do you say, my contractor;
Didn't I tell you I'd be back?
Send me wherever you will,
Because now I bring someone with me.

If you love me, etc.

Well then, Mexican fellow,
I'll know what to tell you.
Of the two jobs that there are,
Where do you want to go?

Don't send me to Kansas
Nor to Oklahoma either,
They are terrible states
Which hate the man who smokes.

If you go to California
Don't bring the good-looking woman,
Because there are many panthers
Who may take her away from you.

(Gamio 1971:90–91)
*i = *allí* (there)
**nagua = *enaguas o faldas* (skirt)
***panteras = (panthers) i.e., good-looking men

The "2ª canción del interior" poses an interesting and very real problem the Mexican immigrant encountered with respect to family relationships and stability. The lonely immigrant worker, far from his wife or girlfriend, sometimes met other women in the United States. Many times these second ties proved more lasting than the first, and the immigrant never returned to his family in Mexico. At other times family ties were stronger and survived the long separation. The immigrant either returned home and stayed or went back to Mexico to pick up his family and bring them back to the United States. The dilemma faced by an immigrant who has acquired a new family in the United States but whose old family ties strongly pull him back to Mexico is evident. In this particular case the immigrant opts to leave his new family and return to the old one in Mexico. The decision reached, however, is obviously a painful one. The social and psychological dislocations the immigrant endures are poignantly spotlighted. "2ª canción del interior" seems to be a combination of the variants just presented and the "Canción del interior."

| 2ª canción del interior | Second Song of the Interior |
|---|---|
| De las tres que vienen ahí<br>cuál te gusta valedor,<br>esa del vestido azul<br>me parece la mejor. | Of those three (women) coming by<br>Which one do you like, sir?<br>That one with the blue dress on<br>Seems to be the best one. |
| De las tres que están allí<br>cuál te gusta, compañero,<br>esa del vestido azul<br>se me hace que me la llevo. | Of those three that are over there<br>Which one do you like, my friend?<br>That one with the blue dress on,<br>I think I will take her with me. |
| Por toda esa calle real<br>todos la vieron pasar,<br>con su rebozo nuevo<br>y su blanco delantal. | Through that street<br>All saw her go by,<br>With her new shawl<br>And her white apron. |
| Ya, ven, deja de moler,<br>ya no muelas nixtamal,<br>vámonos a Estados Unidos<br>que allá iremos a gozar. | Hey, stop now, stop your grinding,<br>Don't grind any more corn,<br>Let us go to the United States<br>Where we shall have fun. |
| Oyes ya, chatita, el tren,<br>óyelo que silbidos da,<br>nomás un favor te pido;<br>que no llores por allá. | Listen, my pugnose one, to the train,<br>Listen to the whistle blowing,<br>I only ask you one favor<br>Please do not cry over there. |
| Querido, ya voy cansada<br>y apenas aquí es Torreón<br>para no sentir cansancio<br>cánteme usted una canción. | Beloved, I am tired<br>And we are only in Torreón,<br>So that I won't feel so tired<br>Sing me a song. |
| Mi vida te cantaré<br>la canción que tú más quieras<br>no más pulsa la guitarra<br>y hay te va una muy tres piedras. | My love, I will sing to you<br>The song that you like the best,<br>Just tune the guitar<br>And here goes a great one (song). |

¡Qué canción tan rebonita
que jamás la había yo oído,
cánteme otra más bonita
y después le canto yo!

Ya llegamos a Laredo,
mira que bonito está,
estas son las oficinas
donde te han de reengachar.

Ahora te voy a mandar
a las yardas a Chicago,
a donde nadie te vea
que traes tu guitarra al lado.

Yo le dije al reenganchista,
yo le dije que volvía,
pero que no me venía solo,
que ahora traería compañía.

No me mandes para Texas
ni al Estado de Oklahoma,
son puntos muy desgraciados
que aborrecen al que fuma.

Pero ya se va a llegar el pago
para que gaste mi querida,
la mitad es para ella
y la mitad para mi familia.

Pues por qué les das a ellos

ningún servicio te dan,
yo te lavo, yo te plancho,
venga el cheque para acá.

Mira, no seas ventajosa;
tú gozas de lo mejor;
supiste que era casado
y que tenía obligación.

Si quieres estar conmigo
guárdame mis centavitos
supiste que era casado
y que tenía tres chamaquitos.

What a beautiful song!
I had never heard it before,
Sing me a nicer song
And I'll sing you one afterward.

We have arrived at Laredo
Look how pretty it is,
Those are the offices
Where you can get a contract.

Now I will send you
To the Chicago stockyards,
Where nobody can see
That you have a guitar by your side.

I told the contractor
I told him I would return,
But that I was not coming alone,
That I would bring company.

Don't send me to Texas
Or to the state of Oklahoma,
They are horrible places
That hate those who smoke.

But payday is getting near
So that my beloved can spend it,
Half is for her
And the other half goes to my
    family.

Well, how come you give them
    money,
They don't do a thing for you,
I wash and iron your clothes, so
Give me that check.

Look, don't take advantage,
You enjoy the very best,
You knew I was married
And had an obligation.

If you want to be with me
Save my money for me,
You knew I was married
And that I had three kids.

Ayer tarde recibí carta
que mis padres me mandaron
en que llorando me dicen
y suplican que me vaya.

Para irme para mi tierra
yo no hallo ni como hacer,
nomás me pongo a pensar
que aquí dejo a esta mujer.

Cuando vayas a tu tierra
que es en San Luis Potosí
te llevas este retrato
de la mujer que dejó aquí.

Si me quieren, se querer,
si me olvidan, se olvidar,
como lo quieran hacer,
para mí todo es igual.

Recuerdos de una ingrata
que en un tiempo yo la amaba
pero mi orgullo ha sido
que no la he vuelto a querer.

Las aves ya no cantan,
los astros ya no alumbran,
las flores no perfuman
porque allí faltó tu amor.

Chinita, lo que te encargo
que cuando de mi te acuerdes
¡ay! nunca, nunca olvides
que fui tu admirador

Pero fui tan desgraciado
con querer a esa mujer,
que he jurado por el eterno
¡no volverla ya a querer!

Tus ojos son dos estrellas
que brillan por el panteón,
yo quisiera abrir tu tumba
para ver tu corazón.

Ya con esta me despido
con tristeza y con dolor
ya les . . .
otra me vuelvo a encontrar.

Yesterday I received a letter
That my parents sent me
Where they tearfully write
And beg me to come home.

Going back home
I do not know what to do.
I just start thinking
That I have to leave this woman here.

When you leave for your hometown
Which is San Luis Potosí
Take this picture with you
Of the woman you left here.

If they love me I love them
If they forget me I forget them,
Anyway you want to do it
Makes no difference to me.

Remembering a cruel woman
Whom I loved at one time,
But I am proud to say
I have not loved her again.

The birds do not sing anymore,
The stars do not shine,
The flowers lost their scent
Because you stopped loving me.

My pretty, I ask you one thing,
That when you remember me
Oh, never, never forget
That I was your admirer.

But I was so unhappy
Loving that woman so,
That I swore by God
Never to love her again.

Your eyes are two stars
That shine at the cemetery,
I wish I could open your tomb
So I can see your heart.

With this I take my leave
With sadness and pain
I have . . .
I will find another (girl).

## Segunda parte

Mis queridas compañeras
pongan bastante atención,
que éstas si no son quimeras
que relato en mi canción.

Yo les voy a aconsejar
con mucha amabilidad
no se dejen engañar
sin saber la realidad.

Lo que a mi me sucedió
lo sufrí con paciencia,
de un consejo que me dió
nuestra madre la Experiencia.

Por andarme yo creyendo
de esos hombres mentirosos
que son puros revoltosos
que siempre andan mintiendo.

Pues un hombre me llevó
con engaños y mentiras
y después me abandonó
causándome muchas iras.

Con cariño me decía:
a Estados Unidos vamos
verás ¡oh vida mía!
como muy bien allá gozamos.

Con lo que a mi me contaba
yo me hacía mil ilusiones
sin saber que me engañaba
con sus malas intenciones.

"Yo te vestiré muy bien
de los pies a la cabeza
tú te pasearás en tren
te lo juro con certeza.

Te traeré muy bien vestida,
gastarás mucho dinero,
serás la consentida
por lo mucho que te quiero.

## Second Part

My beloved friends,
Pay close attention,
For these are not dreams
Which I narrate in my song.

I am going to advise you
With much friendliness,
Do not be deceived
Without knowing the truth.

What happened to me
I suffered with patience
The advice I received
From our Mother Experience.

Because I believed
Those lying men
They are a bunch of troublemakers
Who are always lying.

Well, a man took me
With lies and deceit
And he later abandoned me
Causing me great anger.

Endearingly he would say:
"Let us go to the United States.
You will see, oh darling,
How we will have fun there."

With all he told me
I was full of dreams.
I didn't know he was deceiving me
With his evil intentions.

"I will dress you well
From head to foot.
You will ride in trains,
I swear to you it's true.

I will have you well dressed
You will spend a lot of money
You will be my darling one
Because of the love I have for you.

Te pondré tu bungalito
también tu cocinera,
te compraré tu forcito
con asiento de primera.

Los domingos nos iremos
a pasear a las orillas
alimentos llevaremos
aunque sea de carnes frías.

Para que alegres tu hogar
te compraré tu victrola

y te pongas a cantar
cuando te encuentres ya sola.

Por tanto que me contaba
por fin correspondí
y después con él me fui
de mi hogar yo me ausentaba.

Mi madre me aconsejaba
y con cariño me decía
que si yo la abandonaba
ella de pesar moría.

Me despedí de mi madre
con dolor de mi corazón,
te lo ruego por mi padre
échame tu bendición.

Me dijo, hija querida,
híncate pues, de una vez,
que te doy mi despedida,
cuando vuelvas no me ves.

Con el alma enternecida
me ausenté yo de mi hogar
sin saber la triste vida
que con él iba a pasar.

Nos fuimos a la Estación
a esperar en el andén,
se me hacía dilación
que llegara pronto el tren.

I will get you your bungalow
And also your own cook.
I will buy you a Ford
With a first-class seat.

On Sundays we will go
On a Sunday drive
We will take our picnic lunch
Even though it'll be cold cuts.

So that you will have a happy home
I will buy you a Victrola (record
    player)
And you can sing
When you are by yourself.

With all he told me
I finally agreed
And I went along with him
And left my home.

My mother would advise me
And with love would tell me
If I abandoned her
She was going to die of grief.

I bade farewell to my mother
With pain in my heart.
I beseech you in my father's name
Give me your blessings.

She told me, "Dear daughter
Kneel down, once and for all,
I will bid you farewell,
For when you return I'll be gone."

With my spirit filled with sadness
I left my home
Without knowing the sad life
That I was going to have with him.

We left for the train station.
Waiting on the platform
I could hardly wait
For the train to come by.

Cuando iba yo caminando
para los Estados Unidos
con gusto iba cantando:
Adios, mis padres queridos.

Muy pronto regresaré
para ver a mi mamá,
buen dinero le traeré
que con gusto gastará.

Muy gustosa fui cantando
cuando iba yo en el camino
y mi amante iba pensando
un negocio de gran tino.

Llegamos a la frontera
y al reenganchista le dijo:
mándeme usted a donde quiera
que no es mucho lo que exijo.

Nos fuimos a Colorado
por mayor fatalidad,
a ese dichoso Estado
que es una calamidad.

Para mi mayor tormento
al llegar a ese lugar
se puso muy descontento
y hasta me empezó a pegar.

En México me decía:
ya ven, deja de moler,
pero allá bien me exijía
que le hiciera de comer.

Del pago que recibió
se lo mandó a su mujer,
en un giro que le envió
para poderla sostener.

Lo que en seguida hice yo
fue decirle a mi querido:
ahora ya me sucedió;
valía más no haber venido.

When we were traveling
To the United States
With joy I was singing:
Good-bye, my beloved parents.

I will be back soon
So I can see my mother.
A good amount of cash I'll bring her
Which she'll be happy to spend.

I happily sang away
When I was traveling
And my lover was thinking
About a great business venture.

We arrived at the border
And he said to the contractor:
"Send me wherever you want,
I don't ask for much."

We left for Colorado.
As our bad luck would have it
That infamous state
Is a disaster.

And as my bad luck would have it
When we arrived at that place
He became very displeased
And started to beat me.

In Mexico he would say:
"Come, stop grinding corn."
But there he would badger me
To make him his meals.

The paycheck he received
He sent it to his wife,
A money order he sent to her
So she could feed herself.

What I immediately did
Was to tell my lover:
Now it's happened to me.
I should never have come here.

| | |
|---|---|
| Pues ni modo de llorar | No use crying now |
| por lo que me ha acontecido, | For what has happened to me. |
| ya no puedo remediar | I cannot remedy |
| lo que a mi me ha sucedido. | What has happened to me. |
| | |
| Con trabajos regresé | With great hardships I returned |
| de ese viaje tan penoso, | From that painful trip, |
| siempre de él me acordaré | What I'll always remember about him |
| que fue un hombre mentiroso. | Is that he was a lying man. |
| | |
| Yo me acordaré diciendo: | I will remember saying: |
| Mal haya quien . . . pero no | Damn the one who . . . but no |
| y lo estaré maldiciendo | I will be damning him |
| por lo mal que se portó. | For the bad way he behaved. |
| | |
| Muy llorosa me despido | Full of tears I bid good-bye |
| terminando esta canción; | As I end this song. |
| y lo que ya he referido | And what I have already said |
| que les sirva de lección. | Let it be a lesson to all. |
| | |
| A todas mis compañeras | To all my women friends |
| les daré un buen consejo | I give this good advice: |
| que no sean las primeras | Do not be the first |
| en cargar el aparejo. | To carry the burden. |

(Guerrero 1924b)

## Canción del interior       Song of The Interior

| | |
|---|---|
| Pero ya se va a llegar el pago | But wages are going to begin soon |
| para que gaste mi querida, | So that my mistress may spend them; |
| la mitad es para ella, | Half is for her |
| y la mitad para mi familia. | And half is for my family. |
| | |
| Mira, no seas ventajosa, | Here, don't take advantage, |
| tú gozas de lo mejor; | For you enjoy the best there is; |
| supiste que era casado | You knew that I was married |
| y que tenía obligación. | And under obligation. |
| | |
| Ayer tarde recibí carta | Yesterday afternoon I got a letter |
| que mis padres me mandaron | That my parents sent me. |
| en que llorando me dicen | Weeping, they asked and |
| y suplican que me vaya. | Begged me to come back. |
| | |
| Para irme para mi tierra | In order to go to my country |
| yo no hallo ni como hacer, | I don't know what to do; |
| no más me pongo a pensar | I begin thinking about how |
| que aquí dejo a esta mujer. | I'll be leaving this woman here. |

| | |
|---|---|
| Recuerdos de una ingrata | I have memories of an ingrate |
| que en un tiempo yo la amaba | Whom at one time I loved, |
| pero mi orgullo ha sido | But I take pride |
| que no la he vuelto a querer. | In not having loved her again. |
| | |
| Las aves ya no cantan, | The birds no longer sing |
| los astros ya no alumbran, | And the stars give no light. |
| las flores no perfuman | The flowers have no scent |
| porque allí faltó tu amor. | Because your love is lacking there. |
| | |
| Chinita lo que te encargo | Chinita, I charge you |
| que cuando de mí te acuerdes | That when you think of me, |
| ¡ay! nunca, nunca olvides | Ah, never, never forget |
| que fuí tu admirador! | That I was your admirer! |
| | |
| ¡Pero fuí tan desgraciado | But I was so unfortunate |
| con querer a esa mujer, | In loving that woman, |
| que he jurado por el Eterno | That I have sworn by the Eternal |
| no volverla ya a querer! | Never to love her again! |
| | |
| Tus ojos son dos estrellas | Your eyes are like two stars |
| que brillan por el panteón, | Shining in the cemetery; |
| yo quisiera abrir tu tumba | I would like to open your tomb |
| para ver tu corazón. | In order to see your heart. |
| | |
| Ya con ésta me despido; | And so I bid you farewell; |
| ya me voy a retirar, | I am going to take my leave, |
| pero al cabo que con otro | But I know that with another |
| ¡tú has de llegar a pagar! | You, too, will eventually pay. |

(Taylor 1969:231–232)

A variant collected by Mendoza is a shorter version.

## De "El interior" o "Los enganchados"

—De esas tres que vienen ahí, ¿cuál te gusta valedor?
—Esa del vestido blanco me parece la mejor.
—Ya ven, deja de moler, ya no muelas nixtamal,
vamos a Estados Unidos, que allí iremos a gozar.
—Oyes, ya, chinita, el tren: oye que silbidos da.
nomás un favor te pido: que no llores por allá.
—Querido, ya me cansé y apenas aquí es Torreón.
pa' el cansancio no sentir cánteme usté una canción.
¡Que canción tan *reteflais,* que jamás la había oído yo!
Cánteme otra más bonita y después le canto yo.
Yo le dije al enganchista. Le dije que volvería:
pero que no venía solo, ahora traigo compañía.

(Mendoza 1964:38)

## From "The Interior" or "The Contract Laborers"

"Of those three that are walking by, which do you like, troubadour?
"That one with the white dress seems to be the best."
"Come now, stop grinding, stop grinding corn.
Let us go to the United States, we shall have fun there."
Do you hear, my love, the train? Listen to the whistle blowing.
I only ask one thing of you: do not cry over there."
"My loved one, I am tired, and this is only Torreón.
To relieve my weariness, sing a song to me."
I have never heard such a crazy song! I had never heard that!
Sing me another, prettier one, and then I will sing to you.
I told the one who signed us up that I would return.
But that I would not come alone. I have company now."

The preceding pages demonstrate the importance of the railroad and the train in the Mexican immigrant experience, both as a source of employment and as a mode of transportation. The impact of railroad construction and traveling by train has been duly recorded in folk songs. These ballads provide a glimpse of the world of the immigrant during this particular epoch. They detail the subjective feelings the immigrants experienced and point to important aspects of the Mexican immigrant experience which history books have neglected or glossed over.

# Revolution and
# Hard Times

*Three* After the Wars of Independence (1810–1821), Mexico began the monumental process of trying to integrate the nation into a cohesive whole. This was easier said than done, for the insurmountable problems existing before the battle for independence—the economic disparity among the various castes, the ideological battle between conservatives and liberals, the vastness of the Mexican territory—were issues that continued to loom before the inexperienced leaders of the nation.

The problems of territorial cohesiveness and integrity proved disastrous for the squabbling politicians, and soon the loss of Texas in 1836 jolted the incipient national consciousness. Events began to overtake the young Mexican nation. The ideological stance of "manifest destiny" emanating from the United States was to deal a second blow to the Mexican nation's territorial boundaries. After engaging in combat with the superior forces of the United States in 1848 and losing the war, Mexico was forced to cede half its territory to the United States as specified in the terms of the Treaty of Guadalupe Hidalgo (see Pahissa 1987). The loss of this vast amount of territory inflicted a tremendous psychological blow to the Mexican people. The need for a more unified front was perceived as critical if the nation was to survive. However, the jockeying for power continued unabated between conservatives and liberals, and it was not until President Benito Juárez took office in 1858 that some semblance of order was restored in the nation's capital. But this long-awaited peace did not last long, for soon Mexico was engaged in combat with the French, who were trying to establish an empire in Mexico under the leadership of Archduke Maximilian of Austria and his wife, Carlotta, in the 1860s.

The French, however, were unsuccessful in establishing an empire, and after they were driven out in 1867 Benito Juárez reestablished his government in Mexico City. In 1872, upon the death of Juárez, the jockeying for power resumed between Sebastián Lerdo de Tejada and the up-and-coming

General Porfirio Díaz. In 1876 Díaz, after defeating federal troops at Tecoac, assumed office as president of Mexico. A few months later John W. Foster, minister from the United States to Mexico, officially notified Díaz that the United States had recognized his presidency. Although there is an interval between 1882 and 1884 in which General Manuel González was president of Mexico, Díaz regained the presidency in 1884 and remained in office until the Mexican Revolution of 1910 forced him out of power.

The powderkeg that finally exploded was a result of the Díaz regime's ideological stance toward the masses. The adherence to Comte's philosophy of positivism, the belief on the part of Díaz's científicos in progress through science at whatever the human cost, the pervasive feelings of European superiority and Indian and mestizo inferiority led to excesses in policy detrimental to the majority of Mexicans. While the elite led a life of decadence and luxury, the campesinos were literally starving to death. John Crow, in *The Epic of Latin America* (1980), metaphorically describes the thirty-year relationship between Indian Mexico and the Porfirio Díaz regime:

> Juárez had left the door ajar for Indian Mexico; Porfirio Díaz then appeared on the threshold and made as if to open it wider. When the Indian started to enter his new mansion, the door was slammed on his fingers, mangling them terribly. During the long years of "peace" to follow, the memory of that pain endured. Finally a crippled hand, almost a claw, reached out from nowhere and destroyed the regime of Díaz. (667)

During the years of the Porfiriato, Mexico indeed became known as the "mother of foreigners, stepmother of Mexicans." For while Díaz's policies helped develop the infrastructure of Mexico—its railroad systems, mining concerns, electrical plants, and so forth—it did so at the expense of the hardworking, exploited Indian and mestizo masses. The foreign capital that the Porfiriato administration so eagerly courted and which streamed into Mexico was not provided free but required a tremendous amount of interest payments. For example, it is estimated that although mining production yielded 160 million pesos a year, this money ended up leaving the country and going to foreign investors (Crow 1980:669).

The revival of the hacienda and hacendado life-style is credited to Díaz's politically corrupt system of land distribution. Díaz literally inverted the old axiom of taking from the rich and giving to the poor. His policy of *pan o palo* (bread or stick) rewarded compliance with is policies; any form of protest was ruthlessly crushed. The reward often took the form of parceling out landed estates that had been taken away from the Indians' commune system of ownership. As Crow writes,

> By the end of the Díaz regime there were few ejidos left in the most thickly populated central region of Mexico. Approximately 95 per cent of all rural

heads of families were landless in 1910. In the state of Chihuahua more than 30,000,000 acres were divided among seven recipients; in Durango two grant-ees received over 2,000,000 acres each; in Oaxaca four recipients divided 7,000,000 acres, and so on down the line. Díaz doled out a total of nearly 135,000,000 acres of public lands to private individuals, most of them political favorites or influential foreigners. This was 27 per cent of the total land of the Mexican nation and included practically all of its arable soil. (671)

Coupled with the expropriation of Indian lands was the tremendous rate of inflation that went along with the influx of foreign capital. The Indian and mestizo populations were getting a twofold punch: high inflation rates and wages frozen at late eighteenth-century levels (672).

The festering sore of the poverty-stricken masses eventually erupted, and Mexico experienced a series of violent convulsions for nearly a decade. Many peasants, having nothing to lose, joined the guerrilla movements that sprang up in south, north, and central Mexico. Others, eschewing the violence, opted for emigration to the United States.

The roots of the Mexican Revolution of 1910–1917 thus are traced to the intransigent thirty-year rule of the dictator Díaz. By the turn of the century grumbling and opposition began to sprout in the middle class, which saw its participation in national affairs and in the economy of the nation dwindling to a trickle. Pressure for open elections and a new leader at the helm rumbled through the towns and cities, finally reaching the ears of the dictator. In an interview conducted with a journalist from the United States in 1908, not long before the elections that were to take place in 1909, Díaz intimated that he was ready to step down. The Mexican nation was elated by the welcome announcement and initiated presidential campaigns throughout the country. Among those campaigning for the presidential post was Francisco I. Madero, a gentleman farmer from the north (Chihuahua). However, Díaz actually had no intention of stepping down and announced his candidacy once more. The refusal of the dictator to relinquish the presidential chair unleashed a series of battles across the nation for more than seven years.

Because the Díaz dictatorship with its policies of modernizing Mexico had resulted in extreme hardship for the middle class and most significantly for the working class and the campesinos, many Mexicans deduced that it was to their advantage to emigrate to the United States, where they hoped life would be much better. The tremors and social upheavals resulting from the Revolution of 1910–1917 likewise stimulated a stream of migratory workers seeking refuge and work in the northern neighbor's territory.

### Corridos from the 1910–1920 Decade

Many corridos written during this period describe the conditions in Mexico which drive a man from his homeland to seek a better life; the Mexican immigrant seems compelled to enumerate the reasons for leaving his beloved country. Other songs merely comment on the hardships and psychological sufferings an emigrant feels at the onset of his trip to el Norte. The folk song "Paso del Norte" is such a song.

| Paso del Norte | Northern Pass |
|---|---|
| Que triste se encuentra el hombre | How sad a man becomes |
| cuando anda ausente | When he is far away |
| cuando anda ausente | When he is far away |
| allá lejos de su patria. | From his own country. |
| | |
| *Piormente** si se acuerda | It is worse when he remembers |
| de sus padres y su chata | His parents and his girl. |
| ¡Ay que destino! | What a cruel destiny! |
| Para sentarme a llorar. | One could sit down and cry! |
| | |
| Paso del Norte | Oh, Northern Pass, |
| que lejos te vas quedando | How far I am leaving you! |
| sus divisiones | Your boundary lines |
| de mi se están alejando. | Are getting farther and farther away. |
| | |
| Los pobres de mis hermanos | My poor brothers |
| de mi se están acordando | Are all thinking about me. |
| ¡Ay que destino! | What a cruel destiny! |
| Para sentarme a llorar. | One could sit down and cry! |
| | |
| Paso del Norte | Oh, Northern Pass! |
| que lejos te vas quedando. | How far I am leaving you! |

*piormente = *peormente* (worse)

This theme of homesickness is repeated in the corrido "Despedida de un norteño." The nostalgic worker takes leave of his country, his relatives, and his favorite saints. His reason for leaving: work. This corrido is a "traveling" song. In this category of texts one principal intent is to name as many cities as possible. The more cities cited in the lyrics, the more appeal the song has for an audience, since a member of the audience is likely to identify with the song if his or her hometown is mentioned. The ballad therefore highlights places en route to el Norte (from Mexico City to El Paso): Salvatierra, Celaya, Salamanca, Irapuato, the state of Guanajuato, Ciudad León, Aguascalientes, the state of Zacatecas, Fresnillo, Torreón, Chihuahua, and Ciudad Juárez. Research confirms that indeed most Mexican immigrants came from these areas and many came (and are still coming) by this route (see Carreras de Velasco 1974).

The trepidation experienced by the immigrant, implicit in these lyrics, is significant. In the back of this immigrant's mind are the dangers he may encounter upon reaching the "promised land." Taking no chances, he directs his prayers to all the patron saints of the towns he is passing through. (Plateros is the shrine where the Santo Niño de Atocha is, near Fresnillo, Zacatecas.)

## Despedida de un norteño

Adiós mi patria querida:
yo ya me voy a ausentar,
me voy para Estados Unidos,
donde pienso trabajar.

¡Adiós! mi madre querida,
la Virgen Guadalupana,
¡adiós mi patria amorosa,
República Mexicana!

Pues, en fin, yo ya me voy,
te llevo en mi corazón,
Madre mía de Guadalupe,
échame tu bendición.

Me voy triste y pesaroso
a sufrir y a padecer
Madre mía de Guadalupe,
tu me concedas volver.

México es mi madre patria,
donde nací mexicano;
échame tu bendición
con tu poderosa mano.

Me voy a Estados Unidos
a buscar manutención,
¡adiós, mi patria querida,
te llevo en mi corazón!

Pues yo no tengo la culpa
que abandone así a mi tierra
la culpa es de la pobreza
que nos tiene en la miseria.

Pues ya voy en el camino
ya salí de Salvatierra,
haz, Madre mía de La Luz,
que yo vuelva a mi tierra.

## An Emigrant's Farewell

Good-bye, my beloved country,
Now I am going away;
I go to the United States,
Where I intend to work.

Good-bye, my beloved mother,
The Virgin of Guadalupe;
Good-bye, my beloved land,
My Mexican Republic!

At last I'm going,
I bear you in my heart;
My Mother Guadalupe,
Give me your benediction.

I go sad and heavy-hearted
To suffer and endure;
My Mother Guadalupe,
Grant my safe return.

Mexico is my homeland
Where I was born a Mexican;
Give me your benediction
With your powerful hand.

I go to the United States
To seek to earn a living.
Good-bye, my beloved land;
I bear you in my heart!

For I am not to blame
That I leave my country thus;
The fault lies in the poverty,
Which keeps us all in want.

So now I'm on my way,
I've left Salvatierra;
Grant, Mother of Light,
That I may return again.

Ya llegamos a Celaya
con mucha resolución,
¡adiós, adiós, Madre mía,
Purísima Concepción!

We've already reached Celaya,
Full of resolution;
Good-bye, good-bye, my Mother,
Immaculate Conception.

Llegamos a Salamanca;
adiós, Señor San Pascual,
échame tu bendición
Padre mío del Hospital!

We arrive at Salamanca;
Goodbye, San Pascual;
Give me your blessing,
Patron Saint of the Hospital!

Vamos llegando a Irapuato
de paso para Silado,
Madre mía de Loretito,
¡haz que yo vuelva a tu lado!

We are arriving at Irapuato
En route to Silado;
My Mother of Loretito,
Grant my return to your side!

Adiós, Guanajuato hermoso,
mi Estado donde nací,
me voy para Estados Unidos,
lejos, muy lejos de tí.

Good-bye, fair Guanajuato,
The state where I was born;
I'm going to the United States
Far, far from you.

Ya vamos en el camino
llegando a la ciudad de León,
y admirado me quedé
al ver su iluminación.

We are on our way again,
Arriving at the city of León;
I was filled with admiration
To see its bright lights.

Al llegar a Aguascalientes
con mucho gusto y esmero,
no arreglé mi pasaporte
por la falta de dinero.

Upon reaching Aguascalientes
With great pleasure and care,
I didn't get my passport
For lack of money.

Luego pasé Zacatecas
con muchísima atención,
en el tren de pasajeros
se me partió el corazón.

Then I passed Zacatecas,
Giving it much attention,
But in the passenger train
My heart was breaking.

Llegamos a la estación
que se llama de Fresnillo,
donde todo mexicano
visita a un milagroso Niño.

We arrived at the station
That is called Fresnillo,
Where every Mexican
Visits the miraculous Niño.

Pues muy cerca de Fresnillo
se ven los boscosos cerros
donde se encuentra también
ese Niño de Plateros.

And very near Fresnillo
The wooded hills are seen,
Where there is also found
That Holy Child of Plateros.

Santo Niño del Fresnillo,
tú me has de favorecer,
Santo Niño de Plateros
tú me concedas volver.

Holy Child of Fresnillo,
You must grant my request;
Holy Child from Plateros,
Allow me to return.

Ya va caminando el tren
hasta llegar a Torreón,
Santo Niño de Fresnillo,
échame tu bendición.

Ya llegamos a Chihuahua,
pues ya de aquí me despido,
¡adiós, mi patria querida!
¡adiós, todos mis amigos!

Ya con ésta me despido
de mi Patria Mexicana,
he llegado a Ciudad Juárez,
¡oh Virgen Guadalupana!

Now the train takes off
Till it reaches Torreón;
Holy Child of Fresnillo,
Give me your benediction.

Now we've reached Chihuahua,
So here I bid you farewell;
Good-bye, beloved country,
Good-bye, all my friends!

And so I take leave
Of my country, Mexico.
I have reached Ciudad Juárez.
Oh, Virgin of Guadalupe!

(Guerrero 1924a)

This farewell song commences with the formulaic phrase "Adios mi patria querida" and cites the reason for leaving Mexico: to secure employment in the United States. The parting is full of pathos, with the Norteño reiterating his patriotism, his love for Mexico, and his love for the Virgin of Guadalupe, the symbol par excellence of the Mexican nation. However, the constant underlining of the immigrant's patriotism and love for Mexico implicitly veils a deep-seated and perhaps unconscious guilt about leaving Mexico. The protagonist attempts to assuage his guilt feelings and simultaneously answer future criticism by detailing his rationale for leaving his land.

Pues yo no tengo la culpa
que abandone así mi tierra
la cupla es de la pobreza
que nos tiene en la miseria.

For I am not to blame
That I abandon my country thus;
The fault is that of poverty
Which keeps us all in want.

It was inevitable that with the large number of immigrants leaving for the United States during the 1910–1920 decade, a bitter debate should arise regarding the advantages and disadvantages of leaving Mexico for a better life in el Norte. In "Consejos a los norteños" we find the beginnings of such a debate. The song is extremely important for the issues it highlights.

### Consejos a los norteños

Ahora sí no llorarán
vayan juntando el transporte,
Muchachos aficionados,
esos que les gusta el Norte.

### Advice to the Northerners

Now you can cease your crying
Start saving money for your ticket
All of you young men
Who love the North (USA).

| | |
|---|---|
| Arreglen su maletita, | Get your luggage ready |
| ya váyanse preparando | Start preparing yourselves |
| cepillen bien la gorrita | Brush well your hat |
| para entrar de contrabando. | So you can cross illegally. |
| | |
| Porque si entran por el puente | 'Cause if you cross the bridge |
| les han de tronar los huesos | Your bones will creak |
| ahora no entran de gollete | You can't cross free no more |
| les cobran dieciseis pesos. | The fee is sixteen pesos. |
| | |
| Báñense hasta con legía | Bathe well even with lye |
| pa' quitarse lo mugroso, | To get the dirt off |
| ya no den en qué decir | Don't get a bad reputation |
| con el gringo pretencioso. | With those pretentious gringos. |
| | |
| Ahora sí van a lonchar | Now you will be lunching |
| y a comer buenos jamones, | And eating good ham. |
| porque aquí en nuestro terreno | 'Cause here in our country |
| no compran ni pantalones. | You can't even buy pants. |
| | |
| Llévense también su vieja, | Take your women too |
| no vayan a abrir la boca | Don't go with your mouths wide open |
| porque las güeras de allá | 'Cause there the blondes |
| no se enamoran de coca. | Don't fall for poor guys. |
| | |
| Vamos a Estados Unidos | Let's go to the United States |
| a ganar buenos salarios, | To earn good money |
| que los señores patones | 'Cause the big-footed ones |
| necesitan operarios. | Need (machine) operators. |
| | |
| Porque los ricos de aquí | Because the rich here |
| no mueven ningún quehacer, | Don't stimulate employment |
| con el reparto de tierras | With the new land distribution |
| me los pusieron a leer. | They've been put to reading. |
| | |
| La cosa está del demonio, | Things are like hell here |
| ya no hay ni revolución, | The Revolution is over |
| nomás lo que está aumentando | What is increasing here now |
| son ladrones de a montón. | Are thieves by the bushel. |
| | |
| Amigos, vamos al Norte; | Friends, let's go up north, |
| no lo estén tanto pensando, | Don't waste time thinking about it |
| si no hay dinero pa'l* tren | If there's no money for train fare |
| nos iremos caminando. | We will travel on foot. |

| | |
|---|---|
| Adentro, machetes pandos, | Come on, you men, |
| no se vayan a rajar. | Don't give up. |
| éntrenle poco a poquito, | Do it little by little |
| ya es tiempo de trabajar. | It's time to work now. |
| | |
| Vamos a portar chaqueta, | Let's go wear jackets |
| la que nunca hemos usado, | Which we've never worn before |
| camisas de pura seda | Pure silk shirts |
| como también buen calzado. | And good quality shoes. |
| | |
| Aquí si nos afanamos | Here even if we work hard |
| siempre andamos encuerados, | We are always naked. |
| por allá en el extranjero | Over there in foreign land |
| parecemos diputados. | We'll look like senators. |
| | |
| Ahora sí, amigos, nos fuimos | Now's the time to go |
| a atravesar las fronteras, | To cross the border. |
| no le hace que luego digan | It doesn't matter if they say |
| que somos chuchas cuereras. | We are stray dogs. |
| | |
| Ese no vió que el país | That dude didn't see that |
| está peor que los infiernos, | Our country is worse off than hell. |
| todas son bullas y habladas | Everything is noise and talk |
| y de comer solo cuernos. | And food is nowhere found. |
| | |
| Ya por la falta de plata | 'Cause of lack of money |
| hasta las viejas se van | Even the women leave |
| creyendo que en otra casa | Thinking that in another house |
| no falta tortilla y pan. | They'll not lack tortillas and bread. |
| | |
| En esto no tengo duda, | In this I have no doubts |
| muy bien lo pueden hacer, | They (women) will do it |
| es más fiel un perro amigo | A dog is much more faithful |
| que una traidora mujer. | Than a treacherous woman. |
| | |
| Pero al fin que por allá | But in the end over there |
| muy al pelo se vacila, | One can have a real good time |
| con esas güeras grandotas | With those big blondes |
| que les gusta la maquila. | Who like factory work. |
| | |
| No pierdo las esperanzas | I don't lose hope |
| cuando venga de regreso | That when I return |
| vendré de todo bombín | I'll be dressed in a bowler hat |
| y con el cuello muy tieso. | And with a stiff collar. |

| | |
|---|---|
| Para enamorar una rica | To court a rich girl |
| y darle bien la canción | And sing her a swan's song |
| de esas de la enague corta | Those women with short skirts |
| que ensañan el zancarrón. | That show off their bony legs. |
| | |
| Qué dicen, amigos, vamos | What do you say, friends, shall we go? |
| por allá es la pura miel, | Over there the honey is easy, |
| se toma buena cerveza | One drinks great beer |
| y se come en el hotel. | And eats at hotels. |
| | |
| Qué dicen, gorras de maíz | What do you say, straw hats? |
| no quieren usar tejano, | Don't you want to wear a Texan hat? |
| los convido a trabajar | I invite you to work |
| con el Gringo americano. | For the American gringo. |
| | |
| No crean que soy pretencioso | Don't think I am a braggart |
| ni tampoco fanfarrón, | Or a showoff. |
| de trabajar muy barato | From working so cheap |
| me duele mucho el pulmón. | My lungs hurt me so. |
| | |
| Aquí no hemos de hacer nada, | Here we wouldn't advance |
| tómenlo por experiencia, | I say from experience |
| porque el dinero se esconde | 'Cause money hides from us |
| y perdemos la paciencia. | And we lose our patience. |
| | |
| Me duele hasta el corazón | My heart aches so |
| dejar mi patria querida, | To leave my beloved country. |
| adios, mi padre y mi madre, | Good-bye, my father and mother, |
| ya les doy la despedida. | I bid you farewell. |
| | |
| Adiós, México lucido, | Good-bye, my illustrous Mexico, |
| con su hermosa Capital, | With its beautiful capital, |
| ya me voy, ya me despido, | I am leaving, farewell, |
| no te volveré a mirar. | I shall never see you again. |
| | |
| Adiós, muchachas hermosas, | Good-bye, beautiful girls, |
| adiós, todos mis amigos, | Good-bye to all my friends. |
| regresaré de Fifí | I shall return a dandy |
| portando muy buen abrigo. | Wearing a fine coat. |

(Guerrero 1924a)
*pa'l = *para el* (for the)

The first stanza implicitly informs us that a significant number of men were eager and willing to emigrate to the United States. The corrido is narrated from a third-person point of view and is addressing a particular audience— those young men interested in traveling northward ("esos que les gusta el Norte"). The second stanza addresses the issue of crossing illegally—"de contrabando." That meant entering the United States without paying the toll charged by customs officials.

The subject of racial snobbery and prejudice is broached in stanza 4, and the term *gringo* appears for the first time in Mexican immigrant songs. Mexico suffered an invasion by U.S. forces in 1914, and the bitter feelings left are extant in the song. Previously, U.S. citizens were called "americanos" (see Herrera-Sobek 1979 and Simmons 1957).

Although the general tone of the first six stanzas toward those leaving Mexico is hostile and mocking, the narrator begrudgingly admits that life is better in the States (stanza 5). Furthermore, there is a sharp change in attitude in stanza 7. The poetic voice changes to the first-person plural, while there is also a dramatic veer toward viewing the trip northward as a change for the better ("Vamos a Estados Unidos / a ganar buenos salarios"). A call to emigrate to the United States, where there is work, is enunciated. The Mexican ruling class is castigated for its lack of initiative to change the situation in Mexico. The breaking up of the huge landed estates after the Revolution, which had promised land to the peasants, is commented upon sarcastically, since the rich are kept busy reading their land grants and trying to retain their estates intact.

The song reflects the ambivalent attitude toward Mexican emigration. President Alvaro Obregón at one point actively encouraged Mexican emigration. He even went so far as to offer free railroad transportation to those desiring to work in the United States (see Carreras de Velasco 1974). Soon, however, this policy changed, and emigration to the United States was discouraged.

The material advantages of working in the United States are enumerated: jackets, silk shirts, shoes, and so forth are within reach if one is willing to work hard in el Norte. Furthermore, according to the corridista's perspective, women are more likely to admire and love you if you have money. Of course the would-be emigrant realizes the disadvantages—you have to work hard, really hard, and leaving one's beloved nation and family is no easy task ("Me duele hasta el corazón / dejar mi patria querida / adios, mi padre y mi madre / ya les doy la despedida"). The bracero's farewell includes an implicit promise to return.

The immigrant's intuition about the negative reaction his emigrating to the United States was going to elicit proved correct. A strong antipathy developed toward those leaving the country to work in "Yankeeland" and returning to show off their acquired goods. "Los norteños" exemplifies these negative attitudes toward the returned braceros.

## Los norteños

Ya llegaron los norteños
del punto de la frontera,
todos vienen presumiendo
que son la chucha cuerera.

Porque ahora traen pantalón

ya se creen que son catrines,
se fueron patas de perro
y hoy presumen de botines.

También se ponen chaleco
con cuello postizo y saco
aunque se pongan levita
no se les quita lo naco.

Con sus camisas de seda
se quieren dar gran paquete,
pero aquí en nuestro terreno
la verdad, valen bonete.

Muchos hablan tarasco,
pero hoy pronuncian el YES,
mas no saben otra cosa;

son puros pata de res.

Si van a las estaciones
dicen al despachador
para probar que saben mucho;
déme un "tíquete," señor.

Aquí pídame boleto,
que no está en el extranjero,
aquí se habla el castellano
no me venga hablando en perro.

La verdad que es de dar risa
con estos recién llegados,
que ya porque traen camisa

La quieren dar de ilustrados.

## The Northerners

The northerners have come
From the (U.S.) border
All are showing off
Thinking they are top dogs.

Because now they're wearing
    pants
They think they are dandies
They left barefooted
And now they show off their half
    boots.

They're also wearing a vest
With a false collar and a coat
Even if they wear frock coats
They are still lower-class dudes.

With their silk shirts
They want to put on airs
But here in our land
The truth is they aren't worth a
    penny.

Many speak Tarascan
But now they speak YES
But they really don't know anything
    else.
They're just oxen hoofs.

They go to the railroad stations
And ask the clerk
(To prove how learned they are),
Give me a "ticket," Mister.

Ask me for a ticket here
You are not in a foreign country
We speak Spanish here
Don't speak to me in dog language.

To tell the truth, it's really funny
Those recent arrivals,
Who think just because they're wear-
    ing a shirt
They are learned people.

Los gringos habilitados
aquí no valen ni tlaco,
aunque vistan de fifí
siempre dan pasos de sapo.

Pues no porque van y vienen

de algún poblado extranjero
con esto quieren decir
que se quitan lo ranchero.

Cuando se van para el Norte
le dicen a su mujer;
para ajustar el trasporte

la casa voy a vender.

Al fin que primero Dios
desde allá te he de mandar
muchos puños de dinero
para que puedas gastar.

Si su mujer es legal
sufre y tiene que aguantar,
pero si es de pocas pulgas
los tiene que coronar.

Qué tal, cómo se verán
con grandes cuernos de chivo,
no más pónganse a pensar
si es cierto lo que les digo.

Venden burros y cobija

para hacerse de centavos
porque piensan ir por lana
pero vienen trasquilados.

Y llegan con su familia
diciendo que los robaron
al pasar por la frontera;
nomás las patas alzaron.

Si te subes en el trén
luego los oyes hablar
Yo, nomás que se componga
me tengo que regresar.

The gringos are very able
But here they're not worth a cent
Even if they dress like dandies
They always walk like toads.

Don't believe that because you
    travel
Back and forth to foreign cities
Your peasant background
Is going to disappear.

When they go up north
They tell their wives:
"In order to have enough money for
    my transportation
I am going to sell the house."

"Believe me, God will provide.
From the U.S. I will send you
Many a handful of money
So that you can spend it here."

If their wife is faithful
She suffers and waits,
But if she has few scruples
She cuckolds him.

How do you think they'll look
With those goat horns?
Just stop to think
If what I say is not the truth.

They sell their donkeys and their
    blankets
In order to raise some funds
'Cause they think they'll make dough
But they return home flat broke.

And they come and tell their families
That they were robbed
Upon crossing the border
They were only able to save their skin.

If you board a train
You can hear them talking:
"As soon as things get better
I will have to return."

Los gringos pagan muy bién
y son muy considerados,
aquí no he de trabajar
con los ricos hacendados.

Otros piensan diferente,
esos que no hicieron nada,
dicen no he de regresar
porque vale una trompada.

Hay de distintos pensares
y de varias opiniones,
unos bien y otros mal
platican de los patones.

Pero en verdad les diré
que para ganar medio o un real
no se necesita el Norte,
aquí hay en que trabajar.

Al fin, como dijo aquél,
metiendo el maíz en trojes,
"si naciste para tamal
del cielo te caen las hojas."

Pues muchos de los que vienen
como bien lo dijo Trejo,
"No traen ni un peso en la bolsa

nada más el *aparejo*\*."

Que las ropas y el abrigo,
la corbata y el calzado,
no crean que los compran nuevos,
son gallos que les han dado.

Unos sí vienen gastando
porque llegan como hidalgos,
pero aquellos fanfarrones
que ahora tratan de hacer menos
a los que portan calzones.

Sin saber que los ingratos
que *agora*\*\* la dan de pomada,
si se quitan los zapatos
les ves la pata rajada.

"The gringos pay very well
And are very considerate
I shall not work here (in Mexico)
For the landed rich."

Others feel differently.
Those that didn't make a penny
Say they will not return
Because it's not worth a damn.

There're many ways of thinking
And there are many opinions
Some speak well, others do not
About the big-footed ones.

But in truth I must tell you
That to earn half a bit or one bit
You don't need to go up north.
There's plenty of work here.

In the end, as the man said
As he put his corn in the barn,
"If you were meant to be a tamal
The corn husks will fall from heaven."

Many who have returned,
As Mr. Trejo well put it,
"They don't have a cent in their pock-
ets
Only the harness."

The clothes and the coat
The tie and their shoes
Don't believe they bought them new
They are hand-me-downs someone
gave them.

Some do come back spending
They arrive here like squires.
But there are those braggarts
Who try to put down
Those who wear Indian trousers.

Without realizing that those ingrates
Who put on airs,
If they take off their shoes
You can see their cracked feet.

| | |
|---|---|
| Ya con ésta me despido | Now I take my leave |
| aquí se acabó el recorte, | I have finished cutting down |
| de los famosos catrines, | Those famous dandies, |
| de esos que vienen del Norte. | Those coming back from the North. |

(Guerrero 1924a)
*aparejo = harness, meaning that the men were working like beasts of burden
**agora = *ahora* (now)

This ballad is probably the first song strongly criticizing the men who went up north to work. Evidently by this time some were returning home for visits. This of course is a very important process of Mexican migration—the immigrant works for a period in the U.S., perhaps engaged in seasonal agricultural work, then returns for a visit. The immigrant may return bringing gifts for relatives—clothing, money, utensils, electrical gadgets, radios, cameras. The song in this instance depicts the experience of the returning norteño in very aggressive, hostile terms. The lyrics present a poetic persona that seems to resent the returnee and his money, his clothing and his speech.

Another corrido also called "Los norteños," by Nomelazo, Saul deftly parodies the Mexican immigrant worker. The bracero is ridiculed for leaving his wife alone in Mexico. In stanzas similar to those in the previous corrido, it is underscored that if she is not of the faithful stripe she will cuckold him; he is chastised for his newly acquired vocabulary and his "uppity" ways.

| Los norteños | The Northerners |
|---|---|
| Voy a cantarles señores | I am going to sing to you sirs |
| estos versos divertidos | These funny verses; |
| de todos los mexicanos | About all the Mexicans |
| que van a Estados Unidos. | Who go to the United States. |
| Por conocer muchas tierras | Because they want to know many lands |
| Y ganar harto dinero | And to earn lots of money, |
| se enrolan en los enganches | They enroll and contract themselves |
| a tierras del extranjero. | To go to foreign lands. |
| Los que no pueden lograr | Those that cannot obtain |
| su tarjeta de bracero | Their bracero card |
| se pasan de contrabando | Go across illegally |
| por El Paso o por Laredo. | Through El Paso or Laredo. |
| Si su mujer es legal | If his wife is faithful, |
| sufre y tiene que esperar | She suffers and has to wait; |
| pero si es de pocas pulgas | But if she has no scruples |
| lo tiene que coronar. | She cuckolds him. |

En ranchos y en ciudades
encuentran luego que hacer
en el traque o en los plantíos

y corte de betabel.

En Waco y en Corpus Christi
en Houston y Nuevo Orleans
conocen lo que es avena
los *sanquequis** y los flans.

Cuando regresan del norte
muchos no quieren ni hablar
porque traen muy buena ropa
y harto dólar que gastar.

Al llegar a una estación
dicen al despachador (hablando):
*Camo vegier, guime guan tiquete*
*Mr., tenquio may fren*
*orray, beri gut, gut bay*
mascando el inglés le piden
un billete por favor.

Hábleme usted castellano
les contesta el boletero
y dígame lo que quiere
ya no me hable como perro.

La verdad que causa risa
con esos recien llegados
que porque vienen del norte

la quieren dar de ilustrados.

Si te subes en el tren
luego los oirás hablar
vengo a ver a mi familia
y me vuelvo a regresar.

Los gringos pagan muy bien
y son muy considerados
yo no vuelvo a trabajar
a los ricos mexicanos.

Otros resuelven quedarse
en la tierra de Tío Sam
porque dicen *q'en*** su patria
no se consigue ni pan.

On the ranches and in the cities,
They find work to do;
On the railroad tracks or in agriculture,
Or in the beet-cutting business.

In Waco and Corpus Christi,
In Houston and New Orleans,
They get a taste for oatmeal,
Pancakes and custard pudding.

When they return from the North
Many do not even want to speak
Because they bring good clothing
And plenty of dollars to spend.

Upon arriving at the station
They tell the clerk (speaking):
*Come over here, give me one ticket,*
*Mr., thank you my friend*
*All right, very good, good-bye.*
In broken English they ask him
For a ticket, please.

Speak to me in Spanish,
The clerk answers them;
And tell me what you want,
Don't speak to me like a dog.

To tell the truth, it's really funny,
Those recent arrivals;
Because they're coming from the North,
They pretend they are learned.

If you get on the train
You can hear them talking:
"I came to see my family,
But I am returning."

"The gringos pay us well
And they are very considerate;
I shall never work again
For the rich Mexicans."

Others decide to stay
In the land of Uncle Sam
Because they say in their country
You can't even find bread.

| | |
|---|---|
| Pero en verdad les diré | But in truth I'll tell you, |
| para no ir a aventurar | One need not go on adventures; |
| no se necesita el norte | We don't need the North, |
| si aquí hay en que trabajar. | There is work here. |
| | |
| Al fin como dijo aquel | And as the saying goes, |
| aunque el dinero recojas | Even if you shovel money, |
| "si naciste para tamal | "He who is born to be a tamal, |
| del cielo te caen las hojas." | The tamal leaves will come to him from heaven." |
| | |
| Ya con ésta me despido | Now I take my farewell, |
| aquí se acabó el recorte | I have finished cutting down |
| de los famosos catrines | Those famous dandies, |
| de esos que llegan del norte. | Those coming back from the North. |

(Guerrero 1924a)
*sanquequis = pancakes
**q'en = *que en* (that in)

A corrido answering the charges brought in "Los norteños" soon appeared. In it the bracero delineates his reasons for leaving: hunger, poor wages, the rich getting richer and the poor getting poorer. He points out the benefits accrued from working up north. The bracero, however, admonishes his counterparts not to be flashy about their good fortune. He reiterates his loyalty to Mexico and states his wish to return if only things were better. He ends by inviting others to see for themselves and go work up north.

| Defensa de los norteños | Defense of the Emigrants |
|---|---|
| Lo que dicen de nosotros | What they say about us |
| casi todo es realidad; | Is mostly the truth, |
| más salimos del terreno | But we left the country |
| por pura necesidad. | From sheer necessity. |
| | |
| Que muchos vienen facetos | So many come back boasting, |
| yo también se los dijera; | I too can tell you that; |
| por eso la prensa chica | That is why the local press |
| tuvo donde echar tijera. | Speaks harshly about them. |
| | |
| Pero la culpa la tienen | But those who are to blame |
| esos ingratos patrones | Are those unkind employers |
| que no les dan a su gente | Who don't give their people [work] |
| ni aun cuando porte chaqueta. | Even when they wear a jacket. |
| | |
| No es porque hable del país: | I'm not criticizing the country, |
| pero claro se los digo | But I frankly will tell you |
| que muchos trabajadores | That many of the laborers |
| enseñan hasta el ombligo. | Are naked to their navels. |

El rico en buen automóvil,
buen caballo, buena silla,

y los pobrecitos peones
pelona la rabadilla.

Siempre el peón es agobiado,
tratándolo con fiereza,
donde le miran los pies
quieren verle la cabeza.

Lo tratan como un esclavo.
no como útil servidor
que derrama para el rico
hasta el último sudor.

Yo no digo que en el norte
se va uno a estar muy sentado,
ni aun cuando porte chaqueta
Lo hacen a uno diputado.

Allí se va a trabajar
macizo, a lo Americano,
pero alcanza uno a ganar
más que cualesquier paisano.

Aquí se trabaja un año
sin comprarse una camisa;
el pobre siempre sufriendo,
y los ricos risa y risa.

Los cuarenta y el tostón
no salen de su tarifa,
no alcanza para comer;
siempre anda vacía la tripa.

Que lo digan mis paisanos,
si yo les estoy mintiendo,
porque no hay que preguntar
lo que claro estamos viendo.

Mucha gente así lo ha dicho:
*dizque** no somos patriotas
porque les vamos a servir
a los infames patotas.

The rich ride in good automobiles,
They ride a good horse and a good
      saddle,
While the poor peons
Go about with a naked tail.

The peon is always burdened,
Is treated with cruelty;
Where the rich see his feet
They would like to see his head.

They treat him like a slave,
Not like a serviceable person
Who pours out for the rich
His last drop of sweat.

I don't say that in the North
One is going to be taking it easy,
Even though one wears a jacket
One is not made a congressman.

One has to work there,
Hard, in the American fashion,
But one succeeds in earning
More than any of our countrymen.

Here one works a year
Without earning enough for a shirt;
The poor always suffer
And the rich laugh and laugh.

Paid forty or fifty cents,
Never more than that,
He can't get enough to eat,
His stomach is always empty.

Let my countrymen say
If I am telling a lie,
For it's needless to ask about
What we can all clearly see.

Many people have said
That we are not patriotic
Because we go to serve
The accursed big-footed ones.

Pero que se abran trabajos
y que paguen buen dinero,
y no queda un Mexicano
que se vaya al extranjero.

Ansia tenemos de volver
a nuestra patria idolatrada,
pero qué le hemos de hacer
si está la patria arruinada.

Si han hablado de nosostros
es por muchos fanfarrones
que andan sonando los pesos
cual si trajeran millones.

Si no hubieran presumido
ni quien nos dijera nada,

porque todos comprendemos
que nuestra patria es sagrada.

Ya tenemos entendido
que en caso de intervención
vendremos de tierra extraña
a servir en su ocasión.

Que no vengan de facetos
les digo a mis compañeros;
amigos, yo no presumo
porque soy de los rancheros.

Orden guarden y decoro
esos que vienen del norte;
si no quieren que la prensa
a toditos nos recorte.

Porque todo están oliendo—
no crean que son ellos sordos—
y nos pudieran cazar
como si fuéramos tordos.

Yo ya me voy para el norte
amigos, no se los niego;
ahí les dejo a sus riquitos
a que los toree Juan Diego.

But let them give us jobs
And pay us decent wages;
Not one Mexican then
Will go to foreign lands.

We're anxious to return again
To our adored country;
But what can we do about it
If the country is ruined?

If they've talked about us,
It is because of all the braggarts
Who go jingling their dollars
As if they'd brought back millions.

If they had not put on airs,
There would have been no
        comment,
Because we all understand
That our country is sacred.

We all know well
That in case of intervention
We'd come back from abroad
To serve our country in her need.

"Don't come back boasting,"
I say to my companions;
"Friends, I don't put on airs
Because I am just a ranchero."

Let them behave themselves,
Those who come back from the North
If they don't want the newspapers
To speak ill of us.

Because they smell this all out—
And don't believe they are deaf—
They could shoot us down
As though we were turtledoves.

Now I am leaving for the North;
Friends, I do not deny it;
I leave you with your rich fellows—
Let who will be bothered with them.

Muchachos, yo los convido
a la Nación extranjera;
no le hace que algunos digan
que somos chucha cuerera.

Boys, I invite you
To the foreign nation;
Don't be bothered if they say
That we are mercenary.

(Guerrero 1924a)
*dizque = *dicen que* (they say)

The controversy was not over, however. A third corrido appeared which incorporated the two opponents in a duel of words.

## Plática entre dos rancheros

## Conversation between Two Ranchers

No critiques a tu patria,
no rebajes la nación,
procura siempre tener
de ideal, la emancipación.

Don't criticize your country,
Don't run down the nation;
Try to have always,
As an ideal, emancipation.

Plática de dos rancheros
de calzón y sombrero ancho,
uno que había ido al norte
y otro no salía del rancho.

A talk between two rancheros
In pajamas and broad-brimmed hats,
One of whom had been in the North
And one who had not left the ranch.

*Norteño:*

*The man who had journeyed north:*

Si vieras como es bonito
esos Estados Unidos,
por eso los Mexicanos
por allá estamos *engreidos.**

"If you could only see how nice
The United States is;
That is why the Mexicans
Are so fond of it there.

No te imaginas lo que es
vivir como un licenciado
buena camisa, buen traje,
buen abrigo y buen calzado.

"You can't imagine how it is
To live like a lawyer,
With good shirt, good suit,
Good overcoat and shoes.

Tu reloj con su leontina,
y tu fistol de corbata,
los bolsillos siempre van
bien retacados de plata.

"Your watch on its chain
And your scarf-pin in your tie
And your pockets always filled
With plenty of silver.

No se conoce la crisis
por allá en el extranjero,
todos los trabajadores
ganan siempre buen dinero.

"Depression is unknown
There in the foreign land;
All the workers
Always earn good pay.

No me quedó que desear,
conocí el estado de Texas,
allí yo llegué a tener
una docena de viejas.

De esas mujeres bonitas
puras güeras de primera
esas que van por las calles
todas vestidas de seda.

Luego me pasé a S. Luis,
a Kansas a Santa Fé,
en Wuasintón** que primor
de gozar me fastidié.

Los Angeles conocí
al derecho y al revés,
tuteándome con los gringos
porque sé hablar el inglés.

Cuando conocí Arizona
ya era un gran boxeador;
no más mira que conejos
me porto, mi valedor.

Lo que es con esta canilla
pocos se paran el cuello,
no más con una guantada
los hago estampar el sello.

Todo esto que yo te digo
en nada te lo exajero;
ojalá me huvieras visto
por allá en el extranjero

Pero tú nunca has salido
del rancho y de tu doctrina
creyendo en monos de palo
y *isque*** en la virgen divina.

No hombre quítate esa venda,
no te dejes explotar
de hombres que dicen ser sabios
y que estudian para robar.

Vieras que bonito el norte,
hay mucha electricidad,
hay máquinas para todo
que es una barbaridad.

"I had nothing more to wish;
I knew the state of Texas,
And there I got as many
As a dozen women.

"Some of these pretty women,
Classy blondes—the kind
Who go through the streets
All dressed in silk.

"Then I went to St. Louis,
To Kansas and Santa Fe;
In Washington, how swell!
I got tired of so much pleasure.

"I knew Los Angeles
Forward and backward;
I go thick with the gringos,
As I know how to talk English.

"When I was in Arizona
I was a great prize-fighter;
Just take a look at the biceps
That I carry around, partner.

"Few have my right to brag
About their muscles;
With a single blow of my fist,
I would put my mark on them.

"All this that I'm telling you
Is no exaggeration at all;
I wish you'd seen me
There in the foreign country.

"But you have never left
The ranch, or your parish school;
Still believing in wooden images
And in the divine virgin.

"Come, man, unbandage your eyes;
Don't let yourself be exploited
By men who claim to be wise
And who study only to rob.

"Look how splendid the North is—
Lots of electricity,
Machines for everything,
An enormous number of them.

Con el aire comprimido
levantan en el espacio,
no sólo rieles, durmientes
se levanta hasta un palacio.

La verdad que esos patones
se las jalan como astutos,
no son como esta nación
que está plagada de brutos.

Por allá hay protección
inteligencia y dinero,
por eso es que le suspiro
y le lloro al extranjero.

Aquí por un veinticinco
trabaja uno de sol a sol

no pasa uno de comer
puras gordas con frijol.

México será bonito
pero está muy arruinado,
se trabaja noche y día
y no sale uno de pelado.

Pero si cree uno en milagros
y en las ánimas benditas
y en irle a besar la mano
a los señores curitas.

Y creelo que el capitalista
aquí nos tiene cegados
para podernos robar
porque son muy desgraciados.

No es que yo hable de más
de los ricos cabezones
pero tú ya bien lo ves
que son puritos bribones.

Hay nos pintan el infierno
y al diablo con mucha cola.
*qisque*\*\*\*\* á San Ramón Nonato
y también la ánima sola.

"With compressed air
They raise up into space
Not only rails and ties
But even whole palaces.

"The truth is those big feet
Are considered very smart;
They are not like this country,
Which is plagued with stupid people.

"Over there they have protection,
Intelligence, and wealth;
That is why I sigh for it,
And yearn for that foreign land.

"Here for twenty-five cents
One works from sun up to sun
        down;
There is nothing else to eat
But tortillas and beans.

"I grant that Mexico is very pretty,
But it's down and out;
One works day and night
And never ceases to be a bum.

"But they do believe in miracles
And in the blessed souls
And in going to the priest
In order to kiss his hand.

"But believe me, the capitalists
Have blinded us
In order to be able to rob us:
They are a lot of scoundrels.

"It isn't that I want to talk
About those rich men,
But you can see for yourself
That they are terrible thieves.

"They picture hell to us
And the devil with a big tail,
As well as San Ramon Nonato
And also the immortal soul.

Nada de eso valedor
no te creas de esas boberas,
son puritas vaciladas
son puras conseguideras.

"Pay no attention to that, pardner;
Don't believe those follies;
They are simply nonsense,
They are simply frauds."

*El que no había ido al norte:*

*The man who had not gone north:*

Ya cáyate pues el osico
no hables de la religión,
se me hace que te despacho
a traer changos al Japón.

"You had better shut your mouth
And quit talking about religion,
Or I'll have to send you
To bring monkeys from Japan.

Voy que con este instrumento
yo te quito lo relajo
aunque seas gran boxeador
ahorita te saco el cuajo.

"With this little tool
I'll change your tune;
Even though you're a great boxer,
I'll cut out your rennet."

Y le enseñó un puñalón
al norteñito payaso,
que luego se le engrifaron
todos los del espinazo.

And he showed him such a knife,
To the clown from the North,
That it gave him the shivers
Up and down his spine.

Y le agarró tal temblor
al ver tan filoso acero,
que se incó a pedir perdón,
el uno al otro ranchero.

It gave him such a fright
To see such a terrible blade
That he knelt to beg
The pardon of the other ranchero.

*Norteño:*

*The man who had journeyed north:*

No vayas a dar por Dios
por San Antonio bendito,
no vayas a dar con fierro
no me pegues hermanito.

"Don't hit me, for God's sake;
In the name of blessed San Antonio,
Don't strike me with the blade,
Don't hit me, little brother."

*El que no había ido al norte:*

*The man who had not gone north:*

No que eres la colmillona
que en el norte te has rifado
para que te incas de rodillas
levántate desgraciado.

"Aren't you the bold fellow
Who's done so much in the North?
What are you on your knees for?
Get up, miserable wretch.

No que no crees en los santos
ni tampoco en el demonio,
para que invocas cobarde
al glorioso San Antonio.

"Since you don't believe in saints
Nor even in the devil,
Then, coward, why invoke
Glorious San Antonio?

Se me hace que eres maldito
nada más de puro pico,
por eso de compasión
no te doy en el osico.

"It seems to me your bravery
Is just a loud mouth;
That's why I am sorry for you
And don't punish you in the mouth."

(Taylor 1969:241–245)
*engreidos = *engreídos* (spoiled, fond of)
**Wuasinton = Washington
*** isque = *dicen que* (they say)
****quisque = *dicen que* (they say)

In spite of the acrimonious recriminations hurled at the Mexican immigrant by his own people and in spite of the charges of being a traitor, he continued to emigrate to the United States. "Despedida de los reenganchados" again depicts a man who under the duress of poverty leaves his land. The protagonist reiterates at every opportunity that he retains his loyalty to religion and country ("pero llevo al frente mi fé y mi bandera"). The song also points out two historical events: the process of recruiting by U.S. companies who worked in Mexico and the rumors associated with recruitment—mainly that Mexicans were being drafted to fight in the trenches of World War I.

## Despedida de los reenganchados

Adiós muchachos me voy de mi tierra,
salgo en el enganche mañana en el tren,
pero llevo al frente mi fé y mi bandera
y a donde yo vaya irá ella también.

Voy a ver a los gringos para ver qué quieren
con los mexicanos que vienen a traer;
al fin que los hombres donde quiera mueren
y voy a su tierra, pues qué me han de hacer.

Dicen que me quieren para que trabaje,
cuatro pesos dólar me van a pagar;
si es para otra cosa no crean que me raje
que también el rifle lo sé manejar.

Tres meses de plazo llevo en mi contrato,
si no me conviene luego volveré
y si son legales y me dan buen trato,
algo de más tiempo les ayudaré.

(Prieto Posada 1944:109)

## A Farewell from a Recontracted Crew

Good-bye, my friends, I leave my country,
I leave on a work crew tomorrow by train,
But I carry with me my faith and my flag
And wherever I go she shall go, too.

I am going to see the gringos to see what they want
With us Mexicans whom they come and recruit;
Anyway, I do say men die everywhere,
I shall go to their land, I am not afraid.

They say they want me to work there,
Four dollars they will be paying me;
If they have something else in mind I will not back down,
For I know how to handle a rifle, too.

Three months does my contract last;
If I do not like it I shall return,
And if they are honest and treat me well
I will help them one more time.

It is obvious in reading these canciones and corridos that the Mexican immigrants had their own versions of the experience and sought to portray it in their own words through the lyrics. The Mexican immigrants thus were successful in inserting themselves into the pages of history through their folk songs.

# Of Migrants and Renegades

*Four* The 1920s was a period of both consolidation and expansion for the Mexican-American population. Its numbers continued to increase until 1929, when the economic crisis in the United States became manifest. The process of migration, job opportunity, and settlement described by historian Albert Camarillo for the Santa Barbara area in California applies also to other sectors of the United States.

> Prior to World War I much of the area on the lower east side was occupied by small-scale vegetable farming, marsh lands, the city dump, and vacant land. However, it was this area that by 1920 became the large Mexicano barrio (the approximately ten-block area bounded by Milpas, Ortega, and State Streets). The Mexicanos there established an early pattern of work and residence based upon economic necessity and racial segregation. Mexicanos increasingly established residence near work opportunities (the railroad and lumber yards, the fruit packing houses) in the least desirable and cheapest areas of the city. As Mexicano migration increased, the area of the barrio expanded and at the same time became more densely populated. The process replicated itself throughout the 1920s. (Camarillo 1979:145–146)

The upheaval, violence, and disruption caused by the Mexican Revolution and the great need in the United States for Mexican labor during World War I were the primary factors stimulating Mexican immigration. In a study conducted by Gilberto Loyo in 1926–1927, sixty-one immigrants were extensively interviewed on why they left Mexico. He reported these results (see Carreras de Velasco 1974:29):

| | |
|---|---|
| Because of the Mexican Revolution. | 17 |
| In search of adventure. | 9 |
| Because of higher wages. | 21 |
| Because of unemployment or underemployment. | 3 |
| To study. | 2 |
| Other reasons. | 9 |

These figures correlate well with the reasons stated in folk songs. In addition, Camarillo (1979:146) indicates that relatives who had settled during previous decades encouraged their kin to emigrate.

Folk songs appearing during the 1920s cover three aspects of Mexican immigration: Mexican migratory movements, crime and the Mexican immigrant, and the beginnings of Mexican assimilation and acculturation into U.S. society and the reaction to this process.

## Migratory Movements

Various migratory streams or routes began to develop as Mexicans' search for work led them to various areas of the United States. Some routes started in southern Texas, in the Rio Grande border region, and expanded northward to Illinois, Michigan, Minnesota, and the Midwest in general. Other routes took immigrants to Arizona, California, and the Northwest. Some immigrants preferred the Colorado, Montana, and Idaho areas. The accompanying table shows the rate of immigration from Mexico to the United States for 1900 or earlier through 1930.

The folk songs "Versos de los betabeleros," "Corrido de Pennsylvania," and their variants describe the migrant experience from Texas to other states. In "Versos de los betabeleros" the hardships and plain hard work endured by the migrant worker are enumerated. The year is 1923; the destination, Michigan;

### U.S. Immigration Rate for Foreign-Born Mexicans by Residence, to 1930

| Residence | 1900 or Earlier | 1901– 1910 | 1911– 1914 | 1915– 1919 | 1920– 1924 | 1925– 1930 | Total 1930 |
|---|---|---|---|---|---|---|---|
| United States | 100.0 | 100.0 | 100.0 | 100.0 | 100.0 | 100.0 | 100.0 |
| Urban | 52.3 | 56.8 | 59.8 | 58.5 | 57.2 | 60.1 | 57.6 |
| Rural | 47.7 | 43.2 | 40.2 | 41.5 | 42.8 | 39.9 | 42.5 |
| Arizona | 9.3 | 7.4 | 6.3 | 8.0 | 8.1 | 7.6 | 7.8 |
| California | 18.3 | 30.9 | 25.7 | 33.4 | 35.4 | 32.2 | 31.0 |
| Colorado | 0.9 | 1.8 | 1.9 | 2.7 | 2.3 | 1.4 | 2.1 |
| New Mexico | 3.9 | 2.9 | 2.7 | 2.6 | 2.6 | 1.5 | 2.6 |
| Texas | 64.5 | 49.3 | 55.1 | 41.2 | 36.1 | 30.4 | 42.6 |
| Illinois | 0.4 | 1.3 | 1.5 | 2.7 | 3.8 | 7.1 | 3.3 |
| Indiana | 0.1 | 0.4 | 0.5 | 0.7 | 1.6 | 3.0 | 1.2 |
| Kansas | 0.2 | 1.3 | 1.3 | 2.1 | 1.7 | 2.4 | 1.8 |
| Michigan | 0.3 | 0.6 | 0.9 | 1.1 | 1.9 | 3.2 | 1.5 |
| All other states | 2.1 | 4.1 | 4.0 | 5.4 | 6.7 | 10.3 | 6.1 |

Source: U.S. Bureau of Census, *Fifteenth Census of the United States: 1930, Reports on Population*, vol. 2, chap. 9, p. 512.
States for which figures are presented are those having a foreign-born Mexican population of 5,000 or more in 1930.

the work, beet cutting. The migrant worker complains about the deceit involved in recruitment: promises of a luxurious life and easy work, but once there, backbreaking work and hard looks from the foreman are all that is reaped. And to complicate matters, even the weather does not cooperate. The men yearn to return home to Texas.

## Versos de los betabeleros

Año de mil novecientos
veinte y tres en el actual,
fueron los betabeleros
a ese Michiga a llorar.

Aquí vienen y nos cuentan
que nos vayamos para allá,
porque allá nos tienen todo
y no vamos a batallar.

Pero son puras mentiras.
Cuando ya estamos allá,
empiezan a regañarnos
y queremos regresar.

Cuando llegamos a Jiusto
no hallábamos qué hacer.
El tiempo estaba muy duro.
No se quería componer.

Cuando llegamos a Jiusto,
trabajando noche y día,
no nos daban de comer
no más que pura sandía.

Al pasar del Estado de Tejas
a las dos de la mañana,
le pregunté al enganchista
que si íbamos a Luisiana.

Gritaba Juan el Coyote,
con su sombrero de lado:
—Yo no volveré a Kansas
a trabajarle al condado.

Gritaba Juan el Coyote
con esa boca de infierno:
—Yo no volveré a Kansas
a trabajarle al gobierno.

## Verses of the Beet-Field Workers

In the year 1923
Of the present era,
The beet-field workers went
To that Michigan, to their grief.

Here they come and they tell you
That we ought to go up there
Because there we will have everything
And we will not have a hard time.

But these are nothing but lies.
When we are over there
They begin to scold us
And we want to return.

When we arrived at Houston
We didn't find anything to do,
The weather was quite bad
And it didn't want to clear up.

When we arrived at Houston,
Working night and day,
They didn't feed us anything,
Nothing more than watermelon.

While leaving the state of Texas
At two in the morning,
I asked the boss contractor
If we were going to Louisiana.

Juan el Coyote yelled out,
With his hat on one side:
"I will not go back to Kansas
To work for the county."

Juan el Coyote yelled out
With that mouth of hell:
"I will not go back to Kansas
To work for the government."

Despedida no la doy
porque no la tengo aquí.
La dejé en el Estado de Tejas
para que se acuerden de mí.

I shall not sing my farewell
Because I do not have it with me;
I left it in the state of Texas
To make them remember me.

(Goodwyn 1944)

The variant "Los betabeleros" focuses on the same theme.

## Los betabeleros

Año de mil nuevecientos
Veinte y tres en el actual
Fueron los betabeleros
A ese Michiga a llorar.

Porque todos los señores
Empezaban a regañar
Y don Santiago les responde:
Yo me quiero regresar.

Porque no nos han cumplido
Lo que fueron a contar.
Aquí vienen y les cuentan
Que se vayan para allá.

Porque allá les tienen todo

Que no van a batallar,
Pero son puras mentiras
Los que vienen y les dicen.

Cuando ya estamos allá
Empiezan a regañarnos
Y luego les respondemos:
"Nosotros nos regresamos

Porque allá en San Antonio
Nosotros sólo gozamos.
El 18 de febrero,
Ah que día tan señalado!"

Cuando llegamos a Houston
No hallábamos ni que hacer
El tiempo estaba muy duro
No se quería componer.

## The Beet-Field Workers

In the year 1923
Of the present era
The beet-field workers went
To that Michigan, to their grief.

Because all the bosses
Began to scold,
And Mr. Santiago says to them:
I want to return.

Because they haven't done for us
What they said they would;
Here they come and they tell you
That you ought to go up there.

Because there you will have every-
thing
Without having to fight for it.
But these are nothing but lies,
From those who come and say those
things.

When we get there
They begin to scold us,
And then we say to them:
"We are going back

Because there is San Antonio
We just enjoy ourselves.
The 18th of February,
Oh, what a day to remember!"

When we arrived at Houston
We didn't find anything to do.
The weather was very harsh,
And it was not getting better.

| | |
|---|---|
| Cuando llegamos a Houston | When we arrived at Houston, |
| Trabajando noche y día | Working night and day, |
| No nos daban de comer | They didn't feed us |
| No más que pura sandía. | Nothing more than watermelon. |
| | |
| Al pasar el estado de Texas | On leaving the state of Texas |
| A las dos de la mañana | At two in the morning |
| Le pregunté al enganchista | I asked the boss contractor |
| Que si íbamos a Louisiana | If we were going to Louisiana. |
| | |
| Llegamos a Kansas City, | We arrived at Kansas City. |
| Gritaba Juan "El Coyote" | Juan "El Coyote" yelled out, |
| Con su sombrero de lado, | With his hat on one side, |
| Yo no volveré a Kansas | I will not go back to Kansas |
| A trabajarle al condado | To work for the county. |
| | |
| Gritaba Juan "El Coyote" | Juan "El Coyote" yelled out |
| con esa boca de infierno: | With that mouth of hell, |
| Yo no volveré a Kansas | I will not go back to Kansas |
| A trabajarle al gobierno. | To work for the government. |
| | |
| Despedida no la doy | I shall not sing my farewell |
| Porque no la traigo aquí | Because I do not have it with me; |
| La dejé en el estado de Texas | I left it in the state of Texas |
| Para que se acuerden de mí. | To make them remember me. |

(Gamio 1971:86–88)

Sources substantiate the Mexican immigrants' involvement in the beet sugar industry. In an article published August 14, 1929, Robert N. McLean writes:

> I was recently called upon to make a survey of the Mexican colony in Saginaw, Michigan. In the foundry of the General Motors Corporation, I found a group of four hundred men. Most of them had been recruited from the beet-workers that the sugar companies had brought from Texas. They were now earning four dollars and a half per day, and their work was permanent. It was only natural that many of the other Mexicans in the neighborhood should have been eager to graduate from the agricultural to the industrial group. And this is going on all over the country. The farmers go to considerable expense to recruit Mexican labor, only to see it taken away from them by the industries. For the movement is from the farm to the factory and the foundry, leaving the farmers to hold the bag. (335)

Similarly, Carreras de Velasco reports:

> In California, Colorado, and Michigan one found the main regions of beet cultivation. Toward the end of the nineteenth century tariffs were levied on the sugar beet which stimulated the expansion of the [domestic] beet-growing

industry. The production of sugar beet is labor intensive. Labor is needed for planting and weeding during the spring season and for harvesting in the fall. The working conditions associated with sugar beet growing were very harsh and salaries very low. Public health facilities were totally absent. Aside from the Mexicans, no one wanted to do that type of job. (1974:40)

But not all migrant workers were engaged in agricultural pursuits. In 1923 the Bethlehem Steel Company in Bethlehem, Pennsylvania, contracted a large number of men to work in the steel mills. Remsen Crawford reported that the "Mexicans are forming colonies as far north as Pennsylvania" (1930:902). Crawford further amplified on a particular Mexican colony in Pennsylvania:

> The reaction to Mexican immigration in the more northerly States should also be noted. A reply from a tract foreman on a railroad at Erie, Pa., where there is a colony of about 100 Mexican workers, states that they went there during a labor boom, that they leave in times of labor reductions, that the wages paid them are the same as are paid to white workers, that they have displaced no native laborers, and that only three out of the 100 brought their families with them. This report gives the Mexicans a clean bill of health and says their standards of living are about the same as those of native whites. (907)

The journey to Pennsylvania is immortalized in the stanzas of the corrido "La Pensilvania" and two variants.

## La Pensilvania

El veintiocho de abril
a las seis de la mañana
salimos en un enganche
pa'l* Estado de Pensilvania.

Mi chinita me decía:
—Yo me voy en esa agencia,
pa' lavarte tu ropa
pa' darte tu asistencia.

El enganchista me dijo:
—No lleves a tu familia
para no pasar trabajo
en el Estado de West Virginia.

—Para que sepas que te quiero
me dejas en Fort Worth
cuando ya estés trabajando
me escribes de donde estés.

## Pennsylvania

The 28th of April
At six o'clock in the morning
We went on a labor contract
To the state of Pennsylvania.

My beloved said to me:
"I want to go on that job,
So I can wash your clothes
And cook your meals."

The contractor told me:
"Do not take your family
So that we don't have problems
In the state of West Virginia."

"So that you know I love you
You can leave me in Forth Worth
And when you are working
Write to me wherever you are.

Cuando ya estés por allá
me escribes, no seas ingrato,
de contestación te mando
de recuerdo mi retrato.

Adiós, Estado de Texas,
con toda tu plantación:
yo me voy a Pensilvania
por no pizcar algodón.

Adiós, Fort Worth y Dallas
pueblos de mucha importancia:
me voy para Pensilvania
por no andar en la vagancia.

Al llegar al steel *mill worque*\*\*
que vemos la locomotora,
¡y que salimos corriendo,
ochenta millas por hora!

Cuando llegamos allá
y del tren nos bajamos,
preguntan las italianas:
—¿De dónde vienen mexicanos?

Responden los mexicanos,
los que ya saben *inglear*\*\*\*;
—Venimos en un enganche
del pueblo de Fort Worth.

Estos versos son compuestos
cuando yo venía en camino,
soy un muchacho mexicano,
nombre das por Constantino.

Ya con ésta me despido
con mi sombrero en las manos
de mis fieles compañeros,
son trescientos mexicanos.

"When you arrive over there
Write to me, don't be mean,
And in return I shall send you
My picture to remember me by."

Good-bye, state of Texas,
With all your planted fields,
I am going to Pennsylvania
So as not to pick cotton.

Good-bye, Fort Worth and Dallas,
Towns of great importance,
I am going to Pennsylvania
So as not to be a bum.

When we arrived at the steel mill
We saw the locomotive
And we started traveling
At eighty miles per hour!

When we arrived over there
And we got down from the train
The Italian ladies asked,
"Where are you coming from, Mexicans?"

The Mexicans answered,
Those that knew some English,
"We come with a labor contractor
From the town of Fort Worth."

These verses were composed
When I was on my way here.
I am a young Mexican man
By the name of Constantino.

With this I bid farewell
With my hat in my hands
And my faithful companions
Are three hundred Mexicans.

(Campos 1962:329–330)
\*pa'l = *para el* (to the)
\*\*mill worque = possible confusion with Milwaukee
\*\*\*inglear = *hablar inglés* (speak English)

## Corrido de Pensilvania

El día veintiséis de abril
a las séis de la mañana,
salimos en un enganche
para el Estado de Pensilvania.

## Ballad of Pennsylvania

On the 26th of April
At six o'clock in the morning
We left on a contract
For the state of Pennsylvania.

Mi chinita me decía:
yo me voy en esa agencia,
para lavarles la ropa
y pa' darles su asistencia.

El reenganchista me dijo:
No lleves a tu familia,
para no pasar trabajos
al Estado de Pensilvania.

Pa' que sepas que te quiero
me dejas en Fort West,
cuando ya estés trabajando
me escribes de donde estés.

Cuando ya estés por allá
me escribes, no seas ingrato,
de memorias yo te mando
de recuerdos mi retrato.

Adiós, Estado de Texas,
con toda su plantación,
ya me voy pa' Pensilvania
por no pizcar algodón.

Adiós, Fort West, de Jara
pueblo de mucha importancia,
ya me voy pa' Pensilvania
por no andar en la vagancia.

Al llegar a Piquíleque,
cambiamos locomotora,
de ahí salimos corriendo
a ochenta millas por hora.

Cuando llegamos allá
que del tren ya nos bajamos,
preguntan las italianas,
¿de dónde vienen, mexicanos?

Responden los mexicanos
los que ya sabían inglés:
Venimos en un enganche
del Estado de Fort West.

My beloved said to me:
"I will go on that job
So as to wash your clothes
And cook your meals."

The contract boss told me:
"Do not take your family
So as not to have a hard time
In the state of Pennsylvania."

"So that you know I love you
You can leave me in Fort West
And when you are working
You write to me from where you are.

"When you arrive over there
Write to me, don't be mean,
And in return I shall send you
My picture to remember me by."

Good-bye, state of Texas,
With all your planted fields,
I am going to Pennsylvania
So I don't have to pick cotton.

Good-bye, Fort West, Dallas,
A town of great importance,
I am going to Pennsylvania
So as not be a bum.

Upon arriving at Kentucky
We changed train engines,
From there we started to travel
At eighty miles per hour.

When we arrived over there
And we got down from the train,
The Italian ladies asked us:
"Where are you coming from, Mex-
        icans?"

And the Mexicans responded,
Those that knew English:
"We came here on a labor contract
From the state of Fort West."

Estos versos los compuse
cuando ya venía en camino,
son poesías de un mexicano
nombrado por Constantino.

Ya con esta me despido,
con mi sombrero en las manos;
y mis fieles compañeros
son trescientos mexicanos.

These verses were composed
When I was traveling,
They are the poetry of a Mexican
By the name of Constantino.

With this I bid farewell
With my hat in my hands
And my faithful companions
Are three hundred Mexicans.

## La Pensilvania

El día veintiocho de abril
a las seis de la mañana,
salimos en un enganche
para el estado de Pensilvania.

Mi chinita me decía:
—Yo me voy en esa agencia,
para lavarle su ropa,
para darle su asistencia.—

Y el enganchista nos dice:
—No se lleven la familia,
para no pasar trabajos
en el estado de West Virginia.—

—Pa' que sepas que te quiero,
me dejas en Foro West;
cuando ya estés trabajando
me escribes de donde estés.—

—Cuando ya estés trabajando
me escribes, no seas ingrato;
de contestación te mando,
de recuerdo, mi retrato.—

Al llegar a West Kentockle
cambiamos locomotora,
de allí salimos corriendo
ochenta millas por hora.

Adiós Foro West y Dalas,
pueblos de mucha importancia;
ya me voy pa' Pensilvania
por no andar en la vagancia.

## Pennsylvania

On the twenty-eighth day of April,
at six o'clock in the morning,
we left on a labor contract
for the state of Pennsylvania.

My beloved said to me,
"I want to go on that job,
so I can wash your clothes,
so I can cook your meals."

But the labor contractor told us,
"Don't take your families along,
so you won't have any trouble
in the state of West Virginia."

"Just to show you that I love you,
leave me, then, in Fort Worth;
when you are settled and working,
write to me, wherever you are."

"When you are settled and working,
please write to me, don't be mean;
when I answer I will send you
my picture to remember me by."

When we got to West Kentucky,
we switched locomotives;
we went out of there going
at eighty miles per hour.

Farewell, Fort Worth and Dallas,
Towns of great importance;
I'm going to Pennsylvania
to avoid a vagrant's life.

Adiós estado de Texas,
con toda su plantación;
ya me voy pa' Pensilvania
por no pizcar algodón.

Farewell, you state of Texas,
    with all your planted fields,
I'm going to Pennsylvania
so I won't have to pick cotton.

Cuando llegamos allá,
que del tren ya nos bajamos,
nos dicen las italianas:
—¿Di 'ónde* vienen, mexicanos?—

When we arrived there,
once we had got off the train,
the Italian girls asked us,
"Mexicans, where are you from?"

Contestan los mexicanos,
los que ya sabían inglés:
—Venimos en un enganche
de la ciudad de For West.—

And the Mexicans answered,
those who already knew English,
"We have come on a labor contract
from the city of Fort Worth."

Estos versos son compuestos
cuando ya venía en camino,
poesías de un mexicano
de nombre de Constantino.

These stanzas were composed
while I was still on the way;
they're the verses of a Mexican
by the name of Constantino.

Ya con ésta me despido,
con mi sombrero en las manos,
y mis fieles compañeros
son trescientos mexicanos.

Now with this I say farewell,
with my hat in my hands,
and my faithful companions
are three hundred Mexicans.

(Paredes 1976:56–57)
*¿Di'ónde? = ¿de dónde? (where from?)

Again in the "Corrido de Texas" the contracted worker is leaving Texas "so as not to pick cotton." The men travel from Texas to Lousiana and on to Indiana and Chicago.

## Corrido de Texas

Mi chinita me decía
Ya me voy para la agencia—
a pasearme por el norte
y para hacerle su asistencia.

## Texas Corrido

My woman used to tell me,
"I am going to the agency—
I'll roam around the north
And take care of you.

De la parte donde estés
me escribes, no seas ingrato
y en contestación te mando
de recuerdos mi retrato.

"Wherever you may be,
Write to me, don't be forgetful;
And in reply I'll send you
My picture as a forget-me-not."

Adiós estado de Texas
con toda tu plantación,
me retiro de tus tierras
por no pizcar algodón.

Good-bye, state of Texas,
With all your growing crops;
I am leaving your fields
So I won't have to pick cotton.

| | |
|---|---|
| Esos trenes del *Tipí*\* | These trains of the T & P |
| que cruzan por la Lusiana | That cross Louisiana |
| se llevan los mejicanos | Carry the Mexicans |
| para el estado de Indiana. | To the state of Indiana. |
| | |
| El día 22 de abril | On the 22nd of April |
| a las dos de la mañana | At two o'clock in the morning |
| salimos en un renganche | We left in a renganche |
| para el estado de Lusiana. | For the state of Louisiana. |
| | |
| Adiós estado de Texas | Good-bye, state of Texas, |
| con toda tu plantación, | With all your growing crops; |
| me despido de tus tierras | I bid farewell to your fields |
| por no pizcar algodón. | So I won't have to pick cotton. |
| | |
| Adiós For Worth y Dallas, | Good-bye, Fort Worth and Dallas, |
| poblaciones sin un lago, | Cities without a lake; |
| nos veremos cuando vuelva | We'll see each other when I return |
| de por Indiana y Chicago. | From Indiana and Chicago. |
| | |
| El enganchista nos dice | The contractor tells us |
| que no llevemos mujer | Not to take a woman along, |
| para no pasar trabajos | So as to avoid difficulties |
| y poder pronto volver. | And so as to return soon. |

(Taylor 1969:227–228)
\*Tipí = Texas and Pacific Railroad

## Crime and the Mexican Immigrant

As might be expected, the Mexican immigrant at times tangled with the law. Such is the topic of the corrido "Vida, proceso, y muerte de Aurelio Pompa," from Gamio's collection. The corridista commences the tragic tale of a young man, Aurelio Pompa, a native of Caborca, Sonora, who left for the United States to escape from civil strife in Mexico: "Vámonos, madre," le dijo un día, / que allá no existe revolución." The leave-taking comes in an omnious atmosphere, with all the participants—girlfriend, friends, town priest—regretting the drastic actions of the young immigrant. However, the incentive for Aurelio was too strong: "Vámonos, madre, que allá está el dollar; / y mucho, juro, que he de ganar." Aurelio leaves for California and gets into a brawl with a carpenter, who so provokes him that in self-defense Aurelio shoots him. The jury convicts the young immigrant, and although 20,000 signatures are collected in his behalf and even President Obregón from Mexico requests clemency, it is all to no avail.

## Vida, proceso, y muerte de Aurelio Pompa

Voy a contarles la triste historia
de un mexicano que allá emigró

Aurelio Pompa, así se llamaba,
el compatriota que allí murió

Allá en Caborca, que es de Sonora,

el pueblo humilde donde nació,

"Vámonos, madre," le dijo un día
que allá no existe revolución.

Adios, amigos, adios, María,"
dijo a la novia con gran dolor,
yo te prometo que pronto vuelvo,
para casarnos, mediante Dios.

Adios, Aurelio, dijo la novia,
que sollozando se fue a rezar,
cuídalo mucho, Virgen María,
que yo presiento no volverá.

El señor cura y sus amigos,
junto a la novia fueron a hablar,

a suplicarle al pobre Aurelio
que no dejara el pueblo natal.

Fueron inútiles tantos consejos
también los ruegos de su mamá

vámonos, madre, que allá está el
    dollar
y mucho, juro, que he de ganar.

El mes de mayo de hace cuatro años
a California fueron los dos
y por desgracia en la misma fecha

en una cárcel allá murió.

## Life, Trial, and Death of Aurelio Pompa

I am going to tell you the sad story
of a Mexican who emigrated out
    there—
Aurelio Pompa, so he was called.
Our compatriot who died there.

Out there in Caborca, which is in
    Sonora,
The humble village where he was
    born,
"Come on, mother," he said one day,
"Over there there are no revolutions.

Good-bye, friends; good-bye, María,"
He said to his betrothed very sadly.
"I promise you that I will return soon,
So we can get married, God willing."

"Good-bye, Aurelio," said the girl,
And she went sobbing to pray.
"Look after him, Virgin Mary,
I have a foreboding he will not come
    back."

The priest and his friends
Along with his sweetheart went to
    talk
And to beg poor Aurelio
Not to leave his native village.

Such advice was useless
And so were the entreaties of his
    mother.
"Let's go, mother, over there is the
    dollar,
And I swear I am going to earn a lot
    of them."

Four years ago in the month of May
The two of them went to California
And through misfortune on the very
    same date
He died there in prison.

| | |
|---|---|
| Un carpintero que era muy fuerte, | A carpenter who was very strong |
| al pobre joven muy cruel golpeó, | Struck the poor young fellow cruelly, |
| y Aurelio Pompa juró vengarse | And Aurelio Pompa swore to be revenged |
| de aquellos golpes que recibió. | For those blows he had received. |
| Lleno de rabia contó a la madre | Filled with rage he told his mother about it |
| y la pobre anciana le aconsejó | And the poor old woman advised him, |
| "por Dios, olvida, hijo querido," | "Por dios, forget it, dear son." |
| y el buen Aurelio le perdonó. | And good Aurelio forgave him; |
| Pero una tarde, que trabajaba, | But one afternoon, when he was working |
| con tres amigos en la estación | With three friends at the railroad station |
| el carpintero pasó burlando | The carpenter came by mocking at him |
| y al pobre Pompa le provocó. | And aroused poor Pompa. |
| Los tres amigos le aconsejaban | The three friends advised him |
| que lo dejara y fuera con dios | To leave him alone and go his way, |
| y el carpintero, con un martillo | And then the carpenter, with a hammer, |
| muy injurioso lo amenazó. | Very offensively threatened him. |
| Entonces Pompa, viendo el peligro, | Then Pompa, seeing the danger, |
| en su defensa le disparó | Fired in self-defense |
| con un revólver y cara a cara, | With a revolver and face to face |
| como los hombres él lo mató. | Like a man he killed him. |
| Vino la causa, llegó el jurado. | The case came to court, the jury arrived, |
| y el pueblo Yanqui lo sentenció. | And the Yankee people sentenced him. |
| "Pena de muerte" pidieron todos, | "The death penalty," they all demanded, |
| y el abogado no protestó. | And the lawyer did not object. |
| Veinte mil firmas de compatriotas | Twenty thousand signatures of compatriots |
| perdón pidieron al gobernador | Asked for his pardon from the governor |
| todo la prensa también pedía | All the newspapers asked for it too, |
| y hasta un mensaje mandó Obregón. | And even Obregón sent a message. |

Todo fue inútil, las sociedades,
todas unidas pedían perdón.
La pobre madre, ya casi muerta,
también fue a ver al gobernador.

"Adios, amigos, adios, mi pueblo

Querida madre, no llores más,
dile a mi raza que ya no venga
que aquí se sufre que no hay piedad."

El carcelero le preguntaba:
español eres? y el contestó
"soy mexicano y orgullo serlo

aunque me nieguen a mi el perdón."

Esta es la historia de un compatriota
que hace cuatro años allí llegó
y por desgracia en la misma fecha

en una cárcel muy mal murió.

(Gamio 1971:104–107)

All was useless; the societies,
All united, asked his pardon.
His poor mother, half-dead already,
Also went to see the governor.

"Farewell, my friends, farewell, my
    village;
Dear mother, cry no more.
Tell my race not to come here,
For here they will suffer; there is no
    pity here."

The jailer asked him:
"Are you Spanish?" and he answered,
"I am a Mexican and proud of being
    so
Although they deny me a pardon."

This is the story of a compatriot
Who four years ago came there
And through misfortune on the same
    date
Died in a dreadful way in a prison.

"Vida, proceso, y muerte de Aurelio Pompa" is narrated in the third person, since the protagonist is dead. The structure therefore follows that of heroic-type corridos in which a third-person omniscient narrator recounts the life and death of the protagonist. The corrido adheres to Duvalier's basic formulas. The corridista first addresses the audience, introduces the main character, Aurelio Pompa, cites his place of birth, and delineates the main events leading to Aurelio's death. Aurelio states his reasons for leaving Mexico: the turmoil and violence of the revolution. The prospective immigrant bids good-bye to his girlfriend (see also chapter 11 for this theme) and promises to return with enough money to marry her. The dollar is highlighted as the strong magnet that impels Aurelio to leave home, country, and loved ones. While in the United States Aurelio is beaten severely by a carpenter and later mocked by this same anonymous carpenter. The protagonist evidently kills or hurts the carpenter, for the next sequence is that of Aurelio in jail. The protagonist bids farewell in the manner of the classic corrido and delivers a message: "dile a mi raza que ya no venga / que aquí se sufre que no hay piedad." The message is unequivocal: do not come to the United States. The issue of racial conflict is approached in this ballad as well as the controversial issue of identity ("I am a Mexican"–type assertion).

In this next corrido, another immigrant lands in jail.

## Ramón Delgado
### Primera parte

Año de mil novecientos
veintitrés que se contó,
en ese pueblo del Hondo
Ramón Delgado murió.

Y ese pueblo del Hondo
está corriendo mala fama,
que matan al mexicano
nomás porque les da gana.

Ahí su esposa lo lloraba,
su hijita con más razón,
de ver a su padre muerto
preso su hermano Ramón.

En esa cárcel del Hondo
Ramón chico se encontraba,
y el estaba inocente
lo que en su casa pasaba.

El carcelero le dijo:
—¿No sabes lo que ha pasado?
que en el rancho donde vives
a tu padre lo han matado.—

Al oír esa noticia
pues, ¿cómo se quedaría?
preso en la cárcel del Hondo
porque así le convendría.

Me dispensarán los gringos
que hablo de su gran valor,
que matan al mexicano
por quitarle su labor.

Yo les digo la verdad,
estoy bastante ofendido,
al cabo si a mí me matan
ya mi padre está tendido.

### Segunda parte

Yo lo siento por mi hermana
y por mi madre querida,
ya a mi padre lo mataron,
yo ya no quiero la vida.

## Ramón Delgado
### First part

The year nineteen hundred and
twenty-three that just past,
in the town of Hondo,
Ramón Delgado was killed.

That town of Hondo
is getting a bad reputation;
there they kill Mexicans
just because they feel like it.

His wife wept for him
and his daughter cried even more
seeing her father dead
and her brother Ramón in jail.

In that Hondo jail
young Ramón found himself
and he was innocent
of what was happening at home.

The jailer asked him,
"Have you heard what's happened?
Over at your ranch where you live
they've killed your father."

When he heard the news,
well, how do you think he felt?
Locked up in the jail of Hondo
because he was better off that way.

The gringos will forgive me
if I speak of their brave deeds;
they kill the Mexicans
to take away their work.

I tell you the truth,
I am deeply offended
so if they want to kill me
my father is already dead.

### Second Part

I am sorry for my sister
and my dear mother,
they've killed my father,
life is not worth living now.

| | |
|---|---|
| Y si yo paro en la misma | If I pay with my life |
| porque digo la verdad, | for speaking the truth, |
| ruéguenselo a Dios sagrado | pray to the Holy Lord |
| que ese día se llegará. | that the day will come. |
| | |
| Todos debíamos de unirnos | We should all be united |
| y mirarnos como hermanos, | and treat each other like brothers, |
| ahi miren lo que nos pasa, | look at what is happening |
| a todos los mexicanos. | to all of us Mexicans. |
| | |
| El mexicano es tan hombre | The Mexican is very manly, |
| y lo es en cualquier terreno, | he's like that anywhere, |
| porque se sabe morir | because he knows how to die |
| en su pueblo y en el ajeno. | in his own town and in a foreign land. |
| | |
| Aquí en el estado de Texas | Here in the state of Texas |
| no nos juzgan con conciencia, | they don't judge us with a conscience, |
| si no nos mandan al 'orca* | when they don't send us to the gallows, |
| se nos da una penitencia. | they sentence us to a jail term. |
| | |
| Vuela, vuela palomita, | Fly, fly, little dove, |
| vuela para el otro lado, | fly to the other side, |
| anda avisarle a mis padres | tell my parents that |
| que murió Ramón Delgado. | Ramón Delgado has died. |
| | |
| Ya con ésta ahi me despido | Now with this I bid farewell |
| al pie de este verde prado, | at the edge of this green field. |
| aquí termina el corrido | Here ends the corrido |
| del señor Ramón Delgado. | of Mr. Ramón Delgado. |
| | |
| Ya con ésta ahi me despido | Now with this I bid farewell |
| porque mi suerte es así, | because this is my fate, |
| les encargo a mis amigos | I leave it up to you, my friends, |
| que hagan recuerdo de mí. | to keep a remembrance of me. |

(Hernández 1978:16–18)
*'orca = *horca* (hanging noose)

The issue of Mexican "criminality" is an interesting one because it underscores the major part politics and ideology play in the perception of a phenomenon and how "scientific" theories are bandied about in an effort to support or refute one's ideological position. During the early part of the twentieth century, when Mexicans began to be perceived as competition in the workplace, the bogeyman of the Mexican with an inherent criminal mind began to surface. Two currents of thought predominated vis-à-vis the "nature" of the Mexican. One current saw Mexicans as passive, obedient, and easily controlled, while the other attributed to Mexicans an inherent inability to distinguish right from wrong and thus a proneness to crime.

Some of those who defended the Mexicans had economic interests at heart, and this colored their view of these people. George P. Clements, manager of the agriculture department of the Los Angeles Chamber of Commerce, for instance, was a strong advocate of Mexican immigration, for he deemed this group indispensable for work in the agricultural fields in California. Clements characterized the Mexican "peon" in these terms:

> No labor that has ever come to the United States is more satisfactory under righteous treatment. He is the result of years of servitude, has always looked upon his employer as his padron [sic] and upon himself as part of the establishment. His great difficulty with the employer in the United States is the lack of the employer's understanding. The Mexican peon is never ordered, outside of the army, in his own country; he is requested. He is strictly honest according to his light, thoroughly responsible, and considerate of his employer's property. He is tribal in thought and habit, and his standards are not ours. He has the greatest capacity for happiness of any people coming to us. By nature he is dignified, gentle, kind, generous and courteous. His troubles are mainly those of his employer. He is in no way criminal. Being totally ignorant of the law and customs of our country, without our language, having totally different ethics of life, he finds himself frequently in the petty court.
>
> In his own country he is a free agent. If he wants a fruit he picks it. If he wants to take a bath, he takes it. If he wants to use a tool and finds one out of use, he appropriates it. If he picks a fruit in California, he is a petty thief. If he takes a bath in one of our ditches or aqueducts, he has polluted the water. If he borrows a hoe, an axe or a plow, he is a petty thief. These in the main are his infractions of the law. (1929:28)

The opposite view was held by Remsen Crawford, who was vehemently opposed to Mexican immigration. In an article called "The Menace of Mexican Immigration" published in 1930, Crawford reported on a survey undertaken by Judge Box and Thomas A. Jenkins of Ohio, members of the Immigration Committee of the U.S. House of Representatives.

> A questionnaire was sent out to several thousand persons including local retail merchants or country storekeepers, to ascertain what effect the trade of Mexican laborers is having upon business; to town and country school teachers for their views on the influence of Mexican families in the local educational institutions; to doctors and sanitation experts in regard to local health conditions as affected by the influx of so many Mexicans; and to judges of local courts in regard to the influence upon crime of the Mexican settlements. (1930:904)

The responses were almost unanimously negative. "On the question of crime there is likewise almost complete concurrence that the Mexicans commit more offenses against law and order, both petty and serious, than do the native whites or negroes"(905). But the author grudgingly admitted that "some of the replies show that the offenses of the Mexicans are mainly of the minor sort, such as fights among themselves and petty larceny" (ibid.).

### Early Concern over Acculturation

On a more cheerful note, a series of songs appeared before the 1930s which parodied the Mexican immigrant experience. A certain anxiety can be detected with respect to the acculturation many of the Mexicans were undergoing in the United States. The songs sought to remind the immigrant of his "roots" and to extol that which was Mexican as opposed to that which was Yankee. "Las pollas de California" is a good example of this type of corrido.

## Las pollas de California

Bonito California,
donde gocé de placeres,
lo que no me gustó a mí
que allí mandan las mujeres.

Voy a hablar de California
y del Estado de Nevada
donde no se habla español
sino pura americanada.

Las pollas de California
gastadoras de dinero,
para salirse a pasear
piden guantes y sombrero.

A la primer carta que hice
a una novia a quien pedí,
dijo que quería buena estufa
y buena cama de dormir.

Cuando la saqué a pasear
en un carrito,
que me va diciendo la indina,
quiero un vestido bonito.

Las pollas de California
no saben comer tortilla,
lo que les gusta en la mesa
es el pan con mantequilla.

## The Chicks from California

California is beautiful,
I had a great time there;
The thing I did not like,
Women are boss there.

I want to tell you about California
And about the state of Nevada,
Where Spanish is not spoken,
Only the American language.

The chicks from California
Like to spend money;
When they want to go out,
They ask for glove and hat.

The first (love) letter I sent
To a girlfriend I wanted to marry;
She said she wanted a good stove
And a good bed to sleep on.

When I took her for a ride
In a car,
She insolently tells me
That she wanted a pretty dress.

The chicks from California
Do not know how to eat tortillas;
What they like on the table
Is bread and butter.

| | |
|---|---|
| Y a la hora de la comida, | And at lunch time, |
| si les falta la cerveza, | If they don't have any beer, |
| luego luego van diciendo | Immediately they say |
| que les duele la cabeza. | That their head aches. |
| | |
| México es horrible, dicen, | Mexico is horrible, they say, |
| por la revoltura que hay, | Because of all the mixtures; |
| hablando en su propio idioma, | They speak in their own language, |
| y luego dicen *good bay*. | And then they say "good-bye." |
| | |
| Los gringos son tan simples | The gringos are so simple, |
| que no saben a Sonora | They do not know Sonora; |
| y para decir diez reales | And when they want to say ten bits, |
| dicen *dolar a necora*. | They say "dollar and a quarter." |
| | |
| Los gringos son tarugos, | The gringos are stupid, |
| y no saben a Teocaltiche, | They do not know Teocaltiche; |
| cuando se enojan con uno | When they get mad at us, |
| le dicen *Sana va biche*. | They say "son of a bitch." |
| | |
| No aprenden al mexicano | They should learn from the Mexican |
| que el corazón se le abre, | That with an open heart, |
| cuando se enoja con alguien | When he gets mad at somebody, |
| le dice . . . *vuelve á la tarde*. | He tells them . . . "Come back this |
| | afternoon." |
| | |
| Si fueran a California, | If you go to California, |
| les encargo compañeros | I advise you, friends, |
| que no se crean de las pollas, | Do not believe those chicks; |
| mejor vivan de solteros. | Better live as bachelors. |
| | |
| Si el marido va a cantina | If the husband goes to a bar, |
| a parrandas o al billar, | On a drinking spree or to a pool hall; |
| y si su mujer lo sabe | And if his wife finds out, |
| ante el juez se va a quejar. | She goes complaining to the judge. |
| | |
| Ya con ésta me despido, | Now I take my leave, |
| ya están saliendo los coches, | The cars are taking off; |
| ya les canté a mis amigos | I have sung to my friends |
| los versitos de las poches. | The verses about the *poches*. |

(Guerrero 1924b)

As the Mexican community took roots and became more established, concern over the loss of one's "Mexicanness" began to surface. Such social institutions as the *mutualistas,* which were organizations initiated by Mexicans in the United States to aid each other, perceived one of their fundamental functions as the "promotion of cultural, social, patriotic, and recreational activities" (Camarillo 1979:148). The founding members of some of these organizations "wanted to ensure that the mutualista remained a nationalistic Mexicano organization that would benefit only those who were actually Mexican citizens. It was also apparently a guarantee against the admission of the U.S.-born Mexican population and the second generation of foreign-born who might introduce a diluted Mexican culture into the mutualista" (149).

Nevertheless, in spite of efforts to prevent a "dilution" of Mexican culture, two distinct communities began to form in the 1920s within the Mexican population: the native born and the more recently arrived immigrants. Camarillo describes the schism that developed in Santa Barbara during this period.

> The political and socioeconomic position of the native-born Mexicans of Pueblo Viejo during the early twentieth century in Santa Barbara was essentially analogous to that of their foreign born counterparts in the lower eastside barrio. The native-born and foreign born, however, often viewed each other as two separate social groups. In part, the schism that developed within the Spanish speaking community was caused by the external prejudice of Anglo society, which caused native-born Mexicans to react negatively against foreign-born Mexicans. The nineteeth-century legacy of racism against Mexicans was carried over into the twentieth century and revitalized by the mass media's derogatory emphasis on the Cholo immigrants from Mexico. (188)

Native-born Chicanos, in trying to escape the stigma ascribed by Anglos to Mexicans, sought to avoid any contact or identification with *lo mexicano.* Camarillo writes:

> A principal reason why many native-born residents of Pueblo Viejo kept their distance from the foreign-born was to try to avoid this negative association. The foreign-born Mexicans saw this aloofness as clannishness and rejection. "They [the foreign-born] resented that we wouldn't say we were Mexican," a native-born woman recalled; "we always said we were Spanish." Her husband, a native-born son of foreign-born parentage, added that "they [the native-born] were ashamed to say they were Mexican." (188)

Songs dating from the 1920s express this conflict. Some songs, like "Las pollas de California," address this issue in a playful mood. Others are vitrolic attacks on assimilated Mexicans.

### Desde México he venido

Desde México he venido
nomás por venir a ver
esa ley americana
que aquí manda la mujer.

### From Mexico Have I Come

From Mexico have I come,
Just to come and see
This American law
That says the woman is boss.

| | |
|---|---|
| En México no se ha visto,<br>ni en la frontera del Norte,<br>que intimiden a los hombres<br>llevándolos a la corte. | This is never seen in Mexico<br>Nor on the northern border,<br>That men should be intimidated<br>By taking them to court. |
| Yo soy un triste pelado,<br>guiado por mi cruel fortuna,<br>he venido a conocer<br>los patos en la laguna.* | I am just a poor bum,<br>Guided by my cruel fortune;<br>I have come to get acquainted<br>With the ducks in the lagoon. |
| Y ¡ay ay! qué bonito es Texas<br>en tiempo que hay elección,<br>verás los yanquis de puro<br><br>y a los de nuestra nación. | Ay, ay! But Texas is a fine place<br>During election time;<br>You will see the cigar—smoking<br>Yankees<br>And our own people as well. |
| En tiempo que hay elección<br>son puro *aló y hay mai fren,* | During election time<br>They are nothing but "hello" and "hi,<br>my friend." |
| *¡ay, navaja, no te amelles!*<br>*ya viene llegando el tren.*** | Razor, don't lose your edge!<br>The train is just coming in. |
| Ya pasada la elección<br>ya no hay *mai fren* ni hay *aló.* | But once elections are past,<br>There's no more "my friend" or<br>"hello"; |
| pongan cuidado, señores,<br>que ese tiempo se acabó. | Better look out, gentlemen,<br>For that time is no more. |

(Paredes 1976:163)
*"I've come to meet the cuckolds in their own surroundings."
**"Flattery, do your stuff! Success is in sight."

| ## Los mexicanos que hablan inglés | ## Mexicans Who Speak English |
|---|---|
| En Texas es terrible<br>por la revoltura que hay,<br>no hay quién diga "hasta mañana,"<br>nomás puro *good-bye.* | In Texas it is terrible<br>How things are all mixed up;<br>No one says "hasta mañana,"<br>It's nothing but "good-bye." |
| *Y jau-didi-dú mai fren,*<br>*en ayl sí yu tumora,*<br>para decir "diez reales"<br>dicen *dola yene cuora.* | And "howdy-dee-do my friend,<br>And I'll see you tomorrow";<br>When they want to say "diez reales"<br>They say "dollar and a quarter." |

Yo enamoré una tejana,
y de esas de sombrilla,
le dije: —¿Te vas conmigo?—

y me dijo: —¡*Lunque jia!*—

Enamoré otra catrina,

d'esas de garsolé,
le dije: —¿Te vas conmigo?—

y me dijo: —¿*Huachu sei?*—

Luego me fui *pa'l\* dipo\*\**
a hablar con doña Inés,
yo le hablaba en castellano
y me contestó en inglés.

Todos queremos hablar
la lengua americana,
sin poder comprender
la nuestra castellana.

Y en Texas es terrible
por la revoltura que hay,
no hay quién diga "hasta mañana,"
nomás puro *good-bye.*

I made love to a Texas-Mexican girl,
One of those with a parasol;
I said to her, "Will you come along
    with me?"
And she told me, "Looky heah!"

I made love to another fashionable
    lady
One of those with a garsolé;
I said to her, "Will you go along with
    me?"
And she told me, "What you say?"

Then I went to the depot
To talk to Doña Inés;
I talked to her in Spanish,
And she answered me in English.

All of us want to speak
The American language,
Without understanding
Our own Spanish tongue.

In Texas it is terrible
How things are all mixed up;
No one says "hasta mañana,"
It's nothing but "good-bye."

(Paredes 1976:164)
\*pa'l = *para el* (to the)
\*\*dipo = depot

These stanzas are from a border zarzuela:

Como estamos en Texas
el inglés hay que aprender,
para que con nuestros primos
nos podamos entender.

Y venderles charamuscas
en la lengua del Tío Sam:
—Mucho bueno palanquetas,
piloncillo *very fine.*

—*One cent the* merengues,
*one cent the* pastel,
*one cent the* turrones,
*and* todo *one cent.*—

Since we are in Texas,
We must learn the English language,
So that we can make ourselves
Understood to our cousins.

So we can sell candy twists
In the language of Uncle Sam:
"Mucho bueno palanquetas,
Piloncillo very fine."

"One cent the meringues,
One cent the pie,
One cent the nougats,
And everything one cent."

| | |
|---|---|
| Hace pocos días<br>que aquí vino un *lord*<br>que cargaba las pilas de *money*<br>en puro *American gold;*<br>vio a una muchachita<br>y le dijo así:<br>—Mí te dar todo este dinerito<br>si tú quieres mí.— | It was a few days ago<br>That a lord came here,<br>Who carried big heaps of money<br>In pure American gold;<br>He saw a little girl,<br>And he spoke to her like this:<br>"Me give you all this nice money<br>If you me like." |
| Al momento la muchacha<br>nada supo contestar,<br>pero viendo que le daban<br>mucho *American gold,*<br>le dijo ella muy resuelta:<br>—*Very well, all right.*— | For a moment the girl<br>Did not know what to say,<br>But seeing that she was offered<br>Much American gold,<br>She told him quite resolutely,<br>"Very well, all right." |

(Paredes 1976, pp. 166–167)

## Mucho me gusta mi novia

Y mucho me gusta mi novia,
me gusta nomás porque me habla in-
    glés;
anoche le preguntaba
que si me amaba
y me dice: —*Yes.*—

*Oh, my little darling,*
*please* dime que sí,
mamacita linda,
*she belong to me.*

(Paredes 1976:167)

## Much Do I Like My Sweetheart

And much do I like my sweetheart,
I like her especially because she talks
    English to me:
Last night I asked her
If she loved me,
And she says to me, "Yes."

Oh, my little darling,
Please say yes,
Beautiful mama,
She belong to me.

## La Pochita

En San Antonio yo la conocí,
en San Antonio yo la enamoré,
en San Antonio me dijo que sí
y por desgracia en San Antonio me
    casé.

Me dijo que no hablaba el español
y yo le dije que no hablaba inglés,
y a todo lo que ella me decía
le contestaba con *Oh Laidi, Laidi yes.*

## The Pochita

I met her in San Antonio
I courted her in San Antonio
In San Antonio she said "yes"
And unfortunately in San Antonio I
    got married.

She told me she did not speak Spanish
And I told her I did not speak English
And everything she told me
I answered her: "Oh Lady, Lady yes."

| | |
|---|---|
| Tú tienes que aprender el español, | You have to learn Spanish, |
| le dije con dulzura a mi mujer, | I sweetly told my wife, |
| y a la cabeza un plato me tiró, | And she threw a plate at me, |
| y yo le dije muy humilde: *Laidi yes.* | And I humbly told her: "Lady yes." |

| | |
|---|---|
| No saben el aprieto en que me vi, | You can't imagine the trouble I got in |
| no saben los trabajos que pasé | You can't imagine all the problems I had |

| | |
|---|---|
| y aquella decepción que yo sufrí, | And the deception I suffered |
| por no saber ni una palabra del inglés. | Because I did not speak one word of English. |

Coro

Chorus

| | |
|---|---|
| Mas luego ya verán lo que pasó, | But listen to what happened later on |
| que no era americana mi mujer, | My wife was not American |
| pos era de Jalisco la Pochita, | She was from Jalisco, my Pochita, |
| y sucedió lo que tenía que suceder. | And it finally happened. |

| | |
|---|---|
| Y un día nos llamó Gobernación, | One day the government called us, |
| no saben la sorpresa que me dió, | You don't know how surprised I was, |
| mandaron pa' Jalisco a la Pochita | To Jalisco they sent the Pochita |
| y yo le dije: "Pos contigo me voy yo." | And I told her: "I will go with you." |

(Calleja 1963)

## Radios y chicanos
## Primera Parte

| | |
|---|---|
| En estos tiempos modernos | |
| de electrizar el sonido, | |
| me entretengo buenos ratos | |
| componiendo este corrido. | |

## Radios and Chicanos
## First Side

In these modern times
Of electrified sound,
I pass the time away
Writing this corrido.

| | |
|---|---|
| Ver a un buen amigo mío | Watching a good friend of mine |
| que al dejar mi pueblo grato, | Leaving my pleasant hometown, |
| creyó que al cruzar el río | Who thought that by crossing the river |
| se le iría lo zurumato. | He'd stop being a hick. |

| | |
|---|---|
| Sí será, sí será, | That's how it is! |
| parece mentira | It's hard to believe |
| que siendo chicano, | That a Chicano, |
| tan hombre y tan sano, | So wholesome and manly |
| se vino de allá. | Would come over here. |

| | |
|---|---|
| Y al llegar a la frontera, | Arriving at the border |
| le dicen que el emigrado | He is told that the immigrant |
| necesita regadera | Has to shower |
| para pasar a este lado. | In order to come to this side. |

Llega al fín a este condado
y alquila un apartamento,
sin saber que en este estado
se termina en el cemento.

Sí será, etc.

Y al sentirse con tostones
se va haciendo de confianza,
y al comprar trajes rabones
se siente casi Carranza.

Se compra caja de fierro
especial para itacates,
ya no piensa en el destierro
ni en ninguno de sus cuates.

Sí será, etc.

Viene ahora lo verdadero
pero se los canto aparte,
me quito pues el sombrero
y *ahi** va la segunda parte.

Sí será, etc.

## Segunda Parte

Se alquila un radio victrola
con foquitos y botones,
pues su casa está muy sola
sin música ni canciones.

Y a la hora que le transmiten
los conciertos al chicano,
resulta que anuncian puercos
y el mejor mole poblano.

Sí será, sí será,
parece mentira
que en vez de canciones
anuncien melones
los de la cíudad.

—Nosotros recomendamos
parteras bien tituladas,
afinadores de piano
pa' las señoras casadas.

Finally he gets to this county
And he rents an apartment,
Little does he know that in this state
You end up in the cement.

That's how it is, etc.

When he gets a little money
He gains confidence
And buying tight-fitting suits
He almost feels like Carranza.

He buys himself a metal box
Especially made to carry his lunch,
He forgets about the old country
And the friends he left behind.

That's how it is, etc.

Now comes the real thing
But I'll sing it next,
A tip of my hat
And here's the second part.

That's how it is, etc.

## Second Side

He rents a radio-phonograph
With little lights and buttons
Because his house is too lonely
Without music or songs.

But when they're supposed to play
Music for the Chicanos
They end up advertising pigs
And the best mole from Puebla.

That's how it is!
It's hard to believe
That instead of playing songs
They advertise melons,
Those city people.

"We recommend
Midwives who are licensed
And piano tuners
For all you married ladies."

—Llame usted al ochenta y cuatro
si tiene dolor de muelas,
por un dólar veinticinco
le ponemos medias suelas.—

Sí será, sí será,
parece mentira
que se oigan tan lejos
los buenos consejos
que da la ciudad.

Al fín de tres cuartos de hora
nos cantan algún mariachi,
luego anuncian la señora
que fabrica buen tepache.

Siguen luego otros asuntos
demostrando las rebajas,
que le hacen a los difuntos
si les compran buenas cajas.

Sí será, sí será,
parece mentira
que en vez de mariachi
nos manden tepache
los de la ciudad.

Ya termino este corrido
poniéndole punto y coma,
dejando a mi amigo creido
chiflando atrás de la loma.

Sí será, sí será,
parece mentira
que nos hagan majes
en estos parajes
los de la ciudad.

(Hernández 1978:30–32)
*ahi = ahí [there]

"Please call telephone 84
If you have a toothache,
For a dollar twenty-five
We'll repair your half sole."

That's how it is!
It's hard to believe
That the good advice
From the city
Can be heard so far away.

After forty-five minutes
A mariachi will sing
Then they advertise the lady
Who sells the best tepache.

Other ads follow
That offer a discount
To the dead
When they buy a good coffin.

That's how it is!
It's hard to believe
That instead of mariachi
They send us tepache
Those city people.

Now I end this song
By placing a semicolon,
Leaving my credulous friend
Whistling from behind the hill (look-
ing like a fool).

That's how it is!
It's hard to believe
How we're treated like dummies
In these parts
By the city people,

In "El rancho donde yo nací" the theme of Mexican superiority is underlined. Everything Mexican is compared to newfangled inventions of the gringo, and of course that which is Mexican is much better, according to this corridista.

## El rancho donde yo nací

No me gusta bailar en salones
Como al estilo de por aquí
a mi me gusta piso de tierra
como en el rancho donde yo nací.

No me gusta la pistola escuadra
como al estilo de por aquí
a mi me gusta carabina negra
como en el rancho donde yo nací.

No me gusta camisa de seda
como al estilo de por aquí
a mi me gustan las *yompas** azules
como en el rancho donde yo nací.

No me gusta coche ni automóvil

como al estilo de por aquí
a mi me gusta carreta de bueyes
como en el rancho donde yo nací.

No me gustan los calzones anchos
como al estilo de por aquí
a mi me gustan pegados al cuero
como en el rancho donde yo nací.

(Gamio 1974:88–89)
*yompas = jackets

## The Farm Where I Was Born

I don't care to dance in the halls
That you have here;
What I want is an earth floor
Like on the farm where I was born.

I don't care for your automatic pistols
That you have here,
What I want is a black rifle
Like on the farm where I was born.

I don't care for your silk shirts
That you have here;
What I want is a suit of blue jackets
Like on the farm where I was born.

I don't care for your carriages or auto-
    mobiles
That you have here;
What I want is a cart with oxen
Like on the farm where I was born.

I don't like your wide trousers
That you have here;
I like them close to the skin
Like on the farm where I was born.

## El rancho

### Primera parte

A cantar vamos unos cuantos versos
de lo que ahora se usa por aquí,

donde más valiera que se usara todo

como en el rancho donde yo nací.

Por aquí todos con el automóvil
matando gente pasan por ahí,
¡cuánto más valiera carreta con bueyes

como en el rancho donde yo nací!

## The Ranch

### First Side

We're going to sing a few lines
About the new trends used around
    here,
But it'd be much better if things were
    done
Just like on the ranch where I was
    born.

Around here they all ride in cars,
Killing people as they pass by,
It'd be much better to use ox-drawn
    carts,
Just like on the ranch where I was
    born.

Por aquí todos presumiendo idiomas

andan diciendo: —*Suit ja ri di di.*—
¡cuánto más valiera: —Prieta, dame un
  beso.—
como en el rancho donde yo nací!

Por aquí todos con chico sacote
de atrás abierto hasta por aquí,
¡cuánto más valiera con chaqueta de
  hombre
como en el rancho donde yo nací!

Por aquí mucho pantalón campana

todos los tipos usan por allí,
¡cuánto más valiera pegados al cuero

como en el rancho donde yo nací!

Por aquí todos estilo borrego
mascando chicle pasan por ahí,
¡cuánto más valiera no tragar saliva

como en el rancho donde yo nací!

Adiós paisanos, ya nos despedimos

aunque volvamos luego por aquí,
para cantarles otros cuantos versos
como en el rancho donde yo nací.

Around here they all brag of foreign
  languages,
Saying, "Sweet-ha-reedeedee,"
It'd be much better to say "Dark girl,
  give me a kiss,"
Just like on the ranch where I was
  born.

Around here they all wear huge coats
With the back slit up to here,
It'd be much better to wear a man's
  jacket,
Just like on the ranch where I was
  born.

Around here you see all these characters
Wearing bell-bottom pants,
It'd be much better if they wore them
  tight fitting,
Just like on the ranch where I was
  born.

Here they all look like sheep
When they pass by chewing gum,
It'd be much better not to swallow
  spit,
Just like on the ranch where I was
  born.

Farewell, countrymen, now we take
  our leave,
But we'll be right back
To sing you a few more lines,
Just like on the ranch where I was
  born.

## Segunda parte

Por aquí todas con crema y colores

se ponen bellas como un maniquí!

¡cuánto más valiera muy bien baña-
  ditas
como en el rancho donde yo nací!

Por aquí todas con blusas de seda

van escotadas hasta por aquí,

## Second Side

Around here the women use creams
  and paints
To make themselves pretty as man-
  nequins,
It'd be much better to see them fresh
  from the bath,
Just like on the ranch where I was
  born.

Around here the women wear silk
  blouses
That are low cut all the way down to
  here,

| | |
|---|---|
| ¡cuánto más valiera ordeñando vacas | It'd be much better to see them milking cows, |
| como en el rancho donde yo nací! | Just like on the ranch where I was born. |
| | |
| Por aquí todas usan el sombrero | Around here the women wear hats |
| que se sanfurran hasta por aquí, | Pulled all the way down to here, |
| ¡cuánto más valiera rebozo terciado | It'd be much better to see them wrapped in a shawl, |
| como en el rancho donde yo nací! | Just like on the ranch where I was born. |
| | |
| Por aquí todas al estilo mula | Around here the women look like mules |
| andan tusadas hasta por aquí, | With their hair chopped up to here, |
| ¡cuánto más valiera con chica trenzota | It'd be much better to see them with a long braid, |
| como en el rancho donde yo nací! | Just like on the ranch where I was born. |
| | |
| Por aquí todas pestañas con rimel | Around here the women wear eye makeup, |
| cejas pintadas pasan por allí, | With painted eyebrows they pass by, |
| ¡cuánto más valiera ojo sin retoque | It'd be much better to see eyes without makeup |
| como en el rancho donde yo nací! | Just like on the ranch where I was born! |
| | |
| Por aquí todas faldas muy rabonas | Around here the women wear short skirts |
| van enseñando hasta por aquí, | Showing all the way up to here, |
| ¡cuánto más valiera para no ver cosas | I'd be better off not seeing such things |
| volverme al rancho donde yo nací! | By returning to the ranch where I was born. |
| | |
| Adiós paisanos, ya nos despedimos, | Good-bye, countrymen, we take our leave |
| este corrido se termina aquí, | As this corrido ends here; |
| no volveremos a cantar canciones | No longer will we sing songs |
| como en el rancho donde yo nací. | Like on the ranch where I was born. |

(Hernández 1978:20–22)

The tongue-in-cheek mocking and friendly rib-poking and banter soon yielded to bitter recriminations and acid-tongue abuse for those who were deemed too assimilated or acculturated. In the latter half of the twenties decade, songs expressing a vitriolic view of the "agringado" or "ayankado" (Yankeelike person) surfaced. The pejorative term *renegado* (renegade) came into vogue, and resentment was clearly articulated by the Mexican population.

The renegado crystallized as a result of the early repatriation efforts the Mexican government and consular offices were making to resettle unwanted Mexicans from the United States. The system of deportations and a general hostile environment toward Mexicans became visible in the United States during this period. Mexico after the revolutionary years wanted to reintegrate those nationals who had left their country and were now adrift in a nation that did not necessarily want them.

Since Mexico was not in the best of economic conditions, however, the repatriation programs were not working as desired. Frequently lands were made available to the returnees but the would-be farmers lacked the necessities with which to function successfully. No fertilizer or seed was provided, equipment was lacking, and there were insufficient funds to the *repatriado* over the long haul of planting and harvesting. Furthermore, the land was often arid and unproductive. One immigrant expressed his disillusionment in this way: "Yes, if I could make money here, I'd like it here, . . . *mi tierra más bonita*. But I want to go back there and make something, there is no chance here. Me no likee. As soon as *se compone vamos pa' allá*" (quoted in Carreras de Velasco 1974:135).

The Mexican press among others viewed this attitude as a rejection of Mexico and unpatriotic. Carreras de Velasco elucidates:

> At the same time that the process to effectuate the Repatriation Program was taking place and when many persons were returning to Mexico, there were cases where Mexicans were emigrating back to the United States even though they were aware of the existing situation in that country. The press and the consulates began classifying these Mexicans [who were returning to the U.S.] as renegades, ungrateful, and unpatriotic. (1974:135)

Soon Mexican authorities and others viewed the returnee as abusing the system and merely asking for repatriation so as to visit Mexico, stay a while, then emigrate anew.

> It is a well-known fact that for the repatriated Mexicans the desire to return to the United States was the normal state of affairs. Few felt any resentment towards that country. Not even the "love for Mexico" which they had ardently declared [when applying for repatriation aid] posed any contradiction with their desire to return to the United States. Their own country they remembered here and there through songs. They had arrived with great optimism and happy to return to Mexico but in the back of their minds was the idea they would emigrate back to the United States. (135)

This attitude provoked a backlash against the repatriated Mexicans and those viewed as being assimilated to Anglo ways: "to the general population in Mexico the *repatriados* were 'members of La Raza' and were to be given all the opportunities possible to reintegrate themselves in the national life of the country. The renegades were included in this national plan" (137). Children in rural schools were warned to beware of the repatriated Mexicans. A rural school text entitled "Emigrados y Repatriados" (Immigrants and repatriated Mexicans) classified returnees in two categories: "those that came eager and willing to cooperate and the renegades who were ungrateful." The text concluded that both types of returned Mexicans were to be treated well.

> This situation, coupled with the differences in customs and dress between stay-at-home Mexicans and of the repatriated Mexicans, created a climate of tension between the two groups. The former were unwilling to accept any claimed superiority on the part of the latter and would call the assimilated Mexican Americans "ayankados" or "gringos." (141)

The general social climate gave rise to the corrido "El renegado." This folk song vividly captures the tension and hostility between the two groups. The corridista accuses the immigrant of acting "uppity" and snobbish, reminding him of his humble roots. The lyrics upbraid the "renegade" in the strongest language possible for denying his Mexican origin. The corridista ends by reaffirming his own loyalty to Mexico.

## El renegado

(Se canta con música mexicana "Dame
 un beso")
Andas por hay luciendo
gran automóvil
me llamas desgraciado,
y muerto de hambre
y es que ya no te acuerdas

cuando en mi rancho
andabas casi en cueros
y sin huaraches.
Así pasa a muchos
que aquí conozco

cuando aprenden un poco de americano
y se visten catrines
y van al baile.
Y el que niega su raza
ni madre tiene,

pues no hay nada en el mundo tan
 asqueroso

## The Renegade

(Sung to the tune of the Mexican song
 "Dame un beso")
You go along showing off
In a big automobile.
You call me a pauper
And dead with hunger,
And what you don't remember is

That on my farm
You went around almost naked
And without sandals.
This happens to many
That I know here

When they learn a little American

And dress up like dudes,
And go to the dance.
But he who denies his race
Is the most miserable creature.

There is nothing in the world so vile
 as he,

| | |
|---|---|
| como la ruin figura del renegado. | The mean figure of the renegade. |
| Y aunque lejos de tí, | And although far from you, |
| Patria querida, | Dear Fatherland, |
| me han echado | Continual revolutions |
| continuas revoluciones, | Have cast me out— |
| no reniega jamás | A good Mexican |
| un buen mexicano | Never disowns |
| de la Patria querida | The dear Fatherland |
| de sus amores. | Of his affections. |

(Gamio 1971:93–94)

In a more playful vein, "El padre del Charro Vargas" (credited to T. A. Soto) ridicules an effete young man, Charro Vargas. The father of this young man arrives in San Antonio, Texas, and exposes the humble beginnings of his son. Evidently, although the son was posing in the States as a journalist, he was nothing but a humble herder looking after pigs—and living like one, to boot.

| El padre del Charro Vargas | The Father of Charro Vargas |
|---|---|
| Ya está en San Antonio | There is here in San Antonio |
| el padre del Charro Vargas, | The father of Charro Vargas. |
| éste sí que es un demonio | He is a regular devil |
| con uñas y barbas largas. | With long nails and a beard. |
| | |
| Esto nunca lo tolero | "This I will never tolerate," |
| dice el padre de Varguitas, | Says the father of Varguitas, |
| que en lugar de ser bolero | "That instead of being a cowboy |
| ande con los periodistas. | He goes about with writers. |
| | |
| Pues en su tierra señores | "Because in his own country, sirs, |
| sólo cuidaba marranos, | He just looked after the pigs, |
| era el peor de los pastores | He was the worst of the herders |
| entre todos sus hermanos. | Among all his brothers. |
| | |
| Y mugroso como él solo | "And dirty without peer |
| con su tazota de atole, | With his big bowl of atole, |
| siempre estaba sobre el lodo | He was always on top of the mud |
| masticando su pinole. | Eating up his pinole. |
| | |
| De charro no tiene tal, | "There is nothing of the charro in him, |
| | |
| en cambio en las fiestas patrias | But on national holidays |
| se vistió con un costal | He dressed up in a sack |
| muy ajustado en las patas. | Very tight around the legs. |

De todos era la risión
con su endiablado caballo,
Y dijo allí un huasón
que era el charro más payo.

"He was the laughingstock of all
With his runt of a horse,
And a joker there said
That he was the most comical charro
   of them all.

Por esa muy justa razón
yo tu padre, ahora quiero
de tu vida explicación;
aquí en el extranjero.

"For this very good reason
I, your father, now wish
An explanation of your life
Here in this foreign land.

Más te digo por trasmanos
que sé que vendías terrenos,
y también moles poblanos
y algunos zapatos buenos.

"I will tell you, by secret ways
I know that you sold land
And also moles poblanos
And good shoes besides.

Supe que fuiste inventor
de un Cemáforo muy bueno,
pero eso de escritor
eso sí que es retebueno.

"I know that you were the inventor
Of a very good semaphore,
But this thing of being a writer
Is quite a good thing.

Pero para otras gentes
que tengan tantito seso,
pues tu solo tienes dientes
pa' masticar con exceso.

"All right for other people
Who have at least some brains,
But you have only teeth
To eat too much with."

(Gamio 1971:94–96)

The twenties decade saw both a consolidation and an expansion of the Mexican-American population in the United States. The great waves of immigrants who had entered during the previous decades had settled in various parts of the Southwest and had carved out the many "Mexican" neighborhoods, or barrios, in the urban sectors. As the population took root and identity, members of the younger generation became more and more identified with the United States. Often they lived far from the border, in the Northwest and Midwest. Many of these young men and women had never been to Mexico and had acquired the customs and manners of the majority population in the States. Newer immigrants constantly arriving from Mexico were shocked at the "strange" mode of living these supposed "Mexicans" displayed. The figure of the *pocho*, or Americanized Mexican, thus begins to emerge, and the songs duly record the event. Conflicts between Americanized pochos and Mexican immigrants were bound to arise. The ballads and songs written during this era capture the conflicts in their lyrics. Thus an important aspect of the acculturation and assimilation of Mexican immigrants and their children is portrayed in the songs which were popular during that era.

# Repatriation and Deportation

The Wickersham Report finds that "the apprehension and examination of supposed aliens are often characterized by methods
unconstitutional, tyrannic and oppressive." In particular, the
Report finds that it is often customary for the immigrant inspectors to jail suspects without any warrant; that in apprehend-
ing suspects, immigration officials have gone to the length of
forcibly detaining groups of people, many of whom are aliens
lawfully in this country or United States citizens, without any
warrant of arrest or search; that these methods have included
raids on lawful institutions and gatherings where a large number
of people are peaceably assembled.

"The Deportation Terror"
Reuben Oppenheimer, (1932:232)

And then these words, spoken in perfect English, floated
through the window [of the departing train]: "I don't want to go
to Mexico! All my friends are in Brooklyn Avenue school, and I
want to stay here!" But the train gathered momentum and swept
out of the yards.

"A Dike against Mexicans"
Robert N. McLean, (1932:165)

*Five* One of the most painful episodes in Mexican-American
immigration history is the 1929–1939 decade; it was the era of the Great
Depression in the United States and the epoch that heralded a severe worldwide financial crisis that adversely affected Mexican Americans and their
status in U.S. society. It was during this period that thousands of Mexicans
and Mexican Americans were "repatriated," or deported back to Mexico.

This era produced one of the highest unemployment rates in U.S. history,
and since jobs were scarce, Mexican workers became personae non grata in
the States. They were perceived not only as unfair competition (some em-

ployers were said to have preferred the hardworking, productive, low-paid Mexican) but also as burdens on the taxpayer, the school system, welfare services, and other social services (see McWilliams 1933:322–324). Regarding the change in attitude toward Mexican immigrants who had been recruited and encouraged to come to work in the United States during prosperous times, Carey McWilliams wrote:

> But a marked change occurred since 1930. When it became apparent last year that the programme for the relief of the unemployed would assume huge proportions in the Mexican quarter, the community swung to a determination to oust the Mexican. Thanks to the rapacity of his overlords he had not been able to accumulate any savings. He was in default in his rent. He was a burden to the taxpayer. At this juncture, an ingenious social worker suggested the desirability of a wholesale deportation program. (1933:324)

In Mexico the government since the end of the Mexican Revolution (1910–1917) had been concerned about the exodus of able-bodied men and women to the United States. One goal of several presidential administrations had been to populate Mexico.

Thus two political currents converged to "encourage" Mexican immigrants who had settled in the United States to return to Mexico. One current was the Mexican nation's embarrassment at having its nationals expelled from the neighboring country and its consequent repatriation program, which was a response to the deportations and news of the unwanted Mexicans. The repatriation program ostensibly offered land, money, farm equipment, and so forth to the would-be returnee (see Carreras de Velasco 1974). The other major movement against the Mexican and Mexican-American population came from various groups and institutions with a vested interest in "getting rid of the Mexican," as McWilliams bluntly put it.

Robert N. McLean, editor of the *Nation* and a critic of the deportation drive, categorized the returning Mexicans into five groups:

> First, there are those who are being deported—and Mexican deportations have reached as high as half of all those in the country. Second, there are those who are going because they have been told they will be deported unless they go voluntarily. Third, there is the great class made up of those who know they are here illegally, and who tremble everytime there is a knock at the door or an American speaks to them upon the street. Composing the fourth class are those whose way is being paid to the border by county relief agencies, which often make their grants of relief dependent upon the promise to return to Mexico at some later date. And the fifth class is made up of those who have long been out of work, and having sacrificed their homes for a fraction of what they are worth, are using the proceeds to go back to Mexico in the hope that things may be a little better and in the conviction that they cannot be any worse. During the first ten months of 1931 the number returning to Mexico outnumbered those entering the United States by 75,337. (McLean 1932:166)

Indeed, Mexican and American citizens of Mexican descent received strong stimulus to repatriate from various U.S. agencies. Abraham Hoffman reported that it was President Herbert Hoover's policy of curtailing legal and illegal immigration which led some administration officials to deport aliens as a means of solving the unemployment problem.

> [William S.] Doak promised to find a way to solve the national unemployment problem. Soon after taking office on December 9, 1930 the new Labor Secretary proclaimed his solution. One way to provide work for unemployed Americans, he announced, was to oust aliens holding jobs. There were 400,000 aliens who were illegal residents in the United States, asserted Doak, and, under current immigration laws, 100,000 were deportable. Following upon the creation of the United States Border Patrol in 1925 and the high rejection rate of visa applications from prospective immigrants in 1928 and afterward, Doak's announcement launched a campaign which one writer called a "gladitorial spectacle." More aliens left the United States in the first nine months of 1931 than entered it. (1973:206–207)

William N. Doak's campaign to oust aliens prompted Charles P. Visel, coordinator of the Los Angeles citizen's relief committee, to offer the services of the police and sheriff's offices in helping in the mass arrests and deportation of Mexicans and Mexican-American citizens. Visel's plan was to create a psychological reign of terror fostered by fear and intimidation that would impel Mexicans to leave the Los Angeles area. Hoffman elucidates:

> It was not Visel's intention to press the Bureau of Immigration into actually conducting an indefinite number of deportation hearings, but rather to establish an environment hostile enough to alarm aliens. "This apparent activity," Visels' telegram promised Doak, "will have a tendency to scare many thousand alien deportables out of this district which is the result desired." (208)

A plan was devised whereby a few well-publicized arrests would be made in order to scare aliens into leaving (209). Los Angeles newspapers carried headlines announcing the proposed deportation drive and encouraging Mexicans to leave of their own accord.

As might be expected, there was general outrage among Mexican-American civic groups as well as the Mexican government. Nevertheless, and in spite of objections from several sources including supervisor W. F. Watkins of the Bureau of Immigration and other government officials, a raid was conducted in the El Monte, California, area. On February 13, 1931, 300 Mexicans were stopped and questioned. Hoffman reported that this effort netted a total of twelve Mexicans who could not prove legal entry (214). On February 26 a raid was conducted at the downtown plaza in Los Angeles; "about 400 people were detained within the grounds of the small circular park for over an hour. Eleven Mexicans, five Chinese, a Japanese were held; nine of the Mexicans were released the following day" (216).

Although these raids were obviously a failure, the climate generated by the publicity on deportations created an environment of fear, tension, and hostility. The end result was an exodus of Mexicans from the Los Angeles area. As Hoffman sums it up,

> The effect of the drive on the Mexican community in Los Angeles was traumatic. Many of the aliens apprehended had never regularized an illegal entry that might have been made years before, at a time when no penalties for illegal entry were even provided for by law. Other than that, to call them criminals is to misapply the term. The pressure on the Mexican community contributed significantly to the huge repatriation movement from Los Angeles that followed upon the anti-alien drive. Beginning in March 1931, the Los Angeles County Bureau of Welfare inaugurated a series of repatriation trains to transport indigent Mexican families as far as Mexico City. By the end of the year four shipments had taken over 2,300 people, including American-born children, out of the country. A similar, though uncounted, number left during 1931 with the aid of the Mexican consulate and charitable Spanish-speaking organizations. . . . Estimates of the exodus from southern California varied between 50,000 and 75,000 people during 1931. (218–219)

U.S. agricultural concerns that had used Mexican labor for three decades were against the mass deportations. Although extremely racist, they saw the loss of Mexican workers as a detriment to their business. In a speech to the Lemon Men's Club on October 2, 1929, George P. Clements, manager of the agricultural department of the Los Angeles Chamber of Commerce, expounded on the danger of losing Mexican workers:

> Much of California's agricultural labor requirements consist of those tasks to which the oriental and Mexican due to their crouching and bending habits are fully adapted, while the white is physically unable to adapt himself to them. (1929:3)

He further cited the transient labor requirements for the San Joaquin Valley as 35,000 workers, the Imperial Valley as 15,000, and the coastal districts as 10,000.

> Why do we need Mexican labor? We can get no other. Common white labor will not enter this field, nor is it capable of doing the work. The Asiatic is denied us. The Filipino has not given general satisfaction—his susceptibility to disease has necessitated federal restrictions.
> The Mexican is our only recourse and the present tightening up of the border has already created embarrassment since it has made of California the labor market for the fruit, truck crop and cotton growing states.
> This class of agricultural labor must be at all times considered the surplus of industrial needs. (3)

Clements painted a dire picture of loss of crops and income for the farmers and posed a rhetorical question:

> What would you do without this army of 72,000 dark skinned workers. Already you are being embarrassed. Tightening up of the border, anti-Mexican progaganda in the United States, misunderstanding of the immigration regulation known as the Vincent-Copeland Act and the attitude of the Mexican government in an endeavor to keep their people, have resulted in a minus figure for Mexicans in the United States in 1929. (28)

In terms tinged with racism, Clements had the highest praise for the Mexican peon. Interestingly, Clements did not see the Mexican as a "biological problem." "He rarely marries out of his own people. A Mexican never marries a white woman. Some white men marry Mexican girls. The Filipino is complicating matters here" (28).

On the other side of the border, Mexico was trying to cope with the massive influx of people suddenly dumped on it. Repatriation programs had been proposed at various times. Basically Mexico deemed that its economic prosperity depended on the development and colonization of its uninhabited lands, and schemes to entice Mexicans to stay home and to lure them back from the United States had been aired. The most prevalent and viable one was that of offering free parcels of land to those "repatriated" Mexicans who wanted to return to Mexico from the United States (see Carreras de Velasco 1974).

Promises of land, agricultural equipment, and materials were made but often not kept. This was due to the economic crisis in Mexico itself. The economic depression was a worldwide financial disaster deeply affecting most nations. In addition, Mexico was struggling to emerge from the chaos and destruction the Mexican Revolution had left in its wake. Thus, although Mexico felt morally obligated to provide for its nationals who were being coerced, cajoled, or forcefully deported from the United States, its economic situation did not provide the means with which it could carry out its repatriation programs successfully. People were therefore being dumped at the U.S.-Mexican border and left destitute.

The terms *repatriation* and *deportation* used in several corridos of this era are an effective means of evaluating the political processes that were uprooting families that had lived (some for generations) on U.S. soil and were now being "encouraged" to leave. From the point of view of the Mexican government, *repatriation* was the less embarrassing or painful term. Mexico did not want the world to think its people were being "kicked out" or deported—a more shameful term—from the United States. Mexico wanted to let it be known it was welcoming back its long-lost brethen. The U.S. goverment perceived the term *repatriation* as more neutral than the heavy-handed term *deportation*, which implies the use of force or coercion in its implementation. Lyrics using the term *repatriation* tend to be more sentimental toward Mexico and less hostile to the process. Those that see the process for what it was—the expelling of Mexicans from the United States—use the term *deportation* and are generally filled with bitter recriminations toward a nation that had first welcomed Mexicans, indeed recruited them unabashedly, and then threw them out.

The corrido "Deportados" describes the travails in first leaving Mexico, the hardships encountered, the sufferings experienced by the kinfolk left behind, and the immigrant embarking upon a new and unknown adventure. The second part of the corrido portrays the deportation of women, children, and old people. Closure is achieved with the optimistic observation that there are no more revolutions in Mexico and therefore the deportees will be welcomed in their own beautiful country.

## Deportados

Voy a contarles, señores,
voy a contarles, señores,
todo lo que yo sufrí,
cuando dejé yo a mi patria,
cuando dejé yo a mi patria,
por venir a ese País.

Serían las diez de la noche,
serían las diez de la noche
comenzó un tren a silbar;
oí que dijo mi madre
Ahí viene ese tren ingrato
que a mi hijo se va a llevar.

Por fin sonó la campana,
por fin sonó la campana;
vámonos de la estación,
no quiero ver a mi madre
llorar por su hijo querido,
por su hijo del corazón.

Cuando a Chihuahua llegamos
cuando a Chihuahua llegamos,
se notó gran confusión,
los empleados de la aduana,
los empleados de la aduana
que pasaban revisión.

Llegamos por fin a Juárez,
llegamos por fin a Juárez
ahí fué mi apuración
que dónde va, que dónde
    viene

## Deported

I am going to sing to you, gentlemen,
I am going to sing to you, gentlemen,
All about my sufferings
When I left my native land,
When I left my native land,
In order to go to that country.

It must have been ten at night,
It must have been ten at night,
When a train began to whistle;
I heard my mother say,
"Here comes that hateful train
To take my son away."

Finally they rang the bell,
Finally they rang the bell.
"Let's go on out of the station;
I'd rather not see my mother
Weeping for her dear son,
The darling of her heart."

When we reached Chihuahua,
When we reached Chihuahua,
There was great confusion:
The customshouse employees,
The customshouse employees,
Were having an inspection.

We finally arrived at Juárez,
We finally arrived at Juárez,
Where I had my inspection:
"Where are you going, where are you
    from,

cuánto dinero tiene
para entrar a esta nación.

Señores, traigo dinero,
señores, traigo dinero
para poder emigrar,
su dinero nada vale,
su dinero nada vale,
te tenemos que bañar.

Los güeros son muy maloras,
los gringos son muy maloras,
se valen de la ocasión,
y a todos los mexicanos,
y a todos los mexicanos,
nos tratan sin compasión.

Hoy traen la gran polvadera,
hoy traen la gran polvadera
y sin consideración,
mujeres niños y ancianos
los llevan a la frontera
los echan de esa nación.

Adiós, paisanos queridos,
adiós, paisanos queridos,
ya nos van a deportar
pero no somos bandidos,
pero no somos bandidos,
venimos a camellar.

Los espero allá en mi tierra,
los espero allá en mi tierra,
ya no hay más revolución;
vámonos cuates queridos
seremos bien recibidos
en nuestra bella nación.

(Taylor 1969:225–227)

How much money have you
In order to enter this country?"

"Gentlemen, I have money,
Gentlemen, I have money
Enough to be able to emigrate."
"Your money is worthless,
Your money is worthless;
We'll have to give you a bath."

The blonds are very unkind;
The gringos are very unkind.
They take advantage of the chance
To treat all the Mexicans,
To treat all the Mexicans
Without compassion.

Today they are rounding them up,
Today they are rounding them up;
And without consideration
Women, children, and old folks
Are taken to the border
And expelled from that country.

So farewell, dear countrymen,
So farewell, dear countrymen,
They are going to deport us now,
But we are not bandits,
But we are not bandits,
We came to work.

I'll wait for you there in my country,
I'll wait for you there in my country
Now that there is no revolution;
Let us go, brothers dear,
We will be well received
In our own beautiful land.

A contemporary variant of this song written by Eugenio Abrego, appears on an album recorded by the popular norteño group Los Alegres de Terán.

## El emigrado

Voy a contarles señores
Todo lo que yo sufrí.
Despúes que dejé mi patria
por venir a este país.

## The Immigrant

I am going to tell you men
All that I suffered
After leaving my country
In order to come to this country
(USA).

| | |
|---|---|
| Serían las diez de la noche | It was about ten o'clock; |
| comenzó un tren a silbar | A train began to whistle. |
| Hay viene ese tren ingrato | There comes that wretched train |
| donde nos van a llevar. | Where they will take us. |
| | |
| Adios mi madre querida | Good-bye, my beloved mother, |
| écheme su bendición. | Give me your blessings. |
| Ya me voy al extranjero | I am going to a foreign land |
| donde no hay revolución. | Where there is no revolution. |
| | |
| Al fin sonó la campana | At last the bell rang; |
| dos silbidos pegó el tren | Two whistles the train gave. |
| No lloren mis compañeros | Do not cry, my friends, |
| que me hacen llorar también. | You will make me cry too. |
| | |
| Al recordar esas horas | Upon remembering those hours |
| me palpita el corazón. | My heart begins to beat. |
| Cuando divisé* a lo lejos | Suddenly I see at a distance |
| ese mentado Torreón. | That famous Torreón. |
| | |
| Llegamos por ciudad Juárez | We arrived by way of Juárez; |
| Allí fue mi apuración | There my worries began. |
| qué cuánto dinero tienes | They asked: How much money do you have |
| para entrar a esta nación? | To enter this nation? |
| | |
| Señores traigo dinero | Gentlemen, I have money |
| para poder emígrar. | So that I can enter. |
| Tu dinero nada vale | Your money is not worth anything, |
| te tenemos que bañar. | We have to bathe you. |
| | |
| Crucé por fin la frontera | I finally crossed the border |
| y en un enganche me fui | And in a contract gang I left. |
| Ay mis queridos paisanos | Oh, my beloved countrymen, |
| fue mucho lo que sufrí. | It was much I did suffer. |

*divisé = devisé [saw]

The effects the Depression had on Mexicans is detailed in "Efectos de la crisis." First is the ever-present hunger—there is nothing to eat. People are resorting to eating a lot of *nopal* (cactus). Second, people are poorly dressed and the music has stopped; there is no more dancing or singing. The bill collectors are busy plying their trade, and no one is getting fat. To top it all off, divorce is increasing. The picture painted by this corridista is indeed a sad one.

## Efectos de la crisis

En este tiempo fatal
la crisis ya nos persigue;
se come mucho nopal,
lo demás no se consigue.

Como todos ya sabrán
estos males tan prolijos;
que hay hogares sin pan
donde lloran nuestros hijos.

Las pianolas ya no tocan
los bailes han disminuido,
las flappers tristes invocan
que vuelva otra vez el ruido.

Se pierden casas algunas
porque los pisos no pagan;
han muerto varias fortunas
de algunas que las poblaban.

La crisis no nos afloja
y el remedio no parece;
nos ayuda la Cruz Roja
que tanto se le agradece.

No se ve luz en las casas
ni llave de agua potable.
La gente de malas trazas
en estado lamentable.

Antes se fumaba puro,
era una alegría en las calles;
hoy de hambre se mira obscuro
y se escuchan muchos ayes.

Los aboneros no aflojan
siguiendo su profesión.
y los deudores se enojan
cuando van a su cantón

Esta crisis decidida
al mundo está desafiando.
Si te falta la comida,
no llores, sigue ayunando.

## Effects of the Crisis

In these unhappy times
Depression still pursues us;
Lots of prickly pear is eaten
for lack of other food.

Probably everybody knows
About these many evils;
That there are homes without food,
In which our children cry.

The pianolas no longer play,
The dances are fewer and fewer;
The sad little flappers pray
To have the gaiety return.

Some lose their houses
Because they can't pay rent;
The fortunes have collapsed
Of some who lived in them.

Depression does not turn us loose,
And the remedy does not appear;
The Red Cross gives us aid,
For which we are very grateful.

No light is seen in the houses
Nor flows the water from the tap;
The people are in tatters
And in a deplorable state.

They used to smoke cigars,
There was gaiety in the streets;
Now faces are clouded with hunger
And many sighs are heard.

The bill collectors do not relent
In pursuit of their profession,
And the debtors get angry
When they come to the house.

This sharp crisis
Is defying the world;
If you have nothing to eat,
Don't cry, keep on fasting.

Ya nadie verás que engorde
con las chuletas guisadas
porque nunca es bueno el *borde**
aquel de "Las Tres Hambreadas."

You'll see no one now who grows fat
From eating broiled chops,
Because the fare never is good
At "The Three Hungers."

Divorcios han aumentado
en estos últimos años;
la crisis lo ha decretado
con sus tristes desengaños.

Divorces have increased
In these last years;
Depression has decreed it
With its sad disillusion.

Ya con ésta me despido,
que sean ustedes felices.
Aquí termina el corrido
y sigue siempre la crisis.

And so I take my leave,
May you all be happy.
Here ends the song,
But the Depression goes on forever.

(Taylor 1969:232–233)
*borde = board

A few songs appeared urging Mexicans living in the United States to voluntarily leave and return to Mexico. However, those who do qualify for legalization are advised to go ahead and try their best to comply with the law by answering all questions asked to the best of their ability.

## La emigración

### Emigration

Vamos a México mis compatriotas

porque es la nuestra propia nación;
ya no nos quieren los Americanos
y nos exigen con la emigración.

Let's go back to Mexico, my compa-
triots,
Because that is our own country,
The Americans don't want us
And they are imposing immigration
laws on us.

Ay, amados compañeros,
pongan toda su atención:
la ley de esta gran nación
se impone a los extranjeros;
en apuros verdaderos
nos vimos en esta ocasión,
quizá haya compasión
para los pobres braceros,
porque si no compañeros . . .

Dear friends,
Listen carefully,
The law of this great land
That is imposed on foreigners
Makes this a time
Of great trouble,
Maybe there'll be compassion
For the poor braceros,
Otherwise, friends . . .

Vamos a México, etc.

Let's go back to Mexico, etc.

Respecto a la emigración
que tanto se oye decir,
todos debemos cumplir

With regard to the immigration
That is so much talked about,
We all should comply

con la ley, sin excepción;
Con la mayor atención
debemos de contestar
lo que habrán de investigar
al cumplir con su misión,
pues si no hay justificación . . .

Vamos a México, etc.

Para no irnos a enredar
en negocios que ignoramos,
con paciencia aquí esperamos
lo que nos venga a tocar;
porque el día se va a llegar
de dar toda información
a la ley de inmigración
que es la que nos va a arreglar,
pues si le vamos a errar . . .

Vamos a México, etc.

Apunta, querido hermano:
cuándo y por dónde pasaste,

amo con quién trabajaste

y conserva esto a la mano,
porque esto tarde o temprano

a la luz tiene que salir,
y te lo vuelvo a decir
guarda, hermano, el papelito,
porque si no en un ratito . . .

Vamos a México, etc.

Está bien que muy derechitos
aquí podemos vivir;
la verdad hay que decir
sin andar con enreditos:
prepara los papelitos,
con ellos hay que probar
que cumplimos al pasar
con todos los requisitos,
y si no con todo y pitos . . .

With the law, without exception,
With the greatest attention
We must answer respectfully
Whatever they might ask,
They're only doing their job,
Otherwise, it'll be justified . . .

Let's go back to Mexico, etc.

So, to avoid getting involved
In business that's not our concern,
We will wait patiently
For whatever befalls us,
Since the day will arrive
When we will be questioned
By the laws of immigration,
Which should straighten us out,
Otherwise, if we make mistakes . . .

Let's go back to Mexico, etc.

Write down, my dear brother,
When and where you crossed the
    border,
The employer with whom you
    worked,
And keep all this at hand
'Cause sooner or later it will have to
    be
Brought to light
And let me tell you again, brother,
Save that little paper,
Otherwise, in no time . . .

Let's go back to Mexico, etc.

It's true that we can
Live here legally,
The truth ought to be said
Without going around the bush,
Get the records ready
That will help prove
That we fulfilled the requirements
When we crossed over,
Otherwise, with all of our
    possessions . . .

Vamos a México, etc.

Let's go back to Mexico, etc.

Pues bien se llega a creer
que se encuentra solución;
las cámaras en acción
se unen para ver que hacer,
cumpliendo con un deber
piden más moderación,
las cosechas a perder
están en vasta región,
y aunque nos de compasión . . .

It is believed
That a solution will be found,
The legislative bodies
Deliberate the bill,
Fulfilling their obligation,
They ask for moderation,
The harvest that is at stake
Covers a large region,
And while we might feel
     compassion . . .

Vamos a México, etc.

Let's go back to Mexico, etc.

Sírvase tener cuidado
con quien le va a interrogar;
con atención hay que hablar
y todo bien explicado,
quien le pregunta es empleado,
sin dudas de inmigración,
pide justificación,
cuándo y por dónde ha pasado,
si no está legalizado . . .

Just be careful
With whoever questions you,
Be attentive when speaking,
Explaining everything in detail,
The employee who asks you
Is surely from immigration
And will request proof
Of when and where you crossed over,
But if you are not lawfully here . . .

Vamos a México, etc.

Let's go back to Mexico, etc.

En todo el valle de Texas
se oye que se están quejando,
las manos están faltando
por eso son tantas quejas,

no hay más que fruncir las cejas;
por aquí con rodeos no se anda,
la ley lo exige y demanda
y las lleva y las deja,
o como enjambre de abejas . . .

All throughout the valley of Texas
You can hear everyone protesting,
Workers begin to be scarce,
That's the reason for all the com-
     plaints,
But all they can do is frown,
Since skirting the issue won't do,
And what the law demands
And requires is the final word,
So like a swarm of bees . . .

Vamos a México, etc.

Let's go back to Mexico, etc.

Les pido vuestra atención,
y a conciencia así lo entiendo
que con mis versos no ofendo
ningún grado superior;
perdonen algún error
les suplico de mil modos,

I ask for your attention
And I honestly mean what I say,
My verses are not meant to offend
Any respectable person,
I beg you a thousand times
To forgive any errors,

| | |
|---|---|
| mi respeto para todos | My respect to all of you, |
| por ser de ellos el autor, | Being the author of these lines, |
| y siempre digo, señor . . . | And I will always say, gentlemen . . . |
| | |
| Vamos a México, etc. | Let's go back to Mexico, etc. |

(Hernández 1978:36–40)

Other songs tried to discourage the would-be bracero from leaving his country, given the situation in the United States. Such is the case in the song "Los que vuelven" ["Those Who Return"] in which a man tells his mother he wants to go to the United States to better his life: "Ya yo me cansé mamá / de vivir tan amolado / por qué no vendemos todo / para irnos al 'otro lado?'" ["I am tired, mother, / Living so broke. / Why don't we sell everything / And go to the 'other side'" (USA)?] (Calleja 1963:147). The mother discourages the son from leaving Mexico, telling him not to be fooled by all the talk of the money that is supposedly made in the United States. She advises him that it is better to stay in Mexico and eat tortillas with hot pepper than to eat hot dogs. The mother continues to warn her son that the United States may be a beautiful country but people suffer great hardships there. Her final word is that the young man should stay in Mexico since he will be better off in his own country.

In the song "Los repatriados" a narrator bids farewell to the United States and gives the reasons for leaving Mexico in the first place: civil wars, poverty, etc. However, since life is becoming very difficult in the United States, the returned Mexican hopes to improve his condition in Mexico.

## Los repatriados

Adiós California, adiós,
Adiós tierra de ilusiones,
Anda y ve y te ayude Dios
Ay te dejo tus millones.
Ya me voy pa'l* terrenazo,
ya aquí no puedo vivir,
Ya me voy de un jalonazo,
Que estoy pando de sufrir.
Ay . . . que vida tan perra,
Maldita sea la finanza
Ya me voy para mi tierra,
Cálmate dolor de panza.
Si en mi tierra paz hubiera,
Y calmaran su ambición,

El mexicano no fuera
A sufrir a otra nación.

## The Repatriated Ones

Good-bye, California, good-bye,
Good-bye, land of dreams.
Go, may God help you,
I leave you your millions.
I am going to my land
I can live here no more
I shall take off now
My body is bent from suffering.
Oh, what a dog's life,
Damn those finances.
I am going to my land,
Be quiet now, stomachaches.
If in my land there was peace
And they would quiet down their ambition
The Mexican would not go
To suffer in another country.

| | |
|---|---|
| Porque el pueblo mexicano | Because the Mexicans |
| Cobra plata y cobra oro, | Charge silver and charge gold, |
| Para que cada chicano | So that each Chicano |
| Tenga en su casa un tesoro. | Can have in his house a treasure. |
| Por eso californianos, | That is why, Californians, |
| Repatriado voy de aquí | I have been repatriated |
| A mis lares mexicanos | To my Mexican homeland |
| A luchar donde nací. | To fight on where I was born. |
| A levantarme al pasito | To better myself slowly |
| Y a rezar de corazón, | And to pray with all my heart |
| Y a pedirle a Dios bendito | And to ask the blessed Lord |
| La paz de nuestra nación. | To bring peace to our nation. |
| Con tus labios consagrados | With your blessed lips |
| Ay Virgen Guadalupana, | Oh, Virgin of Guadalupe |
| Ruega por los repatriados | Pray for the repatriated ones |
| De tu tierra soberana. | People from your own homeland. |
| Señores nos retiramos; | Sirs, we take our leave, |
| Que los santos nos concedan | May the saints grant us |
| Buena suerte a los que vamos, | Good luck to those who go |
| También a los que se quedan. | And also to those who stay. |

(Calleja 1956:75–76)
*pa'l = *para el* (to the)

"Corrido de la emigración" details an unexpected appearance of the United States Border Patrol in Miami, Arizona. The corridista advises how best to handle immigration officers and what lawful procedures to follow in order not to be deported. Particularly humorous is the advice given to those operating bootleg beer stills. The corrido ends by extending an invitation to all Mexicans in exile to return to Mexico.

| Corrido de la emigración | Corrido of the Immigration Officers |
|---|---|
| Miami es la población | Miami is the town |
| que se haya muy atrasada; | Which has suffered many reverses; |
| pues llegó la Emigración | For the "Emigration" arrived |
| cuando menos se esperaba. | When it was least expected. |
| Se oyen no más las quejas | You hear only the complaints |
| de todos sin distinción; | Of all without distinction; |
| hombres, niños y viejas, | Men, children, and old people, |
| todos van a la prisión. | All have to go to prison. |
| Si tú no estás bien casado | If you are not legally married, |
| no te sirve el pasaporte; | A passport is of no use to you; |
| te llevan los del condado, | The county authorities will take you |
| a dormir allá en la corte. | To sleep there in the jail. |

Llevan las mujeres solas
y algunas que no lo son,
pobrecitas amapolas
que cortó la Emigración.
Con la mano en la cintura
se paran a investigar
como si fueran el cura,
cuando te va a confesar.

Yo voy a dar un consejo
a todo joven soltero,
que se mire en este espejo
aquí en suelo extranjero.

Que arregle su pasaporte,
no viva amancebado
porque va a dar a la corte
siendo al final deportado.

En el Globe, las mujeres
aclaman a Cristo Rey,
se olvidan de sus deberes
y algunas violan la ley.

Si tú quieres ser feliz,
Cuando el Bravo hayas pasado
muestrale a este país
que sus leyes no has violado.

Si antes has hecho cerveza
y has vivido de alambique,
hoy te rascas la cabeza
no tiene ni que te explique.

Así, paisanos queridos,
en México los espero
y allá todos reunidos
en aquel suelo sincero.

Labraremos nuestro suelo
y olvidemos esta angustia;
bajo aquel bendito cielo,
protejamos nuestra industria.

Por fin llegó ya la era
de que me arrastrara el viento,
adiós, México de afuera,
ya me voy para el de adentro.

They take away the single women,
And sometimes those who are not;
Poor little poppies
Cut down by "Emigration."
With hand on belt they pause
To make investigation
As though it were the priest
About to hear confession.

I am going to give advice
To every young bachelor;
Let him look in this mirror
Here on this foreign soil.

Have your passport in order;
Do not live with a mistress;
Because you'll land in jail
And at last you'll be deported.

In Globe, although the women
Acknowledge Christ the King,
They forget their religious duties
And some of them break the law.

If you want to be happy
When you have crossed the Bravo,
Show this country clearly
That you have not broken its laws.

If you used to make beer
And operate a still,
Just scratch your head
And don't admit anything.

Thus, dear countrymen,
I await you in Mexico,
And there we'll be reunited
In that true country.

We will till our own soil
And forget our misery here;
Under that blessed sky
Let us protect our own industry.

At last the time has come
For the wind to carry me away;
Good-bye, Mexicans in exile,
Home to Old Mexico I go.

| | |
|---|---|
| Ya con ésta me despido, | And so I take my leave, |
| raza de mi estimación; | Race that I hold in esteem, |
| sin poder dar al olvido, | Without being able to forget |
| que me echó la Emigración. | That "Emigration" deported me. |

(Taylor 1969:234–235)

The optimistic vision that the deported Mexican worker would be received by compatriots in Mexico with open arms is shattered by the corrido "Los deportados." Here the narrator acidly comments that the Mexican immigrant is getting what he deserves for being so stupid as to leave his country to go work for a foreign nation. He chastises the Mexican for becoming acculturated and acquiring U.S. styles and manners.

## Los deportados

Les cantaré un corrido
de todos los deportados,
que vienen hablando inglés
y vienen de desgraciados.

Los tiran en donde quiera
a puro mendigar,
da lástima verlos
que no traen ni para almorzar.

Marchan para el Norte
con gran gusto y afán,
trabajan en el campo
como cualquier gañan

Se van al algodón
y dan muy mala cala,
trabajan en el traque
o en el pico o la pala.

Pue eso y más merecen
esos pobres paisanos,
sabiendo que este suelo
es para los Mexicanos.

Se tumban el bigote,
y mascan su tabaco,
parecen la gran cosa y no
cargan ni . . . tlaco.

## The Deportees

I shall sing you a song
Of all who were deported,
Who come back speaking English
And come back as hopeless wretches.

They are dumped anywhere
And have to beg their way.
It's a pity to see them
With nothing to eat.

They set out for the North
With high hopes and eagerness,
But they work in the fields
Like any fieldhand.

They go to pick cotton
And get on very badly;
They work on the track
Or with shovel or with pick.

So they deserve that and more,
Those poor countrymen,
For they knew that this land
Is for the Mexicans.

They lop off their mustache
And chew their tobacco;
It seems the thing to do
And they don't have a cent.

| | |
|---|---|
| Se pelan a la Boston | They cut their hair close |
| como burros tuzados, | Like a clipped donkey; |
| se van a las segundas | They go to secondhand stores |
| y compran trajes usados. | And buy worn-out clothes. |
| | |
| Los corren los maltratan | They're insulted, mistreated, |
| los gringos desgraciados, | By those gringo wretches; |
| no tienen vergüenza | They have no shame, |
| siempre allá están pegados. | They keep going there. |
| | |
| Por eso yo me quedo | That is why I remain |
| en mi patria querida, | In my beloved country: |
| México es mi país | Mexico is my country |
| y por el doy la vida. | And for it I give my life. |

The "Corrido de inmigración" details some of the reasons men and women left Mexico for the United States, i.e., lack of employment opportunities and poverty. The lyrics are specific about the bonanza found in the United States during the 1923–1930s period. However, during the years of the Great Depression the immigrant population is hit particularly hard and people are seen milling around former work sites seeking employment to no avail. Various regions in California are specifically mentioned in the song: San Francisco, San Diego, and San Joaquín Valley. The situation becomes progressively more desperate, and many people are deported or leave under the prodding of U.S. government agencies and the Mexican government.

An interesting aspect of this corrido is the point made regarding immigrants joining the Communist party in desperation. In fact, the Communist party was quite active during this period in the United States. Another important point made in this song is the loss of property the deported immigrants suffered. Many Mexicans and Mexican Americans indeed had to sell their property at very low prices or were forced to leave their property without any compensation when they were deported or forced to leave "voluntarily." The immigration raids visited upon the Mexican and Mexican-American population exerted a great toll of suffering in physical, material, and psychological terms, as the child's voice in the corrido attests.

### Corrido de Inmigración

| | |
|---|---|
| Señores, voy a contarles | Sirs, I want to tell you |
| con dolor del corazón, | With pain in my heart |
| lo que sufre nuestra raza, | How our poor people suffer |
| causa de la inmigración. | Because of the immigration (officers). |

### The Immigration Corrido

Por cuestión del Presidente
o las grandes compañías,
desocupan mucha gente
todos los más de los días.

Por la escasez de trabajo
o casos comprometidos,
abandonan sus hogares
pa' salir de Estados Unidos.

Desde el año viente y trés
hasta la fecha en que estamos,
eso duró la bonanza,

pero ahora sí ya nos vamos.

En S. Francisco y S. Diego
no haya la gente que hacer,
ocurren al Comité
a que les den de comer.

Los mexicanos se van
por la falta de quehacer,
van para su patria libre,

fué la que los vió nacer.

Unos van con sus familias

como se presenta el caso,
y otros van deportados
de California hasta El Paso.

En las plantas de cemento
o en obras de construcción
se junta gente de a diario
que parece procesión.

En el Valle San Joaquín
hasta duele el corazón,
de ver las pobres familias
ahora en la inmigración.

Unos van a San Francisco,
otros al Valle Imperial,
los jefes de inmigración
del gobierno federal.

Because of the President
Or because of the big corporations
They are firing many people
Almost every day.

Because of lack of work
Or because of other pressures
They abandon their homes
And leave the United States.

Ever since the year 1923
Up until the present date
We were having a prosperous
     time
But now we have to leave.

In San Francisco and San Diego
People don't know what to do
They go to the Committee
To get something to eat.

Mexicans are leaving
Because there is no work
They are going to their land of free-
     dom
The land of their birth.

Some are going with their
     families
As the occasion arises
Others are being deported
From California to El Paso.

In the cement factories
And in construction jobs
People gather every day
It looks like a parade.

In the San Joaquin Valley
It pains one's heart
To see the poor families
Now being deported.

Some go to San Francisco
Others to the Imperial Valley,
The officers from the immigration
Of the federal government.

| | |
|---|---|
| Andan miles por las calles | There are thousands in the streets |
| toditos descoloridos, | All of them pale and worn |
| nomás pintando monitas | Without any work to do |
| en los Estados Unidos. | In the United States. |
| | |
| Unos ya son comunistas, | Some have become communists |
| otros platican de guerra | Others talk about war |
| y están deseando el pasaje | And all are desiring free fare |
| pa' regresar a su tierra. | To return to their homeland. |
| | |
| Vuelva, vuelva, palomita | Fly, fly little dove |
| con tu sombrero en las manos, | With your hat in your hands, |
| le noticias a Ortiz Rubio | Go tell Ortiz Rubio |
| que allá van los mexicanos. | Mexicans are coming back. |
| | |
| Ortiz Rubio les promete | Ortiz Rubio is promising |
| de la Frontera pa' allá, | That from the border on |
| que al mexicano que salga | All Mexicans leaving (the USA) |
| su pase se le dará. | Will get a free ride. |
| | |
| Unos van canta y canta, | Some sing and sing as they travel |
| otros pobres van dormidos, | Others fall asleep |
| pensando en su propiedad | Thinking about their properties |
| que quedó en Estados Unidos. | They left behind in the United States. |
| | |
| Unos andan asustados | Some are running around scared |
| les dicen a sus hermanos, | Telling their friends |
| que si quieren trabajar | If they wish to work |
| tienen que ser ciudadanos. | They have to be (U.S.) citizens. |
| | |
| En Mexicali y Nogales, | In Mexicali and Nogales |
| en Piedras Negras y El Paso, | In Piedras Negras and El Paso |
| se ven muchos compatriotas | There are many compatriots |
| que van para el terrenazo. | Leaving for the homeland. |
| | |
| En el pueblo San Fernando, | In the town of San Fernando |
| esto no es cosa de risa, | This is no laughing matter |
| allí bloquearon el pueblo, | They blocked off the whole town |
| el miércoles de ceniza. | On Ash Wednesday. |
| | |
| Hicieron un gran alarme, | They made a big hullabaloo |
| tengan esto muy presente, | Keep this in mind |
| en el Barrio del Rebote | In the Barrio of Rebote |
| allí juntaron la gente. | There they gathered all the people. |
| | |
| Exigían el pasaporte; | They demanded passports, |
| mujeres, niños llorando; | Women and children crying; |

se llevaron a mi papá,
solo Dios sabe hasta cuando.

They took my daddy,
God only knows when I'll see him
        again.

Ya con ésta me despido,
les encargo, mexicanos;
hay que volver a la patria
donde están nuestros hermanos.

I bid you farewell,
I do tell you, Mexicans;
We must return to our homeland
Where our brothers reside.

Es muy triste, compañeros,
vivir en estas esferas,
donde tienen que humillarse
a las ideas extranjeras.

It is very sad, my friends,
Living in this land
Where we are humiliated
By foreign ideas.

Hay que salir de este país
toditos a nuestra tierra,
para no prestar lugar
a que nos echen pa' fuera.

We must leave this country
All must return to our homeland,
So that they don't have the excuse
To kick us out of their country.

El que compuso estos versos,
ese se fué en aeroplano,
lleva ganas de pisar
a su suelo mexicano.

The one who composed these verses
Left (the USA) by airplane;
He is very desirous
Of stepping on Mexican soil.

(Guerrero 1931)

In the "Corrido de la triste situatión" the troubadour comments on the deportations and general ill treatment Mexicans were receiving in the United States. The workers are encouraged to leave foreign lands voluntarily. However, the song also tells of hardships encountered all over Mexico.

## Corrido de la triste situación

Señores, tengan presente
pongan mucha atención,
voy a cantarles los versos
de esta triste situación.

## Corrido of the Sad Situation

Sirs, be aware,
Pay close attention,
I am going to sing to you
The verses of a sad situation.

El novecientos treintaiuno
¡ay! señores, qué dolor,
¡qué miseria se presenta!
¡que nos ampare el Señor!

In 1931
Oh, gentlemen, what a pity,
Oh what misery abounds!
May the lord have pity on us!

En Ciudad Juárez se mira,
ya es cosa de lamentar
que anda toda la gente
que no haya en qué trabajar.

In the city of Juárez one can see
And it is truly pathetic
People are everywhere
And cannot find any work.

Madre mía de los Dolores,
en este Juárez ingrato
no más se oyen los clamores.

Dear mother of Dolores,
In this wretched town of Juárez
One can only hear the cries.

Uno al otro se decía:
esa trampa no la supe,
unos van al Porvenír,
otros van a Guadalupe.

One person would tell another
This trap I did not know about;
Some go to the town of Porvenir,
Others go to the city of Guadalupe.

Pues vienen del Porvenír,
de Guadalupe también,
diciéndole a sus familias:
que no encontraron quehacer.

Others came from Porvenir
And from Guadalupe too,
Telling their families
They could not find any work.

Prendiditos quien los ve,
andan colectando el cinco
para tomar un café.

Huddled around one sees them
Runing around collecting alms
So as to buy some coffee.

Llega la gente del Sur

People arrive from the South (of
    Mexico)

sacando sus pasaportes,
y lamentan su fortuna
en las fronteras del Norte.

They take out their passports
And they bemoan their bad fortune
In the northern borderlands.

Se pasan pa'l otro lado
creyendo que son formales,
y allá tan mal que los ven
los ingratos federales.

They cross over to the other side
Thinking they (Americans) are honest,
And there they are so badly treated
By those ingrate federal officers (bor-
    der patrol).

¡Ah! ¡qué ingratos patones!

Oh how cruel those big-foots (Amer-
    icans) are!

ya a la gente vuelven loca,
metiéndose por los ranchos
y llevándolos en troca.

They do drive people crazy,
They come into the farms
And take the men (Mexicans) in their
    trucks.

Luego que ya los agarran
les hacen observaciones
por caminos y condados,
esos ingratos patones.

After they apprehend them
They keep an eye on them
Through roads and through counties,
Those cruel big-footed ones.

Los llevan a Emigración,

They take them to the immigration
    office

los sentencian a la Corte,
los que van de contrabando
aunque lleven pasaporte.

They sentence them in the courts,
Those that are here illegally
And even those with passports.

Pobrecitos prisioneros
que a la Corte van a dar,
a tomar agua caliente
y luego avena sin sal.

Cuando cumplen su sentencia
al puente vienen a dar,

con su corazón alegre
a volver a experimentar.

Anden, ingratos patones,
que no tienen compasión,
ya viene Alemania y Rusia
unidas con el Japón.

En la Colonia Reforma
lamentan la situación
por los fuertes temporales
se les perdió el algodón.

El día siete de Septiembre
¡que suerte sin compasión!

que en S. Francisco Tresjacales
fué la grande anegación.

Agraristas de este valle
ya no hallan ni qué pensar,
quieren entregar las tierras
y salirse a experimentar.

En San Isidro y Sauzal
están acabando su vida,
pues no hallan ni qué vender
para la Cooperativa.

Pobrecitos Sauzaleños,
son dignos de compasión,
ya no les vale la leña
ni las ventas de carbón.

La Forestal les exige
el permiso con razón,
luego, si no lo presentan,
decomisan el carbón.

Poor, pitiful prisoners
Those that end up in the jails,
They'll have to drink warm water
And eat oatmeal without salt.

When their jail term is up
They end up at the bridge (U.S.-
    Mexican border);
With joy in their hearts
They are ready to try again one more
    time.

Hey, you cruel big-footed ones,
You without compassion,
Here comes Germany and Russia
Allied with the Japanese.

In the suburb of Reforma
They bemoan the situation
Because of the drought
They lost their cotton crop.

On the seventh of September
What darn luck—there's no compas-
    sion!
In San Francisco Tresjacales
There was a great flood.

Farmers from this valley
They do not know what to think.
They want to return their land
And try their luck elsewhere.

In San Isidro and Sauzal
They are about to lose their lives
Because they don't have a thing to sell
To the cooperative.

Poor people from the Sauzal
They deserve our compassion;
Their lumber is not worth a penny
Nor is their coal worth anything.

The forest service requires
A permit and with good reason,
And if they do not present it
They confiscate their coal.

| | |
|---|---|
| Ellos tienen esperanzas | They still do have some hope |
| como la flor de alelía | Just as the flower blooms |
| que si les echan drenaje | That if a flood control system is installed |
| otras cosechas tendrían. | They would have another harvest. |
| | |
| Ya me despido de Juárez | I bid farewell from Juárez |
| de la Frontera también; | From the border I say good-bye; |
| ya el Gobierno nos dió pases, | The government gave us a free fare, |
| ya nos vamos en el tren. | We will be leaving by train. |
| | |
| Ya con ésta me despido, | With this I bid farewell |
| encogido el corazón, | With sadness in my heart; |
| aquí termina el corrido | Here I end this corrido |
| de esta triste situación | Of our sad situation. |

(Guerrero 1931)

A more positive view of the repatriation experience is presented in the ballad "Despedida de Karnes City Texas." Of particular significance is the aid given to the repatriated Mexicans by Mexican-American organizations and the Mexican consulate. This indeed was the case, since it has been reported that mutual aid societies began to proliferate during the 1920s and 1930s to render aid to Mexicans and Mexican Americans (see Camarillo 1979 and Del Castillo 1984).

### Despedida de Karnes City Texas     Farewell from Karnes City, Texas

| | |
|---|---|
| Mil novecientos treinta y uno | Nineteen hundred and thirty-one |
| fecha que no olvidaremos, | A date that we shall not forget |
| que por falta de trabajo | Because for lack of work |
| a nuestra patria volvemos. | We return to our homeland. |
| | |
| Día 18 de octubre | Eighteenth day of October |
| Inolvidable mañana, | An unforgettable morning. |
| que regresamos gustosos | We returned happily |
| a la Patria Mexicana. | To the Mexican motherland. |
| | |
| Adios Texas renombrado | Good-bye, renowned state of Texas, |
| con todas tus plantaciones | With all your agricultural fields; |
| gozamos de tus delicias | We enjoyed all your pleasures |
| y hoy de tristes situaciones. | And today experience this sad situation. |
| | |
| Adios Condado de Karnes | Good-bye, county of Karnes, |
| donde siempre residimos | Where we always did reside. |
| nos vamos pobres sin dinero | We leave poor and without money |
| porque ahorras nunca hicimos. | Because we never saved money. |

Todos ganamos dinero
no lo podemos negar,
el defecto que tuvimos
que no lo supimos guardar.

We all did earn money
We cannot deny it;
Our shortcoming was
We did not know how to save it.

Nos despedimos Karnes City
con el sombrero en la mano,
porque todos te contamos
como suelo Mexicano.

We bid farewell to Karnes City
With our hat in hand,
Because we all think of you
As our own Mexican land.

Sociedad Benito Júarez
me voy pero no te olvido,
por los grandes beneficios
que de tí hemos recibido.

Benito Juárez Association,
I take leave but won't forget you,
Because of the great benefits
We received from you.

Adios todos los patrones
que con nuestos buenos fueron,
aunque por nosotros trabajo

siempre nos protejieron.

Good-bye, all the employers
That treated us well,
Even though it was because of our
    work
They always did protect us.

Adios nuestros amigos
y familias de la casa,
procuren el consulado
que es el arma de la raza.

Good-bye, all our friends
And all our relatives;
Seek out the Mexican consulate
For that is the weapon of our race.

El Sr. Rosendo Tórrez
y el Cónsul General,
incansablemente trabajaron
para podernos repatriar.

Mr. Rosendo Tórrez
And the consul general
They worked incessantly
To help us repatriate.

El Cónsul de San Antonio
y el Sr. Rosendo Tórrez,
son distinguidas personas
de glorias merecedoras.

The San Antonio Consulate
And Mr. Rosendo Tórrez
They are two distinguished persons
Worthy of high praise.

La recompensa esperamos
que del cielo les vendrá
por habernos ayudado
con tan buena voluntad.

We hope they shall be repaid
By the heavens above
Because they helped us
With such goodwill.

Juntamente las personas
que nos ayudaron como hermanos
las expresivas gracias reciban
de todos los que nos vamos.

All the people
That aided us like brothers,
Our most expressive thanks to you
From all of us who depart.

Nos despedimos de todos
con muy buena voluntad,
deseamos en lo futuro
años de prosperidad.

We bid all farewell
With plenty of goodwill
We hope in the near future
There'll be years of prosperity.

En fin Texas ya nos vamos
pobres y sin dinero,
creo que el último adios
te lo damos en Laredo.

Well, Texas we are leaving
Poor and without money;
I believe our last good-bye
Will be at Laredo.

Aquí se acabó la historia
y molestias en la ocasión
roguemos a dios no vuelva
la terrible situación.

Here our story ends
And all other inconveniences.
We pray to God
This terrible situation does not return.

(Carreras de Velasco 1974:111)

The repatriation program of the Depression era left a deep scar in the Mexican-American community. The deportations uprooted entire communities, disrupted lives, and generally stunted the growth of the Mexican-American population. The folk songs included here faithfully depict the trials and tribulations of those directly affected.

# The Bracero Program

*Six*   There are various studies on the Farm Labor Supply Program, also known as the bracero program, which was instituted in 1942 and terminated in 1964. Seminal works covering this topic include those by Ernesto Galarza, *Merchants of Labor: The Mexican Bracero Story* (1964) and *Strangers in Our Fields* (1956); Richard B. Craig, *The Bracero Program: Interest Groups and Foreign Policy* (1971); and Richard H. Hancock, *The Role of the Bracero in the Economic and Cultural Dynamics of Mexico: A Case Study of Chihuahua* (1959). (See also my work *The Bracero Experience: Elitelore versus Folklore*, (1979).) More recent studies include Dennis Nodín Valdés, *Al Norte: Agricultural Workers in the Great Lakes Region, 1917–1970* (1988), Erasmo Gamboa, *Mexican Labor and World War II: Braceros in the Pacific Northwest, 1942–1947* (1990), and Leo R. Chávez, *Shadowed Lives: Undocumented Immigrants in American Society* (1992).

The bracero program was initiated by the United States government during World War II in response to the urgent pleas of farmers, who claimed there was insufficient manpower to harvest their crops. The urgency for importing farm laborers was tied to the war effort, since many U.S. workers had been drafted to work in various war industries or recruited to fight on the battle-fields. Thus at the initiative of the U.S. government the Mexican government agreed to engage in the structuring of a program to export workers from Mexico to the United States. After the massive deportations of the 1930s, Mexican officials were leery of sending their nationals to the United States; therefore, before embarking on a new program to send workers, Mexican leaders wanted certain guarantees in writing for their Mexican nationals. The two nations consequently engaged in bilateral discussions and hammered out an agreement on the basic protections to be guaranteed for the imported workers. These benefits included:

1. Mexican laborers shall not be subject to the military draft.
2. Discrimination against braceros is forbidden.
3. They shall be guaranteed transportation, food, hospitalization and repatriation.
4. They shall not be used to displace other workers nor to lower wages.
5. Contracts made by employee and employer will be made under the supervision of the Mexican government and shall be written in Spanish.

6. Expenses incurred for transportation and lodgings from point of origin to destination shall be paid by the employer who will be reimbursed by sub-employer.
7. Salaries shall be the same as those made to citizens of the U.S.A. and shall not be lower than 30 cents an hour.
8. Exceptions as to wages can be made under extenuating circumstances provided authorization by the Mexican government is given.
9. No minors under 14 will be allowed to work.
10. Braceros will be allowed to form associations and elect a leader to represent them.
11. They shall be guaranteed work for 75 percent of the working days.
12. Savings shall be deducted from their pay and the Banco Nacional Agrícola shall take charge of the money until the braceros return. (United States Executive Agreement Series 278, 1943:3)

The agreement was drafted on August 4, 1942, with representatives from both Mexico and the United States participating in the formulation of the agreement. Though it was meant to be an emergency measure, once it was put in place, powerful agricultural concerns and lobbyist continued pressuring Congress into extending it. The basic provisions remained in place until 1951. After 1951 Public Law 78 regulated the importation of farm labor until 1964, when the program was finally terminated as a result of pressure exerted by religious groups, Mexican Americans, and others who perceived the program as detrimental to native farm workers as well as to the braceros themselves.

The number of Mexican workers imported into the United States in the twenty-two years the bracero program was in effect proved to be in the hundreds of thousands. Galarza (1964:70) gives these yearly totals:

| | |
|---|---|
| 1942 | 4,203 |
| 1943 | 53,098 |
| 1944 | 62,170 |
| 1945 | 49,494 |
| 1946 | 32,043 |
| 1947 | 19,632 |
| 1948 | 35,345 |
| 1949 | 107,000 |
| 1950 | 67,500 |
| 1951 | 190,745 |
| 1952 | 197,100 |
| 1953 | 201,380 |
| 1954 | 309,033 |
| 1955 | 398,650 |
| 1956 | 445,197 |
| 1957 | 436,049 |
| 1958 | 432,857 |
| 1959 | 447,535 |
| 1960 | 427,240 |

Equally high were the figures for undocumented workers who lacked official contracts and crossed the border without any legal papers (59):

| | |
|---|---|
| 1940 | 8,051 |
| 1941 | 6,082 |
| 1942 | 5,100 |
| 1943 | 8,860 |
| 1944 | 29,176 |
| 1945 | 69,111 |
| 1946 | 101,476 |
| 1947 | 199,282 |
| 1948 | 203,000 |
| 1949 | 293,000 |
| 1950 | 480,000 |
| 1951 | 509,040 |
| 1952 | 528,815 |
| 1953 | 885,587 |
| 1954 | 1,108,900 |

Even though the period 1942–1964 saw a great number of Mexican immigrants entering the United States, the era produced only a few corridos, such as the "Corrido de los desarraigados" (The Ballad of the Uprooted Ones), written in 1942 but not published until 1976, that depicted the travails of the Mexican worker. The other nine texts that I have garnered from this period are décimas or canciones rather than true corridos. The corrido, although still a viable form, had been appropriated by the movies and commercial record companies. Matinee idols such as Jorge Negrete and Pedro Infante sang many canciones rancheras and corridos from previous eras. Singers such as Miguel Aceves Mejía also sang standard corridos. The canción ranchera mostly focused on love themes. Many corridos which were popular during the 1950s were written by professional writers such as Víctor Cordero, who wrote such hits as "Juan Charrasqueado," "El Ojo de Vidrio," and "Gabino Barrera." The polka and *conjunto*-type music too had superseded in popularity the corrido for the time being (Peña 1985).

Other important factors contributed to the lack of immigrant corridos in this period. One of the most important events that transpired was World War II. The United States entered a period of feverish industrialization. Young men left the farms for military service or big-city industries. At the same time Mexico was experiencing a drive to industrialize. President Lázaro Cárdenas had focused his administration's efforts in the 1930s on the rural sector, i.e., on ejido building, and on the expropriation of petroleum and foreign holdings in Mexico. However, the presidents who succeeded him, Miguel Aguila Camacho (1940–1946), Miguel Alemán (1946–1952), and Adolfo Ruiz Cortines (1952–1958), advocated and promoted a concerted effort toward industrialization.

It was during these three presidential terms in particular that Mexico experienced its greatest industrialization and urbanization growth. The campesinos were leaving their farms and migrating to the United States or to the large cities, principally Mexico City. The rural folkways were being left behind, and the local troubadour began to go out of vogue.

In the United States members of the Mexican-American population who had survived the ravages of forced and voluntary repatriations and outright deportations were now becoming assimilated. Two classes crystallized within the community: the high tones (middle and upper-middle classes) and the raza, pelados, and working class. Peña has written an excellent study of the schism that developed between the two groups and how it prevented any type of solidarity from forming and advancing the Chicano cause. According to Peña's theory, this schism could be seen in the musical discourses of the two groups. In the straightforward words of Narciso Martínez, a participant in the formation of the working-class musical style of the era, this conjunto music was "pa' la gente pobre, la gente de rancho; la orquesta era pa' high society" ("for poor people, rural people; orchestra was for high society"). Peña interprets this assertion:

> In such succint language can the socially defined functions of conjunto and orquesta be summed up. In such clear language also may be discerned the tension between conjunto's proletarian, Mexicanized, and originally rural folk base on the one hand and orquesta's urban, middle-class, and necessarily more Americanized base on the other. It was, in short, a tension born of incipient class differences. (1985:4)

Much of conjunto music consisted of instrumental renditions, i.e., no words accompanied the musical numbers. They were polkas, which did not have lyrics. The corrido, on the other hand, told a story.

Another factor contributing to the scarcity of corridos dealing with the bracero experience during this period is that in the early stages of the program the Mexican immigrant was welcomed with open arms. The United States government itself had urgently requested that Mexico send workers. Farmers and the small-town residents in the various regions where the braceros were desperately needed formed welcoming committees and held small fiestas and receptions for the newcomers. If in the 1930s they had been viewed as not fit to inhabit the same areas where Anglos lived, attend the same schools, or dine in the same restaurants, the 1940s brought a marked change in attitude (although segregationist practices continued in much of the Southwest). The braceros were welcomed as heroes who were going to save the crops—the much-needed crops for the war effort.

A fictionalized biographical account written under the satirical name Máximo Peón describes the arrival in the United States of a newly inducted bracero in glowing terms:

Fortunately, all these itinerant peddlers disappeared as soon as we entered the United States. From that moment on, with great anticipation (by means of the telegraph) they [the Americans] would treat us to hearty breakfasts, lunches, and dinners in elegant restaurants. Some of these restaurants were even bigger and prettier than the Lady Baltimore here. Upon arriving in Colorado we stopped at a beautiful town called Trinidad. Its streets were paved, not like all the others with cement but with huge, red flagstone-type paving material. These "flagstones" were made from certain materials which were shinier than tile. They reflected beautifully the sharp blueness of the clear sky, the greenness of the trees planted along the streets or standing in the gardens of each house, and the colors reflected from the buildings nearby.

   We were taken to a large and roomy building where we found long dining tables covered with extremely white tablecloths. These tables were decorated as if a banquet was about to be served: roses and carnations were placed on top of the tables and decorated the rest of the big hall. Standing by the walls we could see numerous beautiful young ladies who, knowing there was a shortage of waitresses, had volunteered to serve the thousands of men newly arrived. (Peón 1966:12–13)

My interviews with braceros who came to the United States during the initial stages of the bracero program produced accounts similar to this one (see Herrera-Sobek 1979). Both indicate that the demand to hear protest-type corridos may not have been great at that time. The braceros preferred to listen to old standbys, such as "Paso del Norte," "Tierra Mixteca," "De aca de este lado," and a hit by Jorge Negrete, the movie idol and crooner à la Bing Crosby, entitled "México lindo y querido." These songs dealt with the theme of homesickness for Mexico.

The period 1942–1964, thus can be conceptualized as transitional for Mexican immigrant canciones and corridos. Before the 1940s corridos were plentiful. The rural flavor of the Mexican immigrants was definitely strong, and their main vehicle of communication was the songs they wrote and sang articulating their experiences either in optimistic, happy terms or as a means of expressing their grievances against the unjust systems that conspired against their welfare in Mexico—i.e., revolutions, hunger, unemployment—and the discrimination and injustices committed against them in the States, especially in the 1930s, when "getting rid of the Mexican" was the order of the day.

World War II affected living conditions in the United States. Food became scarce, and the U.S. government resorted to rationing staples. "La restrinción del azúcar," written by the folk poet Bartolo Ortiz from south Texas, describes in a humorous manner the effects the rationing of sugar was having on Chicanos.

The use of the term *Chicana* (Raza Chicana, i.e., the Chicano people) should be noted, since these verses were collected in the early 1940s and were written around that period. The writer, however, considers himself a Mexican. It is not certain if he is a Mexican immigrant narrating the events or if he is a Chicano who is following the custom of that time by calling himself a "mexicano."

The narrator explains the situation with respect to the rationing of sugar. People had to register to receive their allotted portion. The allotment consisted of five pounds per family, and with some families having ten members the portion seemed quite small, particularly for those with a sweet tooth, as the corridista explains. The song ends with an exhortion to help the United States in this crisis.

## La restrinción del azúcar

Yo, como buen mejicano,
vengo a traer la alegría
y a que más de algún paisano

de mis tonteras se ría.

Soy de la farsa el payaso,
soy *clown* de la palomilla.
De lo que hablen no hago caso,
ganando algo de pastilla.

No se me agota el aliento
para decir la verdad,
y si en lo que digo miento,
el público juzgará.

Hoy les hablo de bonanza
y mañana de la crisis,
y siempre con la esperanza
de que un día sean más felices.

La cosa se está poniendo
un tanto color de hormiga

ustedes bien lo están viendo,
no vale que yo lo diga.

El azúcar se ha escondido.
Ya es artículo de lujo.
Si el café es desabrido,
que puedo hacer, nomás pujo.

Pero si ya es mi de malas,
*Vale grillo que me cruja.**

## The Rationing of Sugar

Like the good Mexican I am
I come to bring joy
And so that one or two of my
     countrymen
Can laugh at my inanities.

I am the clown of comedy skits
I am the clown of the gang.
What they might say I don't care
As long as I earn a cent.

I'm never out of breath
So as to tell the truth,
And if I should say untruths
The public can be the judge.

Today I talk about bonanzas
Tomorrow I'll tell about the crisis
And always with the hope
That you'll be happy some day.

Things are getting to be
The color of an ant (i.e., tight,
     painful);
You are witness to it,
I don't need to tell you this.

Sugar is not in sight
It is now a luxury item.
If the coffee is bitter now,
What can I do, I just grunt.

But if bad luck is with me
It is good to have someone speak for
     me.

No podré volar sin alas,
aunque esté un día a puja y puja.

I will not be able to fly wingless,
Even though I grunt and grunt.

Yo mucho azúcar no como,
pero me fuí a registrar,
porque dije, si me aplomo,
no sé qué vaya a pasar.

I don't really use much sugar
But I went and registered
'Cause I said if I am not sharp
I don't know what will happen.

Porque dicen que más luego
aunque nos lleve la china,
se va a aparecer Juan Diego
con el límite de harina.

'Cause they say later on
Even though we suffer much
Juan Diego will appear
Telling us flour is rationed.

Que se limita la harina
le importa poco a mi raza,
porque alcabo en la cocona
habrá tortillas de masa.

If they ration flour
My people don't really care,
Because in the pantry
There will be corn tortillas.

El cuatro y cinco de Mayo,
desde una hora temprana,
con la rápidez del rayo,
iba la raza chicana.

The fourth and fifth of May
At an early hour
As quick as a lightning bolt
The Chicano people lined up.

A registrarse a la escuela
pa' que les den su ración,
palabra que ni en una muela

le cabe al que sea glotón.

They went to register at the school
So as to get their ration.
To tell the truth not even enough for
one molar
Was given to the glutton type.

Como una dosis laxante,
en sobres de celofán,
azúcar en el restaurante
ni medio a darme nos dan.

Like a laxative dose
In wax paper envelopes
The restaurants
Hardly give us sugar.

No me gusta el café amargo,
me dijo doña Tomasa
pues no más hágase el cargo,
son diez bocas en mi casa.

I don't like unsweetened coffee,
Doña Tomasa told me;
Can you imagine
In my house there're ten mouths (to
feed).

Cinco libras por semana,
pues no sabe ni a melado
para los que en la mañana
toman el café endulzado.

Five pounds a week
It will never taste sweet
To those who in the morning
Like their coffee sweet.

El día que al registro fuimos,
allí en la Escuela Navarro,
si vieran cómo nos reímos,
uno hacía la trompa jarro.

The day we went to register
There at the Navarro School
You should've seen how we laughed,
One kept puckering his lips.

Le dijo la profesora:
—¿Cómo se llama usted, amigo?
—Me llamo Pancho, señora,
pero no sé dónde vivo.

Hay allí un callejoncito,
no es muy lejos de la plaza.
También hay un arbolito
que le da sombra a la casa.

¿Qué nombre es el callejón?
—Corre de oriente al poniente.
Creo que le dicen Torreón,
yo no tengo muy presente.

—Bueno, ¿cuántos años tiene?
Todo eso quiero saber.
¿Dónde nació, y de dónde viene?

¿Es solo, o tiene mujer?

—Yo estoy creyendo que sea
como mi mamá platicaba
que nací en una zalea
que hasta yo la rasguñaba.

Y me decía que había elotes
en medio de dos lagunas,
y que también había ejotes,
calabacitas y tunas.

Seguiremos discutiendo
del azúcar el problema.
Ya se nos está poniendo
de muy mal sabor la crema.

L'agua** fresca desabrida
eso que ni duda cabe
si así es cuates de mi vida,
mejor tomo de la llave.

Si me voy para Laredo.
el asunto es más sencillo,
ya veré allí si puedo
pasar mucho piloncillo.

The teacher said to him:
"What's your name, my friend?"
"My name is Pancho, ma'am;
But I don't know where I live.

"There is a little alley
It's not far from the plaza.
There is also a small tree
That gives shade for the house."

"What's the alley's name?"
"It runs east and west.
I think they call it Torreón,
I am not too sure."

"Well, how old are you?
I want to know all that.
Where were you born, and where do
    you come from?
Are you single or do you have a
    wife?"

"I think it was like my mother
Used to tell me
I was born on an animal hide
Which I used to scratch.

And she told me there was corn
In the middle of two lakes
And that there were green beans,
Squash, and prickly pears."

We shall continue
The sugar problem
The cream is getting to be
Awful tasting.

The punch is unsweetened
There is no doubt about that
If that's how it is, my good friends,
I'll drink water from the faucet.

If I go to Laredo
Things will be better.
I'll see if I can
Smuggle a lot of brown sugar.

| | |
|---|---|
| Si así sigue este conflicto, | If this war carries on |
| ¡ya nos llevó la trompeta! | We're all damned! |
| Hay que darle a Hiroshito (*sic*) | We'll have to punch |
| muy prontito en la maceta. | Hirohito out. |
| | |
| ¡Hijo de la remolacha, | That son of a beet, |
| pariente del betabel! | Kin to the beet! |
| Que por su puntada gacha | 'Cause of his crazy plans |
| nos está llevando al *jel*.*** | We are all in hell. |
| | |
| Hay que prestar nuestra ayuda | We'll have to give our help |
| a los Estados Unidos. | To the United States. |
| Si así lo hacemos, sin duda, | If we do that, no doubt |
| jamás seremos vencidos. | We'll never be beaten. |
| | |
| ¡Viva el Pendón de las Barras! | Long live the stars and stripes |
| y también el Tricolor, | And also the tricolor flag |
| y el águila con sus garras | And the eagle with its claws |
| haga trizas al traidor. | Shall tear apart the traitor. |

(Goodwyn 1944:430–433)
*vale grillo que me cruja = literally, "A cricket that will chatter for me is valuable"
**L'agua = *el agua* (the water)
***Jel = hell

This song displays a poetic persona who seeks to bring humor and laughter to his compatriots. The topic of sugar rationing is transformed by the *pícaro*-type narrator into a humorous event. The persona denominates himself a "clown," indicating some acculturation by using the English word for *payaso*. Nevertheless, the narrator indicates that although he delivers his message in a humorous manner he is stating the truth and challenges the audience to participate and be the judge of what he says.

The narrator achieves humor through various strategies. One is the dialogic exchange described in the interviewing process carried out by administrative officials in order to be eligible for the rationed sugar. The interview reveals the mocking attitude and disdain the people had for the bureaucratic process and red tape. This of course was due in part to the nature of the questions and the instability of migratory life. Frequently migrants did not have permanent residences, and when children were born in the fields and ranches they were not registered in the official records. When the interviewee is questioned about his address, the answer is both vague and concrete. It is obvious that the pícaro worker is pulling the bureaucrat's leg.

Poetic closure is achieved with a patriotic exhortation to help the United States to win the war and for unity between the two countries—Mexico and the United States—in order to defeat the "treacherous" enemy. The song offers a fascinating glimpse of how Chicanos were dealing with the measures instituted during World War II: with grace, patriotism, and humor.

Two décimas depict the life of the cotton picker in a humorous light. The décima was very popular in the Southwest. It was the main form of singing in the eighteenth and nineteenth centuries until the corrido displaced it in popularity (see Paredes 1976). However, it did not entirely die out in the twentieth century, as is evident in these two texts written by the folk poet Bartolo Ortiz.

"Las puntadas de Canuto en la pizca de algodón" offers a view of a happy-go-lucky cotton picker named Canuto. The décima contains an interesting array of words and phrases used in the cotton fields by Chicanos. For example, the phrases *pizcar a tirón* and *pizcar a limpio* refer to two types of cotton picking. The latter means to pick the cotton fibers cleanly, while the former signifies picking the whole cotton ball. Other words, such as *chanza* (opportunity, from the English *chance*), *wes* (west), *de violín* (big), *guayín* (wagon), *prole* (children), *role* (roll), *chilpayates, chamacos* (children), *cuates* (friends), *morlacos* (dollars), *marqueta* (market), *flirtear* (to flirt), are all characteristic of the Spanish spoken in the Southwest. The cotton picker Canuto is seen as a comical figure who thinks he is a real lady-killer. We see women working in the fields as well as a positive attitude toward family life and children, although Canuto is portrayed as very prone to "mess around," i.e., he likes to flirt with women. The migratory life of the worker is described. Canuto has traveled around the Rio Grande Valley as well as to west Texas.

## Las puntadas de Canuto en la pizca de algodón

Volvió otra vez la bonanza
para el que pizca algodón.
Ya sea a limpio o al tirón,
da hacer pesos tienen chanza.

Canuto está que hasta danza
por ir a pizcar al wes,
porque sabe que esta vez
si pizca nueve quintales
a peso o a doce reales
allá se arma en dos por tres.
Con gusto va Serafín,
Canuto, Lupe y Francisca
porque saben que en la pizca

las sandías son de violín.

Sentados junto al guayín
hacen banquete formal,
Canuto lleva hasta sal

## The Witty Sayings of Canuto while Picking Cotton

The bonanza is here again
For those who pick cotton.
Be it clean picking or straight picking
There is a chance to make money.

Canuto's legs are a-dancing
Ready to go pick cotton out west,
Because he knows this time
If he picks nine hundred
At a dollar or twelve bits,
He'll get rich in a jiffy.
Very happy is Serafín,
So are Canuto, Lupe, and Francisca
Because they know that in the picking fields
The watermelons are huge.

Seated next to the wagon
They make a formal banquet,
Canuto even provides the salt

para echarle a la sandía
pues dice que está muy fría
y salada no hace mal.

Canuto le dijo a Inés:
—Yo quisiera mucha prole
para ir a darle que role
en las pizcas en el wes.

Tú habías de darme de a tres
o cuando menos de a dos
que con agüita de arroz[1]
se crían bien los chilpayates.
Cierto, no se rían mis cuates,
esa es la verdad de Dios.

La casa donde hay chamacos
y que ya son de servicio
no cuesta gran sacrificio
para ganar los morlacos.
Ya estén gordos o estén flacos,
avientan mucho algodón
y allí el papá es el patrón
que, si no va a la cantina,
de diario comen gallina
y nunca falla el jamón.

Por eso es que el buen Canuto
le dijo a Inés que es tan buena:
—De hijos quiero una docena,
como homenaje o tributo.
Ese hombre la da de astuto
y tiene fe y esperanza,
más vale grillo la chanza
porque, aunque Inés es tan buena,

para cuando *haiga** la docena
ya se acabó la bonanza.

Canuto en la noche sueña
que anda con sus chilpayates
y les dice a sus cuates:
—Me los trajo la cigüeña,
luego corre a toda greña
porque su patrón lo llama.
De volador tiene fama.
Vió claro que iba volando

To sprinkle on his watermelon
Because he says it's very cold
And with salt it doesn't make you ill.

Canuto tells Inés:
"I want a whole bunch of kids
So that I can really clean up
During the cotton picking season out
    west;

You should give me triplets
Or at least twins
Since you know that with rice water
The kids grow up very healthy."
The truth, do not laugh, my friends,
That is God's truth.

In the house where children live
And they are old enough to work,
It's no great sacrifice
To earn those dollars:
Be they fat or skinny
They can all pick a lot of cotton
And there their dad is the boss,
And if he doesn't go to the bars
They can eat chicken every day
And there is always ham around.

That is why the good Canuto
Told Inés, who is a great gal:
"I want a dozen kids
As a tribute or as homage."
That man thinks he is real smart
And he has faith and hope,
But his plans aren't worth a cricket
Because even though Inés is a good
    woman,
By the time they have a dozen
The cotton bonanza will be over.

Canuto dreams during nighttime
That he is surrounded by his kids
And he tells his buddies:
"The stork brought them."
Then he runs full speed
Because his boss calls him.
He is famous for his flying
He clearly saw he was flying

nada, es que estaba soñando
y se cayó de la cama.

But no he was only dreaming
And he fell out of bed.

Canuto no entra en cantinas,
no se emborracha ni juega,
pero a lo que sí se niega
es a enamorar catrinas,[2]
y lo quieren las indinas,
a muchas les da de saz[3]
y no lo dejan en paz
cuando le miran fierrada,
pero al no quedarle nada
lo mandan a pizcar más.

Canuto does not go to bars,
He does not drink nor gamble
But what he definitely refuses to do
Is to court fancy dames,
And the darn things do love him,
He drops many of them
And they don't leave him in peace
When they see him with money,
But when he is flat broke
They send him out to work for more.

Canuto siempre respeta
a su querida costilla,
pero teniendo pastilla
le busca el modo a la treta.
Ya lo he visto en la marqueta
de la plaza del zacate.[4]
Pa' flirtear no tiene cuate,
pues dice que es chicanito
y *dizque*** le importa un pito
dormir en cama o petate.

Canuto always respects
His beloved better half,
But when he's got dough
He gives it a good try.
I've seen him at the market
By the Plaza del Zacate.
As a flirt he's got no match,
He says he is a Chicanito
And doesn't give a darn
If he sleeps on a bed or a mat.

Me dijo: —Yo en Robestaun
no creas que soy cualquiera,
pizcando tengo manera
de tomar leche con pan;
pues mis patrones me dan
blanquillos, queso y jamón,
y, como yo soy buscón,[5]
con dos dólares o tres
le traigo la papa a Inés
y el resto pa'l vacilón.

He told me: "In Robertson
I am not just anybody,
When I pick cotton I find a way
To drink my milk with bread;
Well, my employers give me
Eggs, cheese, and ham,
And since I am no laggard
With two or three dollars,
I bring potatoes to Inés
And the rest is for having fun."

Canuto, como es ladino
se ha puesto muy aguzado
y como ya tiene andado,
da buen razón del camino.
Anduvo[6] en el valle[7] y vino,
despúes se fué para el wes,
dijo, lo que es esta vez
no volveré ficha lisa,[8]
voy al tirón a la misa,
que ahí está echada la res.

Canuto since he is a country boy
Has his wits about him
And since he has traveled much
He knows his way around.
He went to the valley once,
Later he went out west,
He said this time
I won't come back broke,
I'll go pick cotton,
That's where the money lies.

(Goodwyn 1964:416–419)
*haiga = *haya*
**dizque = *dicen que*

The second décima by Ortiz, "Vacilada algodonera," focuses on the wages paid per hundred pounds of cotton picked. Like the other décimas he wrote, this one is generously sprinkled with the witty words and phrases that cotton-field workers were keenly aware of.

## Vacilada algodonera

Aquí me tienen mis cuates
después de correr el mundo,
con un amor muy profundo
vuelvo a buscar mis petates;
perdonen los disparates,
si es que lo toman por mal,
pues ya ven que no es igual
el español al inglés.
Pero oigan con interés
los versitos del costal.

—¿Qué costal? dijo don Pancho
¿qué clase de peroratas?
—Pos cual lleva entre las patas
que hasta lo hace hacerse gancho.[9]

Me admiro que sea del rancho

y no entienda mi razón,
a poco ya ni el patrón,
que ni las manos se roza.

—Y usted pos no ha hecho otra cosa

más que pizcar algodón.

Yo algo de campo conozco,
pues también fuí agricultor,
y tenía pa' mi labor
un buey pinto y un buey jocoso.
Mi patrón, don Juan Orozco,
me enseñó la agricultura.
La pizca no será dura,
cualquiera se los dirá,
pero qué barbaridad.
¡Cómo duele la cintura!

No digan que los engaño,
ya saben que así es mi modo,
me gusta decirles todo
sin tratar de hacerles daño.

## Cotton-Picking Jive

Here I am, my friends,
After traveling around the world,
With a deep love
I again look for my (sleeping) mat.
Please forgive the foolish sayings
If you take them the wrong way,
For you know they are not the same,
Spanish and English.
But listen with interest
To the verses of the sack.

"What sack?" says Mr. Pancho.
"What kind of speech is that?"
"Well, the one between your legs.
That which makes you look like a hook.
I am surprised that you, being from a farm,
Do not understand my reasoning.
Even the boss whose hands
Do not even touch this cotton (understands)."
"And you—well you have not done anything else
Except pick cotton."

I know a thing or two about farms.
I too was a farmer
And I had for farm work
A spotted ox and a jocular one.
My boss, Mr. Juan Orozco,
Taught me about farm work.
Cotton picking may not be hard,
Anyone can tell you that.
But damn it all,
How your back hurts!

Do not think I deceive you,
You know this is my style.
I like to tell it all
Without doing anyone harm.

Es mi tarea de cada año
hacer esta vacilada.
Dirán que me importa nada
de ustedes el sufrimiento,
pero yo, con mi talento,
tengo que ganar fierrada.[10]

—¿Qué tal está el algodón?
—¿Hacen sus cuatro quintales?

¿Se los pagan a seis reales,
o lo pizcan a tostón?

—Perdonen lo preguntón,
es que yo vine a pizcar,
pero a mí me han de pagar
por cien libras un morlaco,
ya ven que estoy rete flaco
por falta de qué tragar.

Y que aquí los hallo pizcando
el algodón, dizque a peso,
pues ahora está suave el hueso[11]
asegún estoy mirando,
y también estoy notando
que está algo cara la vida;
pues es profecía cumplida
que cuando abunda el dinero
tan sólo gana el obrero
nomás para la comida.

Pero de cualquier manera
hallo contenta a mi raza,
porque hoy gana la masa
y trae en su billetera
con qué pasear a una güera,[12]
esto, si ella se encandila,
no siendo hermana de pila,
darles un consejo puedo:
que la lleven a Laredo
y la embriaguen con tequila.

Deseo que sus ambiciones,
mis cuates, se les concedan
aunque más de tres se quedan
sin yompa[13] y sin pantalones,
pero los que son gallones

It is my job each year
To do this jiving.
You may say I do not care
About all your sufferings,
But with this talent of mine
I have to earn my money.

"How is that cotton?"
"Do you make your four hundred
    pounds?
Are they paying six bits (a hundred)
Or are you picking at fifty cents a
    hundred?"
"Forgive my meddlesomeness,
But I too came to pick cotton,
And they have to pay me
For each hundred pounds a dollar.
You can see I am quite skinny
From lack of food to eat.

And here I find you picking cotton
At one dollar a hundred.
Well, times are really good now.
I can see that now
And I am also noticing
How living is pretty expensive,
For it sure is prophecy come true
That when money is plenty
The worker barely earns
Enough to buy his food.

In spite of all this
I find my people happy
Because today they earn dough
And have in their billfolds
Enough to take out a blondie.
This if you find her willing
Not being my sister
I can give you some advice:
Take her to Laredo
And get her drunk with tequila.

I hope your ambitions,
My friends, all come true,
Even though some may end up
Without a jacket or pants,
But those that are real men

| | |
|---|---|
| y pizcan sus seis quintales | And can pick their six hundred |
| si cuando era a cuatro reales | If when the pay was four bits |
| nadie quería ser sargento, | No one wanted to be a sergeant |
| pos ahora a dólar el ciento | Now that the pay is a dollar a hundred |
| | |
| se van a creer generales. | They will think they are generals. |
| | |
| ¡Ay, mi cuate Baltasar! | Oh my friend Baltasar! |
| ¡Cómo me duelen las uñas! | How my fingernails hurt! |
| Solo tú no te rasguñas. | Only you do not get scratched (from picking cotton). |
| | |
| Te zumba[14] pare pizcar. | You are a whiz at picking. |
| Yo no puedo adelantar, | I cannot advance too far. |
| se me hacen gancho las patas | My legs begin to feel like hooks |
| y me enredo entre las matas, | And I get entangled in the weeds. |
| y si me hago atrabancado | And if I disregard all this |
| me quedo allí jorobado | I end up all bent over |
| o salgo del surco a gatas. | Or end up crawling out of the cotton row. |
| | |
| ¡Aguilas! ¡No dejen pluma, | Watch it! Do not leave any cotton fibers! |
| | |
| que van a pagar dos grullos?[15] | They are paying two dollars. |
| Extraiga bien los capullos | Take out the cotton bolls |
| tan blancos como una espuma. | They are as white as foam. |
| Esa ley nomás abruma, | That rule only bugs one. |
| nomás que paguen más plata | Just let them pay more, |
| para no meter la pata | And I know I am right |
| si les juro, señores, | When I swear to you, men, |
| que los que son voladores | That those that are really experts |
| atacan hasta la mata. | Attack even the plants themselves." |

(Goodwyn 1944:419–422)

Tomás Rivera, in his classic Chicano novel . . . *Y no se lo tragó la tierra* / . . . *And the Earth Did Not Part,* has a character named Bartolo who is supposed to be the town's (or the Rio Grande Valley in South Texas area's) bard. Bartolo chronicles in verse the daily events touching the Mexican Americans. Rivera's short vignette on Bartolo reads:

Bartolo always came through town around December, when he felt that most of the people had returned from work in other states. He always sold his poems. They were almost completely sold out by the end of the first day because they mentioned the names of the people in town. And when he read the poems out loud he told the people to read his poems out loud because the voice was the love seed in the dark. (1971:171)

One wonders if Rivera took his model for this short sketch of a south Texas folk poet from the real life of Bartolo Ortiz.

The canción "Del viaje de la 'Típica de Policía' a California" depicts a group of musicians leaving for the States. The general tone is happy and confident. The immigrant is proud of Mexico and proud of himself. He looks forward to being a good-will ambassador.

## Del viaje de la "Típica de Policía" a California

¡Adiós, México querido, testigo de mi alegría!
Me mandan a California con mi "Típica" querida.

Yo ya me voy, te digo adiós.
voy a cantar las canciones del pueblo trabajador.

El día dieciocho de julio llegamos a la Estación,
el tren ya estaba formado y había "cuates" de a montón.

—¡Quihúbole, pues! ¿Pa' dónde van?
—Nos vamos a California nuestros sones a cantar.

—¿Adónde vas, Miguel Lerdo?—me dijeron mis amigos.
—Pos ya se los dije, cuates, voy para Estados Unidos.

—¿Qué vas a hacer?—Ya lo sabrán,
dejaremos bien plantada la bandera nacional.

"Diré a los americanos lo que es mi México hermoso,
donde hay trabajo y contento y el pueblo vive dichoso.

"Yo se los digo y es la verdad,
que México es muy hermoso y es tierra de libertad."

—¡A Estados Unidos salen!—nos dijo mi general—,
quiere el señor Presidente que vayan a trabajar.

—¡Ándele, pues, jálenle ya;
muchachos, lo ordena el Jefe, por algo lo ha de ordenar.

Nuestra música preciosa tenemos que propagar,
y nuestros viriles cantos por nuestra raza hablarán.

—Le damos, pues, me canso ya;
ya le estamos dimos dando, comiencen, pues, a afinar.

Huapangos, sones, valonas, del Bajío y de Michoacán;
y los "sones socialistas" que alientan para luchar.

¡A poco sí! ¡Cómo no!
Canciones de hombres sin miedo que dió la Revolución.

Si lejos de nuestra tierra la suerte, los trata mal,
¡Vénganse, pues, camaradas a México a trabajar!

¡No sufran, más, jalen pa' allá!
Pa' que sepan lo que vale tener Patria y Libertad.

(Mendoza 1964:396)

## About the Trip of "Típica de Policía" to California

Good-bye, my beloved Mexico, witness to my happiness!
They are sending me to California with my beloved group.

I am leaving, I bid thee farewell,
I shall be singing the songs of the hardworking people.

On the eighteenth of July we arrived at the station.
The train was ready to go and there were "brothers" all around.

"Hey, hello! Where are you going?"
"We are going to California, our songs there to sing."

"Where are you going, Miguel Lerdo?" my friends asked.
"Well, I told you, brothers, I am going to the United States."

"What are you going to do?" "You shall soon know.
We shall leave a good image of our national flag.

"I shall tell the Americans about my beautiful Mexico.
Where there is work and happiness and the people are contented.

"I tell you this, and it is true,
That Mexico is beautiful and is a land of liberty."

"To the United States you go!" the general told us.
"The President wants you to go to work."

"Come on, get going; boys, the boss tells us so.
He has his reasons for going so."

Our beautiful music we want to spread,
And our virile songs will speak about our race.

"Let's get going, I am getting tired.
We're on our way, start to tune up."

Huapangos, songs, valonas from the Valley of Michoacán,
And the "socialist songs" that inspire us to fight.

It is true! Yes it is!
Songs of men of the Revolution, sired without fear!

If far from our land, luck will treat you badly,
Return to Mexico, friends, to work.

Do not suffer, go over there,
So that you know what it means to have land and liberty.

The "Corrido de los desarraigados" is one of only two protest songs known for this era. (The protest corridos and canciones were revitalized during efforts to form a farm workers' union; see chapter 7.) This corrido was written in 1942 by Arnulfo Castillo, a folk poet from the Midwest who was extensively interviewed by Inez Cardozo-Freeman in the 1970s (see Cardozo-Freeman 1976). The lyrics detail the hardships experienced by the Mexican immigrant. Specific blame is heaped upon the middlemen-contractors and the truck drivers who hauled the workers from field to field and, according to the corrido, shamelessly exploited the workers.

### Corrido de los desarraigados

Señores, pongan cuidado
lo que es verdad yo les digo.
Como México no hay dos
por lindo, hermoso y florido.

Toditos los extranjeros
lo tienen pa' su delirio.
Del cuarenta y tres atrás
no se hallaba complicado.

México, México era muy feliz
sincero, humilde y honrado.
Hasta que empezó a cruzar
la raza pa'l otro lado.

Contratistas y troqueros
pa' mi todos son iguales.
No más 'taban* esperando
que pasaran nacionales.

### The Corrido of the Uprooted Ones

Men, pay attention,
What I say is true.
There is no other country like Mexico,
Beautiful, lush, and green.

All the foreigners
Are amazed by Mexico.
Previous to 1943
There were no complications.

Mexico, Mexico was happy,
Sincere, humble, honest
until our race started crossing
To the other side.

Contractors and truckers
To me they are all the same.
They were only waiting
For nationals to cross.

| | |
|---|---|
| Parecían lobos hambrientos | They resembled hungry wolves |
| fuera de los matorrales. | Outside their thicket. |
| Los creemos con honor | We believe they are honorable |
| pero no lo(s) conocemos. | But we don't know them. |
| | |
| Nos trabajan como esclavos | They work us like slaves |
| y nos tratan como perros. | And treat us like dogs. |
| No más falta que nos monten | All we need is for them to ride us |
| y que nos pongan el freno. | And to put the bridle on us. |
| | |
| Si alguno lo toma a mal | If someone doesn't like what I say |
| es que no lo ha conocido. | It's because he wasn't there. |
| Que se vaya a contratar | Let him go as a bracero |
| a los Estados Unidos. | To the United States. |
| | |
| Y verá que va trabajar | He will see that he will work |
| como un esclavo vendido. | Like a sold slave. |
| Antes éramos honrados | Before we were honorable men, |
| y de eso nada ha quedado. | Now we have lost it all. |
| | |
| Con eso del pasaporte | With our passports |
| nos creemos americanos | We think we are Americans. |
| Pero tenemos el nombre | But we are called |
| de ser desarraigados. | The uprooted ones. |
| | |
| Allí les va la despedida | Here I bid farewell |
| a toditos mis paisanos | To all my countrymen. |
| Si quieren tener honor | If you want to have honor |
| no vayan al otro lado | Don't go to the other side |
| A mantener contratistas | To feed the contractors |
| y los troqueros hambrientos. | And hungry truckers. |

(Cardozo-Freeman 1976:132)
*'taban = *estaban* (they were)

"Canto del bracero" by Rubén Mendéz continues the theme of the hard life endured by braceros. This song appeared during the 1950s as abuses against Mexican immigrants were frequently reported in newspapers along the border. An interesting point is made in the first stanza. The immigrant-narrator mentions that he entered the United States without documentation and without the help of government officials in charge of issuing immigration papers. This of course was a common abuse, particularly in Mexico, where a prospective recruit had to pay *mordida,* or bribe, to officials in charge of processing the workers. Various states where Mexican immigrants went to work are mentioned: Arizona, Texas, Louisiana, Minnesota, Ohio. The song closes with an admonition: if you are in the United States, return to your own country; if you are planning to emigrate, don't.

## Canto del bracero

Cuando yo me fui pa'l norte
me colé por California
yo no tenía cartilla ni pasaporte
ni amigos ni palancas en Migración,

pero me colé con resolución.

Recorrí varios Estados
de la Unión Americana
en Arizona y Texas y por Luisiana

siempre sentí la falta de estimación
*quesque** dicen que es discriminación.

Ay qué triste es la vida
qué triste vida la del bracero
ay cuánta decepción, cuánta desola-
ción.

Lejos de nuestros padres
y de la novia y el compañero

dan ganas de llorar no más de re-
cordar.

Al pasar por Minesota
y por Clivelan y Ojayo
cuánto le suspiré al rancho del Pitayo

rancho que abandoné por aventurar

y al pensar en él fue para llorar.

Si tú piensas ir detente,
o si estás allá regresa
donde está tu cariño y está tu gente

y el rinconcito aquel que te vio nacer

donde está el amor que pueden perder.

## The Bracero's Song

When I left for the North
I slipped through California.
I did not have a card or a passport
Neither friends nor an "in" with im-
migration,
But I slipped in with great resolve.

I traveled through various states
Of the American Union.
In Arizona and Texas and through
Louisiana
I always felt a lack of respect
Which they say is called discrimina-
tion.

Oh how sad is life
How sad the life of a bracero.
Oh how much deception, how much
desolation.

Far from our parents
and far from one's girl and one's
friend
I feel like crying by just remembering.

When I passed through Minnesota
And through Cleveland and Ohio,
How I sighed over the Ranch of the
Pitayo,
The ranch I left behind to seek adven-
ture,
And thinking about it was enough to
make me cry.

If you are thinking of going, stop.
Or if you are there, return
To where your beloved resides and
your people too
And that small corner of the world
where you were born,
Where there is a loved one you might
lose.

(*Libro de oro de la canción* n.d.:12)
*quesque = *que es que*

In contrast to the two songs just presented, "Me voy para el Norte" gives an optimistic view of the bracero's life. The story is that of a would-be bracero, happily in love, who is bidding farewell to his sweetheart. He plans to work in the United States, earn and save money, and return and marry his girlfriend. This did often happen.

## Me voy para el Norte

¿Qué dices mi vida,
nos vamos al Norte?
ya tengo todo arreglado
para que pasemos
tengo el pasaporte
ya me lo dio el Consulado.

¡Qué bonito es querer!
¡qué rechulo es amar
y gozar entre lindas flores!

Tú bien sabes, mi bien,
que no te puedo olvidar,
chatita de mis amores.

Los dos nos iremos en el pasajero
con destino a la Frontera.
Irás en mis brazos, dueña de mi vida,
aunque tu mamá no quera.*

¡Qué bonito, etc.

¡Bonito es el Norte! nunca se me
olvida
porque se gana dinero.
Yo soy mexicano que adora a mi
Patria
que para mi es lo primero.

¡Qué bonito, etc.

Nos vamos al Norte tierra del ensueño,
llorado del repatriado.

(*Libro de oro de la canción* 1953:64)
*quera = *quiera* (like)

## I Am Going Up North

What do you say, my love,
Shall we go up north?
I have everything all fixed up
In order to cross over;
I have a passport
The consulate gave it to me.

How beautiful it is to love!
How great it is to love
And take pleasure among beautiful
flowers!
You know well, my love,
That I cannot forget you,
My beloved little one.

We shall both take a passenger train
Toward the border.
I'll hold you in my arms, my love,
Even if your mother objects.

How beautiful, etc.

The North is beautiful, I never forget
it,
Because you earn a lot of money.
I am a Mexican who loves his
country,
My country comes first.

How beautiful, etc.

We shall go up north, land of dreams,
Cried over by the repatriated ones.

The last three songs in this chapter were written by Eulalio González, commonly known by the nickname "El Piporro." A singer and writer-performer particularly popular with the working class in the borderlands of northern Mexico and the Southwest, González had many hits in the late fifties and after. He dressed in the typical norteño style, with cowboy boots, western shirt, tie, pants, and leather jacket, and used the regional dialect of the norteño.

"Chulas Fronteras" portrays a pícaro-type bracero who travels widely along the U.S.-Mexican border. The lyrics follow the tradition of the traveling-song text. Several cities are mentioned: Ciudad Juárez, Laredo, Matamoros, Reynosa. The main theme is that of the trickster bracero confronting the immigration officer and getting the best of him. The bracero is witty, smart, and confident; he does not fit the stereotype of the downtrodden bracero (see Herrera-Sobek 1979). Humor predominates in the imaginary confrontation between the two main characters. Verbal play and dialogue are used in structuring the humorous situations.

| Chulas Fronteras | Beautiful Borders |
|---|---|
| *Hablado:* | *Spoken:* |
| Chulas Fronteras del Norte como las extraño. No las miro desde hace un año. | Beautiful Northern Borders. How I miss you! I haven't seen you in a year. |
| *Cantado:* | *Sung:* |
| Andándome yo pasiando (paseando) por las Fronteras del Norte ¡hay que cosa tan hermosa! de Ciudad Juárez a Laredo de Laredo a Matamoros sin olvidar a Reynosa. | I was traveling Around the border cities. Oh, what a beautiful sight! From Ciudad Juárez to Laredo, Then from Laredo to Matamoros Without forgetting Reynosa. |
| *Hablado:* | *Spoken:* |
| Me acuerdo la primera vez que fui a United States of America. "¡Qué no me fui a pasiar (pasear), me fui a pizcar!" Le escribí a mamá, "Amá ya compré *saco*."* Una argüenda que armó mi mamá: "¡Mi hijo anda muy bien vestido. Trae saco nuevo!" ¡Nada, pos (pues) el saco de pizcar! | I remember the first time I went to the United States of America. "I did not go on a pleasure trip there, I went to pick cotton!" I wrote my mother, "Mom, I have a new *saco*." And my mother went around town making a big fuss, telling everybody, "My son is well-dressed. He has a new *saco*!" Heck, a new cotton-picking sack! |
| *Cantado:* | *Sung:* |
| Una muchacha en el puente blanca flor de primavera me miraba me miraba. | A young lady at the bridge, Beautiful spring flower she was, Kept looking and looking at me. |

Le pedí me resolviera
si acaso yo le gustaba
pero ella quería otra cosa
¡le ayudara en la pasada!

I asked her to please tell me
If she liked me.
But all she wanted was for me
To help her cross the bridge.

*Hablado:*

Me vio fuerte de brazo ancho de espaldas, me cargó de bulto. Y yo hacién-
dole tercera. Al llegar a la aduana me
dijo el de la cachucha "¿Qué llevas ahí?"
"Ja puro wiskle." "¡Pos si pero llevas
cien cajas!" "Es que ando de parranda y
no soy de botella—¡Soy de caja! Agarra
dos pa' tí." Y no las agarró. ¡Se quedó
con todas!

*Spoken:*

She saw my strong arms, my wide
shoulders. She made me carry her stuff.
Upon reaching the customs office, the
officer with the cap asked me, "What
have you there?" "Only whiskey."
"Yeah, but you have a hundred cases!"
"Well, I am on a drinking spree and I
don't drink by the bottle, I drink by the
case! Why don't you take two of them?"
And he did not take two. He took them
all!

*Cantado:*

Antes iba al otro lao (lado)
escondido de la gente,
pues pasaba de mojado.
Ahora tengo mis papeles
ya estoy dentro de la ley
tomo whisky o la tequila
hasta en medio del highway.

*Sung:*

I used to go to the USA
Hiding from people,
For I was a wetback.
Now with my passport
I am within the law.
I drink my whisky or tequila
Even in the middle of the road.

*Hablado:*

En eso llegó el Cherifón. Un pelao (pelado) que me saca como dos metros de
alto. Y nos vimos cara a cara, bueno eso
de cara a cara es un decir. ¡Lo más que le
alcancé a ver es la hebilla del pantalón!
"Hey tú Mexicano. ¿Tú eres mojado?"
"Wait a minute, Güero. I am working
here. This is my picture, un poco bigo-
tón, pero is my picture." "Güeno
(bueno) sí pero tú estás tomando tequila. Mucho picoso." "Nomás el
primero pica, después se pica uno solo.
Echate un trago." "¡Oh, no otra vez
será!" "Güeno (bueno), I wai(t) for you
or you wai(t) for me. ¡Mejor you
wai(t)!"**

*Spoken:*

At that point the sheriff arrived, a big
fellow about two meters taller than I. We
came face to face, in a manner of speaking. He was so tall I could only see his
belt buckle. "Hey, you Mexican. Are you
a wetback." "Wait a minute, Blondie. I
am working here. This is my picture. My
mustache is big, but this is my picture."
"Well, yes, but you are drinking tequila.
It is very hot." "Only the first gulp, after
that one cannot stop. Here, have a
drink." "Oh, no, another time!" "Well, I
will wait for you. Or you wait for me.
Better yet, you wai(t)!"

| *Cantado:* | *Sung:* |
|---|---|
| Yo les digo a mis amigos | I tell my friends |
| los que vayan a las pizcas | That when they go pick cotton |
| no se dejen engañar. | Not to be deceived. |
| Con los güeros ganen lana | To earn their money there |
| pero no la han de gastar | But to spend it |
| vénganse pa' la frontera | Here on the border |
| ¡donde si van a gozar! | Where they can really have fun. |

*Play on words; *saco* can denote a coat or a cotton-picking sack.
**Play on words; *wai* (wait) sounds like *buey* (ox), which in Spanish denotes a cuckold husband or boyfriend.

The theme of acculturation, common in the second and third decades of the twentieth century (see chapters 4 and 12), is reintroduced in González's "Natalio Reyes Colás," a 1960s parody of a bracero who has been transformed from the Spanish "Natalio Reyes Colás" to the English "Nat King Cole." The narration in the third person tells of the travails of Natalio, who fearlessly swims across the Río Bravo (Rio Grande), leaving his fiancée behind.

The song commences with the singer playfully announcing that he is not emigrating to the United States because he does not speak English and those speaking it do not understand him. That sets the stage for a playful cultural conflict—not between Anglo and immigrant but between the immigrant and a thoroughly assimilated Chicana, Mabel Ortiz, a pochita (the more or less pejorative term for Mexican Americans). It is Mabel who transforms Colás into Cole. This bracero henceforth rejects Mexican culture and desires to hear only rock and roll. Natalio, however, soon suffers cultural shock, since Mabel does not cook Mexican food and Natalio misses his tortillas and hot peppers. Closure of the song is achieved with Natalio's return to Mexico and his dark-skinned girlfriend, Petrita, who, "even though she's ugly, she knows how to love."

The song thus subtly criticizes assimilation and advocates a return to one's culture and people. It is interesting to note how women are represented in two diametrically opposed figures—the Mexican Petrita serving as a metaphor for Mexican culture and the Americanized Mabel the figure incarnating the process of cultural change.

## Natalio Reyes Colás

| *Hablado:* | *Spoken:* |
|---|---|
| Ya no vuelvo al otro lao (lado) porque no sé hablar inglés, y los que lo saben, pos (pues) no me entienden. | I am not going back to the USA because I do not speak English, and those that can speak it do not understand me. |

*Cantado:*

Natalio Reyes Colás
de Tamaulipas nacido,
pelado fino y audaz
el Río Bravo crecido
cruzó sin mirar pa' trás,
dejando novia, comprometido,
con quien casar.

No era flaca, era gordita,
Petra Garza Benavides
llorando dijo a Natalio
Reyes Colás no me olvides,
soy más bien feya (fea) que hermosa
pero no te hallas otra
que seya (sea) más hacendosa.

*Hablado:*

Nomás cruzó la línea divisora por el otro
lao y se encontró con Mabel, Mabel
Ortiz, una pochita que hasta el nombre
le cambió, en vez de Natalio, le puso Nat,
en vez de Reyes, King, y Cole por Colás.
Ahora es Nat King Cole Martínez de la
Garza.

*Cantado:*

Bracero, bracero, ya no quiere polka

con el acordeón, ora (ahora) se desdobla
al compás del rock and roll.
Olvidó a Petrita, quiere a la pochita

y hasta le canta como Nat King Cole.

(Music changes to the tune of "Love Is a
Many-Splendored Thing")

Bracero, Bracero, etc.
Love is a many-splendored thing
It's the April rose
In the early spring
Love is nature's way of giving
A reason to be living.
Bracero, bracero, etc.

(Music changes back to original tune)

*Sung:*

Natalio Reyes Colás,
Native of Tamaulipas,
A bold and fine dude,
Crossed the Río Bravo.
He crossed it without looking back
Leaving his fiancée,
Whom he had planned to marry.

She wasn't skinny, she was chubby,
Petra Garza Benavides.
Crying, she told Natalio:
"Reyes Colás, do not forget me.
I am on the ugly side, I know,
But this I can tell you.
You will not find a better housekeeper."

*Spoken:*

As soon as he crossed the line, he found
another girl, Mabel, Mabel Ortiz, a Chicana, who even changed his name. Instead of Natalio, she named him Nat,
and instead of Reyes, King, and for Colás, Cole. Now he is Nat King Cole Martínez de la Garza.

*Sung:*

Bracero, bracero, he does not like
    polkas,
With the accordions, now he goes wild
With the rhythm of rock and roll.
He forgot Petrita, he likes the little Chi-
    cana:
And he even sings to her like Nat King
    Cole.

(Music changes to the tune of "Love Is a
Many-Splendored Thing)

Bracero, bracero, etc.
Love is a many-splendored thing
It's the April rose
In the early spring
Love is nature's way of giving
A reason to be living.
Bracero, bracero, etc.

(Music changes back to original tune)

*Hablado:*

Pero la pochita lo dejó en la calle no sabía más que cantar y bailar, de cocinar nada, puro ham and eggs, waffles and jambargers with cachup y aquel estaba impuesto a pura tortilla con chile.

*Spoken:*

But the little Chicana left him on the streets. She only knew how to sing and dance. She couldn't cook, only ham and eggs, waffles, and hamburgers with ketchup. And the dude was used to tortillas and hot peppers.

*Cantado:*

Natalio Reyes Colás
se regresó a la frontera,
se vino a pata y en "ride"
diciendo yo no he de hallar
otra prieta que me quiera
como Petrita, aunque feyita (feita)
si sabe amar.

*Sung:*

Natalio Reyes Colás
Returned to the Mexican border.
He walked and asked for a ride
Saying I shall never find
A dark-skinned girl who loves me
Like little Petra; even though she's ugly
She knows how to love.

(González, *Lo Mejor del Piporro*)

"El burro norteño" by González is a parody of both the immigrant experience and corridos about faithful horses who travel thousands of miles. Here the traveling entity is not an immigrant male but a burro. The immigrant theme is touched upon when the burro, on his trip to Guadalajara from Ensenada, Baja California, crosses to the United States to avoid galloping through the mountains. In the states the burro meets a *gringa burrita* who flirts with him—a spoof of the conceptualization common in Mexican immigrant songs of the bracero whom Anglo women find irresistible (see chapter 11).

## El burro norteño

Este es el corrido del burro norteño

que en un martes trece feliz escapara,

aventó su carga y salió de volada

a ver a su burra hasta Guadalajara.

Pegó un rebuznido al salir de Ensenada
y hasta Rosarito se fue esa mañana

sin saber el pobre que la mala suerte

lo estaba esperando al llegar a Tijuana.

## The Northern Donkey

This is the corrido of the northern donkey

Who on a Tuesday the 13th happily escaped.

He threw off his load and took off flying

To see his lady donkey in Guadalajara.

He hee-hawed upon leaving Ensenada

And on to Rosarito he left that morning

Without realizing, poor thing, that bad luck

Was waiting for him in Tijuana.

| | |
|---|---|
| Ahí lo agarraron dos tipos ávaros | There two greedy characters grabbed him |
| le pintaron rayas y ante una carreta; | They painted stripes on him and in front of a cart |
| sacaban retratos a todos los turistas | They took pictures of all the tourists |
| en el pobre burro por una peseta. | On top of him for a quarter a picture. |
| | |
| Después de tres meses logró él escaparse | After three months he managed to escape |
| y hacia Mexicali se fue muy temprano, | And on to Mexicali he left very early |
| no quiso subirse por la rumorosa | He did not want to climb up the rumorosa |
| | |
| y cruzó la frontera del lado americano. | And crossed the border to the American side. |
| | |
| Siguió su camino pensando en su burra | He followed the road thinking of his lady donkey |
| rebuzna y rebuzna, respinga y respinga, | Hee-hawing and hee-hawing and bucking and bucking. |
| cuando de repente en una cañada | When suddenly in a thicket |
| se le atravesó una burrita gringa. | A gringa burrita crossed his path. |
| | |
| Sus ojos azules coquetos bailaban | Her blue eyes coquettishly danced |
| y al burro le dijo ven aquí conmigo | And said to the donkey: "Come here with me." |
| | |
| y entonces el burro así contestó: | And then the donkey answered so: |
| lo siento chiquita ya tengo a mi burra. | "Sorry, honey, I already have my lady donkey." |
| | |
| Llegó a Mexicali siguió pa' Caborca | He arrived in Mexicali and went on to Caborca; |
| y ahí en Hermosillo comió unas mazorcas | There in Hermosillo he had some corncobs. |
| en Bacanora le dieron agruras | In Bacanora he got indigestion |
| y a pesar de todo siguió su aventura. | But in spite of all he kept on going. |
| | |
| Siguió hasta Guamúchil, pasó Sinaloa | He went on to Guamúchil, past Sinaloa, |
| Allá en Nayarit ya se andaba quedando. | There in Nayarit he almost stayed. |
| cuentan que un arriero lo cargó de leña | They say a mule-skinner so loaded him with wood |
| que hasta el espinazo le andaba quebrando. | That he almost broke his back. |
| | |
| Llegó hasta Jalisco y a todos los burros | He arrived in Jalisco and of all the donkeys |

| | |
|---|---|
| por su burra prieta llegó preguntando. | He asked about his brunette lady donkey. |
| y le contestaron: tu burra querida | And they answered him: "Your beloved donkey |
| anoche se fue con un caballo blanco. | Left last night with a white horse." |

(Calleja 1967)

The period in which the bracero program was in effect did not produce as large a corpus of immigrant-type corridos as might be expected given the number of men and women entering the United States to work. Other musical forms of expression were in ascendency during this period (1942–1964). The conjunto-type music (much of which is instrumental), the polka, and the canción ranchera were all competing successfully with the corrido. In addition, the rise of the matinee movie idol and mass-produced music overwhelmed the local troubadours. In spite of all these competing factors, the period produced a number of songs which detail the bracero experience from the worker's perspective.

# PART TWO
## After 1964

# Songs of Protest

*Seven* The turbulent 1960s catapulted numerous men and women who were committed to social change into national prominence. Martin Luther King, Jr., Rosa Parks, Dolores Huerta, César Chávez and others became known for their commitment to bettering the lives of their fellow citizens through radical social change. The civil rights movement affirmed the idea that social justice could indeed become a reality and was not merely an empty promise in the Constitution of the United States. Minority groups had suffered discrimination at a social level and exploitation at an economic one for too long. Blacks, women, Native Americans, Mexican Americans and other marginalized groups all felt the weight of centuries of gender and racial oppression.

King mobilized the African-American population into seeking redress for the discriminatory practices in the United States through various nonviolent activities: sit-ins, boycotts, political pressure, and mass demonstrations. Feminists such as Betty Friedan through their writings began to move women off their stultifying pedestals to more fulfilling roles. And the Mexican-American leader Chávez served as the main catalyst in the farm workers' search for a better life through more equitable wages and working conditions in the agricultural fields. The various techniques Chávez used in organizing the farm workers had a tremendous impact on corrido production. Chávez and his contribution to the "renaissance" of the corrido in the 1960s are the principal focus of this chapter.

César Chávez was born in Yuma, Arizona, in 1929, the son of a migrant farm worker. After the family lost its farm during the Depression, Chávez's early childhood was spent migrating from one agricultural town to another in search of field work in California. The constant traveling the family was forced to undertake allowed Chávez to complete no more than seven years of schooling. The extreme poverty in which he lived and the constant injustices he suffered at an early age instilled in Chávez a deep sense of commitment to those in similar circumstances and a desire to change their conditions.

Chávez became involved in agricultural labor unions early in life. At age nineteen he belonged to the National Agricultural Worker's Union. Unionization efforts in the California fields, however, had failed. Before the 1960s union organizational drives had met with insurmountable obstacles and continued failure. Early in this century, for example, the Wobblies had made tentative efforts to organize the agricultural labor force; strong opposition from farmers as well as national and international events, however, had conspired to defeat any successful unionization attempts. Most noticeably, the need for workers in World War I had brought great numbers of temporary Mexican nationals to labor in the fields, making it impossible to carry out effective strikes against the growers.

The Great Depression and World War II also had made organizing of farm workers difficult if not impossible. As a consequence of the labor shortages claimed by railroad and agricultural concerns during World War II, the bracero program was instituted, and it was to last until 1964 (see chapter 6). It was not until the 1960s that Chávez had some measure of success in organizing agricultural workers.

Chávez received his training in organizing through his work in the Community Service Organization (CSO) in the 1950s under the auspices of Fred Ross, a community organizer with training and experience. The farm workers' leader has described his first encounter with Ross:

> Fred Ross never stopped working. He was very persistent, and it was lucky he was, because I never would have met him otherwise. I was trying to avoid him. It must have been in June 1952 when I came home from work one day, and Helen told me this gringo wanted to see me. That was enough to make me suspicious. We never heard anything from whites unless it was the police, or some sociologist from Stanford, San Jose State, or Berkeley coming to write about Sal Si Puedes. They'd ask all kinds of silly questions, like how did we eat our beans and tortillas. We felt it wasn't any of their business how we lived. (Levy 1975:97)

Voter registration was a priority during the fifties. It was deemed that with the power of the vote Mexican Americans could make radical changes for the better through peaceful means. However, since unemployment was high in the southwestern barrios, Chávez began to perceive the connection between low wages, unemployment, and the bracero program. Toward the end of the fifties, he veered away from merely organizing for community services and embraced the goal of instituting fundamental changes in the farming communities of the United States.

Ideological differences surfaced between Chávez and Ross, since Ross wanted to continue working through the CSO. Chávez had been the director of the CSO for several years, but as he entered the new decade of the 1960s he became serious about organizing a farm workers' union. Since Ross was against this move, Chávez was forced to undertake the project alone. In an interview he recalled his initial attempts at organizing farm workers:

I stayed in CSO as director a couple more years, hoping I could persuade the board to organize farm workers. I thought of doing it alone, but I was discouraged by some friends, mostly some of the priests I worked with. They said I couldn't start a union without the help of the AFL-CIO. "That's the only way it's going to be done," they said.

They had good hearts and a lot of interest and gave a lot of themselves, but I didn't know that they knew less about it than I did. When I met with the priests and Dolores [Huerta], only Dolores encouraged me. (Ibid.:145)

Chávez nevertheless persisted, and the National Workers Association was founded September 30, 1962. His plan was to organize one member at a time until the union was strong enough to attempt striking for better wages and working conditions. The drive for union membership and acceptance of the union (later renamed United Farm Workers of America) by agribusiness continued unabated.

One instrument Chávez used for his membership drives was singing. He learned this technique through his association with a Protestant minister when he was invited to participate in a humble Protestant service. He noticed that there was a considerable amount of singing and clapping of hands. Furthermore, the people looked very happy in spite of their meager circumstances. Chávez deduced correctly that the singing and music would enhance his union meetings and inspire the people. He recalled:

So in that little Madera Church, I observed everything going on about me that could be useful in organizing. Although there were no more than twelve men and women, there was more spirit there than when I went to a mass where there were two hundred. Everybody was happy. They all were singing. These people were really committed in their beliefs, and this made them sing and clap and participate. I liked that.

I think that's where I got the idea of singing at the meetings. That was one of the first things we did when I started the Union. And it was hard for me because I can't carry a tune. (Ibid.:115–116)

The technique proved to be a very successful tactic, and from then on singing songs, especially corridos, was an integral part of union meetings, strikes, and organizational efforts.

With the demise of the bracero program in 1964, the intensified organizing efforts to unionize farm workers began to yield results. Chávez assumed leadership of this movement, and his dedication helped bring the plight of the nonunionized agricultural laborer to the nation's attention. The problems and hardships of the migrant worker were sung in corridos composed by Chicano and Mexican corridistas, such as Rumel Fuentes, Francisco García, Pablo and Juanita Saludado, and Rosa Gloria. The corrido became an important form of expression for airing the farm workers' grievances.

Some of the corridos thematized César Chávez and his struggle to form a union. Two examples bear his name in their titles.

## El Corrido de César Chávez

En un día 7 de marzo
Jueves santo en la mañana
salió César de Delano
componiendo una campaña.

Componiendo una campaña
este va a ser un ejemplo
esta marcha la llevamos
hasta mero Sacramento.

Cuando llegamos a Fresno
Toda la gente gritaba
y que viva César Chávez
y la gente que llevaba.

Nos despedimos de Fresno
nos despedimos con fe
para llegar muy contentos
hasta el pueblo de Merced.

Ya vamos llegando a Stockton
ya mero la luz se fue
pero mi gente gritaba
sigan con bastante fe.

Cuando llegamos a Stockton
los mariachis nos cantaban
que viva César Chávez
y la Virgen que llevaba.

Contratistas y esquiroles
ésta va a ser una historia
ustedes van al infierno
y nosotros a la gloria.

Ese Señor César Chávez
él es un hombre cabal
quería verse cara a cara
con el gobernador Brown.

Oiga Señor César Chávez
su nombre que se pronuncia
en su pecho usted merece
la Virgen de Guadalupe.

## The Ballad of César Chávez

On the 7th day of March
Good Thursday in the morning
César left Delano
Organizing a campaign.

Organizing a campaign
This is going to be an example
This (protest) march we'll take
To Sacramento itself.

When we arrived in Fresno
All the people chanted
Long live César Chávez
And the people that accompany him.

We bid good-bye to Fresno
We bid good-bye with faith
So we would arrive safely
To the town of Merced.

We are almost in Stockton
Sunlight is almost gone
But the people shouted
Keep on with lots of faith.

When we arrived at Stockton
The mariachis were singing
Long live César Chávez.
And the Virgin of Guadalupe.

Contractors and scabs
This is going to be your story
You will all go to hell
And we will go to heaven.

That Mr. César Chávez
Is a very strong man
He wanted to speak face to face
With Governor Brown.

Listen, Mr. César Chávez,
Your name is well known
On your chest you well deserve
The Virgin of Guadalupe.

This ballad, recorded by Francisco García and Pablo and Juanita Saludado, adheres to many of Duvalier's six structural components (see the introduction.) The first stanza provides the date and the name of the protagonist. The main body of the text, that is, the six stanzas that follow the first one, narrates the events: Chávez's march to Sacramento to meet with Governor Jerry Brown. The last two stanzas provide closure by reiterating Chávez's fine leadership qualities. The text is composed of several formulaic phrases.

The second ballad, bearing the same title, "Corrido de César Chávez," was written by a well-known singer-composer from the Southwest, Lalo Guerrero. It contains only one of Duvalier's six basic formulas—the farewell, or despedida. It has fewer formulaic phrases than the first one and displays more of a polished literary style, congruent with the fact that it was written by a professional songwriter. It tells of Chávez's involvement in the union struggle and extols the virtues and courage Chávez demonstrated on a twenty-five-day fast. The song celebrates his dedication to the farm workers' cause and the people's love for him. Thus it continues the corrido tradition of extolling heroes, presenting grievances, and thematizing historical events important in the lives of the common folk.

### Corrido de César Chávez

Gente de mi corazón
en el pecho no me cabe
de regocijo y orgullo
al cantarle a César Chávez.

Inspiración de mi gente
protector del campesino
el es un gran Mexicano
este sería su destino.

De muy humilde principios
organizaste a la gente
y a los hacendados ricos
te paraste frente a frente.

E injustamente te acusan
de intentar de usar violencia
ayuna días veinte y uno
hasta probar tu inocencia.

En el estandard que llevas
mi Virgen de Guadalupe
que viniste ante alabar
de bendiciones te cubre.

### Ballad of César Chávez

My beloved people
My heart is not big enough
For the joy and pride I have
In singing to César Chávez.

He is an inspiration to my people
Protector of the farm worker
He is a great Mexican
This must be his destiny.

From very humble origins
You organized the people
And the rich landowners
You stood up to them face to face.

And they unjustly accused you
Of trying to use violence
Fast twenty-five days
Until they prove your innocence.

In the flag you use
Is the Virgin of Guadalupe
To whom you came to pray
May she bless you.

| | |
|---|---|
| A los 25 días | After twenty-five days |
| el ayuno terminó | The fast ended |
| y en el parque de Delano | In the Delano Park |
| una misa celebró. | A mass was celebrated. |
| | |
| Junto con 8,000 almas | Together with 8,000 folks |
| el parque de días sintió | The park for days felt |
| admiración y cariño | Admiration and love |
| nuestra gente le brindó. | Our people gave to him. |
| | |
| Vuela de aquí de mi seno | Fly from my heart, dove, |
| paloma vete a Delano | And go to Delano |
| y por si acaso no sabes | And in case you don't know |
| Allí vive César Chávez. | César Chávez lives there. |

"Corrido de la causa" focuses on the righteousness of the cause the farm workers have been fighting for. Chávez is highlighted as the leader of this cause. The corrido employs five of Duvalier's six basic formulas: introduction of the corridista ("Señores voy a cantarles"); the date and location of action ("6 de enero . . . este Valle Imperial"); the message (arrest of the protesting farm workers); the farm workers' farewell; and the corridista's farewell. Formulaic phrases are employed throughout the text, demonstrating the continuity of the corrido structure and composition in contemporary ballads.

## Corrido de la causa / The Ballad of the Cause

| | |
|---|---|
| Señores voy a cantarles | Gentlemen I am going to sing |
| lo que nos ha sucedido | What has happened to us |
| nos mandaron a la carcel | They sent us to jail |
| esa compañía de ricos | That rich company |
| por reclamar un derecho | Because we demanded our rights |
| por el bien de nuestros hijos. | For the future welfare of our children. |
| | |
| La fecha tengo presente | The date is clear in my mind |
| la recordarán ustedes | You too will recall |
| fue el mero 6 de enero | It was the very 6th of January |
| el día de los Santos Reyes | The holiday of the Three Wise Men |
| veinte patrullas llevaron | Twenty policeman's cars came |
| repartiendo unos papeles. | Giving out some papers. |
| | |
| Como estaban en inglés | Since they were in English |
| se los tiramos al suelo | We throw them on the ground |
| hablan de leyes injustas | They talk about unjust laws |
| que nos ha puesto el ranchero | That the farmer has imposed on us. |

| | |
|---|---|
| hermano viva la causa | My brother long live the cause |
| mi familia está primero. | My family comes first. |
| | |
| Mi bandera roja y negra | My black and red flag |
| va flotando hacia adelante | Is floating onward |
| liberando a nuestros hijos | Freeing our children |
| campesino tú lo sabes | Farm worker you well know this |
| sigue al pequeño gigante | Follow the small giant |
| nuestro líder César Chávez. | Our leader César Chávez. |
| | |
| Haz vuelo águila negra | Give flight black eagle |
| no te vayas a quedar | Do not stay behind |
| avísale al mundo entero | And tell all the world |
| que nos van a sentenciar | They are going to sentence us |
| a ochenta y un campesino | Eighty-one farm workers |
| en este Valle Imperial. | In this Imperial Valley. |
| | |
| Despedida no les doy | I will not bid you farewell |
| porque no la traigo aquí | 'Cause I do not have it here |
| si no estoy haciendo huelga | If I am not striking |
| al boycott me voy a ir | I will join the boycott |
| por defender a mi raza | In defending my people |
| yo también me sé morir. | I too know how to die. |

Two other social protest songs that mention César Chávez's role in the farm workers' struggle are "Corrido del campesino," by José Luis Carrera, and "El corrido del Rancho Sespe," by Don Jesús Toledo.

| **Corrido del campesino** | **The Farm Worker's Ballad** |
|---|---|
| Tararararara | Tararararara |
| Lai la la la la la la la la | Lai la la la la la la la la |
| Trararaira lailalaila | Trararaira lailalaila |
| Lailalalala talalaila lalala | Lailalalala talalaila lalala |
| | |
| Un humilde servidor | A humble servant |
| lanza sus notas al viento. | sings his notes to the wind. |
| | |
| Un humilde servidor | A humble servant |
| lanza sus notas al viento. | sings his notes to the wind. |
| | |
| A decirle al pizcador | To inform the picker |
| que se siente muy contento | that he feels very happy |
| que se siente muy contento | that he feels very happy |
| de ver que ahora brilla el sol | to see the sun shining bright |
| con rayo resplandeciente. | with resplandecent rays. |

Police arrest farm workers, August 8, 1973.
Photo courtesy of National Farm Worker
Ministry, Los Angeles.

| | |
|---|---|
| Tiempo de revolución | Time of revolution. |
| pa' pelear por nuestra gente. | Time to fight for our people. |
| Ya era tiempo compañeros | It was about time my friends |
| que alguién los organizara. | that someone should help you organize. |
| | |
| El compadre Horencio El Chino | Our compadre Horencio El Chino |
| hombre de Guadalajara. | a native of Guadalajara. |
| | |
| Hay que demostrar con hechos | "We have to show them with action," |
| el Señor Ortiz decía. | Mr. Ortiz did say. |
| | |
| Hay que demostrar con hechos | "We have to show them with action," |
| el Señor Ortiz decía; | Mr. Ortiz did say, |
| reclamando sus derechos | asserting his rights |

a todas las compañías
protección pa'l campesino
protección pa'l campesino
con todas sus garantías.

Consejero muy capaz
conocedor de las leyes
Don Francisco Ortiz decía
nomás no se echen *pa' trás**
pos pa' ganar una lucha
hay que decir ¡si se puede!

¡Sí se puede!
¡Sí se puede!
¡Sí se puede!
¡Sí se puede!

Tararararararará
Tararairararararaararara
Tararararararararará
Tararaí rararararara

Ya viene rayando el sol
por la loma del Encino.
Ya viene rayando el sol
por la loma del Encino,
vamos a cantar con gusto
el tiempo del campesino.

Vamos a cantar con gusto
el tiempo del campesino.

Mayo del 78
recuérdenlo, ya lo saben.
Hay que dar gracias a Dios
y al señor don César Chávez.

Hay que dar gracias a Dios
y al señor don César Chávez.

¡Sí se puede!
¡Sí se puede!
¡Sí se puede!
¡Sí se puede!

to all the companies
protection for the farm worker
protection for the farm worker
with guaranteed rights.

A most capable adviser
knowledgeable of the law
Mr. Francisco Ortiz did say,
"But don't you back off
because if one is to win in a struggle
we have to say: 'Yes, we can!' "

Yes, we can do it!
Yes, we can do it!
Yes, we can do it!
Yes, we can do it!

Tararararararará
Tararairararararaararara
Tararararararararará
Tararaí rararararara

The sun is rising
over the hills of Encino.
The sun is rising
over the hills of Encino,
let us sing with joy
to the time of the farm worker.

Let us sing with joy
to the time of the farm worker.

May of '78
remember it, now you know.
We must give our thanks to God
and to Mr. César Chávez.

We must give our thanks to God
and to Mr. César Chávez.

Yes, we can do it!
Yes, we can do it!
Yes, we can do it!
Yes, we can do it!

*pa' trás = *para atrás* (back)

## El corrido del Rancho Sespe

El día nueve de Mayo
oiga bien lo que decimos
fue ganado el Rancho Sespe
pa' la unión del campesino.

Es que vino César Chávez
a invitarnos a su unión,
pa' acabar con malos tratos
y también la explotación.

Nos decía Mister Lombardo
vénganse mis muchachitos
no ven que esos de la unión
nomás son puros malditos.

Y nosotros nos reímos
de verlo tan compujido
pues le apretaba la soga
que el mismo había tejido.

Andaban muy apurados
mandando cartas de amor
y también unos comprados
nos decían no quiero unión.

Nos mandaron sus agentes
para dar explicaciones.
Cuando oyeron "¡Viva Chávez!"

y se hicieron en sus calzones.

Ahora que ya les ganamos
con honor las votaciones,
lucharemos por contratos
que nos dan más protecciones.

Compañeros campesinos
que votaron por la unión
la Virgen de Guadalupe
les dará su bendición.

Ahora si mis compañeros
ya les canté mi canción.
Ahora griten "¡Viva Chávez!"

y también "¡Viva la Unión!"

## The Ballad of the Sespe Ranch

On the ninth of May
Listen well to what we say
We won the right in the Sespe Ranch
To form a farm worker's union.

César Chávez came to us
To invite us to join his union
To put an end to poor treatment
To put an end to exploitation.

Mr. Lombardo would say,
"Come here my little children.
Can't you see those from the union
Are a bunch of evil men?"

And we laughed
Seeing his discomfort.
The noose was getting tighter
But he had brought this on himself.

They were pretty busy
Sending us "love" letters
And we could hear some sellouts
Telling us, "We don't want a union."

They sent us their agents
To deliver explanations
But when they heard "Long live
      Chávez!"
They shit in their pants.

Now that we have won
With honor the referendum
We will fight for contracts
That will afford us protection.

All of you farm worker friends
Who voted for the union
The Virgin of Guadalupe
Will give you her blessings.

Now my friends
I have sung you my song.
Now you can shout, "Long live
      Chávez!"
And also "Long live the Union!"

When the bracero program officially ended in 1964, the flow of immigrants from Mexico was far from over. The Vietnam War that raged in the sixties diverted the attention of both the government and the public so that the constant trickle of Mexican immigrants was almost imperceptible. It was not until the war had ended and unemployment loomed as a national problem that the Mexican worker began to receive a barrage of mostly negative publicity. The term *undocumented worker,* coined by pro-Mexican immigrant groups, became more acceptable than the more value-laden *illegal alien.*

As the United States began to experience a series of recessions and high unemployment rates, the question of whether Mexican immigrants were taking jobs away from U.S. citizens surfaced as an issue. Those sensitive to Mexican immigration denied that undocumented workers took jobs away from citizens, suggesting that, on the contrary, Mexican workers performed those jobs that no one would take. They posited that the undocumented workers made it possible for U.S. companies to stay in the States instead of relocating to underdeveloped countries with large pools of cheap labor. The other side contested this view with the argument that should the companies pay decent wages, U.S. citizens would be more than happy to fill those jobs deemed undesirable. In spite of all the charges and countercharges leveled at the Mexican immigrant, the flow of people to the United States did not cease. And Chávez continued to carry forth his struggle to organize farm workers.

Numerous corridos likewise continued to describe the travails as well as the victories of the farm workers' struggle. "El corrido del ilegal," for example, not only depicts the travails of the illegal alien and his reasons for journeying to the United States but also delineates the perception by many undocumented workers that the U.S. Immigration and Naturalization Service (INS) was closely allied with U.S. farmers, agribusinesses, and police. Hunger in Mexico is given as the main motive for making the trip to the United States. The stanzas (recorded by García and the Saludados) basically detail how the undocumented worker is being introduced to break the farm workers' strike. The treacherous role of the *contratista* (the middle boss between farmer and farm worker) is expounded upon. Closure is achieved in the last stanza through the despedida, where the main message is imparted: do not cross the border illegally and do not be a strikebreaker.

## El corrido del ilegal

Andando yo en la frontera
Ya me cargaba el hambre.
Dicen que el hambre es canija,
Pero es más del que ya le ande.

Me pasé al otro lado.
Tuve que hacerla de alambre.

## The Ballad of the Illegal Alien

As I was walking along the border
I was already burdened by hunger.
They say that hunger is unrelenting,
But it is even more painful to the
    hungry one.

I crossed over to the other side.
I had to cross the wire fence.

A los poquitos momentos
Me agarra la inmigración.
Me dice, "Tú eres alambre."
Le contesté, "Sí, señor."
"De eso no tengas cuidado
Tal vez tengas tú razón."

"Si tú quieres trabajar
Nomás que no seas Chavista.
Yo mismo te he de llevar
A manos del contratista.
Le estamos dando la chanza
A todos los alambristas."

Nos llevaron para un campo
Juntos con *chavos** de escuela.
Rodeados de policía
Que provocaban la guerra
Para quebrar una huelga
En el Valle de Coachella.

Policías e inmigración
Unidos con los rancheros,
Conspiración contratista
Por el maldito dinero.
En contra de nuestra gente
Parecían unos perros.

Dormíamos bajo las viñas,
Todo el *bonche*** de alambristas.
Y para el peor de la ruina
Nos picaron las avispas
No nos dio ni medicina,
el desgraciado contratista.

Después salimos en huelga
Para ayudar a la unión.
El desgraciado contratista
Nos echó la inmigración.
Esposados de las manos
Nos llevan a la prisión.

Yo les digo a mis amigos,
"Más vale jalar parejo;
Nunca cruzen la frontera
En calidad de conejo,
Menos a quebrar la Huelga.
Que ya no sean tan pendejos."

In a few moments
The immigration officer caught me.
He said to me, "You are illegal."
I answered, "Yes, sir."
"Don't worry about it,
Perhaps you are right."

"If you want to work,
As long as you're not a Chavista,
I myself will take you
To a contractor.
We are giving an opportunity
To all the wire jumpers."

They took us to a field
Together with school kids.
We were surrounded by policemen
Who provoked a fight
In order to break the strike
In the Coachella Valley.

Police and immigration
Together with the growers,
This was the contractors' conspiracy
For the sake of evil money.
Against our people
They acted like dogs.

We slept under the vines,
The whole bunch of wire jumpers.
And to top it all off
The wasps stung us.
That wretched contractor
Did not even give us medicine.

Later we went on strike
In order to help the union.
The wretched contractor
Turned the immigration on us.
They took us handcuffed
To prison.

I tell my friends,
"It is better not to scab;
Never cross the border
Like a rabbit,
Let alone to break the Strike.
Don't be so stupid anymore."

*chavos = *chavalos* (young boys and girls)
**bonche = bunch

A folk bard who identified with Chávez's struggle and wrote many protest songs during the 1960s and early 1970s was Rumel Fuentes of Texas. Two of his songs, taken from a small mimeographed collection I was able to obtain from that period, deal specifically with the undocumented worker and the person who identifies with both the Mexican and U.S. cultures.

### La migra

Ciudadanos *ahi** viene la migra

viene pidiendo papeles
diciendo que eres mojado
si tú no le hablas inglés.

Porque a veces cruzo el río
dices que soy mojado
si tú cruzaste la mar
tú lo traerás más mojado.

Que triste vida la de ellos
con *baterillas*** en la mano
tener que ganar la vida
molestando mejicanos.

Dicen que harán una barda
muy alta como en Berlín
para parar mejicanos
de que vengan por aquí.

Me pararon otra vez
Ya de esto ya estoy cansado
cual es su criterio que usan
pa' reconocer mojados.

Ya con ésta me despido
mis papeles en la mano
soy pobre y color café
y también soy ciudadano.

### The Border Patrol

Watch out, here comes the border patrol

He comes asking for papers
Calling you a wetback
If you don't speak English.

Because I sometimes cross the river
You call me a wetback
If your people crossed the ocean
Your back must be a lot wetter.

It must be a sad life for them
With flashlights in hand
Having to make a living
Harassing Mexicans.

They want to build a wall
High, just like Berlin
To stop Mexicans
From coming over here.

They stopped me again
I am very tired of all this
Just what is their criterion
For recognizing wetbacks.

A farewell to you, my friends,
With my papers in my hand
I am poor and bronze in color
And also a citizen (of the United States).

(Fuentes 1977:6)
*ahi = *ahí* (there)
**baterillas = *baterías* (flashlights)

"La migra" depicts the conflict between the *migra* (the INS officers who patrol the border) and the supposedly undocumented worker who is actually a citizen. The brown Mexican American confronted with the migra's derogatory use of the term *wetback* replies that his back may be wet from crossing the river but the Anglo officers' backs are far wetter from having crossed an ocean. This of course is a reference to European immigration. The song ends with the declaration that he may have brown skin but he is a U.S. citizen.

Fuentes's "México americano" speaks of the double origin of many Mexican Americans.

| México americano | Mexican American |
|---|---|
| Por mi madre yo soy mexicano | Mexican by parentage |
| por destino soy americano | American by destiny |
| yo soy de la raza de oro | I am of the golden race |
| yo soy méxico americano. | I am Mexican American. |
| | |
| Yo te comprendo el inglés | I have learned the English language |
| También te hablo en el chicano | And I also speak Chicano |
| Yo soy de la raza noble | I am of the noble race |
| Yo soy méxico americano. | I am Mexican American. |
| | |
| Zacatecas a Minnesota | From Zacatecas to Minnesota |
| De Tijuana hasta Nueva York | From Tijuana to New York |
| Dos países son mi tierra | Two countries are my own |
| Los defiendo con mi honor. | I will defend them with my honor. |
| | |
| Dos idiomas y dos países | Two languages, two countries |
| dos culturas tengo yo | Two cultures are my own |
| Es mi suerte y es mi orgullo | It is my fate, it is my pride |
| porque así lo manda Dios. | Because it is the will of God. |

(Fuentes 1977:31:32)

César Chávez's impact on corrido production cannot be underestimated. He revived the centuries-old custom of using the corrido to air grievances and simultaneously record the events of the time. He popularized the tradition of corrido singing by encouraging and actively promoting their use at union meetings, strikes, marches, and other activities related to union organizing.

In addition, the corrido-singing tradition reinstituted by Chávez during the early years of union organizing was an important influence on Luis Valdez and the Teatro Campesino (see Huerta 1982). Valdez's career as a dramatist commenced with the farm workers' unionizing efforts. He joined their cause and began to present short skits *(actos)* related to the concerns and activities of the strikers and union members. Many of these skits were punctuated with corridos; sometimes the background music was new or old corridos.

Corrido production thus owes a great debt to César Chávez. Indeed, we can safely conclude that the renaissance of the corrido came about as a result of his unionizing efforts.

# Border-Crossing Strategies

*Eight* It should now be clear that a large corpus of corridos and canciones has evolved over the past 130 years reflecting the adventures and travails of Mexicans immigrating to the United States.[1] They continue to be produced and sung on local radio stations, in bars and restaurants, at fiestas and *tertulias,* and in the privacy of the home.[2] The wave of immigration from Mexico in the past two decades provides an opportunity to observe this immigration process firsthand and to note the attitudes and reactions of immigrants as they face innumerable hardships through the lyrics of their songs. Corridos and canciones play an important role in commenting on the successes and failures of this enterprise.

This chapter focuses on strategies of the immigration process as reflected in 1970s and 1980s Mexican immigrant corridos and canciones. I focus on three themes dominant in discussions of Mexican immigration: the quest for a *mica,* or legal border-crossing card (also called a green card); the role of coyotes, or guides, who serve as mediators (for a fee they smuggle undocumented persons into the United States); and the conflict and tension between the migra, or border patrol, and the immigrant. Popular music commenting on these themes mirrors the strategies used by Mexican immigrants to circumvent their problems and ameliorate their negative status.

Furthermore, the songs symbolically reflect the struggles of aspiring immigrants by objectifying and parodying situations and persons with whom immigrants come into daily contact. Music objectifies the immigrants' experiences through the singing of songs that articulate their concerns, anxieties, and fears; historicize the events of migration to fit them into familiar patterns; and contemporize these events so as to make them relevant to ongoing immigrant experiences. The prevalence of this song tradition reveals the immigrants' awareness of the forces affecting their everyday life and demonstrates the artistic ingenuity of twentieth-century folk bards in creating a world in which realities are confronted.

The rise in corrido production in the past two decades parallels the drastic changes in immigration policy undertaken by the United States in the 1960s. The bracero program instituted in 1942 at the request of the U.S. government was finally terminated in 1964.[3] The legal importation of Mexican labor for all practical purposes ceased, although a provision in the H-2 Temporary Workers Act allowed the entrance of a limited number of temporary workers on U.S. farms (see Kirstein 1977). This law, however, never equaled the scope and extent of the bracero program.

Although the bracero program ceased to exist in the 1960s, the demand for workers did not abate, and consequently the number of undocumented workers rose dramatically in the past two decades. As immigration from Mexico increased, so did the number of songs thematizing the immigrant experience. Two factors contributed to the increase of song production as detailed in chapter 7: César Chávez used corridos in his recruiting efforts, and songs were used in Campesino theater productions. This renaissance of the Mexican-American ballad and the frequent use of the corrido as a protest song stimulated the writing and recording of Mexican immigrant songs. The general popularity and prestige of protest songs during the 1960s and 1970s in the United States through the work of Joan Baez and Bob Dylan helped in the general acceptance of the corrido, which falls in the category of folk songs, as a viable form of expression.

## The Mica

The "illegal alien" phenomenon dates back to the third decade of this century. Before that period no significant restrictions or immigration laws applying specifically to Mexico existed; people crossed the border at will, as had been the custom previous to the loss of Mexican territory. Concern over unimpeded immigration surfaced in the 1880s, but it was principally directed at Asians and not at Mexicans. Various acts passed during the second half of the nineteenth century and first decade of the twentieth century were aimed at stopping the incoming flow of Chinese and Japanese workers. The Immigration Act of 1907 was not geared toward restricting Mexican immigrants, and border officials were lax about enforcing the various provisions of the act when it came to Mexicans.

A decrease in Asian railroad and farm workers, together with increased labor needs of the Southwest's expanding economy, stimulated migration of Mexican men and women northward. The steady surge in numbers of this ethnic group alarmed certain Anglo groups, and pressure was exerted on Washington to enact legislation to "control" the borders. Responding to these pressures, Congress passed the Immigration Act of 1917 (Reisler 1976:12). This act provided for the implementation of a literacy test and an eight-dollar head tax for each prospective immigrant. Since many Mexicans were extremely poor and uneducated, these two stipulations proved insurmountable to a large number of them. The result was that many crossed the border without paying the head tax. Some of the older folks songs discuss the immigrants' cleverness in crossing the border without paying the stipulated entrance fee (see Herrera-Sobek 1979). As Mexican immigrants posed a greater economic threat in the decades that followed, immigration requirements became progressively more stringent and the difficulty of obtaining legal residency increased.

Since job opportunities (except for the years of the Great Depression) continued to increase and attract Mexican labor, the enterprising immigrant through the years devised various strategies for entering the United States. Of course the preferred venue has always been to acquire a legal resident's card, called a mica or green card. The word *mica* metonymically refers to the resident card legally granted through the offices of the Immigration and Naturalization Service. Its dictionary meaning is "any of a group of minerals (complex silicates) that crystallize in thin, somewhat flexible, easily separated layers, translucent or transparent." The dream of all undocumented workers is to legalize their status in the United States so as not to fear deportation or pay exhorbitant prices to those smugglers who help them enter.

The process involved in applying for legal residency is long, expensive, and arduous. There are, however, provisions in the immigration law that facilitate the acquisition of legal resident status. One such provision is marrying a U.S. citizen. The recently popular song "Mi Micaela" of Guillermo de Anda describes in metaphoric terms the extreme yearning and desire on the part of a man to obtain a mica.

## Mi Micaela

Tú eres mi Mica, Mica, mi Micaela
Tú representas todo lo que mi alma
     anhela
esas visicitudes que se han enseñado

por mi pasado las resolveré
se estás a mi lado.

Tú vas a ser mi Mica, mi Micaela

y esto lo arreglamos con mucha
     cautela
sin que nadie se entere de que tú me
     quieres
vamos y nos casamos
y así todo lo arreglamos.

Tienes que ser mi Mica, mi Micaela
Verde como los pastos de las praderas
Siempre aquí mi esperanza

## My Micaela

You are my Mica, Mica, my Micaela
You represent all that my soul desires.

Those vissicitudes that have cropped
     up
In my past I shall resolve
If you are by my side.

You are going to be my Mica, my
     Micaela
And this we shall arrange with great
     caution
Without anyone suspecting you love
     me
We shall go and marry
And fix everything up.

You have to be my Mica, my Micaela
Green like the pastures in the fields
Always with hope here

| | |
|---|---|
| La voz primera que serás un día mi compañera | I voice firstly that you shall someday be my companion |
| Por fin que seas mi Micaela | At last you'll be my Micaela |
| Y todos mis problemas | And all my problems |
| Se irán al demonio | Will go to the devil |
| Sólo con que resuelvas | By your agreeing |
| Lo del matrimonio. | To our matrimony. |
| | |
| Juntos no habrá ya nada que jamás nos duela; | Together there will never be anything that'll hurt us; |
| Serás tan feliz que llegarás a abuela. | You shall be so happy you'll live to be a grandmother. |
| | |
| Yo seré tu amor y tú mi Micaela. | I will be your love and you my Micaela. |

This song portrays a man singing a love song to his "Mica," metaphorically disguised as a woman named Micaela (Michelle). (In the second half of the song the woman answers with basically the same verses.) The suitor suggests that through marriage (or the coming together of the two, man and "Mica") they will live happily ever after. The lyrics of this song linking marriage and mica together reflect what happens in real life: marriage is one way of obtaining a mica. The song cleverly disguises the real nature of the desire through the metaphorization process of transforming the green card into a woman, Micaela.

The first strophe indicates through the nickname "Mica" that there is a double meaning in the lyrics. The plot is complicated by mentioning previous difficulties ("vicissitudes") suffered by the poetic voice. That the marriage has to be arranged with "great caution," as stated in the second strophe, and in a secret manner further underscores the suspicious nature of the proposed marriage. The third stanza conclusively confirms that Micaela is not a person, for "she" is described as "green like the pastures in the fields." Thus the coming together of the green "Mica" through the metaphor of matrimony resolves all the immigrant's problems. Pain and suffering will "go to the devil" and the two "lovers," Mica and immigrant, will live happily to ripe old age.

A portrayal of this type of marriage appeared in the *Los Angeles Times* (August 10, 1984) bearing the headline "Scam to Stay in U.S.: Aliens Find Home with Trip to Alter." It included a humorous "want ad" for prospective spouses: "Wanted: Spouse. Any size or shape. No sex or relationship desired. Must be a U.S. citizen. Will pay $1,000."

The irony of impersonalizing the object of desire is expressed in the canción "La bracera" (Estevan Navarrete), in which a trickster's search for a prospective mate backfires.

## La bracera

Para conseguir dinero
Yo me pasé la frontera
Iba dispuesto a la chamba
Saliera lo que saliera
Pizqué limón y naranja
Subía y bajaba escaleras.

Como no era contratado
Yo quise hallarme acomodo
Pensé que si estaba casado
Sería más sencillo todo
Me dije este año me caso
O no me llamo Teodoro.

Me enteré en un viejo pueblo
de una muchacha cualquiera
para en seguida casarnos
y que ella me consiguiera
la visa y el pasaporte
para cruzar la frontera.

El trato quedó cerrado
Y se citó la ceremonia
Tuvimos mil invitados
Y otros quinientos de gorra
Unos eran mis amigos
Y los otros de la novia.

Ya que estábamos casados
Le digo, "Bueno, mi vida,
Ahora que estamos solitos
Vas a saber de mi vida.
Yo soy purito mojado.
Hay tú sabrás si me *imigras*."*

Apenas oyó mi esposa
Lo que yo le propusiera
Me dijo, "Ya te amolaste.
Pues también yo soy bracera.
Me casé por lo mismo
Para cruzar la frontera."

## The Bracera

In order to make money
I crossed the border.
I was ready to work
Anywhere work was available.
I picked lemons and oranges
I went up and down ladders.

Because I had no legal papers
I tried to find a way to get them
I thought if I were married
Everything would be easier
I said to myself: "This year I marry
Or my name isn't Teodoro."

I found out in an old town
About a girl living there.
I immediately proposed to her
Hoping she would get for me
My visa and my passport
So I could cross the border.

The deal was sealed.
We set the date for the ceremony.
We had a thousand guests
And five hundred party crashers
Some were my friends
The others were the bride's.

After we were married
I said: "Listen my love,
Now that we are alone
You are going to know about my life.
I am really a wetback.
It's up to you to get my documents."

As soon as my wife heard
What I was telling her,
She told me: "You are out of luck.
I too am a wetback.
I married you for the same reason
So that I could cross the border."

*imigras = *emigras* (i.e., gets visa documents)

In other instances the mojado brazenly proposes that marriage is the solution to the "illegal alien" problem.[4] This aspect is clearly delineated in "El corrido de los mojados" (Luis Armenta).

## El corrido de los mojados

Porque somos los mojados
siempre nos busca la ley,
porque estamos ilegales
y no hablamos el inglés;
el gringo terco a sacarnos
y nosotros a volver.

Si uno sacan por Laredo
por Mexicali entran diez,
si otro sacan por Tijuana

por Nogales entran seis;
ai* nomás saquen la cuenta,
cuantos entramos al mes.

El problema de nosotros
fácil se puede arreglar:
que nos den una gringuita
para podernos casar;
y ya que nos den la mica
que se vuelva a divorciar.

Cuando el mojado haga huelga
a no volver otra vez,
quién va a tapar la cebolla,

lechuga y el vetabel;
el limón y la toronja,
se echará todo a perder.

Esos salones de baile
todos los van a cerrar,
porque si se va el mojado
quienes van ir a bailar;
y a más de cuatro gringuitas,
no las podrán consolar.

Vivan todos los mojados,
los que ya van a emigrar,
los que van de vacaciones,
los que vienen a pasar;
y los que van a casarse
para poder arreglar.

*ai = ahí (there)

## The Wetbacks' Corrido

Because we are wetbacks
The law is always after us,
Because we are illegals
And cannot speak English;
The stubborn gringo chases us out
And then we return.

If they kick one out through Laredo
Ten come in through Mexicali,
If another is kicked out through Tijuana
Six come in through Nogales;
You just figure it out,
How many come in each month.

Our problem
Can easily be solved:
All we need is a gringuita
So that we can get married;
And after we get our green card
We can get a divorce.

When the wetback decides
Not to ever return,
Who is going to take care of the onion fields,
The lettuce and the beets?
The lemons and the grapefruit
All will rot in their place.

And the dancing halls
All will close their doors,
Because if the wetback leaves
Who is going to go dancing;
And more than four gringuitas
Will be inconsolable.

Long live all the wetbacks,
Those that are ready to emigrate,
Those that vacation there,
Those that are just passing by;
Those that go there to get married
So they can legally stay.

The *Los Angeles Times*, in the previously cited article, reported the existence of a thriving business offering this type of sham marriage for a fee.

> Brokers may operate from their homes, or out of businesses such as a travel agency, a notary, or law office. Usually advertising by word of mouth, they sometimes employ recruiters, messengers and professional "stand-ins" whose job is to fraudulently impersonate missing brides or grooms.
>
> This underground business has evolved into an increasingly sophisticated and lucrative black market, authorities say. It is yet another symptom of controversial immigration quotas that attempt to restrict the flow of foreigners admitted to this country.
>
> For illegal aliens who want to live here, marrying a U.S. citizen is the fastest and surest way to gain permanent residency, it is generally agreed. The broker capitalizes on the alien's desire to gain a permanent foothold here, authorities say, while pandering to greedy or gullible Americans willing to pose as spouses.

However, only a small percentage of Mexican immigrants take this route to legalizing their status. The expense ($1,000, as stated in the *Times*) is too great for the average Mexican worker.

Still, marriage is not the only strategy available to the prospective immigrant. The use of false or fraudulent documents is integrated into the lyrics of "La patera (Juana La patera)" (Magdaleno Oliva).

### La patera (Juana La Patera)

Soy hembra muy mexicana
y cruzo varias fronteras
ahora la gente me dice
que soy Juana La Patera
porque si cruzo el Río Bravo
ni se las huelen siquiera

He cruzado la frontera
revuelta en la [word unclear]
me voy disfrazada de hombre
y nadie me nota nada
así llego al otro lado
junto con la coyotada.

En Texas y en San Francisco
me agarró la inmigración
pero a mí no me hace nada
yo traigo una mica falsa
y falsa es mi dirección. . . .

### The Woman Smuggler (Juana the Smuggler)

I am a proud Mexican woman
And I cross the borderlands
Now people tell me
That I am Juana the Smuggler
Because if I cross the Rio Bravo
People are nary aware.

I have crossed the border
Mingled among the crowd
I disguise myself as a man
And nobody notices a thing
That is how I get to the other side
Together with the rest of the smug-
    glers.

In Texas and San Francisco
The border patrol caught me
But they couldn't do a thing
I have a false green card
And my address is also false. . . .

Cuando yo me fui a las pizcas
haciéndola de *troquero**
el mero jefe de todos
me andaba *echando los perros***
y como no le hice caso
me regresó hasta Laredo.

When I went to pick cotton
I was a truck driver
And the big boss
Was flirting with me
And since I ignored him
He sent me back to Laredo.

A las fronteras del Norte
yo las estimo y las quiero
y esa cortina de alambre
que andan haciendo los güeros
a mi no me importa nada
yo entro y salgo cuando yo quiero.

The borderlands up north
I do love them so
And that wire curtain
That the blondies are building
I don't care one whit
I come and go as I please.

*troquero = truck driver
**echando los perros = literally, "to sic the dogs"; metaphorically, "to flirt."

Other strategies used in crossing the border are detailed in "Los alambrados" (Antonio Marcos Solís).

## Los alambrados

"Ahora sí muchachos, a ganar muchos
    dólares."

De México habían salido
hasta Tijuana llegaron.
Por no tener sus papeles
de alambristas se pasaron.

Se cruzaron por el cerro
Su rumbo habían agarrado
iban rodeando veredas
como lo habían acordado
era de noche y por eso
la vigilancia burlaron.

Ya por allá en Chula Vista
dos tipos los esperaron
un helicóptero andaba
queriéndolos encontrar
pero entre los matorrales
nada pudieron mirar.
Lo que hay que hacer en la vida
para dólares ganar. . . .

## The Wire Jumpers

"Now, boys, we are going to earn a
    lot of dollars!"

From Mexico City they came,
Arriving in Tijuana.
Because they did not have passports,
As wire jumpers they crossed the
    border.

They went through the hills.
They followed the way
Close to the sideroads
As they had planned.
It was night and that is why
They fooled the border patrol.

Around Chula Vista
Two men waited for them.
A helicopter was circling
Trying to apprehend them,
But hidden in the bushes
They could not see them.
This is what a man must do
To earn his keep. . . .

| | |
|---|---|
| Hasta Encinitas llegaron | They arrived at Encinitas |
| casi ya de madrugada | Around the early dawn. |
| de los que los recojieron | The men who took them |
| no se volvió a saber nada | Disappeared without a trace. |
| allí pasaron dos noches | There they spent two nights |
| y sin poder hacer nada. | Without being able to move. |
| | |
| Más tarde se decidieron | Later they decided |
| a dar la vida o la muerte | To risk life itself |
| la fe que tenían | Their strong faith in themselves |
| los llevó con mucha suerte. | Brought them good luck. |
| Ahora ya andan en Chicago, | Now they are in Chicago, |
| con dólares se divierten. | Having fun with the dollars they earn. |

The song "El bracero" (Rafael Buendía) reiterates the method of crossing the border through the wire fence erected along the California-Mexican border.

## El bracero

*Cantado:*

Cuando las nubes
en el suelo mexicano
se niegan a llover
emigra mi paisano.

A los estados
del suelo americano
dejando su labor
sin cultivar el grano.

Tristes se quedan
las casitas desoladas
los hijos, la mujer
las madres olvidadas.

Por ellos lloran
como pidiendo al cielo
que un día pueda volver
de nuevo a nuestro suelo.

Solo Dios sabe
y el tren que va pa'l Norte
cuando el bracero
se aleja suspirando
sin un amigo

## The Bracero

*Sung:*

When the clouds
On Mexican soil
Refuse to bring rain
My countrymen emigrate.

To the States
To American soil
Leaving their farmland
Without planting seed.

Sad do they leave
Their desolate houses
Their children and their wives
Their mothers quite forgotten.

They all cry for the bracero
As if asking heaven above
To let him one day return
To his homeland once again.

Only God knows
And the train leaving for the North
When the bracero
Leaves a-sighing
Without a friend

| | |
|---|---|
| sin contrato | Without a contract |
| y pasaporte | Without a passport |
| por el alambre | Through the wire fence |
| se pasan arrastrando. | They crawl to the other side. |

| *Hablado:* | *Spoken:* |
|---|---|
| ¡Ay San Isidro Labrador! | Oh, Saint Isidro Laborer! |
| ¡Los campesinos de gira | The farm workers on tour |
| y la tierra abandonada! | And their land abandoned! |

| *Cantado:* | *Sung:* |
|---|---|
| La madre espera | Their mother waits |
| con el rostro marchitado | With her aging face |
| los hijos, la mujer | Their children and their wives |
| mil penas han pasado | A thousand pains have suffered |
| siempre lo esperan | Always waiting |
| devisando pa'l camino | Looking up the road |
| y salen a encontrar | And going out to meet |
| a todo el peregrino. | All traveling people. |

| | |
|---|---|
| Pero el bracero | But the bracero |
| perdido en la distancia | Lost in the distance |
| fue de los muchos | Was one of the many |
| que nunca más volvieron; | Who never returned; |
| tal vez algunos | It may be that some |
| olvidaron sus familias, | Forgot their families, |
| otros muy tristes | Others becoming very sad |
| de pena se murieron. | From deep grief died. |

The ballad "Por el puente," on the other hand, speaks of crossing the border by walking across the bridge. This method entails waiting for a moment when the immigration officers are distracted and then walking over unnoticed. This method presupposes a certain amount of luck, needless to say.

| **Por el puente** | **Over The Bridge** |
|---|---|
| Por el puente voy cruzando, | Over the bridge I am crossing |
| cruzan mis hijos también; | My children cross over too. |
| si la migra está esperando, | If the border patrol is waiting |
| regresamos en el tren. | We shall return by train. |

| | |
|---|---|
| Qué suerte la del bracero, | Woe the luck of the bracero |
| qué suerte fea e ingrata, | What mean and cruel luck it is |
| pizcar en el extranjero | To be a picker in a foreign land |
| queriendo estar en la patria. | Wishing to be in our homeland. |

| | |
|---|---|
| Por el puente voy cruzando, | Over the bridge I am crossing |
| cruza mi mujer también; | My wife crosses over too. |
| si ahorita están deportando, | If they are deporting people now |
| volveremos otra vez. | We shall return again. |

(Vélez 1982:63)

The song "A El Paso" (Mario Ríos) describes walking across the bridge while the immigration officers "sleep."

### A El Paso

Atención, estar alertas
que ya es hora de cruzar,
la migra estará durmiendo,
salga el toro y a pasar.

Por el puente, sobre el río,
y sin dejar de correr,
iremos todos a El Paso
y allí podremos comer.

Sin hablar, sin hacer ruido,
vamos todos a cruzar;
si llegamos sin apuros
ya podremos trabajar.

Atrás se queda la patria,
¡qué lejana que ahora está!
Adiós, Sonora querida,
es la hora de cruzar.

### To El Paso

Attention, we must be alert
It is time to cross now
The border patrol must be sleeping
Let the bull out and let's cross.

Over the bridge, over the river
And do not stop running.
We shall all go to El Paso
There we shall be able to eat.

Without a word, without a sound
Let us all cross.
If we make it in one piece
We shall be able to work there.

Behind us we leave our homeland.
How far away it seems to be!
Good-bye, my beloved Sonora,
It is time to cross over now.

(Vélez 1982:63)

The fear and anxiety the border-crossing process elicits is narrated in "Vamos a cruzar, Julián" (Juana Valdez Patiño).

### Vamos a cruzar, Julián

Allá me están esperando,
esperando, así dicen;
si es verdad que allá me esperan
será verdad lo que dicen.
Dicen que están deportando
a mil braceros por hora;
aunque tengo mucho miedo
yo me meteré en la bola.

### Let Us Cross Over, Julián

They wait for me over there
Waiting for me, that's what they say.
If it's true they wait for me there
It must be true what they say.
They say they are deporting people
One thousand braceros per hour.
Even though fear is with me
I will get in on the action.

| | |
|---|---|
| Cruzar es morir un poco | To cross over is to die a little, |
| dijo el sabio en la frontera; | One wise man said at the border. |
| el sabio tenía razón: | The wise man was right: |
| ellos quieren que me muera. | They would like to see me die. |

| | |
|---|---|
| Vente conmigo, Julián, | Come with me, Julián, |
| iremos al otro lado; | We shall go to the other side. |
| no hay nada peor, Julián, | There is nothing worse, Julián, |
| que un "mojadito" espantado. | Than a scared wetback. |
| Julián, ya estamos llegando, | Julián, we are getting near, |
| ahorita estamos cruzando. | Now we are crossing. |
| ¿Será verdad lo que dicen, | Could it be true what they are saying, |
| que allá me están esperando? | That they wait for me there? |

(Vélez 1982:63)

## The Coyotes

A commonly described border-crossing strategy in contemporary corridos and canciones involves the smuggler who, for a fee, helps the undocumented worker enter the United States. These guides are called coyotes or polleros (*pollero* means one who takes care of chickens; the prospective immigrant wishing to cross is called a *pollo,* "chick"). They represent a recurrent motif in the texts.

The coyote arose out of a definite need. Northern Mexico, or *la frontera* as it is called in Mexico, has been up to recent times sparsely populated. Immigration to the United States tends to originate from more heavily populated states in the interior with high unemployment: Jalisco, Michoacán, Guanajuato, Durango, Zacatecas, San Luis Potosí. An immigrant traveling from the interior of Mexico will not be experienced in crossing the border illegally or knowledgeable about the best routes to select. The coyote thus has been an indispensable middle person (both females and males practice the trade) in helping the uninitiated succeed in crossing over to the United States, as the song "Yo soy mexicano señores" (Juan Manuel Valdovinos) states.

| Yo soy Mexicano señores | Gentlemen, I Am a Mexican |
|---|---|
| *Cantado:* | *Sung:* |
| Yo soy mexicano señores, | Gentlemen, I am a Mexican, |
| nacido en Michoacán | Born in Michoacán, |
| en————para ser exacto. | In————to be exact. |
| Soy Tarasco por gracia de Dios. | I am Tarascan, by the grace of God. |

| | |
|---|---|
| Cuando yo tenía catorce años | When I was fourteen years old |
| mis padres se separaron | My parents were separated. |
| duele tanto que no quiero ni acordarme. | It is so painful I don't want to remember. |
| Sufres tanto si no tienes edad. | You suffer so if you're under age. |
| | |
| Por ahí cantaba la gente que en el Norte | People sang of how in the North |
| el dinero se barría con la escoba. | Money could be swept off the streets. |
| Y nosotros creyéndonos el cuento | And believing this fairy tale |
| decidimos venirnos para acá. | We decided to come to this land. |
| | |
| Y ay señores no quiero ni acordarme | And, oh my dear sirs, I do not want to remember |
| | |
| los trabajos que pasamos en Tijuana | The hard times we had in Tijuana. |
| cuando ya veníamos cruzando | When we were about to cross |
| la migra que nos echa pa' atrás. | The border patrol kicked us out. |
| | |
| Un coyote tienen que conseguirse | You have to find a good smuggler, |
| nos decía la voz de la experiencia. | The voice of experience told us, |
| Un coyote que con su buena lana | A skilled smuggler who with money |
| por fin nos ayudó a cruzar. | Finally helped us cross to the other side. |
| | |
| *Hablado:* | *Spoken:* |
| | |
| Y aquí estoy todavía mi paisano | And here I still am, my countrymen, |
| trabajando pa' hacer rico al patrón | Working to make the bossman rich. |
| Y aquí estoy todavía mi paisano | And here I still am, my countrymen, |
| regando los files con sudor. | Irrigating the fields with my sweat. |
| | |
| *Cantado:* | *Sung:* |
| | |
| Con estas coplas termino mi corrido | With these couplets I end my song. |
| que perdonen si los he ofendido | Please forgive me if I have offended you. |
| se despide su amigo el Michoacano. | Your friend from Michoacán bids you farewell. |

The coyote character is a staple in Mexican, Chicano, and American Indian folklore. It is frequently found in the guise of the trickster who is duped by others. The animal is the Mexican's natural and constant enemy in the ranch country, according to Sarah S. McKellar, and "must get the worst of it in every story" (quoted in Dobie 1969:102). In immigrant lore the brutalizing and dehumanizing process of crossing the border has been reconceptualized and restructured poetically into a cast of archetypal characters belonging to the animal world—to the brutal and irrational sphere. The coyote in animal lore has the reputation of being wily, sly, sneaky, and clever at deceptions; he is the archdeceiver.

Immigrants see themselves in this light. Not allowed to enter legally, they rely on their wits to enter the United States. Many times, however, they are duped by their own countrymen who take advantage of the naiveté of immigrants. The crafty coyote (smuggler) takes advantage of innocent undocumented pollos. In barnyard lore, the coyote is the animal who sneaks in at night and steals the farmer's chickens to eat them. The pollos waiting to be smuggled across the border are thus perceived in this barnyard metaphorization as innocent victims who must fall into the claws of the coyote in order to be guided out of the "chicken coop." The coyote is the figure who can successfully evade the watchful eye of the "farmer" (read INS) and in the dead of night sneak them into the United States.

Although the coyote performs an important service to the prospective undocumented person, he or she suffers from an extremely negative image. Many people view this smuggler as the lowliest form of life on this planet. Coyotes are known to pack people in poorly ventilated trucks or garages and expose them to the danger of suffocating to death. Coyotes also charge high fees to smuggle people. The going rate in the early 1980s was $300 for walking illegals through the hills of southern California and then transporting them to their destination, $600 for smuggling undocumented workers in the comfort of a car through the Tijuana–San Ysidro inspection station.[5] The general population feels that coyotes prey upon innocent, unsuspecting victims, charge them exhorbitant fees, and often leave them stranded in the middle of the desert to die. Of course this occasionally does happen, and it makes the front pages of newspapers.

This song of Magdaleno Rosales clearly states the undocumented workers' feeling about the smuggler and his fees.

### Gana el güero y el pollero

Cruzan y cruzan braceros
en verano y primavera;
en verano y primavera
cruzan y cruzan braceros.

Gana el güero y el pollero

y a mí no me queda nada;
y a mí no me queda nada,
gana el güero y el pollero.

Pero yo sigo cruzando
porque allá tengo trabajo;
porque allá tengo trabajo
por eso sigo cruzando.

### The Blond Man and the Smuggler Profit

Braceros cross over and cross
in springtime and in summer.
In springtime and in summer
braceros cross over and cross.

The blond man and the smuggler profit
and I am left without a thing.
And I am left without a thing,
the blond man and the smuggler profit.

But I keep on crossing over
because my work is over there.
Because my work is over there
that's why I keep on crossing.

| | |
|---|---|
| Voy y vengo, vengo voy | I come and go, I go and come |
| buscando pan pa' mis hijos; | in search of bread for my children. |
| buscando pan pa' mis hijos | In search of bread for my children |
| voy y vengo, vengo y voy. | I come and go, I go and come. |

(Vélez 1982:64)

Since undocumented workers are frequently apprehended by border patrol officers, many quickly learn the safest routes to take and thus no longer need the service of the coyotes. This fact is expressed in the song "No necesito coyote" (Jesús Zermeño).

## No necesito coyote

Con esta van cuatro veces
que he visitado Tijuana.
La ciudad más visitada
de mi tierra mexicana
porque es la puerta de entrada
a la Unión Americana.

Por Tijuana, Mexicali,
Nogales y Piedras Negras
no necesito coyote
para cruzar las fronteras
yo no tengo pasaporte
y paso cuando yo quiera.

Las pochas son muy bonitas
hermosas son las Chicanas.
Las gringas son exquisitas.
Las negritas tienen fama
pero no una se compara
con la mujer mexicana.

De Texas a California
tengo todas mis querencias
en Chicago no me olvidan
también añoran mi ausencia
cuando llego a Sacramento
allí tengo preferencia.
No se me *agüiten** paisanos
hay que seguir trabajando
a darle duro al tomate,
durazno y al chabacano
para poder conseguir
lo que venimos buscando.

## I Don't Need a Coyote

This makes the fourth time
I have visited Tijuana,
The city most visited
In my Mexican homeland
Because it is the gateway
To the American Union.

In Tijuana, Mexicali,
Nogales and Piedras Negras
I don't need a coyote
To cross the border.
I don't have a passport
And I cross whenever I please.

The pochas are very pretty
Beautiful are the Chicanas.
The gringas are exquisite,
Black women are highly esteemed,
But none of them compare
With Mexican women.

From Texas to California
I have all my loves.
In Chicago, they don't forget me
They also miss me a lot.
When I get to Sacramento
They prefer me there.
Don't get sad, my countrymen,
We have to keep on working
Work hard at the tomato,
The peach and the apricot
So that we are able to get
That which we came here for.

*agüitar = become sad, depressed

## The Migra

The immigrant characterizes others as well as himself in the process of typologizing those with whom he comes in contact. Present-day corridos continue the literary tradition of incorporating within their lyrics a formidable foe who challenges, battles, or confronts the protagonists of the songs. In songs of the latter part of the nineteenth century the Texas Rangers (Rinches de Tejas) served as the force of evil in constant pursuit of the Mexican hero. The "Corrido de Jacinto Treviño" and the "Corrido de Gregorio Cortés" are examples (Paredes 1976, 1978). In Mexico during the Porfirio Díaz regime, the Texas Rangers found their counterpart in the *federales* (federal soldiers), who fought against Mexican rebel guerrilla fighters.

During the Depression the forced "repatriation" of Mexicans and Mexican Americans created great bitterness in the Chicano community toward the INS. Corridos written during this period castigate border patrol officers for their "heartless" disruption of family life and their breaking up of families. In the second half of the twentieth century the migra again becomes the villian and is portrayed in corrido lore as the archenemy of the undocumented worker.

It is clear that changes in attitude toward the border patrol corresponded to political and economic events. In the 1940s, when workers were needed to help in the World War II effort and Mexican nationals were heartily welcomed to the United States, the INS maintained a low profile and was not a common topic in corridos. And in the 1950s, when the much-touted "wet-back invasion" occurred, the migra was not generally portrayed as a malevolent force. Rather, it was often the butt of jokes (Herrera-Sobek 1979:92–95). Anglos in general were portrayed as clumsy, dimwitted, and easily duped by sharp-witted Mexicans. The role of the border patrol changed in ballads sung in the 1960s and 1970s, from trickster to villain. The migra was viewed as vindictive and its actions cruel. According to immigration studies by scholars such as Julián Samora, the INS has frequently been subservient to the interests of the surrounding communities dominated by Anglos and has not applied immigration laws in an evenhanded, objective manner. Thus, during periods of peak harvest season, the INS tends to look the other way, allowing "illegal aliens" to harvest the crops; when the harvest season is over, the officers descend on fields and ranches and deport undocumented workers.

An example of the hostile feelings expressed by undocumented workers toward the border patrol and the raids it carries out is expressed in "Las redadas" (Juan Prieto).

| Las redadas | The Raids |
|---|---|
| Los Angeles, California | Los Angeles, California, |
| Mayo del '73 | May of '73 |
| guardo triste en mi memoria | I hold sadly in my memory |

| | |
|---|---|
| las redadas de ese mes. | The raids taking place that month. |
| Mayoría de mexicanos | It was mostly Mexicans |
| agarraron esa vez. | They caught during that time. |
| | |
| Con órdenes federales | With orders from the federal govern-ment |
| para toda la nación | Covering the whole nation, |
| mil redadas de ilegales | A thousand illegal aliens |
| agarró la inmigración | The immigration did apprehend. |
| Descendían a California | They descended into California, |
| Nuevo México y Tucson. | New Mexico, and Tucson. |
| | |
| Los agentes federales | The federal agents |
| sin ninguna compasión | Without compassion |
| despacharon a ilegales | Sent home illegals |
| en perreras y en camión | In vans and buses. |
| por Tijuana y Mexicali | Through Tijuana and Mexicali |
| para su deportación. | They were deported. |
| | |
| Sacaron hasta mujeres | They even grabbed women |
| sin ninguna distinción | Without drawing a distinction. |
| Las redadas son muy crueles | The raids are very cruel |
| pongan todos atención | All of you pay attention. |
| hasta los que traen papeles | Even those with legal documents |
| sufren descriminación | Suffer discrimination. |
| | |
| Mientras pasan las redadas | Until the raids are over |
| me regreso a mi nación; | I am returning to my country; |
| a mi México querido | Back to my beloved Mexico |
| donde hay ley y protección | Where law and protection rule. |
| Ya me voy de California | I am leaving California |
| hay les dejo mi canción. | I leave you my song. |

Equally pernicious to respect for immigration law is the belief that the INS served the interests of employers during the farm workers' attempts to unionize. It is widely believed that during the past three decades whenever unionization efforts have been undertaken by a group of workers, the threat of deportation is immediately held up. Many union leaders point out that whenever incipient unionization movements arise, the employer calls the INS to round up those working without proper documentation. A 1970s ballad, "El corrido del ilegal," details precisely this view (see chapter 7 for the complete text).

| | |
|---|---|
| Policía e inmigración | Police and border patrol |
| Unidos con los rancheros, | Together with the growers, |
| Conspiración contratista | This was the contractors' conspiracy |

| | |
|---|---|
| por el maldito dinero. | For the sake of evil money. |
| En contra de nuestra gente | Against our people |
| Parecían unos perros. | They acted like dogs. |

The belief that the INS and employers conspired either to deport illegal aliens, or to keep them working is reiterated in "A dos dólares la hora."

| A dos dólares la hora | At Two Dollars an Hour |
|---|---|
| A dos dólares la hora | Two dollars an hour |
| ahorita están pagando | That is the current wage. |
| no ser mucho, *manito*,* | It may not be much, my brother, |
| pero estamos trabajando. | But we are working. |
| | |
| La migra no nos molesta | The border patrol does not bother us |
| cuando estamos trabajando; | When we are working. |
| con tarjeta o sin la mica, | With a visa or without a green card |
| aquí mismo nos quedamos. | Here we shall remain. |
| | |
| Cuando el trabajo termina | When the harvest is over |
| entonces viene la migra; | Then the immigration arrives. |
| de a uno nos van corriendo, | One by one they run us out, |
| ¡ay, qué suerte tan cochina! | Oh, what rotten luck! |
| | |
| En el verano, otra vez, | In the summertime once again |
| regresamos por trabajo. | We come back again to work. |
| California nos espera | California waits for us |
| a dos dólares pagando. | Paying two dollars an hour. |

(Vélez 1982:62)
*manito = *hermanito* (brother)

The capricious and racist nature of the INS with respect to its application of immigration laws is humorously pointed out in the recently popular song "Superman es ilegal" (Jorge Lerma).

| Superman es ilegal | Superman Is an Illegal Alien |
|---|---|
| *Hablado:* | *Spoken:* |
| ¿Es un pájaro, es un avión? | Is it a bird, an airplane? |
| No hombre, es un mojado. | No, man, it's a wetback. |
| | |
| (Sound effects of an airplane) | |

| *Cantado:* | *Sung:* |
|---|---|
| Llegó del cielo | He came from the sky |
| vino en avión. | He came by airplane |
| Venía en su nave | Traveling in his spaceship |
| desde Kryptón. | From Krypton. |
| Y por lo visto | And anyone can see |
| no es americano; | He is not an American. |
| sino otro igual | He is just another |
| como yo indocumentado. | Undocumented (worker) like me. |
| | |
| Así es que migra | So, border patrol, |
| él no debe trabajar, | He should not be allowed to work, |
| porque aunque duela | Because even though it hurts |
| Superman es ilegal. | Superman is an illegal alien. |
| | |
| Es periodista | He is a journalist |
| también yo soy | So am I |
| y no *jue** al army. | And he did not serve in the army. |
| ¡A que *camión!*** | What a jerk! |
| Y aquel es *güero,**** | He is fair-skinned |
| ojos azules, | Blue-eyed |
| bien formado; | And has a great physique, |
| y yo prietito | And I am dark-skinned |
| gordiflón y muy chaparro. | Fat and very short. |
| Pero yo al menos | But at least I served |
| en mi patria ya marché | In my country's army |
| con el coyote que pagué | With the smuggler I paid |
| cuando crucé. | When I crossed over. |
| | |
| No cumplió con el | He did not do his |
| servicio militar. | Military service. |
| No paga impuestos | He does not pay taxes |
| y le hace al judicial. | And practices law. |
| No tiene mica | He does not have his green card |
| ni permiso pa' volar. | Nor a permit to fly. |
| Y les apuesto que ni | And I bet he does not |
| seguro social. | Even have a social security card. |
| | |
| Hay que echar a Superman | We have to kick Superman |
| de esta región | Out of this region |
| y si se puede | And if we can |
| regresarlo pa' Kryptón. | Send him back to Krypton. |
| | |
| ¿Dónde está esa autoridad | Where are the immigration |
| de inmigración? | Authorities? |
| ¿Qué hay de nuevo | What's new in the |
| Don Racismo en la nación? | Nation, Mr. Racism? |

¿A cuál borrarón
cuando llegó?
De un colorcito
verde limón
y no era hierba
ni tampoco un agripal.
Más bien agüita
d'esa**** que hace reparar!

Who did they whiten up
When he arrived?
Wiping out his
Lemon-green color
He wasn't a plant
Nor was he an *agripal.*
It was probably water
Firewater that is!

Y que yo sepa
no lo multan por volar
sino al contrario
lo declaran Superman.

And as far as I know
They don't fine him for flying
On the contrary
They declare him Superman.

No cumplió con el
servicio militar.
No paga impuestos
y le hace al judicial.
No tiene mica
ni permiso pa' volar;
y les apuesto que ni
seguro social.

He did not do his
Military service.
He does not pay taxes
And practices law.
He does not have his green card
Nor a permit to fly.
And I bet he does not even have
A social security card.

Hay que echar a Superman
de esta región
y si se puede
regresarlo pa' Kryptón.

We have to kick Superman
Out of this region
And if we can
Send him back to Krypton.

¿Dónde está esa autoridad
de inmigración?
¿Qué hay de nuevo
Don Racismo en la nación?

Where are the immigration
Authorities?
What's new in the
Nation, Mr. Racism?

*jue = *fue* from *ver ir* (to go)
**camión = euphemism for *cabrón* (bastard, fucker)
***güero = fair-skinned, blond
****d'esa = *de esa* (that kind)

Freud has amply demonstrated that humor is an effective instrument by which an important message can be structured in a nonthreatening manner. "Superman es ilegal" encompasses in its lyrics several grievances the undocumented worker has vis-à-vis U.S. society's heroes and villains and the hypocrisy in the nation coupled with unequal treatment of people due to the color of their skin. The poetic persona addresses the border patrol by the slang term *migra,* and by this speech act effectively deconstructs the INS's official status. *Migra* is an epithet that simultaneously divests the agency and its personnel of its status and power; at the same time it confers on it ridicule and disdain. In this process of deconstruction of power through naming, migra and mojado become equal entities in a chess game where each player tries to outwit the other. In the end, however, each participant knows that it really does not matter who wins because the game will continue to be played indefinitely. The immigrant-narrator confidentially exposes the U.S. icon and urges the migra to accept this fact even though the truth hurts.

Furthermore, the poetic persona continues to enumerate Superman's illegal and unethical conduct: he is a journalist without any journalistic credentials, and horror of horrors, he is a draft dodger!—not having served in the army, as most Mexican Americans do. The specter of racism and unequal treatment under the law is raised, for the "superior" racial characteristics of Superman are listed and contrasted with the devalued Mexican ones: Superman is fair-skinned, blue-eyed, with a great physique, while the immigrant is dark-skinned, fat, and very short.

The tension elicited by the confrontation between migra and "illegal alien" is the principal axis structuring many immigrant songs. The immigrant is aware of the nature of the game. His or her life depends on many factors, including luck. The stakes are very high: death may be the end result of the long journey across the borderlands.

The song "Ai viene la migra" tells in heart-wrenching lyrics of the life and death odyssey an immigrant has embarked upon. The Cerberus figure of the migra guards the entrance to the "other side" and is a formidable obstacle for those trying to cross to another life.

| Ahi viene la migra | Here Comes The Border Patrol |
|---|---|
| Esta es la historia del pobre | This is the story of the poor |
| que huyendo de la miseria | Who fleeing from poverty |
| sólo tiene una esperanza | Only have one hope |
| llegar hasta la frontera. | To reach the border. |
| | |
| En el silencio se oía | In the silence one could hear |
| un ulular de sirenas | The piercing sound of the sirens |
| Todo el mundo corría | And all the people ran |
| pidiendo a dios por las buenas. | Asking God in good faith. |
| | |
| Que no me agarre la migra | Please don't let the migra catch me |
| no quiero ser deportado | I don't want to be deported |
| sino de nada ha valido | Otherwise all this will be in vain |
| el sufrimiento pasado. | All the past sufferings I endured. |
| | |
| *Ahi** viene la migra | Here comes the border patrol |
| agarrando ilegales | Catching illegal aliens |
| la Simpson Mazzoli | The Simpson-Mazzoli Act |
| causó nuestros males. | Caused all our suffering. |

Yo quiero mucho a mi tierra
Siento dolor al dejarla
ahi quedaron recuerdos
que no se borran del alma.

Si nos jugamos la vida
con una poca de suerte
o nos ayuda el destino
o nos alcanza la muerte.
Que no me agarre la migra
no quiero ser deportado
si no de nada ha valido
el sufrimiento pasado.

Ahi viene la migra
agarrando ilegales
la Simpson-Mazzoli
causó nuestros males.

I love my country very much
I feel pain upon leaving it
I left memories there
Etched forever in my soul.

If we risk our lives
With a little luck
Either destiny will help us
Or death will reach us.
Please don't let the migra catch me
I don't want to be deported
Otherwise all this will be in vain
All the past sufferings I endured.

Here comes the border patrol
Catching illegal aliens
The Simpson-Mazzoli Act
Caused all our suffering.

*ahi = *ahí* (there); in this case it means "here," the INS is pretty close

At times the migra is victorious in this deadly game and thoroughly routs the mojado, even taking away his very existence, as in "Los que cruzaron," by Víctor Cordero.

## Los que cruzaron

## Those Who Crossed Over

Los que cruzaron el puente
cerca de la madrugada
para enfrentarse a la muerte
traían pistolas cargadas,
eran rancheros valientes
Don Emeterio Benítez,
Domingo y Jesús Zavala
y don Maclovio Ramírez,
Francisco y Javier Taboada
por su ambición al dinero
se fueron al extranjero.
Se decidieron de plano,
querían probar su fortuna
para cruzar el Río Bravo
bajo la luz de la luna,
y con peligro arriesgado
cruzaron pa'l otro lado.

Cuando tocaron la orilla
los guardias les dispararon
y se rifaron la vida

Those who crossed the bridge
Near dawn
Coming face to face with death
They had their guns loaded
They were brave ranch hands.
Mr. Emeterio Benítez,
Domingo and Jesús Zavala
And Mr. Maclovio Ramírez,
Francisco and Javier Taboada
Due to their greed for money
Went to a foreign land.
They made up their minds
They wanted to test their fortunes
In crossing the Río Bravo
Under the light of the moon,
And with danger ever present
They crossed to the other side.

When they touched the river's edge
The guards fired at them
And they pitted their lives

contra los americanos,
y allí quedaron regados
como si fueran gusanos.
Madre mía de Guadalupe
Reina de los Mexicanos,
un gran milagro nos urge
que de tu gracia esperamos,
que no abandonen su tierra
nuestros queridos hermanos.
Es preferible ser pobre
y no andar en tierra ajena,
para el trabajo del hombre,
su patria está *rete güena**
y no buscar el dinero
con la sangre en el extranjero.

Against the Americans
And there they ended up
Like worms.
Mother of Guadalupe
Queen of the Mexicans
We urgently need a miracle
From your grace we wait
That they do not abandon their land
Our beloved brothers.
It is preferable to be poor
And not be in another's land.
For a man to work
His country is just fine
And not look for money
Giving up one's life in a foreign land.

*(Los mejores corridos mexicanos* 1972:40)
*rete güena = *muy buena* (very good)

On other occasions the undocumented worker defeats and eludes the "evil forces" and even mocks them, as in "Los mandados" (Jorge Lerma).

## Los mandados

Crucé el Río Grande nadando
sin importarme dos reales
me echó la migra *pa' juera**
y fui a caer a Nogales
entré por otra frontera
y que me *avientan pa'Juárez.***

Me disfracé de *gabacho****
y me pinté el pelo güero
y como no hablaba inglés
que me retachan de nuevo.

La migra a mi me agarró
300 veces digamos
pero jamás me domó
a mi me hizo los mandados
los golpes que a mí me dió
se los cobré a sus paisanos.

Por Mexicali yo entré
y por San Luis Colorado
todas las líneas crucé

## The Errands

I crossed the Rio Grande swimming
Without caring one bit,
The immigration threw me out
And I landed in Nogales;
I entered through another border town
And they threw me out through Juá-
rez.

I disguised myself as an Anglo
And I dyed my hair blond,
But because I did not speak English
They caught me once again.

The immigration caught me
About 300 times, let us say,
But they never broke me down
I sent them to do my bidding;
The blows I received from them
Their countrymen paid dearly for
them.

Through Mexicali I entered
And through San Luis Colorado,
All the border lines I crossed

| | |
|---|---|
| de contrabando y mojado | By contraband and as a wetback; |
| pero jamás me rajé | But I never gave up |
| y me venía al otro lado. | And I kept coming back. |
| | |
| Conozco todas las líneas | I know all the border routes |
| también los ríos y canales | Also the rivers and canals |
| entre Tijuana y Reynosa | Between Tijuana and Reynosa |
| de Matamoros a Juárez | From Matamoros through Juárez, |
| de Piedras Negras al Paso | From Piedras Negras to El Paso. |
| de Agua Prieta a Nogales. | From Agua Prieta to Nogales. |
| | |
| La migra a mi me agarró | The immigration caught me |
| 300 veces digamos | Three hundred times, let us say, |
| pero jamás me domó | But they never broke me down; |
| a mi me hizo los mandados | I sent them to do my bidding, |
| los golpes que a mí me dió | The blows I received from them |
| se los cobré a sus paisanos. | Their countrymen paid dearly for them. |

*pa' juera = *para afuera* (outside)
**avientan pa' Juárez = idiomatic expression (threw me out through Juárez)
***gabacho = derogatory for Anglo

Not only is "Los mandados" humorous, but the protagonist (the immigrant) also seriously confronts the migra. It seems as if, with each successive historical period, the immigrant gains historical perspective to unmask the evils of a system which is harsh and hypocritical. The immigrant's stance evolves in a symbolic transference, from person to object (the mica), person to trickster (the coyote), then trickster to villain (the migra). This maturation process is paralleled by members of other ethnic groups who become increasingly knowledgable about their civil rights the longer they live in the United States.

The binary structure of hero versus villian predominates in these corridos. Corrido production has cast the immigrant in the role of the hero and the INS in the villain's role. As a protagonist or secondary character in the various narratives, the INS is never portrayed in the guise of the hero. It is always the villain or the buffoon, even though the INS, according to newspaper accounts, has at times saved the lives of undocumented immigrants. This is particularly true in the hot Arizona desert, where Mexicans from the central area with its moderate climate attempt to cross the Arizona desert ill-prepared, with little or no water and not suspecting the deadly danger of the intense heat. Each summer the INS likes to document the lives it saves from the killer desert. The corridos have never acknowledged this side of the INS but instead portray it in a negative light.

The waiting game. Migra (border patrol)
and would-be immigrants keep a vigilant
eye on each other on the San Ysidro–
Tijuana border, January 1991. Photo courtesy of Roberto Córdova Leyva, Studio C.

# Racial Tension

*Nine*   Américo Paredes has perceptively delineated the trajectory of culture conflict between Anglos and *tejanos*, or Texas Mexicans, in *"With a Pistol in His Hand": A Border Ballad and Its Hero* (1978). He attributes the conflict that arose between the two cultures to various factors: the competition for land, the cultural differences between Catholic Mexicans and Protestant Anglo settlers, and the differences in language, skin color, and customs, to name a few.

Raymund Paredes, on the other hand, traced the roots of Anglo-Mexican conflict back to European history (see Paredes 1978). According to this scholar, the many wars between Protestant England and Catholic Spain resulted in antipathy toward each other in the Old World. This antipathy was later transplanted and nurtured in the New World.

Arnoldo de León, in *They Called Them Greasers: Anglo Attitudes toward Mexicans in Texas, 1821–1900,* posits that "from the moment they landed on the American continent, white people in their role as discoverers, settlers, pioneers, and landholders manifested unique feelings toward the colored or *mestizo* (mixed-blood) people they encountered" (De León 1983:ix). He adds:

> Collectively, the many attitudes whites held toward Mexicans went hand in hand with attempts toward oppression. They buttressed the idea that Americans were of superior stock and Tejanos were not, rationalized an elevated place for whites and a subservient one for Mexicans, and justified the notion that Mexican work should be for the good of white society. Those attitudes were at the base of the world that Tejanos had to grapple with in efforts to live a normal life and were among the forces defining what roles those coming from Mexico should assume.
>
> Judging from the few studies that touch upon relations between Anglos and Tejanos in more recent times, these entrenched ethnocentric and racist attitudes held their own for decades into the twentieth century. Segregation, blatant discrimination, disparaging names, and public abuse all reflected a state of mind redolent of the nineteenth century. So did the widely held belief that Tejanos were to keep a place subservient to their benefactors. (102)

These studies depict a society torn by racial conflict from its very inception. Indeed, racial tension in the Americas between Anglos and Mexicans was but a continuation of European Spanish and English animosity. A series of racial epithets began to surface in America—among the earlier ones is the word *gringo*. According to one explanation gringo is a corruption of the Latin word *griego*, or Greek, which in Latin meant "foreigner" or "barbarian." Later terms denoting new conflictive social relations appeared; among these we can include *pocho* and *Chicano*.

Corridos and canciones, particularly those popular among Mexican immigrants, incorporate in their lyrics the racial tensions extant in American society. Their perspective is important in affording us another view of the conflictive and at times explosive Anglo-Mexican relations. Corridos and other popular songs encapsulate theoretical frameworks which seek to explicate racial animosity between the various groups. These theoretical postulates include: (1) racism is an illogical emotion full of contradictions and difficult to explain; (2) it is exacerbated in a competitive market, i.e., competition for women, for jobs, etc.; (3) it is an ideological tool used to keep various populations segregated in specific jobs; (4) it is an ideological tool used by a dominant society to prevent the various ethnic and racial groups from uniting in a common cause; and (5) it is due to differences in skin color. In the pages that follow I will be using examples of corridos and songs which I believe delineate either connotatively or denotatively some of these points.

The song "Mexicano cien por ciento" exemplifies the illogical nature of prejudice.

## Mexicano cien por ciento

Soy amigos cien por ciento mexicano

y a mi raza le dedico mi canción
los que se hayan trabajando en suelo
    extraño
alejados de mi patria y mi nación.

Por mojados nos conocen *d'este*\* lado

y los gringos nos desprecian sin razón

no se acuerdan que esta tierra que
    ahora tienen
fue de México en un tiempo de valor.

Si ese suelo necesita nuestras fuerzas
y los gringos nuestro apoyo pa' valer

## One Hundred Percent Mexican

I am, my friends, one hundred percent
    Mexican
And to my people I dedicate my song
To those working in a foreign land

Far away from my homeland and my
    nation.

We are known on this side (USA) as
    wetbacks
And the gringos despise us without
    reason
They do not remember that this land
    they now have
Belonged to Mexico and was of great
    value.

If that land now needs our manpower
And the gringos need our support for
    their survival

yo no entiendo por qué entonces nos desprecian
si ese suelo lo trabajamos tan bien.

I don't understand why they despise us
If we work that land so well.

De Jalisco, Michoacán y Zacatecas

de Chihuahua, de Durango y de San Luis
de Coahuila, Nuevo León y Tamaulipas
son los que hacen esta tierra producir.

From Jalisco, Michoacán, and Zacatecas
From Chihuahua, Durango, and from San Luis
From Coahuila, Nuevo León, and Tamaulipas
These are the men that made this land productive.

Ofender con mi cantar a *nadien*** quiero
aunque tenga yo motivos y razón

a pelear con estos gringos yo no vengo

aunque late aquí en mi pecho este rencor.

I don't want to offend anyone with my song
Even though I have good reason to do so
I didn't come over to fight with these gringos
Even though I feel a lot of rancor in my heart.

A trabajar yo he cruzado la frontera
recordando a mi familia con dolor

que la Virgen los proteja mientras vuelvo
por las noches le ruego a mi lindo Dios.

I have crossed the border to work
Remembering my family with great pain
May the Virgin protect them until I return
I pray nightly to my beautiful Lord.

Con el alma entristecida me despido
deseando hoy termine un día este rencor
me perdonan las verdades que aquí digo
se las dice un Mexicano con honor.

With sadness in my soul I bid farewell
Hoping one day this hatred will end

Please forgive the truths I say

A Mexican of honor states this so.

Con orgullo mis paisanos adelante

unidos por la confianza y la razón
que este grito se escuche por todas partes
¡mexicano cien por ciento sí señor!

With pride let us go forward, my countrymen,
United with trust and with reason
Let this shout be heard all over the land
(I'm) one hundred percent Mexican, yes sir!

*d'este = *de este* (from this)
**nadien = *nadie* (no one)

Here the concern for a Mexican identity is explored. The title indicates a preoccupation with being Mexican, since it explicitly states that the singer is 100 percent Mexican—possibly as opposed to or in contrast to Chicanos, who are no longer deemed to be 100 percent Mexican, or 100 percent American, for that matter. The poetic voice addresses his "friends," i.e., the audience, by stating from the very inception of the song his nationality. The ballad is addressed to those working in a foreign land (the USA). In the second stanza the poetic persona acknowledges the derogatory epithet with which Mexican workers are known—mojados, wetbacks. But again there is a definite sense of history. The mojado reminds the gringo (Anglo) that the southwestern part of the United States once belonged to Mexico. Therefore, implicit in the song's lyrics is the belief that Mexicans have the right to be in the Southwest by right of conquest and colonization in the sixteenth and seventeenth centuries.

The poetic persona proceeds to expound his arguments in a logical manner: the Anglos need manpower and the Mexicans need jobs. According to this logic, the gringos are irrational in their hatred for the Mexican since they need Mexican strength and labor to work the land and are essential to the U.S. economy. Mexicans from Jalisco, Michoacán, Zacatecas, Durango, San Luis, Coahuila, Nuevo León, and Tamaulipas are the working force that keeps U.S. agricultural lands fertile and productive. The poetic persona is knowledgeable about the Mexican states which send the most workers; emigration from these states is the most numerous.

The ever-polite Mexican singer insists in the fifth stanza that he does not desire to offend anyone with the truth ("a pelear con estos gringos yo no vengo," "I didn't come over to fight with these gringos") but the poetic voice admits there is rancor in his heart because of the ill-treatment received. Having stated the illogical nature of prejudice, the song achieves closure with a call for peace, for more harmonious relations between the two social groups, and with a proud affirmation of his Mexicanness.

The theme of ill treatment and discrimination is reiterated in numerous other songs currently popular, such as "Los ilegales" (Pepe Gavilán).

## Los ilegales

*Cantado:*

Con cuenta tristeza canto
lo que sufre un ilegal
en este país hermano
pero que nos tratan mal.

Para llegar a esta tierra
yo vendí lo que tenía

## The Illegals

*Sung:*

How sadly I sing
About how much an illegal suffers
In this our brother country
But which treats us badly.

In order to come to this land
I sold all that I had

en mi lejano pueblito
dejé lo que más quería.

Después de mil sacrificios
logré cruzar la frontera
con la esperanza en el pecho
de trabajar donde fuera.

Pero ay que triste sorpresa
el destino me tenía
por falta de documentos
no logré lo que quería.

*Hablado:*

Hay como quince fronteras
y por ellas me he cruzado
y ya son como quince veces
que la migra me ha agarrado.

Si algún día la migración*
me llegara a sorprender
más se tardan en sacarme
como yo en volverme a meter.

*Cantado:*

Los ilegales sufrimos
mucha *descriminación***
nos persiguen como a ratas
agentes de migración.

Para conseguir trabajos
vergüenza y humillaciones
se aprovechan de nosotros
los que se dicen patrones.

Y yo que tanto soñaba
con venir hasta esta tierra
que antes era mexicana
pero que vendió Santa Ana.

Pero hay que triste sorpresa, etc.

In my far-away village
I left that which I loved the best.

After a thousand sacrifices
I managed to cross the border
With hope in my heart
To be able to work anywhere.

But what a sad surprise
Destiny had for me
Because I lacked documents
I could not get what I wanted.

*Spoken:*

There are about fifteen border towns
And I have crossed them all.
And fifteen times it's been
That the border patrol has caught me.

If one day the border patrol
Should take me by surprise
It will take them longer to take me out
Than for me to come back.

*Sung:*

Illegals like us suffer
Much discrimination
They hunt us like rats
Those immigration agents.

In order to get work
We go through shame and humiliation
They take advantage of us
Those that call themselves bosses.

And I who dreamed so much
In coming to this land
That used to be Mexican
But that Santa Ana sold.

But what a sad surprise, etc.

*migración = migration (in the song it means immigration officers)
**descriminación = *discriminación* (discrimination)

If the song "One Hundred Percent Mexican" presented gringo prejudice, the next song, "Pocho," is an example that implicitly points out intragroup conflict and racism. The *Pequeño Larousse Illustrado* defines the term *pocho* as *descolorido*, "pale." The *Diccionario General de Americanismos* (1942) provides a more detailed definition:

> Word used to designate those North Americans of Spanish origin, especially those of Mexican descent. It is used in the southern part of the United States, particularly in California, also applied to Mexicans or Spanish citizens residing in the United States. (In Mexico, *poche* and *pocha* are more commonly used. It probably has the same origin as *pochie,* a word native to Sonora, Mexico, and probably comes from the Yaqui language. It also has the meaning of being limited in intelligence, more bluntly, stupid.) 2. Corrupted Castilian. Mixture of bad English and terrible Spanish that is spoken by the North American residents of Spanish origin, mainly Mexicans in California (United States).

As can be seen, even the dictionary entry has a negative description of what a pocho/a is. It offers a value judgment regarding the English and Spanish spoken by Mexican Americans. The word has been pejoratively used by Mexicans against Chicanos. The song "Pocho" (Eulalio González) reiterates the concern with identity. This time the poetic persona is a Mexican American who is appealing to the two groups that directly effect him: Mexicans and Anglos. The poetic persona proceeds to define himself first as Pocho.

**Pocho**

*Cantado:*

Pocho
Soy Americano y Mexicano
dos en uno soy.

Chicano,
Tiéndeme la mano mexicano
que tu hermano soy.

Gringo,
veme sin distingos
tan americano como tú soy yo.

Texas, Arizona, todo California

y Nuevo México;
eran mis terrenos antes que
los güeros allí estaba yo.

**Pocho**

*Sung:*

Pocho
I am American and Mexican
Two in one I am.

Chicano,
Give me your hand, Mexican,
For I am your brother.

Gringo,
Look at me without prejudice
For I'm as American as you are.

Texas, Arizona, all of California

And New Mexico:
This was may land, before
The blonds came, I was there.

Gringo,
veme sin distingo
tan americano como tú soy yo.

Gringo,
Look at me without prejudice
For I'm as American as you are.

*Hablado:*

"Oye tu sabes eso paisa
(i.e., paisano).

*Spoken:*

"Say, did you know that friend?

You know that ¿qué si quiero a México?
Sí, lo llevo en el color de mi piel y por
dentro de mis venas. ¿Tú sabes eso
*paisa\*?*"

You know that. Do I love Mexico you
ask me? Yes, I carry Mexico in the color
of my skin and inside my veins. You
know that, partner?

"Oh yeah, Chicano power!"
*paisa = *paisano* (countryman)

The double identity of the pocho, Mexican and American (i.e., U.S. citizen), is highlighted. Furthermore, by utilizing the word *pocho* the poetic voice is addressing those Mexicans who are prejudiced against Mexican Americans. In the second stanza the poetic persona reminds Mexicans that he, the pocho, is their brother. Furthermore, the political term *Chicano* is now introduced to differentiate the legal status of Mexican citizens and U.S. citizens of Mexican descent. However, the emphasis is on unity and solidarity; an appeal is made to the blood relationship that ties the Chicano and Mexican together.

The third stanza zeros in on the haughty gringo. Here a request for racial justice is articulated. A call for social, economic, and political equality is made, since both the Anglo and the Chicano are U.S. citizens. Again the Anglo is reminded of his *parvenu* status: "Texas, Arizona, all of California and New Mexico: / This was my land, before / the blonds came, I was there." The theme of having the right to live in the Southwest by right of conquest and colonization before the Anglo came is reiterated. The troubadour is obviously cognizant of historical facts and his rightful place in history. History, therefore, is an important structuring element in immigrant song construction.

The Chicano movement of the 1960s and 1970s raised the consciousness of many Mexicans vis-à-vis the sufferings of their Mexican-American brothers. Previously, pochos were perceived as traitors (see Herrera-Sobek 1979). However, the civil rights movements of the 1960s reached the Mexican press and the injustices committed against Mexican Americans in the United States became more real and widely known. Various Mexican administrations in recent decades have met with Chicanos to discuss issues of mutual concern. A special office was created to deal with issues related to Mexicans residing in foreign countries (which means mostly those Mexicans living in the United States). Various Mexican universities, such as the Universidad Nacional Autónoma de México, have sponsored conferences dealing with Mexican-Chicano issues. Mexico is beginning to perceive the Chicano population as a possible ally and political force that could conceiveably pressure the U.S. government toward more favorable treatment of Mexico in export and import trade, petroleum prices, and so forth.

A song depicting this newfound consciousness on the part of Mexicans is "El chicano" (Juan Zalazar). It details much empathy and solidarity on the part of the Mexican-speaking subject toward his Chicano brothers.

## El chicano

Hay va un corrido señores
señores hay va un corrido;
Quiero que cruce el Río Bravo,
y llegue hasta los oídos;
De aquel que llaman Chicano,
*d'ese** que tanto ha sufrido.

D'ese que tanto ha sufrido,
de sangre y raza es mi hermano;
Su padecer me ha dolido,
por eso en me triste canto;
Que se le brinde yo pido,
un trato justo y humano.

Que acaben ya sus pesares,
que acabe su sentimiento;
Que brille un sol de justicia,
que sea la razón su aliento;
Que vea la luz de la aurora,
que vea que está amaneciendo.

Un grito sordo se escapa,
desde mi pecho angustiado;
Y en él a Dios le pregunto,
por que sufre aquí este hermano;
Que nace un ser culpable,
sobre suelo Americano.

Sobre suelo Americano,
se ha de seguir mi corrido;
Y hasta en lejanos poblados,
habrán de escuchar seguido;
Este mensaje al hermano,
que tanto, tanto ha sufrido.

## The Chicano

Here goes a corrido, gentlemen,
Gentlemen, here is a corrido.
I want it to cross the Rio Bravo
And to reach the ears
Of those they call Chicano,
He who has suffered so much.

The one who has suffered so much
By blood and race he's my brother;
His sufferings have pained me so
That is why in my sad song
I want him to be granted
A just and humane treatment.

I want his hardships to end
I want his sufferings to end;
That justice shine his way,
That reason be his guide;
That he see the light of dawn,
That he see morning is coming.

A deep and soundless gasp
From my anguished heart does come
And through it I ask God
Why my brother suffers so;
(Why) he is born guilty
Upon American soil.

Upon American soil
My corrido shall arrive
And even in far-away places
They shall all hear
The message I send my brother
Who has suffered so very, very much.

Desde este México mío,
te tiendo firme mi mano;
No tuerzas nunca el camino,
no temas a los fracasos;
Cambia mi hermano querido
tendrás el triunfo en tus brazos.

From my own Mexican land
I extend to you my hand;
Don't take the wrong road,
Don't be afraid of failure,
Change, my beloved brother,
You shall have victory in your arms.

*d'ese = *de ese* (that one)

In spite of the snobbery, racial prejudice, and haughtiness of the Anglo as perceived by Mexican immigrants, nothing pains them more than the prejudice and ill treatment received from those they view as brothers—the Mexican Americans. In Gil García Padrón's "Ciriaco el mojado," grievances are articulated against the sufferings received at the hands of those Mexicans legally residing in the United States ("There are times when the enemy / Is found in your own home").

### Ciriaco el mojado

### Ciriaco the Wetback

*Cantado:*

*Sung:*

Los que tienen migración
y los que son ciudadanos
sienten descriminación
por los que son sus hermanos
si América la hizo Dios
tienen derechos humanos.

Those who have their documents
And those who are citizens
Have discriminatory feelings
For those who are their brothers
If God made America
All have human rights.

Sienten dolor y martirio
en dejar su gente amada
pero más triste se sienten
cuando regresan sin nada
la esperanza los golpeó
la decepción los amarga.

(Those who leave) feel pain and anguish
Leaving their beloved people
But they even feel more sad
When they return without a penny
(Loss of) hope crushed their spirit
And disillusionment made them bitter.

Ciriaco duró tres meses
para llegar a Merced
quince días sin trabajar
y cuatro más sin comer
y a los tres días de trabajo
lo reportó una mujer.

It took Ciriaco three months
To arrive at Merced (California)
Fifteen days without work
And four days without food
And after working three days
A woman turned him in (to the INS).

Hay un dicho que es muy cierto
y se lo digo a mi raza
hay veces el enemigo
se encuentra en su propia casa.

There is a proverb that is very true
And I tell it to my people
There are times when the enemy
Is found in your own home.

| *Hablado:* | *Spoken:* |
|---|---|
| Yo quisiera que colgaran<br>a todos los que traicionan mi raza<br>para que al serio se vea<br>por lo que Ciriaco pasa. | I wish they would hang<br>All who betray my people<br>So that people take seriously<br>The (hardships) Ciriaco experiences. |
| *Cantado:* | *Sung:* |
| Andaban diez Mexicanos<br>cuando la migra cayó | There were ten Mexicans<br>When the immigration officers came<br>    upon them |
| para salvar sus hermanos<br>Ciriaco mejor corrió<br>aviones, carros y perros<br>pobre del que se escapó. | In order to save his brothers<br>Ciriaco decided to run<br>Airplanes, cars, and dogs<br>Pity those who try to escape. |
| Como estaba el campo abierto<br>y no podía esconderse<br>Ciriaco siguió corriendo<br>siquiera pa' defenderse<br>y a las tres millas corridas<br>Ciriaco empezó a caerse. | Since it was open country<br>And he could not hide<br>Ciriaco continued to run<br>Trying to defend himself<br>And after running three miles<br>Ciriaco started to fall. |
| Hombre ¿por qué corres tanto?<br>la migra le preguntó<br>    Ciriaco<br>pero no le contestó<br>la emigración enojado<br>Ahí en cuanto lo golpeó. | Man, why do you run so much?<br>The immigration officers asked<br>    Ciriaco<br>But he did not answer them<br>The immigration officers became angry<br>And started to beat him up. |
| Hay un dicho que es muy cierto<br>y se lo digo a mi raza<br>hay veces que el enemigo<br>se encuentra en su propria casa. | There is a proverb that's very true<br>And I tell it to my people<br>There are times when the enemy<br>Is found in your own home. |

The theme of betrayal by one's own people is reiterated in "La descriminación," written by Juan Manuel and Leobrado Pérez. The hardships encountered by a hardworking immigrant are expounded, and the advice to return to Mexico is firmly stated.

## La Descriminación

Dejé mi patria por mi afán aventurero
Y a California me marché sin dilación
Por la ilusión calenturienta del dinero
partí en pedazos de mi madre el corazón.

Y lavaplatos, ayudante y cocinero
sin hacer caso de la *descriminación*\*
en el trabajo por mi origen extranjero
se iba *empiorando*\*\* cada día la situación.

En una noche que a mi casa regresaba
frente a una iglesia me aprendió la inmigración
me denunciaron por envidia mis vecinos
y me mandaron de regreso a mi nación.

Sólo un consejo yo les doy a mis hermanos
A los que se hallan de aventura por allá
que se regresen que en su patria los esperan
sus familiares y también su libertad.

Cuando a mi rancho nuevamente regresaba
con intenciones de ponerme a descansar
mi madre enferma agonizante me esperaba
era tan triste el panorama de mi hogar.

Al Santo Niño le rogué que la curara
y hasta juré que no la vuelvo abandonar
Solo un consejo yo les doy a mis hermanos, etc.

## Discrimination

I left my country because of my adventurous spirit,
To California I went without delay.
With the burning illusion of making money,
I broke in a thousand pieces my mother's heart.

And as a dishwasher, helper, and cook,
Without heeding the discriminatory treatment
I got at work for being a foreigner,
Each day the situation became worse.

One night when I was returning home
In front of a church the immigration officers caught me.
My envious neighbors had turned me in
And I was returned to my country.

I have but one word of advice for my friends,
The ones that are still over there:
To return, for here in your country,
Your family and your liberty await you.

When I returned to my ranch
With the intent of resting

My sick dying mother was waiting for me.
It was a sad picture I found indeed.


I begged Santo Niño to cure her.
I even promised I would never leave her.
I have but one word of advice, etc.


*descriminación = *discriminación* (discrimination)
**empiorando = *empeorando* (worsening)


The ballad "Frontera internacional" of Enrique Valencia recapitulates the themes already discussed: the sufferings poverty-stricken Mexicans have to endure to come to the United States and earn "a little bit of money," the color barrier that divides the two peoples, the call for solidarity between the two neighbor nations, the affirmation that all men and women are created equal regardless of the color of the skin.


## Frontera internacional

*Cantado:*

Frontera, tú que ves hombre llorar
sin abrigo y sin hogar
porque dejaron su tierra.
Quisiera que cuando pase mi amor

en el nombre del Señor
esa puerta se cayera.


Frontera, dejo mi patria y mi hogar

todo por querer ganar
un poquito de dinero.
Dinero esa es la causa fatal
de que mi hermano al pasar
haya muerto allá en el cerro.


Frontera, frontera internacional
abre que voy a pasar
con el amor de mi vida.


Frontera, frontera internacional
si somos hombres igual
¿por qué divides la tierra?


## International Border

*Sung:*

Frontera, you who see men crying
Without food or shelter
Because they left their land.
I wish that when my beloved crosses over (to the USA)
In the name of God
That door would fall.


Frontera, I leave my country and my home
All because I want to earn
A little bit of money.
Money, that is the fatal reason
That my brother upon crossing
Died there in the hills.


Oh border, oh international border!
Open up I am crossing over
With the love of my life.


Oh border, oh international border!
If all men are created equal
Why do you divide the land?

| *Recitado:* | *Spoken:* |
|---|---|
| Cuantas madres se han quedado | How many mothers have waited |
| llorando aquel hijo amado | Crying for their beloved sons |
| y muriendo de dolor | And dying from the pain? |
| yo te pregunto frontera: | I ask you, frontera, |
| ¿Por qué en lugar de trinchera | Why instead of a dividing trench |
| no eres la línea que uniera | Aren't you the line that unites |
| sin importar el color? | Without regard to the color of the skin? |

| *Cantado:* | *Sung:* |
|---|---|
| Frontera, frontera internacional | Oh border, oh international border! |
| abre que voy a pasar | Open up I am crossing over |
| con el amor de mi vida. | With the love of my life. |
| | |
| Frontera, frontera internacional | Oh border, oh international border! |
| si somos hombres igual | If all men are created equal |
| ¿Por qué divides la tierra? | Why do you divide the land? |

In the ballad "Los hijos de Hernández" a confrontation between a hostile immigration officer and a would-be border crosser is narrated. Mr. Hernández attempts to cross the border and hears the resentful remarks of the customs official who fears Mexicans are taking away jobs from "Americans." The immigrant, wounded in his pride, proceeds to lecture the official on how Mexican Americans, including his son, have died for this country. The lyrics are preceded by the playing of reveille and a voice calling out names of soldiers:
  "Smith."
  "Sir."
  "Garza."
  "Sir."
  "Johnson."
  "Sir."
  "López."
  "Sir."
  "Hernández."
  "Missing in action."

## Los hijos de Hernández

| | |
|---|---|

### Hernández's Sons

| Regresaba de mi tierra | I was coming back from my country |
|---|---|
| y al cruzar por la frontera | And upon crossing the border |
| me pregunta un oficial | An official asks me |
| que cumpla mis deberes | To do my duty |
| que si yo tenía papeles | And if I had my papers |
| se los tenía que enseñar. | I had to show them to him. |

Y mientras los revizaba
escuché que murmuraba
algo que me hizo enojar
"Ya con tantos emigrados
muchos norteamericanos
no pueden ni trabajar."

Le dije muy enojado
eso que tú has murmurado
tiene mucho de verdad
Los latinoamericanos
a muchos americanos
le han quitado su lugar.

Sí muy duro trabajamos
tampoco no nos rajamos
si la vida hay que arriesgar
en los campos de combate
nos han echado adelante
porque sabemos pelear.

Aquí nacieron mis hijos
que ignorando los prejuicios
y la descriminación
su patria los reclamaba
y en el campo de batalla
pusieron el corazón.

Allí nadie se fijaba
que Hernández ellos firmaban
eran carne de cañón
quiza mis hijos tomaron
el lugar que no llenaron
el hijo de algún sajón.

Si en la nomina de pago
encuentras con desagrado
mi apellido en español
lo verás en otra lista
que a la hora de hacer revista
son perdidos en acción.

Mientras esto le gritaba
el emigrante lloraba
y dijo con emoción
"Puedes cruzar la frontera
esta y las veces que quieras
tienes más valor que yo."

And while he checked them
I heard him murmur
Something that made me mad:
"With so many immigrants
Many North Americans
Cannot find work."

I answered him angrily
That which you have said
Has a lot of truth in it
Many Latin Americans
Have taken the place
Of these American citizens.

Yes we work very hard
We don't give in
And we take our chances
In the battlefields
They have placed us on the front lines
Because we know how to fight.

My sons were born here
And ignoring all prejudice
And discrimination
Their country called on them
And in the battlefields
They fought with their hearts.

There, no one paid attention
That their signature was Hernández
They were cannon fodder
Perhaps my sons took
The place not filled by
The son of an Anglo-Saxon.

If in the payroll
You find with displeasure
My Spanish surname
You will also see it in another roll call
That when called upon
Are missing in action.

While I yelled this out
The immigration officer cried
And said with emotion
"You can cross the border
This and as many times as you want
You are more brave than I."

Tijuana Estuary National Wildlife Refuge, February 1990. Migrants (particularly the men) had stripped off much of their clothing and attempted to cross the Tijuana River toward the east. A border patrol helicopter forced the migrants back with the air from its rotors. Photo courtesy of Daniel Ituarte.

Tijuana Estuary National Wildlife Refuge, May 1990. At low tide, where the Tijuana River meets the ocean, migrants were preparing to attempt a shallow crossing. Mounted border patrol agents surrounded them from the south.

Patrol trucks approached the north bank of the river; the migrants gave up readily and were herded across the river and loaded into trucks. Photo courtesy of Daniel Ituarte.

Conflict over women has also been a recent topic, as in "El gringo y el mexicano" (Adolfo Salas). In this song, a married couple—Cipriano and Rosa María—cross the Rio Grande. "Y como espaldas mojadas/se cruzaron pa'l otro lado ["And as wetbacks/cross to the United States"]." They find work in McAllen, Texas, but soon Rosa María is sexually harassed by her employer, an Anglo, who threatens to deport her if she does not yield to his sexual advances. The young woman yields and Cipriano finds out. Outraged, Cipriano first kills the "gabacho," that is, the Anglo boss, and then proceeds to kill his wife, Rosa María. The husband is imprisoned for twenty years.

The shocking aspect in the drama that unfolds in this song (besides the Mexican's cold-blooded murder of his wife and the boss) is the reaction to the events demonstrated by a son who had been left in Mexico when the couple migrated to the States. When the son learns of his mother's death and the circumstances surrounding it, he agrees that the mother should have died for her transgression.

In "Tierras de California" (Pascuala Paredes) a bracero details all the sufferings he experienced in California. Nevertheless the immigrant still has faith in humanity and believes there are both good and evil people everywhere. In California, we are told, the immigrant can find people who have a good heart and those who hate Mexicans.


### Tierras de California

Voy a narrarles paisanos

lo que a mí me sucedió
en estas tierras del norte
las que tanto quiero yo.

Por la ilusión al dinero
dejé mi pueblito bello
mis padres y mis hermanos
y Isabel lo que más quiero.

Miles de agentes había
cuando crucé la frontera
la ley es muy dura amigos
regresáronme a mi tierra.

Pues insistí varias veces
hasta que logré pasar
a trabajar en el campo
en ese Valle Imperial

### California Lands

I am going to tell you, my country-
men,
All that happened to me
In those northern lands
Those which I love so.

Because of the dream of money
I left my beautiful town,
My parents, and my brothers,
And Isabel, my most beloved.

Thousands of agents were there
When I crossed the border.
The law is very strict, my friends,
They deported me back to my home-
land.

Well, I insisted on returning
Until I managed to cross over
To work in the fields
In that Imperial Valley.

Este California amigos
tumba de tantos hermanos
que deben ser recordados
por todos los mexicanos.

This California land, my friends,
Tomb to so many brothers
Who should be remembered
By all Mexicans.

Aquí encontré gente mala
y gente buena también
gente que odia a la raza
y gente que le hace el bien.

Here I met mean people
And good-hearted people too,
People who hate Mexicans
And people who help them too.

Madrecita yo te pido

que al regresar al terruño
encuentre a todos los míos
y que no falte ninguno.

My dearest Mother (of God), I beg
        you
That when I return to my homeland
I shall find all my kinfolk
And not be missing a single one.

Cuídame a mis viejecitos
ya mi hora llegará
cuídamelos madre mía
del cerro del Tepeyac.

Take care of my aged folks
My time is almost up
Take care of them, oh Mother,
Mother of the Hill of Tepeyac.

Este California amigos
tumba de tantos hermanos
que deben ser recordados
por todos los mexicanos.

This California land, my friends,
Tomb to so many brothers
Who should be remembered
By all Mexicans.

Aquí encontré gente mala
y gente buena también
gente que odia a la raza
y gente que le hace el bien.

Here I met mean people
And good-hearted people too,
People who hate Mexicans
And people who help them too.

Mexican ballads and songs dealing with racism seem to veer toward a structural theory to explain U.S. racism. According to this theory, racism occurs because the institutions of a society are so structured as to keep one group economically and socially inferior to the other. For example, ghetto schools are inferior so as to prevent ghetto dwellers from acquiring an adequate education. Furthermore, recent songs point to the color of the skin as a determining factor in racial prejudice toward Mexicans. A prime example of this is "Superman es ilegal" (see chapter 8).

It is obvious that these contemporary lyrics discuss the problem of prejudice from a unique perspective: that of the Mexican immigrant. At times the subject of racism is approached with anger, at others with pathos; still a third approach is biting humor. The people, through centuries-old folk genres, continue to expound on subjects close to their hearts and well-being.

# Poverty, Petroleum, and Amnesty

> Migration, the movement of peoples through space and time, influences almost every social process including the expansion of urban areas, mixing of cultural traditions, changes in social identities, and supply and demand labor. Despite its recognized importance, migration proves to be a dismally confusing topic for scholarly discussion. After decades of collecting, counting, censusing, surveying, sampling, and modelling migrations in every corner of the earth, scholars have created a migration literature still characterized by unarticulated perspectives, data, models, and explanations. The absence of anything approaching "migration theory" has troubled most reviewers.
>
> Theodore E. Downing, "Explaining Migration in Mexico and Elsewhere" (1979:159)

*Ten* A primary thesis of this study is that Mexican immigrants are well aware of their historical position as immigrants. They are conscious of their position as subjects in the historical process. Immigrants force this self-reflexive consciousness on the pages of history through the Mexican ballad, the only viable instrument they have at their disposal; it is the only medium they have for articulating their condition in the world. They are not helpless spectators in the flow of historical currents but very much aware of their selves as acting subjects.

## The Poverty Issue

Migration scholars have proposed various theoretical models to explain the phenomenon of human migration. But Mexican immigrants have their own explanatory models, or theoretical constructs, which provide logical reasons for migrating. The migrating workers explicitly state the primary reason for leaving Mexico: poverty.

For example, the Mexican immigrant in the song "Tanto tienes, tanto vales" (Pablo Botello) comments philosophically on contemporary society's propensity for judging individuals on the basis of their material worth. The song expounds on an immigrant's experience in selling his meager possessions in order to emigrate to the United States in hopes of a better life. Life in the United States, however, is harsh although the immigrant's eternal optimism, hardwork ethos, and belief in self-help aid him somewhat in coping with life in his new country. The song is impregnated with a strong message. Money is not everything, the acquisition of money should not change one's personal dealings with people. However, the immigrant believes in bettering oneself and working hard to attain one's goals instead of waiting for luck to come by. The song depicts a strong, honest, hardworking person who knows human beings deserve respect whatever their social position may be.

### Tanto tienes, tanto vales

Cansado de no ser nadie
decidí rifar mi suerte
vendiendo lo que tenía
que era muy poco por cierto.

Abandoné mi familia
y me aventuré pa'l norte
no llevaba documentos
ni tampoco pasaporte.

Tanto tienes tanto vales

en este mundo es la ley.
Pero no piensen señores

que el dinero que gané
cambiaría mis sentimientos
por los que tanto luché
Mis amigos son los mismos
y mis costumbres también.

La cosa nunca fue fácil
pero siempre tuve fe.
Donde quiera que yo anduve
en mil cosas trabajé,
pero siempre me acordaba
de lo que lejos dejé
de mi tierra de mi gente
que nunca los olvidé.

La riqueza más que nada
debe llevarse en el alma.

### Your Worth Is Measured by Your Wealth

Tired of being a nobody
I decided to take a gamble
I sold everything I had
Which wasn't much to tell the truth.

I left my family
And traveled to the North
I did not have any documents
Nor did I have a passport.

How much do you have? That's how much you're worth.
That's the law of the land.
But do not for a moment think, gentlemen,

That the money I earned
Would change my beliefs,
For which I fought so hard.
My friends are the same
And my customs I retain.

Life was never easy
But I always had faith.
Everywhere I went
In a thousand jobs I worked,
But I always did remember
That which I left far away
My land and my people
I never did forget.

Wealth of all things
Should be a spiritual wealth.

La pobreza no es pecado
pero siempre hay que luchar
por ser alguien en la vida
y alguna meta alcanzar.
La buena suerte no vino
pero yo la fui a buscar.

Poverty is not a sin
But one always should work hard
To make something of oneself
And to reach a worthwhile goal.
Good luck did not come my way
But I went out to look for it.

In a similar fashion the "Corrido del inmigrante" narrates the reasons for leaving Mexico.

### Corrido del inmigrante

México, mi patria,
donde nací mexicano,
dame la bendición
de tu poderosa mano.

Voy a Estados Unidos
para ganarme la vida;
adiós, mi tierra querida,
te llevo en mi corazón.

No me condenen
por dejar así mi tierra;
la culpa es de la pobreza
y de la necesidad.

Adios, lindo Guanajuato,
estado en que yo nací,
voy a Estados Unidos,
lejos, muy lejos de tí.

### The Immigrant's Corrido

Mexico, my country,
Where I was born a Mexican,
Give me your blessings
With your powerful hands.

I am going to the United States
To earn by daily bread.
Good-bye, my beloved country,
I will keep you in my heart.

Please do not blame me,
For leaving my country.
Poverty is to blame
And my great need.

Good-bye, my beautiful Guanajuato,
The state in which I was born.
I am going to the United States
Far, far away from thee.

(Vélez 1982:61–62)

Many would not leave their country if it were not for dire conditions in Mexico. Economic need is underscored in "El bracero" (Rafael Buendía), cited in chapter 8.

Another song thematizing the bracero who leaves his land is "Campesino asalariado," written by Víctor Cordero.

### Campesino asalariado

Campesino mexicano
no abandones a tu pueblo,
en el banco ejidatario
tu respaldo es el gobierno;

### Salaried Farm Worker

Mexican farm worker,
Do not leave your people.
In the Farmer's Bank
The government will back you.

| | |
|---|---|
| no abandones el arado | Do not leave the plow |
| porque México es tu dueño. | Because Mexico is your country. |
| Si las tierras que has sembrado | If the land you've planted |
| no rindieron tu cultivo, | Is not producing your crops |
| no te rajes campesino | Do not give up, farm worker, |
| ha de ser que no ha llovido; | It must be for lack of rain |
| el sudor de tu trabajo | The sweat of your work |
| lo respalda el agrarismo. | The agrarian cooperative backs. |
| Yo ambiciono de esas tierras | I wish I had those lands |
| que'l* gobierno ha repartido, | The government has given away. |
| si el que tiene no la siembra | If the one who has them doesn't plant them |
| | |
| es un mal agradecido | He is just ungrateful |
| porque yo sólo le sirvo | Because I only serve |
| a mi México querido. | My beloved Mexico. |
| | |
| Compadezco a los braceros | I feel sorry for the braceros |
| que se alejan de sus tierras, | Who leave their land, |
| los arrean como becerros | They are driven like calves |
| pa' que crucen la frontera | So they can cross the border |
| y los tratan como perros | And they treat them like dogs |
| pa' que cumplan su faena. | So they can get their work done. |
| | |
| La Virgen Guadalupana | The Virgin of Guadalupe |
| que es patrona de mi tierra | Who is the patron saint of all this land |
| a mi raza mexicana | Will defend my Mexican people |
| la defiende donde quiera | Wherever they may be |
| y es Reina soberana, | She is the Sovereign Queen |
| porque en ella no hay frontera. | Because with her there are no borders. |
| | |
| Los braceros que han dejado | The braceros who have left |
| sus familias y su tierra, | Their families and their land |
| luego van al consulado | They go to the (Mexican) consulate |
| a llorar por su bandera | To cry for their flag |
| su bandera mexicana | Their Mexican flag |
| que los salva donde quiera. | That saves them wherever they go. |

(*Los mejores corridos mexicanos* 1972:39)
*que'l = *que el* (that the)

"El corrido del chicano mexicano" (Ramón Fajardo) and "La opinión de unas gringas" (Bulmaro Bermúdez) underscore the theme of need as a primary force in impelling the immigrant to leave home. In the latter the uncontrolled natural catastrophes of drought and frost ruining the farmer's crops are given as compelling reasons for leaving Mexico.

## El corrido del Chicano Mexicano

Voy a cantar un corrido
del Chicano Mexicano,
porque este apodo le pusieron
en este país hermano.

Fue el 29 de Agosto
mil novecientos setenta,
cuando mataron a un grande
que hacía por el Mexicano.

Como un héroe en la historia
su nombre ha sido grabado
nunca será olvidado
como el apodo "mojado."

El Mexicano señores
es raza muy poderosa,
porque se parten el alma
por conseguir cualquier cosa.

Siempre abandonan su tierra
para venirse al norte
a conseguir el sustento
aun sin tener pasaporte.

Yo también soy Mexicano
y he recorrido fronteras

pero me gusta esta tierra
sobre todo este condado.

Les contaré que el condado
lleva por nombre Ventura
su gente es noble y pura
su orgullo es la agricultura.

El Mexicano señores
es raza muy poderosa
porque se parten el alma
por conseguir cualquier cosa.

## The Corrido of the Mexican Chicano

I am going to sing a ballad
Of the Mexican Chicano,
Because this is how they call him
In this our neighbor country.

It was the 29th of August
Nineteen hundred and seventy
When they killed a great one
Who worked for the betterment of
    Mexicans.

Like other heroes in history
His name will be engraved.
He will never be forgotten
Nor his nickname, "Wetback."

The Mexican, gentlemen,
Is a mighty race
Because they'll break their backs
To earn their keep.

They always abandon their homeland
In order to come up north
To find work for their sustenance
Even though they have no passport.

I too am a Mexican
And have traveled throughout the
    borderlands
But I do love this land (USA)
In particular this county.

I will tell you that this county
Is called Ventura.
Its people are noble and pure
They're proud of their agriculture.

The Mexican, gentlemen,
Is a mighty race
Because they'll break their backs
To earn their keep.

## La opinión de unas gringas

Solamente sin Dios y sin patria
se puede aguantar lo que sufre un mojado.
A pesar de que tanto trabaja
solo causa lástimas al otro lado.

Esa fue la opinión de unas gringas
de las que protejen al desamparado.
Yo no se si hay razón pa' que digan
tantas cosas tristes de un pobre mojado.

Aunque yo ando legal de bracero
al oirlas le lloré a mi tierra.
Pero en mi parcela no hay siembra de riego
lo poco que siembro se seca o se hiela.

Esas gringas seguían criticando
y hablaron lo peor reclamando justicia.
Yo entendí que se estaban burlando
porque algo decían de los bancos de Suiza.

Nos dijeron primores y encantos
y hablaron de tierras que son de extranjeros
los señores dueños de los bancos
son los que fabrican miseria y braceros.

Yo creí que las gringas hablaban
criticando solo a los mojados
pero les oí (decir) que se desperdiciaban
los ríos y los mares y hombres preparados.


## In Some Gringas' Opinion

Only those without a god and without a country
Can withstand the travails a wetback suffers.
Even though he works very hard
All he reaps is the pity of all on the other side (USA).

That was the opinion of some gringas
The kind that protect the dispossessed.
I don't know if there is any truth in what they say
All those sad things about a poor wetback.

Even though I am legally here as a bracero
Upon hearing them I cried for my homeland.
But in my farm I don't have irrigation
The little I plant dries up or freezes.

Those gringas kept on criticizing
And they spoke harshly demanding justice.
I thought they were making fun of us
Because they said something about Swiss banks.

They told us everything
They talked about lands belonging to foreigners
About the gentleman bank owners
Who are responsible for all the poverty and for the braceros' (hard life).

I thought the gringas speaking
Were criticizing only the bracero
But I heard them talk about the waste
Of rivers and oceans and well-prepared men.

In spite of the poverty suffered by Mexican immigrants, they never lose their sense of humor, their ability to laugh at themselves and their precarious condition. The song "Uno más de los mojados" (José Manuel Figueroa) is a case in point. Although the song narrates the travails and poverty of one immigrant, Pancracio—the story is told tongue-in-cheek and with a great sense of humor. The song gently pokes fun at the immigrant's dream of fleeing poverty in Mexico and "making it" in the United States. It follows the trajectory of earlier songs which criticized immigrants for coming to the United States and forgetting their language.

## Uno más de los mojados

## One More Wetback

*Hablado:*

*Spoken:*

¡Hay mis cuates! Esta canción se llama "Uno más de los mojados" dedicado a tanto pelao que han entrado ilegalmente a United States. ¡Ay te va pa' mi compadre Pancracio! ¡Ay te voy compadre!

Oh, my "brothers!" This song is called "One More Wetback." It is dedicated to all those dudes who have entered the United States illegally. Here goes! For my compadre Pancracio! Here I go compadre!

*Cantado:*

*Sung:*

Cuando Pancracio
vino a este país de güeros
sólamente agujeros
él traía en el pantalón.

When Pancracio
Came to this country of blondes
He carried only holes
In his pants.

No se sorprendan
que esta es la verdad
y al cabo se coló por el Río Bravo
y escapó del azadón.

Don't be surprised.
This is the truth
And anyway he crossed the Río Bravo
And escaped the hoe.

Era Pancracio
uno más de los mojados
que traían siempre asoliados
a la heroica migración.

Pancracio was
One more of those wetbacks
Who always kept
Those heroic immigration officers jumping.

Y ahora Pancracio
con los años que ha pasado
me dirán si no ha progresado
mírenlo en televisión.

Now Pancracio
With the passing years
Has progressed quite a bit;
You can see him at the TV station.

*Hablado:*

¡Limpia los baños! ¡Limpia los baños!

*Spoken:*

He cleans bathrooms! He cleans bathrooms!

*Cantado:*

"Good morning prieta,"
le decía a cualquier güereja
que encontraba en la banqueta
y ella no le hacía jalón.

*Sung:*

"Good morning, honey,"
He would tell any blonde
He saw on the sidewalk,
And she would ignore him.

Y ahora las gordas
como estamos en carencia
andan buscando su herencia
y él les dice, "Leave me alone!"

But now that we are
In a recession
They are looking for money
And he tells them, "Leave me alone."

*Hablado:*

Sí porque el viejo aprendió inglés. Sí
amigo. Saben que Pancracio se fue a los
United States y a los seis meses les es-
cribió a todos sus cuates acá en el rancho
del Pujido y les decía, "Olvídaseme el
español y dificúltaseme el inglés." Y sus
cuates le dicen: "Pos regrésate güey.
¡Antes que te quedes mudo!"

*Spoken:*

Yes, you see, the old man learned English. Yes, my friend. You see, Pancracio
went to the United States and after six
months he wrote back home to all his
buddies here at the Ranch of the Grunt.
He wrote: "I am forgetting Spanish, and
English is getting more difficult." And
his buddies replied: "Well, you have better return before you forget how to
speak, you ox!"

*Cantado:*

Pero un güen día
se encontró a Doña María,
le juró que la amaría
y le entregó su corazón.

*Sung:*

But one fine day
He met María.
He swore he would love her
And gave her his heart.

Y así pusieron
un puestote de cacahuates
compartieron el petate
y comparten el colchón.

And that is how
They set up a peanut stand.
They shared a straw mat
And now share a mattress.

*Hablado:*

¿No qué te ha ido tan bien?

*Spoken:*

Aren't you well off?

*Cantado:*

"Good morning, prieta,"
le decía a cualquier güereja
que encontraba en la banqueta
y ella no le hacía jalón.

Y ahora las gordas
como estamos en carencia
andan buscando su herencia
y él les dice, "Leave me alone!"

*Sung:*

"Good morning, honey,"
He would tell any blonde
He saw on the street
And she would ignore him.

But now that we are
In a recession
They are looking for money
And he tells them, "Leave me alone."

*Hablado:*

Como el pelao está trabajando en el traque allá en "Arkenso." Allá en "Arkenso" allá anda el viejo. ¡Allá les voy!

*Spoken:*

You see, the "dude" is working on the
railroad tracks over there in Arkansas.
There in Arkansas the old man is! Here I
go!

*Cantado:*

"Good morning, prieta,"
(Repeat verse)

*Sung:*

"Good morning, honey"
(Repeat verse)

*Hablado:*

Que quiere decir: ¡Déjenme en paz! ¡Déjenme en paz! "Go away, güey!"

*Spoken:*

Which means: "Leave me in peace, leave
me in peace. Get lost, creep!"

In a similar manner the song "La cucaracha mojada," written by Luis
Cuéllar, uses humor to address a painful issue: hunger. The song is a parody
of the famous Mexican Revolution folk song "La cucaracha," which was
popular with the men and women involved in the fighting.

## La Cucaracha Mojada

La cucaracha, la cucaracha
ya no quiere caminar,
porque no tiene, porque le falta

Coca-Cola que tomar.

La cucaracha, la cucaracha
también se quiere pasar,
para engancharse, para engancharse
y unos pesos así ganar.

## The Wetback Cockroach

The cockroach, the cockroach
Does not want to walk.
Because it doesn't have, because it
    lacks,
Coca-Cola to drink.

The cockroach, the cockroach
Also wants to cross the border
To get a contract, to get a contract,
And a few dollars to earn.

| | |
|---|---|
| Todos se van de la patria, | All are leaving the motherland, |
| la cucaracha también, | The cockroach is leaving too, |
| unos van por el desierto | Some are leaving through the desert |
| y otros cruzan con el tren. | Others are crossing by train. |
| | |
| Atravesando en Tijuana | Some are crossing through Tijuana |
| y por El Paso también | And through El Paso also. |
| vamos como cucarachas, | We are crossing like cockroaches |
| porque no hay que comer. | 'Cause there's nothing to eat. |

## The Petroleum Issue

The respected folklore scholar Merle E. Simmons accurately observed that

Only rarely have efforts been made to use the *corridos*, Mexico's historical ballads, to gain an understanding of modern Mexican life or an insight into the reaction of the common folk to what has transpired in the Mexican scene. This omission is the more surprising since probably no better means exist of penetrating the collective mind of Mexico's masses. Inaccurate though they may be as to specific historical details, the *corridos* do undoubtedly mirror with a high degree of fidelity the trends and directions of popular thought, and they reveal truth as the pueblo has seen it. (Simmons 1953:34).

The petroleum issue is a case in point. Historically, petroleum always has been a sensitive, emotionally charged political problem. Stanley Ross (1984:249–256) pointed out that questions regarding petroleum are not strictly based on dollars and cents but involve questions of national pride and sovereignty. Mexican folk songs expounding on political events related to petroleum offer interesting commentaries and focus sharply on the emotional hues enveloping the oil question. From the days of the hated Porfiriato and early twentieth-century foreign exploitation to President Cardenas's expropriation era, corridos vehemently denounce "Yankee meddling," exploitation, and unwanted intrusions in national affairs. It is here that the sharpest differences in attitude toward the United States arise. A definite hostile attitude is assumed in ballads dealing with U.S.-Mexican petroleum issues.

We are unequivocally made aware of these feelings in these emotionally charged stanzas from the corrido "De los ambiciosos patones" ("About Those Greedy Big-Footed Ones," Guerrero 1924b):

| | |
|---|---|
| Por ahí vienen "los patones" | The "big-footed ones" are coming, |
| los gringos americanos, | The American gringos, |
| diciendo que han de acabar | Saying they'll wipe out |
| con los indios mexicanos. . . . | The Mexican Indians. . . . |
| | |
| La verdad yo les diré | The truth is, let me tell you, |
| que hay unos malos vecinos | That there are some bad neighbors |

| | |
|---|---|
| que se les van a vender | And some of them will sell out |
| como si fueran cochinos. . . . | As if they were pigs. . . . |
| | |
| Dicen que quieren petróleo | They say they want petroleum, |
| mucho oro y mucha plata, | Lots of gold and lots of silver. |
| no se vayan a quedar | I hope they don't end up |
| nomás bailando en la reata. | Dancing from a rope. |
| | |
| Después que metan la pata | After they stick their foot in |
| no la'n de poder sacar, | They won't be able to take it out. |
| fígense que hay treinta-treinta, | Be aware we have 30-30 rifles |
| máusseres para pelear, | And Mausers for fighting. |
| pues no sea que los inditos | It may be that these little Indians |
| los vayan a hacer rajar. | Will make you give up. |

These lyrics convey a fighting spirit against U.S. ambitions vis-à-vis petroleum found on Mexican soil.

Similarly in "El peligro de la intervención americana" ("The Danger of American Intervention," Guerrero 1924b), written during the U.S. occupation of Vera Cruz in 1914, the injured feelings of a weak nation being overtaken by a more powerful one are vividly expressed:

| | |
|---|---|
| Si fuera una cosa justa | If it were a just thing |
| lo que ellos vienen peleando; | That they fight for— |
| pero eso no puede ser, | But that cannot be |
| porque nos están robando. . . . | Because they're stealing from us. . . . |
| | |
| Ya la mitad del terreno | Half of our territory |
| les vendió el traidor Santa Anna, | Was sold off by the traitor Santa Anna |
| con lo que se ha hecho muy rica | With that the American nation |
| La nación americana. | Became very wealthy. |
| | |
| Qué, ¿acaso no se conforman | Aren't you satisfied |
| con el oro de las minas? | With the gold from the mines? |
| Ustedes, muy elegantes | You, [dressed] very elegantly |
| y aquí nosotros en ruina. . . . | And us here in ruins. . . . |
| | |
| Búsquenle por otro lado, | Look elsewhere, |
| ya no sean tan ambiciosos, | Do not be so greedy, |
| porque aquí no nos sobraron | Because here we don't have anything |
| más que reatas de los pozos. | Except holes in the ground. |
| | |
| El petróleo se acabó, | The petroleum is all gone, |
| se lo consumieron todo. | You have used it all up. |
| Caminen por lo parejo, | You'd better follow the straight path now. |
| | |
| no se atasquen en el lodo. | Don't get stuck in the mud. |

And when Mexicans realized that what they had perceived only as a threat or possible danger became in fact a reality, their anger, their unbounded rage, found expression in these stanzas from the corrido "Llegada de buques americanos a Tampico" ("The Arrival of American Ships in Tampico," Guerrero 1924b):

| | |
|---|---|
| Gringos malditos patones | Damned big-footed ones |
| huerotes patas de perros, | Blond dog-footed ones |
| que mandan de sus naciones | You who send from your nation |
| a Tampico sus cruceros. . . . | To Tampico your battleships. . . . |
| | |
| Los petroleros han jurado | The petroleum companies have sworn |
| boycotear a este gobierno, | To boycott this government |
| el gringos muy desgraciado | The gringo is a disgraceful person |
| y es nuestro enemigo enterno. . . . | And is our eternal enemy. . . . |
| | |
| Compraron los petroleros | The petroleum companies bought off |
| a los jefes Chao y Herrera | The officials Chao and Herrera |
| Pero el Gobierno no es tonto | But the government isn't dumb |
| y les zurró la cuera. | And whipped their hide. |

Another more literary type of corrido emerged during the petroleum expropriation crisis. "Literary" corridos date back to the Mexican Revolution. As a result of the tremendous popularity and upsurge of corrido production during this tumultuous period, learned poets began to take interest in the popular genre and began composing songs imitating the corrido style and structure. Their songs, critics agree, generally lack the flavor of campesino and pueblo; they often appear stilted and unnatural, even to one not deeply acquainted with the style and form of the true corrido. Literary corridos are interesting, nevertheless, because the poet does try to incorporate and capture the feelings of the pueblo. Often, too, the poet may have pronounced socialist leanings, and these are conveyed in the songs.

One such example is the "Corrido del petróleo" ("The Petroleum Corrido," Campos 1962, vol. 2:462–464). A cursory reading of some of the lyrics makes evident the differences in style, but the antiforeign feelings are deeply embedded, just as they are in the typical pueblo corrido.

| | |
|---|---|
| Los pesares olvidando | Let's forget our painful memories |
| hoy cantamos ciudadanos | Today let us sing, citizens, |
| el triunfo que está vibrando | To the triumph that is vibrating |
| en los pechos mexicanos. . . . | In Mexican hearts. . . . |
| | |
| Así creciste: oprimida | Thus you grew: oppressed |
| bajo el yugo del magnate, | Under the yoke of the magnate |
| y tu carne mal vestida | And your body poorly dressed |
| tuvo por cama un petate. . . . | Had a straw mat for a bed. . . . |

De los campos petroleros
los burgeses se adueñaron
explotando los veneros
que en el subsuelo encontraron.

The petroleum fields
The bourgeoisie grabbed
Exploiting the riches
That under the soil they found.

Un vil mendrugo de pan
era el sueldo del obrero
era el fruto de su afán
¡buen pago del usurero! . . .

A miserly piece of bread
That was the workers' wage
That was all he earned
From the exploiter! . . .

Mientras tanto los millones
de pesos al extranjero
se llevaban los patrones
con escarnio verdadero.

Meanwhile millions of pesos
Left for foreign lands
Taken by the owners
With great glee.

Finally the Mexican government expropriates the petroleum fields from foreign ownership, and the poet exults:

Decretó la expropriación
de la industria petrolera
reintegrando a la Nación
lo que para ella surgiera.

Expropriation was decreed
Against the petroleum industry
Returning to the nation
All that belonged to her.

Mexico's long and painful tradition of foreign concerns extracting its mineral wealth without giving much thought to the needs and wishes of the native population weighs heavily on the Mexican mind. The Spanish conquistadores who melted down artistic creations in gold and silver to facilitate their shipment to Spain were barely cognizant of the fact that these precious metals and other mineral riches found in America rightfully belonged to the local Indians. And late in the nineteenth century and early in the twentieth, when British and American companies dominated the Mexican oil market, the general feeling was that industrialized countries had a right to the raw materials of the underdeveloped ones. The problem of mineral rights, therefore, carries with it strong emotional overtones of national pride. The ballads just excerpted most aptly transmit these emotions through their caustic lyrics.

The theme of Mexican petroleum resurfaced in the 1970s with the discovery of rich petroleum deposits in southern Mexico. The discovery produced a feeling of euphoria in the Mexican nation. The rich deposits were deemed to be Mexico's ticket to the good life, to becoming a developed, industrialized, wealthy nation. Mexico believed that petroleum revenues would ensure the future well-being of its citizens. Unfortunately the dreams were never realized. The oil market crashed, and Mexico was left with a huge foreign debt, one of the largest in the world. Mismanagement, corruption, and overspending in setting up the drilling and processing facilities all contributed to Mexico's woes in the 1980s, when inflation was rampant and the value of the peso fell precipitously.

The song "El petróleo (ahora sí), by Enrique Franco, explodes with great optimism for the future of Mexico and a possible end to the sufferings of the bracero. But it was written before the devaluation of the peso began.

## El petróleo (ahora sí)

Ahora sí esos del otro lado

Ahora todo será muy diferente
Ahora ustedes van a ser los mojados
Ya lo dijo todita la gente.

Ya verán si no cruzan el río
cuando vean que es de puro petróleo
Ya los veo temblar tiesos de frío

Y sin esa miradita de odio.

Quieren nuestro petróleo
Y quieren nuestro hogar
más come dijo el indio
eso les va a costar.

A ver ahora que dicen
esos de Puputlán
inflados como globos
tienen que reventar.

Ahora que bueno es estar prieto

Ahora sí que lindo Mexicano

Ahora sí ya no somos braceros
Ahora sí ya somos como hermanos.

Es mejor así de lejecitos
Aunque estén unidas las fronteras

Ahora ya no comemos bolillos
que nos den ahora pura telera.

## Petroleum (Now It's Our Turn)

Now you will see, you from the other side (the USA),
Things will be very different now.
Now you will be the wetbacks
Everyone is saying it now.

You'll see how you'll cross the river
When you see it's filled with pure oil
I'll be seeing you shivering from the cold
And without that look of hatred.

You want our oil
And you want our homes
But as the Indian said,
"That'll cost you."

Now we'll see what they say
Those from Puputlán
Filled up like balloons
You will have to explode (give in).

Now (everyone thinks) it's great to be dark
Now (everyone thinks) what beautiful Mexicans
Now we are no longer braceros
Now we are like brothers.

It's best you keep your distance
Even though the borders are connected
Now we won't eat white bread
Let them give us only wheat bread.

The theme of reversal of roles is highlighted here: North Americans will become the future wetbacks in search of oil. As the United States becomes unable to obtain oil from other sources and as the oil-rich Mexican nation becomes glutted with oil, it is the North Americans who will be crossing the river begging for the precious commodity. And the poetic voice predicts a change in attitude: it will be chic to have dark skin and wonderful to be Mexican. Sweet revenge is the theme.

Equally optimistic about the future of Mexico and of the bracero is the song "De bracero a petrolero" (Melesio Días), recorded in 1980.

| De bracero a petrolero | From Bracero to Oil Rigger |
|---|---|

*Cantado:*

Adios fronteras de El Paso
de San Ysidro y Laredo.
Ya me voy con rumbo al sur
voy a hacerme petrolero
Adios todas las fronteras
se acabaron los braceros.

Adios a los emigrantes
que casi son mis amigos
tantas veces me agarraron
en los cargueros dormido
soñando con las riquezas
ya no sentía ni el ruido.

Este bracero se va
en un avión de *catego**
Voy a hacerme petrolero
y a ganar mucho dinero.
Adios todas las güeritas
del Viejo y Nuevo Laredo.

*Hablado:*

¡Y nos vamos pa'l Sur Panchito!

*Cantado:*

Jamás volveré a brincarme
los alambres con garrocha
ni a prenderle veladoras
al Santo Niño de Atocha
para que en el Río Bravo
no enciendan ni las antorchas.

A mis patrones de Texas
los dejo con sus maquilas.
He de verlos por mi patria
buscanco la gasolina

*Sung:*

Good-bye borderlands of El Paso
Of San Ysidro and Laredo
I am southward bound
I'm going to be an oil rigger.
Good-bye all the border towns
The braceros will all be gone.

Good-bye to the INS officers
For they are almost my friends
They caught me so many times
Sleeping in the train's boxcars
Dreaming of great wealth
I did not even hear the noise.

This bracero is taking off
In a first-class airplane
I'm going to be an oil rigger
And earn a lot of money.
Good-bye to all the blonde girls
From the Old and New Laredo.

*Spoken:*

And we'll go down South, Panchito!

*Sung:*

I will never jump
Across the fences with a wire cutter
Nor will I light any more candles
To the blessed Niño de Atocha
So that in the Rio Bravo
They won't light up the torches (flood-
     lights).

I leave my bosses from Texas
I leave them with their factories.
I shall see them in my country
Looking for gasoline

| | |
|---|---|
| nomás a ver como se siente | Then they'll know how I felt |
| andar como me traían. | When they had me working so hard. |

*catego = *categoría* (i.e., first class)

The ballad "Oro verde por oro negro" (Pedro Ulloa) approaches the petroleum topic from a different angle: the political maneuverings of two presidents, Jimmy Carter of the United States and Luis Echeverría of Mexico.

## Oro verde por oro negro

Con destino a tierra Azteca
y oro verde en el bolsillo
salió de la Casa Blanca
un emisario de amigo
pa' negociar oro negro
como si fueran bolillos.

Los presidentes reunidos
en la Casa de los Pinos
para llegar a un acuerdo
de los puntos principales
hablaron largo y tendido
de petróleo y de ilegales.

De todos los ilegales
que cruzamos la frontera
pero cual fue la sorpresa
para asombro de la gente
sin importarle un comino
no se vendió el Presidente.

Aquí se termina amigos
la historia ya estaba escrita.
El oro negro ha ganado
y el oro verde no brilla

¡Viva nuestro Presidente!
No hay muralla de tortillas.

Los americanos pensaban comprarnos

petróleo barato y en sus ambiciones
Mas mi Presidente sin más pretensiones
se sentó en su macho
y amarró calzones.

## Green Gold for Black Gold

With a destination toward Aztec land
And with green gold in his pockets
An emissary from the White House
Took off and came as a friend
To negotiate for black gold
As if it were bread.

The presidents met
In the House of Pines
In order to reach an accord
On the principal points
They conferred long and seriously
About petroleum and illegal aliens.

About us illegal aliens
Who cross the border
But what a surprise
To the astonishment of all
Without caring a whit
The President did not sell out.

Here the story ends my friends.
History had already been written.
The black gold has won
And green gold does not shine any
more.
Long live our President!
There is no Tortilla Curtain.

The Americans thought they would
buy
Cheap petroleum and in their greed,
But our President without pretensions

Sat on his horse
And tightened his pants (firmly said
no).

The U.S. president is once more seen as an enemy of Mexico who tries to buy off Mexican presidents and cut an advantageous deal. This had happened in the past, according to corridos such as "Llegada de buques americanos a Tampico," quoted earlier. But this time the Mexican president is viewed as the real "macho" (strong man) who did not yield to bribery and stood his ground on the important issues of petroleum and immigration.

### The Amnesty Issue

"Late last year, after a decade of often-emotional political debate, Congress approved, and President Reagan signed into law, a major revision of the nation's immigration laws," the *Los Angeles Times* reported on May 4, 1987. "This week, millions of people across the nation will begin to feel the impact of those changes."

> Under provisions of the Immigration Reform and Control Act of 1986, illegal aliens who have been in the United States for at least five years can begin the process of legalizing their status on Tuesday [May 5, 1987]. The doors to legalization will remain open for a year afterward.
>
> It is estimated that 3,000,000 to 4,000,000 people may qualify for legalization, or "amnesty," as it is often referred to.

The political issue of amnesty for undocumented workers which was hotly debated in the U.S. Congress during President Carter's and President Reagan's administrations, was not lost on the Mexican immigrants themselves but was debated and aired through the medium of song. The immigrants took the subject of amnesty and added their own comments and personal viewpoints.

Basically the immigrants have distrusted government, being suspicious and incredulous regarding the proposed amnesty. Amnesty is seen as a trick, as yet another maneuver to hoodwink and hurt the immigrant. It is perceived as a threat and as a means to expel immigrants; overall, such a program is not to be trusted.

In an editorial, Jorge G. Castañeda, one of Mexico's foremost authorities on Mexican immigration, commented:

> The Simpson-Rodino Immigration Act of 1986 was a source of constant debate and acrimony in Mexico long before it actually took effect. A significant number of Mexican observers of the U.S. legislative process were sure that the American Congress would never pass an immigration reform bill; when, after years of postponement, the law came into being last November, many in Mexico predicted that it would be inoperable, thanks to its loose and confusing regulations and application procedures. Once the law took effect in May, however, this attitude changed, and a serious discussion on U.S. immigration policy gradually is emerging in Mexico.

Originally this debate was dominated by a widespread fear of massive deportations from the United States, and by the more well-founded concern that the new legislation would have a deterrent effect on the flow of new undocumented Mexican workers to the United States. Committees were hastily set up to receive deportees; politicians swore that those expelled from the United States would be given preference in finding new jobs in Mexico and in receiving assistance from the government. All in all, there seemed to be a generalized perception that the law was directed against Mexico and would cause the country severe damage. There were calls from a united national effort to protect Mexican citizens from a racist, xenophobic piece of U.S. legislation that was unilateral and highly contrary to Mexico's interests. (*Los Angeles Times,* July 5, 1987:5)

The song "La amnistía" presents a jaundiced view of the amnesty program. The ballad, written in 1978 by R. M. Gutiérrez, was a strong predictor of how the amnesty program would be viewed when it was eventually implemented. The fears and suspicions of the immigrants became a reality in 1987, and the amnesty program suffered from the reluctance of illegal aliens to step forward and apply for amnesty.

## La amnistía

El problema del mojado
muy pronto se va arreglar
con eso de la amnistía
que dicen nos van a dar
pa' mi que eso es puro cuento
es pura publicidad.

Con ese cambio de leyes
Y cambio de posesión
ya no se habla de otra cosa
que no sea de inmigración
si lo hacen por asustarnos
ya cámbienle de canción.

Los que tengan su permiso
y esperan saque arreglar

tengan muy buenos trabajos
dinero pa' colectar
estampillas de comida
y también el medical.

La cosa se puso dura
ya no encuentro ni que hacer
ya pusieron a los cucos

## The Amnesty

The wetback problem
Is going to be solved shortly
With that amnesty
They say they'll grant us.
To me that sounds like all talk
And merely a publicity ploy.

With that change in laws
And change in possessions
No one speaks of anything else
Except immigration talk.
If they are trying to scare us
Please change your tune.

Those of you with a permit
And who are hoping to get your legal
        papers
You'd better have a good job,
Money to collect,
Food stamps available,
And also your Medi-Cal.

Things are getting pretty hard.
I don't know what to do.
They've brought those bogeymen (bor-
        der patrol)

| | |
|---|---|
| pa' podernos detener | In order to detain us |
| cuando crucemos la línea | When we cross the border |
| y eso no se va a poder. | And we can't have that happen. |
| | |
| Si se aprueba la amnistía | If the amnesty program is approved |
| muy pocos van a arreglar | Very few are going to get it. |
| los que no la conseguimos | Those of us who don't get it |
| pa' fuera nos van a echar | Will be kicked out. |
| lo que yo les aseguro | What I do assure you |
| es que todos volverán. | Is that we will all return. |

The song was recorded right after President Carter initiated proposals for an amnesty program. On November 6, 1986, President Reagan signed the act. It took effect on May 5, 1987, and lasted until May 5, 1988. Immigrants did not eagerly flock to apply for amnesty but were reluctant even to approach the agencies which provided the application forms. As the *Los Angeles Times* reported on June 21, 1987 (page 10):

> In Los Angeles' sprawling community of illegal aliens, life has always been edged with fear and stress. Dogged by the constant fear of discovery by bosses and government officials and the threat of arrest and deportation by immigration agents, the region's estimated 1 million *indocumentados* have endured by conducting their lives with caution.
>
> Now, caution is no longer enough. The 6-week-old amnesty program has raised new fears about the future, confronting many undocumented aliens with painful decisions about coming out into the open and many others with deadlines that will force them to either return to their homelands or burrow deeper into the immigrant underground.
>
> Those who work with these immigrants, in schools, in mental health clinics, in immigration offices, say these fears are increasingly emerging in classic symptoms of stress. . . .
>
> Officials of the Immigration and Naturalization Service and private groups working with illegal aliens worry that along with other factors, these new fears, realistic or unfounded, have impeded the early success of the new law, contributing to the low turnout of applicants in the early weeks of the program.

Obviously the song "La amnistía" was an excellent predictor of immigrant behavior.

Another canción ranchera dealing with the same topic (written by Jesús Armenta) assumes a more optimistic stance.

### Ya nos dieron permiso

### They've Given Us a Permit

| | |
|---|---|
| Ya nos dieron un permiso | They've given us a permit |
| para estar bien con la ley. | So we can be within the law. |
| Más vale que se decidan | They'd better decide |

| | |
|---|---|
| a emigrarnos de una vez | To grant us legal status once and for all |
| porque por más que nos sacan | Because no matter how much they deport us |
| nos volvemos a meter. | We always return. |
| | |
| De Laredo hasta Tijuana | From Laredo to Tijuana |
| Matamoros y Nogales | Matamoros and Nogales |
| De Agua Prieta, Piedras Negras | From Agua Prieta, Piedras Negras |
| De Mexicali hasta Juárez | From Mexicali to Juárez |
| Es por donde los coyotes | That's where the smugglers |
| pasan a los ilegales. | Cross the illegal aliens. |
| | |
| La migra nos dio permiso | The INS gave us permission |
| Hay que salir a gozar | Let's go have fun |
| con más de cuatro del welfare | With more than four (women) on welfare |
| lo vamos a celebrar | We are going to celebrate |
| ya pronto será el día quince | Soon it'll be the 15th of the month |
| y el cheque ya va a llegar. | And their checks will arrive. |
| | |
| Dicen que si hallan mojados | They say if they find wetbacks |
| al patrón van a multar | They'll fine the boss |
| las fábricas y los campos | The factories and the fields. |
| hoteles y restaurantes | Hotels and restaurants |
| como pagan muy barato | Since they pay such low wages |
| solos se van a quedar. | Are going to be empty. |
| | |
| Se va a perder la cebolla | The onion will rot |
| el limón y la lechuga | The lemon and lettuce crops |
| pues si sacan al mojado | Because if they deport the wetback |
| quienes van a trabajar | Who is going to work? |
| nosotros los ya legales | Those of us who are legally here |
| no vamos a ir a pizcar. | Are not going to go work in the fields. |
| | |
| Si nos quitan el permiso | If they take our permits |
| Uuuyyy y uy uy que dolor | OOOhhhh, oh, oh, what pain! |
| mientras que estemos casados | As long as we are married |
| y nos prefiera el patrón | And the bosses prefer us |
| nos van a hacer los mandados | The INS officials will |
| los jefes de inmigración. | Be unable to touch us. |

In predicting the futility of trying to stop undocumented workers from migrating to the United States, this song was right on target. The *Los Angeles Times* (July 19, 1988:1) announced that "Fear of New Law Apparently Abates: Central Americans Flock to U.S. Border, INS Says."

As detailed in this chapter, corridos and canciones are important indicators of Mexicans' feelings about political issues. The songs not only reveal the Mexicans' reasons for migrating—chiefly poverty—but also zero in on the amnesty program, accurately reflecting deep-seated feelings toward specific government programs.

# Love

*Eleven* An underlying assumption in this study is that corridos and canciones present the Mexican immigrant as a well-rounded person as opposed to a stereotyped unidimensional individual. We encounter in these songs a full spectrum of emotions shared by all human beings. It should not surprise us, therefore, to encounter the Mexican immigrant fully engaged in love relationships.

The song "De California te escribo" (José Luz Alamís Cantú) depicts an immigrant as he is about to embark on his journey to California; we meet him as he is bidding farewell to his beloved. Unending love and the promise of marriage to his sweetheart are voiced in the lyrics of the song. Great optimism at finding employment and saving money in order to eventually support his future bride is evident in the song. The song is lighthearted and gay and displays self-confidence and an optimistic outlook on life and the future.

**De Californai te escribo**

*Hablado:*

Hermanos de California
que andan por allá;
de California y todos sus alrededores,

hay les voy. ¡Ayyya ju ju!

*Cantado:*

Te vengo a decir adiós
Te vengo a decir adiós
No quiero verte llorando.
Estoy viendo tus ojitos

**From California I'll Write to You**

*Spoken:*

My brothers from California,
You who are over there;
From California and the surrounding area
Here it goes. Ayyya, hoo, hoo!

*Sung:*

I've come to say good-bye
I've come to say good-bye
I don't want to see you crying.
I am looking at your eyes

| | |
|---|---|
| Estoy viendo tus ojitos | I am looking at your eyes |
| que de agua se están llenando. | That are welling up with tears. |
| Mañana mismo | Tomorrow without a doubt |
| me voy pa' California | I am going to California, |
| de allá te escribo | From there I'll write to you; |
| cuando ya esté trabajando | When I am working there |
| mucho dinero tendré | A lot of money I will have |
| porque voy a estar ahorrando | Because I shall be saving (it) |
| pa' cumplirle a mi Chatita | So that I can fulfill my promise |
| pa' cumplirle a mi Chatita | So that I can fulfill my promise |
| que me ha de estar aguardando. | To my girl who'll be waiting for me. |

| | |
|---|---|
| *Hablado:* | *Spoken:* |
| Queridos hermanos de California, | My beloved brothers from California, |
| Arizona, Colorado, Nuevo México, | Arizona, Colorado, New Mexico |
| Texas, Illinois, Nueva York, | Texas, Illinois, New York, |
| Florida, Arkenso, | Florida, Arkansas, |
| Illinois y Miguaje, | Illinois and Milwaukee; |
| Pa' todos ustedes con mucho amor. | To all of you with all my love, |
| No se olviden de México, *pelaos.** ¡Ay, ja ja! | Don't forget Mexico, you dudes. Ay ha, ha! |

| | |
|---|---|
| *Cantado:* | *Sung:* |
| Te vengo a decir adiós | I've come to say good-bye |
| (Se repite el primer verso) | (Repeat first verse) |
| | |
| Yo no quisiera | I do not want |
| separarme de tu lado | To leave your side, |
| Me parte el alma. | My heart breaks in two. |

| | |
|---|---|
| *Hablado:* | *Spoken:* |
| ¡Llorar dan ganas, pelao! | Makes you want to cry, dudes! |
| ¡Lloren, lloren! | Cry! Cry! |

| | |
|---|---|
| *Cantado:* | *Sung:* |
| El dejarte tan solita | Leaving you all alone |
| volver contigo mi amor | To return back to your love, |
| Ojalá Dios lo permita. | I hope God wills it |
| Pa' estrecharte entre mis brazos. | So I can hold you in my arms. |
| Pa' estrecharte entre mis brazos | So I can hold you in my arms |
| y besarte tu boquita. | And kiss your lips. |

*pelaos = *pelados* (slang for men)

The songs "Me voy a California," by A. Villagómez, "Adiós México queri-do," by Juan José Molina, and "Me voy pa'l Norte," by Manuel Esquivel, display basically the same sentiments as the previous ditty. The women are left home sad and crying over the departure of their loved ones.

## Me voy a California

Ya me voy a California
voy a cosechar dinero.
Aunque dejo aquí a mi novia
la prenda que tanto quiero.

Ella me dice llorando
no te vayas amorcito
dame como despedida
un abrazo y un besito.

Cuando ya pase algún tiempo
y si la suerte es muy buena
que regrese yo a mi pueblo
a cumplirle a mi morena
entonces nos casaremos
ay que vida tan hermosa
Si te llevo a California
pasaremos por Reynosa.

## I Am Going to California

I am going to California
I am going to reap lots of money.
Even though I leave my girl here
The treasure I love the most.

She does tell me sobbing
Please don't go my love
Please give me a farewell token
A hug and a kiss.

After a short time
And if luck is good to me
I shall return to my hometown
To keep my promise to my brunette
Then we shall marry
Oh what a beautiful life
If I take you to California
We shall pass by Reynosa.

## Adiós, México querido

Adiós, México querido,
me voy muy lejos de tí:
voy buscando otros destinos,
quizá allá yo sea feliz.

Te dejo aquí mis amores
y todo mi corazón,
adiós, México querido,
con tu recuerdo me voy.

Te dejo también mis hijos,
mi mujer y hasta mi hogar:
adiós, México querido,
quizá pueda regresar.

Adiós, México querido,
ya vendré por mi familia,
si la migra no nos ve,
habrá pan todos los días.

## Good-bye, My Beloved Mexico

Good-bye, my beloved Mexico,
I am traveling far away from you.
I am looking for another way of life
Perhaps there I will be happy.

I leave you all my love
And all my heart.
Good-bye, my beloved Mexico,
Memories of you will linger on.

I also leave you my children,
My wife and even my home.
Good-bye, my beloved Mexico,
Perhaps I shall return.

Good-bye, my beloved Mexico.
I shall come back for my family.
If the border patrol doesn't see us
There will be bread everyday.

(Vélez 1982:62)

| Me voy pa'l Norte | I Am Going Up North |
|---|---|
| Adios chaparrita | Good-bye, little one, |
| me voy para el Norte | I am going up north |
| voy en busca de fortuna, | I am going in search of fortune |
| tan pronto regrese | As soon as I return |
| luego nos casamos | We'll get married |
| porque como tu ninguna. | Because there's no other like you. |
| | |
| Ya está tu casita | Your house is there |
| allá en el potrero | On the plains |
| donde tu serás la reina, | Where you will be the queen |
| donde muy feliz | Where you will happily |
| serás para siempre | Forever be |
| De mi corazón la dueña. | The keeper of my heart. |
| | |
| En esa famosa | In that famous |
| frontera del Norte | Land of the North |
| voy a ganar mucha plata, | I am going to earn lots of money |
| compro tu vestido | I'll buy your dress |
| bordado de azares | Embroidered with orange blossoms |
| y nos casamos mi chata. | And we will marry, my pugnose dear. |
| | |
| Acércate mi alma | Be near my soul |
| y dame un besito | And give me a kiss |
| pa' llevarlo de recuerdo, | So I can take it as a souvenir. |
| que yo como prenda | I in turn give you |
| mi vida te entrego | My life as a token |
| y mi corazón entero. | And my whole heart. |

Of course the immigrant does have the option of taking his girlfriend or fiancée to the United States. Many Mexican women emigrate to the United States in this manner (see Herrera-Sobek 1983). In "Dos pasajes" the lyrics present a would-be immigrant enticing his girlfriend to join him on his trip to the States ("otras tierras" in generally a metaphor for the United States).

| Dos pasajes | Two Tickets |
|---|---|
| Qué dices, prieta querida, | What do you say, my dark love? |
| vámonos para otras tierras, | Let us go to another land. |
| aquí traigo dos pasajes, | I have two tickets for us, |
| o me sigues o te quedas. | Will you follow me or stay? |
| | |
| Vámonos para otras tierras | Let us leave for other lands |
| a gozar de los amores, | To enjoy the fruits of love. |
| viviremos muy felices | We shall live so happily |
| sin agravios ni rencores. | Without affronts or hatred. |

No te ofrezco las estrellas
ni tampoco un mundo nuevo,
soy muy pobre, tú lo sabes,
jugador y parrandero.

I don't offer you the stars
Nor do I offer you a new world.
I am a poor man, this you know,
A gambler and a reveler.

Pero si, por Dios te digo,
a cambio de tu cariño,
que me dedico a quererte
y a dejar todos los vicios.

But this, by God, I do tell you,
In exchange for your love
I shall dedicate myself to love you
And leave all my vices behind.

Ya están silbando los trenes
dile adiós a tus parientes,
viviremos muy felices,
verás que no te arrepientes.

The train whistle does blow
Tell your relatives goodbye.
We shall live very happily
In truth you will not be sorry.

(Vélez 1982:65)

In a light vein and using much *caló*, i.e., street jive, "Concha la mojada" (Ernesto Pesqueda) also depicts a would-be immigrant contemplating taking his girlfriend to the United States.

## Concha la mojada

En la calle donde vivo
vive Concha la muchacha
más bonita de mi barrio
y me dicen los muchachos
que le caigo a toda mecha
porque el bato que la sigue
es un *chavo*\* muy borracho.

Como yo no tengo coche
pa' pasearla por las calles
voy a ver si me entra un lazo

me consigo una chaqueta
que me tape el espinazo
le presumo unos billetes
para ver si le changazo.

Conseguí una guitarrita
chiquitita y re bonita
para echarnos una rola
porque yo no tengo radio
mucho menos grabadora
cantaremos algo nuevo
cual si fuera sinfonola.

## Concha the Illegal Alien

In the street where I live
Lives Concha, the prettiest girl
In my neighborhood,
And the guys tell me
That she thinks I am great
Because the dude who courts her
Is a drunkard.

Since I don't have a car
To take her out riding
I am going to see if I can make a connection
And find a jacket
That will fit me well
And I will show off some bucks
To see if I can catch her.

I found a little guitar
Very small and very pretty
So we can sing a song
'Cause I don't have a radio
Let alone a tape recorder.
We shall sing something new
As if we were a phonograph record.

La Conchita tiene fama
de echarla de trompada
pero a mí me vale gorro
lo canijo se lo quito
hay me voy poco a poquito
que la cosa sea calmada
para que salga a mi modo.

Conchita is famous
For being a fighter
But I don't care
I can tame her
A little bit at a time
In a calm manner
So that I can have my way.

Si me voy pa'l otro lado
me la llevo de bracera
hay la paso de mojada
nos pasamos por el Bravo
a la Unión Americana
y derecho hasta Chicago
nos iremos de volada.

If I go to the USA
I will take her as a bracera
I will take her as a wetback
We will cross the Rio Grande
To the United States
And straight to Chicago
We will go real fast.

*chavo = *chavalo* (young man)

Once the immigrants are in the United States, many do not forget their relatives or girlfriends, as the song "Desde el México de afuera" (José Vaca Flores) testifies.

## Desde el México de afuera

*Hablado:*

¡Ayyyy! ¡Ora Huertas, cántenle a mi México lindo! ¡YYYjajuy, Ay amor!

*Cantado:*

Desde el México de afuera los saludo
y aunque no los alcance les extiendo mi mano
ya tengo hambre de andar allí en mi tierra
de estar con mis viejitos, mi novia y mis hermanos.

Dos años tengo de andar por estas tierras
y cada día que pasa me siento más extraño
Y cada día que pasa me duele más la ausencia
el día que yo me vaya me voy en aeroplano.

Estando tan lejos de mi pueblo tan lejos de mi gente
tan lejos de mi tierra
se mete más hondo aquí en el alma
el verde, blanco y rojo de mi linda bandera.

Cuando oigo un quince de septiembre
el himno de mi patria mi corazón no aguanta

se asoma el llanto por mis ojos
y un nudo que me aprieta
yo siento en la garganta.

*Hablado:*

¡Ay, ganas me dan de llorar de sentirme tan lejos de mi México!

*Cantado:*

Es muy bonito andar en la aventura
dándole rienda suelta al amor y a las paseadas
pero se siente padre saber que ya regresas
hasta donde se encuentran los que ya te esperaban.

Estando tan lejos de mi pueblo
tan lejos de mi gente, tan lejos de mi tierra
se mete más hondo aquí en el alma
el verde, blanco, y rojo de mi linda bandera.

Cuando oigo un quince de septiembre
el himno de mi patria, mi corazón no aguanta.

*Hablado:*

¡Viva México!

*Cantado:*

Se asoma el llanto por mis ojos
y un nudo que me aprieta
yo siento en la garganta.

*Hablado:*

México, mi México lindo, aunque este lejos mi corazon siempre estará contigo.


## From the Other Mexico

*Spoken:*

Aayyy, come on Huerta sisters, sing to my beautiful Mexico! Aayy ha juy, oh my love!


*Sung:*

From the other Mexico I bring you greetings,
And even though from far away I extend my hand to you
I hunger to be there in my land
And to be with my parents, my girlfriend, and my kinfolk.

Two years it has been since I roamed around this land
And each day that goes by I feel more out of place,
And each day that goes by I feel the pain more of being away.
The day I return I will take an airplane.

Being so far from my hometown and my people,
So far from my homeland,
I can feel deep inside my soul
The green, the white, and the red of my beautiful flag.

When I hear a fifteenth of September,
My country's national anthem, my heart cannot bear it.
The tears begin to fall from my eyes
And a knot that tightens
I feel in my throat.

*Spoken:*

Oh, I feel like crying upon feeling so far from my Mexico!

*Sung:*

It is very exciting going out on adventures
Roaming free, enjoying love and fun.
But one feels great knowing one is returning
To those who have been waiting for you.

Being so far from my hometown,
So far from my people, so far from my homeland,
I can feel deep inside my soul
The green, the white, and the red of my beautiful flag.

When I hear a fifteenth of September,
My country's national anthem, my heart cannot bear it.

*Spoken:*

Long live Mexico!

*Sung:*

The tears begin to fall from my eyes
And a knot that tightens
I feel in my throat.

*Spoken:*

Mexico, my beautiful Mexico, even though I am far from you my heart will always be with you.

Not all the women who are left behind are in Mexico. Some are left behind in the United States as returning braceros or immigrants head south to their homeland. The pain is nevertheless the same, as can be felt in the lyrics of the song "Cruzando el puente" (R. Hernández). It is interesting to note, in addition to the motif of the sweetheart left behind, the positive representation of the United States. I have discussed this aspect more fully in *The Bracero Experience: Elitelore versus Folklore*.

## Cruzando el puente

Ya parece que voy cruzando el puente
de Matamoros con rumbo a Valle Hermoso,
se divisan las praderas, y mis ríos
y los cantares de los pájaros hermosos.

Adiós Estados Unidos, me despido
de tus bellezas y tus artes tan preciosos,
tus edificios, aeropuertos y otras cosas,
y tus mujeres son las rosas más hermosas.

Adiós, adiós, adiós, adiós.
Yo ya me voy pa' no volver.
Lo que más quise se quedó
por no saberme comprender.

## Crossing the Bridge

I feel like I am crossing the bridge
At Matamoros on my way to Valle Hermoso.
I can see the meadows, the rivers,
And hear the singing of the beautiful birds.

Good-bye, United States, I say good-bye.
To your beauty and your precious art,
Your skyscrapers, your airports, and other things,
And your women are the most beautiful roses.

Good-bye, good-bye, good-bye, good-bye.
I am leaving, I will not be back.
That which was dearest to me I leave behind,
Because she did not understand me.

Some Mexican immigrants meet women after arriving in the United States and fall in love with them. However, the girl who is a U.S. citizen may lose her boyfriend to the INS when he is deported for lack of proper documents. "Dejé mi amor allá en el Norte," by Isidoro Coronel, tells of the brokenhearted immigrant who was deported and left his sweetheart behind. The poetic persona is optimistic that he will acquire his visa and will join his fiancée shortly. This of course is a common occurrence. When the INS deports a member of the family the rest stay behind and wait for his or her return. Sometimes even children are deported and separated from their parents. At other times, when the parents are deported the children are left behind to fend for themselves until the parents return.

### Dejé mi amor allá en el Norte

Dejé mi amor al otro lado
No tengo yo mi pasaporte
Y es que mi fui así de mojado.
La quiero yo y ella me quiere
con un amor desesperado;
quisiera ser, ser como el ave
para volar siempre a su lado.
Pero ya pronto si Dios quiere
amorcito consentido
arreglaré bien mis papeles
para estar siempre contigo
y así los dos juntitos
embriagarnos de cariño.

### I Left My Love in the North

I left my love on the other side
I do not have my passport
For I went there as a wetback.
I love her and she loves me
With a desperate love.
I wish I were, were like a bird
So I could always fly by her side.
But very soon if God wills it,
My dearest beloved,
I shall get my papers in order
So that I may always be with you
And together the two of us
We'll be dizzy with our love.

In "La Chicanita," by Catarino Lana Benavídez, the Mexican immigrant falls in love with a young lady from Michoacán. He wonders why she is called a Chicana, since she is really a Mexican citizen. Chicanos, as opposed to other immigrant groups such as Japanese Americans, who have different terms for first-, second-, and third-generation native-born citizens, are not overly concerned about which generation a Mexican American belongs to. Perhaps this lack of snobbishness is derived from the fact that to the Anglo population Chicanos have always been "Mexicans," no matter what generation. Californios and their descendents were considered "foreigners" in spite of the fact that they were the original settlers! A Chicano may be any person usually of Mexican descent who calls himself a Chicano, even though he may not have been born in the United States. The song reflects this quite open attitude toward the use of the term.

## La Chicanita

¡Ajaa! ¡Ajaa! ¡AJAA!
¡Ora! ¡Ora! ¡Ora!
¡Empujen!
¡Ayaaaa!

Tiene unos ojos
rete bonitos
es morenita
y sus belleza
es natural
boca chiquita
nariz bonita
cuerpo bonito
y estatura regular.

Todos le dicen
la Chicanita
no se porque
si ella es nacida
en Michoacán.

Es para todos
la más bonita
dicen que tiene
un modo a todo dar.

Que suerte tengo
de conocerla
de estar con ella
y que me quiera como yo.

La quiero mucho sí
me tiene loco
con su mirada
me ha robado el corazón.

¡Ayaaaa!
¡Lléguele mi chavo!
¡Qué cosa!
¡Nada! ¡Nada! ¡Nada! ¡Nada!

## The Chicanita

Ahaa! Ahaa! Ahaa!
Now! Now! Now!
Move it!
Ayaaa!

She has
These beautiful eyes.
She is a brunette
And her beauty
Is natural:
Small mouth,
Pretty nose,
Pretty figure,
And regular height.

All call her
The Chicanita.
I don't know why
Since she was born
In Michoacán.

Everyone agrees
She is the prettiest.
They say her personality
Is out of sight!

How lucky I am
To know her,
To be with her,
And that she loves me so.

I love her very much, yes.
She drives me crazy.
With her looks
She has stolen my heart.

Ayaaaa!
Hit it, my friend!
What a beauty!
Yea! Yea! Yea!

The Mexican immigrant is generally portrayed as emigrating for financial reasons. The song "Fronteras del Río Bravo," by Benjamín Sánchez Mota, presents another reason for emigrating to the United States—to find his girlfriend who has gone to live in the States. The lovesick would-be immigrant is portrayed as brokenhearted and dismayed at not finding his girl.

## Fronteras del Río Bravo

Me voy pa' la Frontera,
voy tras de tus amores,
Si quieres que te quiera
olvida los rencores.

Morena de ojos negros,
morena encantadora,
por ti muere de celos
el hombre que te adora.

Estoy desesperado
y no hallo qué hacer
y allí del otro lado,
me habrán de comprender.

Regresa morenita,
regresa por favor
que mi alma me palpita
nomás de puro amor.

Las flores se secaron
desde que tú te fuiste
y luego me dejaron
dime por qué lo hiciste.

Fronteras del Río Bravo,
dónde está mi amada,
por ahí se las encargo
ya que no encuentro nada.

Estoy desesperado
y no hallo qué hacer
y allá del otro lado,
me habrán de comprender.

## The Rio Bravo Borderlands

I am going to the border
I am seeking your love
If you want me to love you
Forget all the hate between us.

My dark-eyed brunette
My enchanting brunette
For you I die from jealousy
The man that adores you.

I am a desperate man
I do not know what to do
And over there on the other side
They shall understand me.

Return my little brunette
Return I beg of you
My heart does beat
From all the love I have.

The flowers they did die
Since you are gone
And they left me
Tell me why did you do it?

Rio Bravo borderlands
Where my beloved lives
I bid you take care of her
Since I cannot find her.

I am a desperate man
I do not know what to do
And over there on the other side
They shall understand me.

(*Cancionero Mexicano* 1980:483–484)

Another lovesick immigrant is depicted in "Voy a cruzar la frontera" (J. Maldonado and J. Villa). His girlfriend, Dolores, has been taken to the States and he is desparately trying to locate her.

## Voy a cruzar la frontera

Voy a cruzar la frontera,
voy a buscar a Dolores,
ella juró que sería

## I Am Going to Cross the Border

I am going to cross the border
I am going to look for Dolores
She swore she would be

la dueña de mis amores;
voy a cruzar la frontera,
voy a buscar a Dolores.

Hace tres días que se fue
sus padres se la llevaron,
a mí tristeza me dio
cuando llegaba al Río Bravo;
hace tres días que se fue
sus padres se la llevaron.

Un retrato ella me dio
aquí lo traigo en el pecho,
cada vez que yo lo miro
lloro, suspiro y lo beso;
un retrato ella me dio
aquí lo traigo en el pecho.

Voy a cruzar la frontera
la cita se está llegando,
de Reynosa le escribí
debe de estarme esperando;
voy a cruzar la frontera
la cita se está llegando.

Voy a cruzar la frontera,
ya estoy arriba del bos,
ya voy con rumbo a McAllen
me voy buscando a mi amor;
después les sigo contando
porque ya se arranca el bos.

The owner of my love;
I am going to cross the border
I am going to look for Dolores.

It's been three days since she left,
Her parents took her away;
I became very sad
When she was nearing the Rio Bravo;
It's been three days since she left
Her parents took her away.

She gave me her picture
I carry it next to my heart,
Each time I see it
I cry, sigh, and kiss it;
She gave me her picture
I carry it next to my heart.

I am going to cross the border
The date is getting near,
I wrote her from Reynosa
She must be waiting for me;
I am going to cross the border
The date is getting near.

I am going to cross the border
I am inside the bus
I am traveling toward McAllen,
I go looking for my love;
I shall sing to you later
Because the bus is now leaving.

A parody of the "Latin lover," the ladykiller stereotype, is depicted in the song "Jacinto Pérez de la O" (José Manuel Figueroa). Reiterating the theme of the preceding songs, Jacinto falls in love with a "blondie" and is compelled to swim the Rio Grande to join his beloved. Of interest is the suggestion that Jacinto might be "limp-wristed," that is, a homosexual.

### Jacinto Pérez de la O

Voy a relatar señores
de la vida y los amores
de un mexicano
que una mañana de mayo
se montó en su fiel caballo
y su pueblo dejó.

### Jacinto Pérez de la O

I'll tell a story, gentlemen,
about the life and loves
of a Mexican
who one morning in May
saddled his faithful horse
and left his hometown.

Su caballo era retinto
el nombre del era Jacinto Pérez
   de la O
Suspiraba a la frontera
porque en sueños de una güera
él se enamoró.

His horse was jet black,
his name was Jacinto Pérez de la O.

He sighed for the border
because in his dreams
he fell in love with a blonde.

Cruzó valles y montañas
con sacrificios y mañas
siempre continuó.

He crossed valleys and mountains.
With sacrifices and skill
he steadfastly continued.

Era un gran macho mexicano
Era un gran macho si señor
nunca se le cayó la mano
puede que sí, que no,
que sí, que no,
era Pérez de la O.

He was a great Mexican macho,
he was a great macho, yes sir;
he never was limp-wristed,
well, maybe yes, maybe no,
maybe yes, maybe no,
he was Pérez de la O.

*Hablado:*

¡Vamos Pérez!

*Spoken:*

Let's go Pérez!

*Cantado:*

Comentaba con un huerco
para mí el Río Bravo es charco
fácil de brincar.
Como era aventado y terco
arrepíntose de barco
y logró cruzar.

*Sung:*

He commented to a kid:
"To me the Rio Grande is a puddle,
Easy to jump."
Since he was daring and stubborn
he took a ship
and managed to cross.

Le gustaba mucho Texes
porque habían muchas viejas
cosas que observar.
Se salió bien con las suyas
y al llegar hasta Falfurrias
no paró.

He liked Texas very much
because there were many women there,
things to observe;
he got his own way
and when he arrived at Falfurrias
he didn't stop.

Era un gran macho mexicano, etc.

He was a great Mexican macho, etc.

Para no contar con malas
no quería pasar a Dallas
pero al fin pasó
y al llegar a San Antonio
esa migra del demonio
lo pescó.

Since he did not want bad luck
he did not want to pass by Dallas,
but in the end he did
and upon arriving in San Antonio
that devil of the immigration
caught him.

Era un gran macho mexicano, etc.

He was a great Mexican macho, etc.

In "La boda fatal," by Paco Camacho, deception and death run hand in hand, with tragic results. The immigrant narrates his sad tale of betrothal and betrayal.

## La boda fatal

Una tarde nublada de marzo
para el Norte me fui de bracero,
a mi novia dejé ya pedida,
porque me iba a casar en enero
y por eso me fui de mi tierra
a buscar el famoso dinero.
Mi viejita, mi madre querida,
me abrazaba y llorando me dijo:
—Vuelve pronto, hijito de mi alma

tú bien sabes que te necesito,

esa novia que dejas pedida
no merece de tí el sacrificio.

Ocho meses duré por el Norte
trabajando con mucho entusiasmo,
la ilusión que llevaba en el alma:
que mi novia me estaba esperando
con el pecho y los brazos abiertos,
pa' llevarla a la iglesia de blanco.

Al llegar a mi pueblo querido
las campanas oí repicando
y la gente pasaba de prisa,
pregunté lo que estaba pasando,
me dijeron con mucha malicia:
—Es tu novia que se está casando.

Paso a paso llegué hasta la iglesia
conteniendo mi furia inaudita
y en presencia del cura y la gente

los maté cuando estaban en misa
y lloré come lloran los hombres
cuando queda su vida marchita.

Aquí estoy encerrado entre rejas,
sollozando por mi viejecita,

## The Fatal Wedding

On a cloudy March afternoon
I left to go north as a bracero.
My fiancée I left behind
I was to marry her in January.
And that is why I left my homeland
In search of almighty money.
My dear old beloved mother
While hugging me and crying did say:
"Please come back soon, my beloved
    son.
You know very well how much I need
    you.
That girlfriend you are engaged to
Is just not worth this sacrifice."

Eight months I did stay in the North
Working well with great enthusiasm.
The dream I did have in my soul
Was my fiancée waiting for me
With open arms and an open heart
Ready to be taken to the church dres-
    sed in white.

Upon arriving in my dear town,
I did hear the church bells pealing,
And people passed by hurriedly.
I asked what was going on.
And they answered with great malice:
"It's your girlfriend who is getting
    married."
Step by step I arrived at the church,
Repressing my audacious fury.
And in the presence of the priest and
    the people
I killed them while they were at mass.
And I cried like only a man can cry
When his life has withered away.

Here I am imprisoned behind bars
Sobbing for my dear old mother.

| | |
|---|---|
| que andará ya pidiendo limosna | She must be begging alms |
| por las calles muy triste y solita, | On the streets very sad and alone |
| y rezando porque ya termine | And praying for my prison term |
| mi condena en la carcel maldita. | To end from this cursed jail. |

(Vélez 1982:65–66)

Again this is another tragic aspect of the immigrant experience. Many men upon returning to sweetheart or wife find the nest empty, their women having found someone new to replace them, as in this song by Salomón Valenzuela Torres.

## El mojado fracasado

## The Wetback Who Failed

*Cantado:*

Una mañana
de mi casita
yo me alejé.
Dejé a mis padres
dejé a mis hijos,
también mi esposa,
todo dejé.

Me fui pa'l Norte
con la esperanza
de hacer fortuna
luego volver.

Pero mis planes,
todos fallaron;
pues me agarraron
los de la ley.

Cuando volví
mi jacalito
solo encontré
mis viejecitos
habían muerto
y con otro hombre
hallé a mi mujer.

*Sung:*

One morning
My little house
I left.
I left my parents,
I left my children,
And also my wife.
I left everything.

I went up north
With the hope
To make a fortune
And then return.

But my plans
All failed
Because the law
Caught me.

When I returned
My little hut
Was all alone,
My poor parents
Had died,
And with another man
I found my wife.

*Hablado:*

Cinco años me tuvieron preso
por haberme pasado de mojado.
Tiempo que ha bastado

*Spoken:*

Five years I was imprisoned
Because I crossed illegally;
Time enough for me to

| para perder a mis padres, | Lose my parents, |
|---|---|
| hijos y a mi esposa. | My children, and my wife, |
| Para que hoy me llamen | So that today they call me |
| "El mojado fracasado." | "The Wetback Who Failed." |

| *Cantado:* | *Sung:* |
|---|---|
| Quise matarme | I wanted to kill myself |
| al ver que solo | Upon seeing how alone |
| yo me quedé. | I was left; |
| pero matarme | But to kill myself |
| es ser cobarde | Is to be a coward |
| como los hombres | And like a man |
| me resigné. | I resigned myself. |
| Dios mío, ¿por qué? | My God, why? |
| ¿por qué has deshecho | Why have you destroyed |
| mi porvenir? | My future? |

| Si soy tu hijo | If I am your son |
|---|---|
| igual que todos | Just like everyone else |
| ¿por qué permites | Why do you permit |
| sufra yo así? | That I suffer so? |

The ballad "De aquellas idas al Norte" (Dagoberto Castillo) reiterates the theme of the brokenhearted bracero.

| **De aquellas idas al Norte** | **Those Trips to the North** |
|---|---|
| De aquellas idas al Norte, | Those trips to the North |
| no me quisiera acordar; | I do not want to remember, |
| todos los días con sus noches, | Every day and every night |
| todo se me iba en pensar. | I just kept thinking about them. |

| Hasta que un día en la mañana, | Until one morning |
|---|---|
| pa' la frontera salí; | I left for the border |
| en un camión a Chihuahua, | In a bus to Chihuahua, |
| ¡hay desgraciado de mí! | Oh, poor wretched me! |

| De México a ciudad Juárez, | From Mexico to Juárez, |
|---|---|
| de ciudad Juárez a El Paso; | From Juárez to El Paso |
| porque yo tenía pensado, | Because I had planned |
| tomar el vuelo a Chicago. | To take a flight to Chicago. |

| Antes de lograr mi intento, | Before reaching my goal |
|---|---|
| me agarró emigración; | The immigration caught me; |
| me esposaron al momento, | They handcuffed me on the spot |
| pa' llevarme al corralón. | And took me to the detention camp. |

| | |
|---|---|
| Del corralón al condado, | From the detention camp to the county |
| me llevaron a encerrar; | They took me to lock me up; |
| cargadito de cadenas, | I was all chained |
| como a cualquier criminal. | Like a common criminal. |
| | |
| El juez dictó mi sentencia | The judge read my sentence |
| sin ninguna dilación: | Without delay; |
| para pasar sin clemencia, | I was sentenced without clemency |
| tres años en la prisión. | To three years in jail. |
| | |
| Los gritos de prisioneros, | The screams of the prisoners |
| no me dejaban dormir: | Kept me awake |
| y yo tirado en el suelo, | And there I was on the floor, |
| mejor deseaba morir. | I wanted to be dead. |
| | |
| Cuando regresé a mi pueblo, | When I returned to my village |
| con que tristeza y dolor; | With sadness and pain, |
| encontré mi hogar deshecho, | I found my home all broken up |
| sin dignidad y sin honor. | Without dignity or honor. |
| | |
| Mis padres ya se habían muerto, | My parents had died, |
| mi mujer me abandonó; | My wife had abandoned me; |
| cuando yo me hallaba preso, | When I was in jail |
| con otro me traicionó. | With another man she betrayed me. |
| | |
| Pobres de los Mexicanos | Those poor Mexicans |
| que agarra la emigración; | That the immigration catches, |
| en manos de esos Texanos, | At the hands of those Texans |
| sufren sin comparación. | They suffer very much. |
| | |
| De aquellas idas al Norte, | Those trips to the North |
| no me quisiera acordar; | I do not want to remember, |
| todos los días con sus noches | Every day and every night |
| solo se me iba en pensar. | I just kept thinking about them. |

The song "De sangre mexicana" (Francisco Trujillo) describes a relationship between a Mexican-American man and a Mexican woman. The Chicano in this instance portrays himself as a Don Juan who has multiracial lovers although his preference is for a Mexican immigrant woman.

| **De sangre mexicana** | **Of Mexican Descent** |
|---|---|
| He nacido en California | I was born in California |
| territorio norteamericano | North American territory |
| y aunque nací entre los gringos | And even though I was born among gringos |
| soy moreno como el mexicano. | I am dark like a Mexican. |

| | |
|---|---|
| Las gabachas me apodan El Pocho | The Anglo women call me "The Pocho" |
| y las *parnas** me dicen chicano | And the black women call me "Chicano." |
| yo con todas mi amor lo derrocho | I give them all my love |
| pero a nadie le pido su mano. | But I don't ask any of them to marry me. |
| | |
| San José, mi Fresno, Sacramento | San Jose, my Fresno, Sacramento |
| los condados donde yo fui criado | Are the counties where I was raised, |
| Los Angeles ya ni les cuento | And Los Angeles, I don't even have to tell you, |
| y en San Francisco allí fuí bautizado. | In San Francisco, I was baptized there. |
| | |
| Quise mucho a una mexicana | I fell in love with a Mexican woman. |
| que un domingo conocí en Chicago | Whom I met on a Sunday in Chicago |
| ella dijo que era Michoacana | She told me she was from Michoacán |
| de un pueblito llamado Santiago. | From a small town called Santiago. |
| | |
| Es por eso que la ando buscando | That is why I am searching for her |
| si es posible rastrearé su huella | If possible I'll track her down |
| La soñé que vivía en San Fernando | I dreamt she lived in San Fernando |
| La he de hallar pa' casarme con ella. | I shall find her and marry her. |
| Mexicano yo soy por mis padres | I am Mexican because of my parents |
| y orgulloso le canto a la vida | And very proud I do sing of life |
| por mis venas me corre la sangre | Through my veins Mexican blood does flow |
| mexicana como el buen tequila. | As Mexican as good tequila. |

*parnas = black people; probably Spanish pronounciation of "partner"

The "Latin lover" type is again depicted in "Rumbo al Norte" (J. Enciso and A. Gastelum).

| **Rumbo al Norte** | **I Am Northward Bound** |
|---|---|
| Voy rumbo al norte | I am northward bound |
| a San José | To San Jose |
| a ver amores | To see the loves |
| que allá dejé | That I left there. |
| dejé mi vida | I left my life, |
| mi corazón | My heart, |
| muchos recuerdos | Many memories |
| y mi ilusión. | And dreams. |

| | |
|---|---|
| A San Mateo | To San Mateo |
| volver deseo | I wish to return. |
| recuerdos gratos | Pleasant memories |
| los que viví | Lived there |
| hermosas hembras | Beautiful women |
| claro que sí | Oh yes siree! |
| las quiero a todas | I love them all. |
| nomás pa' mí. | All are for me. |
| | |
| En San Francisco | In San Francisco |
| yo me encontré | I found |
| a una morena | A brunette girl |
| que yo adoré | That I adored. |
| la quise tanto | I loved her dearly. |
| recuerdo aquel | I remember how |
| dejé una güera | I left a blondie |
| en San Rafael. | In San Rafael. |
| | |
| En Santa Rosa | In Santa Rosa |
| yo me encontré | I found |
| a una trigueña | A brown-skinned woman |
| que siempre amé. | I always did love. |
| Si ella me quiso | If she loved me |
| nunca sabré. | I'll never know. |
| Yo por sus besos | But for her kisses |
| lloré y lloré. | I cried and cried. |
| | |
| A Sacramento | To Sacramento |
| también llegué | I also went. |
| a mi Rosita | And little Rosa |
| besé y besé. | I kissed and kissed. |
| Ella me quiso | She really loved me |
| con devoción | With much devotion, |
| fue realidad | I tell you truly |
| esta canción. | In this my song. |
| | |
| Por Colorado | Through Colorado |
| yo pasaré | I will pass. |
| iré hasta Texas | I head for Texas |
| a basilar. | To have some fun. |
| A Kansas City | To Kansas City, |
| luego a Ilinoi | Then to Illinois, |
| y a saludarlos | And just to say hello |
| iré a Detroit. | I'll go to Detroit. |

The "love at every port" theme is broached in "Amor norteño," by Rafael Buendía.

## Amor norteño

Bonita la primavera
cuando hay amor y dinero,
lo que yo siento en mi tierra
lo digo en el extranjero,
para mi amor no hay fronteras,
lo doy en el mundo entero.

De México salgo al Norte
con destino a la frontera,
yo no cargo pasaporte,
tampoco traigo chequera,
pero me sobra transporte
para pasear cualquier güera.

Morelos, Ciudad del Mante,
Limón y Ciudad Victoria,
Hidalgo con Villa Grande
me dieron amor y gloria,
Linares, Montemorelos,
yo los guardo en mi memoria.

En Allende y Monterrey
conocí un amor sincero,
pero en Sabinas Hidalgo
le conseguí su relevo,
se me quedó en San Antonio
y agarré barco en Laredo.

Amores en Ciudad Lerdo,
Torreón y Parras, Coahuila,
por Saltillo y Cadereyta
sin olvidar Villa China,
en Reynosa, Tamaulipas,
tengo un amor *gachupina*.*

Bonitas en Ciudad Juárez,
en Chihuahua a todo dar,
las Delicias y Camargo
y Jiménez del Parral;
si aguantan las de Durango
en Zacatecas ni hablar.

(Vélez 1982:86)

*gachupina = derogatory word for Spaniard

## Northern Love

Springtime is beautiful
When you have love and money.
The feelings I have in my homeland
I'll repeat them in foreign lands.
For my love there are no borders
I give it freely all over the world.

From Mexico I am going up north
My destination is the borderlands
I don't have a passport
And I don't have a checkbook
But I have enough fare money
To ride with any blondie.

Morelos, Ciudad del Mante,
Limón, and Ciudad Victoria,
Hidalgo and Villa Grande
Gave me love and glory.
Linares, Montemorelos,
I do keep you in my memory.

In Allende and Monterrey
I met a sincere lover
But in Sabinas Hidalgo
I met her replacement.
She stayed in San Antonio
And I met someone new in Laredo.

Many loves in Ciudad Lerdo,
Torreón and Parras, Coahuila,
By Saltillo and Cadereyta
Without forgetting Villa China
In Reynosa, Tamaulipas,
I have a Spanish sweetheart.

Beautiful girls in Ciudad Juárez
And really great ones in Chihuahua,
In Delicias and Camargo
And Jiménez del Parral;
Those from Durango can take it
And in Zacatecas, needless to say.

Female lettuce workers with
faces covered (*caritas tapadas*)
to avoid dust and insecticide.
Photo courtesy of Herlinda
Cancino.

At times the male immigrant farm worker expresses genuine admiration
for female immigrant workers. The song "La carita tapada" (Oscar Curiel
Aladaiz) is an example.

### La carita tapada

De Tejas a California
por las fronteras del Norte
existen ciertas mujeres
que cuentan con pasaporte.

Con sus caritas tapadas
y sus mochilas de "lonche"

### Covered Face

From Texas to California
On the northern borderlands
Live certain women
Who have passports.

With their little faces covered
And their lunch sacks,

| | |
|---|---|
| se pasan de madrugada | They cross at daybreak |
| a sus labores del Norte. | To their jobs in the North. |
| | |
| Se distinguen estas damas | These women distinguish themselves |
| con su grande corazón | Because of their great heart. |
| al igual que cualquier hombre | Just like any man |
| trabajan de sol a sol. | They work from sun up to sun down. |
| | |
| No le tienen miedo al frío | They are not afraid of the cold |
| ni tampoco a la calor, | Nor are they afraid of hot weather. |
| son mujeres de trabajo | They are working women |
| cumpliendo su obligación. | Fulfilling their obligation. |
| | |
| Desahijan melón y limpian | They weed and clear melons |
| y también el coliflor. | And also cauliflower. |
| El limón y la lechuga | Lemon and lettuce |
| lo dan al mismo sol. | Grow under the same sun. |
| | |
| En el "fil" o los empaques | In the fields or packinghouses |
| son obreras de valor. | They are hardworking laborers. |
| No conocen el rajarse | They do not give up |
| porque mexicanas son. | Because they are Mexican women. |
| | |
| La fuerza de los obreros | The labor of the workingman |
| se completa con honor | Is done with honor, |
| con las caritas tapadas | Together with the "little covered faces" |
| que también sueltan sudor. | Who also perspire. |
| | |
| Gastan bien estas mujeres | They spend well, these women, |
| y también alegres son, | And they are cheerful, too. |
| en sus cases son pilares | In their homes they are pillars |
| pues también traen pantalón. | For they wear the pants, too. |

Immigrant love songs generally portray an aggressive young man in search of fortune and happiness. The immigrant invariably leaves his country on an optimistic note. At times reality overwhelms him and he returns a broken, bitter man. The women in such songs frequently appear in a passive mode, as waiting sweethearts or wives, although in some songs the wife tires of the waiting game and leaves the bracero for another man. The songs included in this chapter present the immigrant from a different angle: involved in a love relationship. These songs humanize braceros and provide a better light in which we can appreciate these workers as multidimensional individuals instead of unidimensional stereotypes.

# Acculturation and Assimilation

*Twelve*  For Mexican immigrants one of the greatest fears is cultural loss. Their intense love for their homeland creates a tremendous psychological pressure to be loyal to their culture, language, traditions, and customs. The journey to the United States is viewed as a transitory state of affairs, not as final. The goal of many Mexican immigrants is to travel to the United States, work hard, and save enough money to return to Mexico and lead an economically better life thereafter. As immigrants leave their home-towns and familiar surroundings, however, they are bombarded with new experiences and modes of living. As they enter the United States the dif-ferences between what they grew up with and cherished and what they have traded it for become even more accentuated. Great fear develops within the immigrants' psyche over loss of identity—of self. The fear of transforming themselves into an unknown factor creates great anxiety. This stress produces a reaction which seeks to reject the new and cling to what was familiar. Most immigrants therefore become critical of those who desire a change and are eager to assimilate themselves into their new environment. Peer pressure is exerted on all Mexicans and Chicanos to be loyal to race, language, and customs.

In this chapter I explore how the Mexican immigrant through the medium of song criticizes those Mexicans who evince a propensity for adopting their new country's culture and become Americanized or, using the pejorative term, become *agringados*. First I look at songs dealing with women, then at songs dealing with men, and finally at recent songs that speak about children.

### Acculturation of Mexicanas

Three stanzas from the corrido "Los paños colorados" ("Red Bandannas," Gamio 1971:89) vividly portray in a humorous vein the acculturation of Mexicanas and Chicanas:

| Los paños colorados | Red bandannas |
| Los tengo aborrecidos | I detest, |
| y ahora las pelonas | And now the flappers |
| los usan de vestidos. | Use them for their dress. |
| | |
| Las muchachas de S. Antonio | The girls of San Antonio |
| son flojas pa'l metate | Are lazy at the metate; |
| quieren andar pelonas | They want to go bobbed, |
| con sombreros de petate. | With straw hats on. |
| | |
| Se acabaron las pizcas, | The harvesting is finished, |
| se acabó el algodón | So is the cotton. |
| Ya andan las pelonas | The flappers stroll out now |
| de puro vacilón. | For a good time. |

This process is viewed in a negative light by their male counterparts, the Mexican and Chicano. Manuel Gamio, author of one of the first studies done on Mexican immigrants and their experiences in the United States, collected "Los paños colorados" in the 1920s. He makes this assertion regarding this sensitive point: "Perhaps no subject arouses the distaste and even disgust of the immigrant as the free-and-easy conduct of the Americanized Mexican girl, contrasting as it does with the traditional restraint upon the Spanish-American woman" (1971:89).

Corridos depicting the acculturation of Mexican-American women date back to the early conflict between the Texas Mexican and the Anglo Texan in the eighteenth century. In *A Texas-Mexican Cancionero: Folksongs of the Lower Border* (1976:xvii), Paredes writes: "The Anglos who came down to us as conquerors saw us as abysmal savages—benighted by papistry (priest-ridden, as that great Texas liberal, J. Frank Dobie, used to say) and debased by miscegenation (with ditchwater instead of blood in our veins, as another great Texas liberal and scholar, Walter Prescott Webb, once put it)." With this type of attitude on the part of the Anglo, it was inevitable that aversion to Anglo-American culture and hostility to those seeking to adopt it (the agringados) should develop in the fiercely proud Texas Mexican.

It is interesting to note, however, that the supposedly passive, retiring Mexican female, who is presented in social science literature as a stay-at-home not daring to peek out of her cloistered life, seeks acculturation even at the risk of strong censorship from her peers, as evidenced in the songs. The folk songs offer a perspective totally different from the sociologist's. In the songs it is the women who are becoming acculturated to the dominant culture or seeking acculturation and the men who seek to exert social control and pressure to conform on these "recalcitrant" women. This is not to suggest that the ballads never criticize the acculturated male. These songs are very democratic in that respect; they zero in on young and old, rich and poor, and of course male and female. Several corridos, such as "El renegado" (Gamio 1971:93–94; discussed in chapter 4) and "Los deportados" (Taylor 1969), are critical of male acculturation, as I will illustrate in the next section of this chapter.

Songs with female acculturation themes collected from the late nineteenth and early twentieth centuries concentrated their criticism on the language factor and the supposed superior role of Mexican-American women in marital affairs—or, as Paredes (1976:154) asserts, "the permissiveness of Anglo husbands." The folk song "Desde México he venido" is a fine example of this attitude, as these stanzas reveal (ibid.:162–163):.

| | |
|---|---|
| Desde México he venido | From Mexico have I come |
| nomás por venir a ver | Just to come and see, |
| esa ley americana | This American law |
| que aquí manda la mujer. | That says the woman is boss. |
| | |
| En México no se ha visto, | This is never seen in Mexico |
| ni en la frontera del Norte | Nor on the northern border, |
| que intimiden a los hombres | That men should be intimidated |
| llevándolos a la corte. | By taking them to court. |

This subject is reiterated in this stanza from "Las pollas de California" (Guerrero 1924b):

| | |
|---|---|
| Bonito California | Pretty California |
| donde gocé de placeres | Where I enjoyed many pleasures |
| lo que no me gustó a mí | What I did not like |
| que allí mandan las mujeres. | Is that the women rule there. |

And in "Los mexicanos que hablan inglés" (Paredes 1976:163–164) the language theme is highlighted:

| | |
|---|---|
| En Texas es terrible | In Texas it is terrible |
| por la revoltura que hay, | How things are all mixed up: |
| no hay quien diga hasta mañana, | No one says hasta mañana |
| nomás puro goodbye. | It's nothing but good-bye. |

I could find only one of the older folk songs dealing with the subject of acculturation that appears not to be highly critical of Mexican-American women who speak English: "Mucho me gusta mi novia" (ibid.:156).

| | |
|---|---|
| Y mucho me gusta mi novia | And I like my sweetheart very much |
| me gusta nomás porque me habla in-glés | I like her 'cause she speaks English to me. |
| anoche le preguntaba | Last night I asked her |
| y me dice, Yes. | And she says, "Yes." |

Beneath the light banter, however, there is a critical tone that may pass undetected by those outside the culture but is readily recognized by Chicanos.

These early satirical corridos found in south Texas bear a close resemblance in content to a more virulent type of song popular in Mexico, generally known as the *bola*, which surfaced in the early part of the twentieth century. The Mexican corrido scholar Celedonio Martínez defined the bola as "a long corrido which generally encompasses thirty to seventy strophes or verses" (Colín 1952:79). The bola is one of the oldest forms of the corrido and is perceived by Martínez as a transitional form between the romance and the modern corrido. It was highly developed and widely used in the southern part of Mexico, particularly around Guerrero and Morelos (states claiming to be the birthplace of the bola). Thus the songs are commonly known as *bolas surianas* (often shortened to bolas). This term frequently appears in the title ("La bola de las viudas"), the first verse ("Por ahí va la bola muchachos / de gusto y de buena gana"), or the last verse (78–79):

| | |
|---|---|
| Aquí terminó la bola | Here the bola ends |
| que con placer he cantado, | I have sung it with pleasure. |
| ustedes dispensarán | You will have to forgive |
| mi saber tan limitado. | My limited knowledge. |

Bolas frequently concentrate on the acculturation or urbanization of lower-class women. Points of acculturation most odious to the Mexican male as expressed in these songs are the fashionable short dress, the equally fashionable short hair, high-heeled shoes, makeup, poor housekeeping, interest in dancing and drinking, unfaithfulness, and in general the more fashionable and liberated Mexican woman. "Rejuego de las pelonas" is a good example.

| Rejuego de las pelonas | A Playful Flapper's Song |
|---|---|
| Cuanta pelona se ve | How many bobbed women there are |
| en todo México entero | All over Mexico, |
| con cabeza de plumero | With feathered heads! |
| ahora se las retraté. | I took a picture of them. |
| | |
| A muchos les causa risa | Many find it funny |
| ver flacas y gordiflonas | To see skinny and fat ones, |
| blancas y prietas, pelonas; | Fair and dark-skinned, bobbed, |
| | |
| aunque hay muchas sin camisa | Even though many are shirtless |
| y se las ve la panza eriza | And one can see their stomach |
| como un sapo o camaleón | Like a toad or chameleon; |
| pero andan de vacilón | But they are all having fun, |

| | |
|---|---|
| dando a todos malos ratos | Giving everyone a hard time; |
| y algunas usan zapatos | Some of them use shoes |
| de los que cuestan tostón. | The kind that cost fifty cents. |

(Guerrero 1924a)

In stanzas from "Las pelonas vaciladores" ("The Fun-Loving Flappers," also from Guerrero 1924a), we hear the same harangue:

| | |
|---|---|
| Estas viejas remalditas | These damned women |
| les gusta la imitación | Like to imitate; |
| por eso andan peloncitas | That's why they are bobbed |
| con su vestido zancón. | And wear short skirts. |
| | |
| Vergüenza habían de tener | They should be ashamed, |
| esas viejas asquerosas | Those disgusting women; |
| que parecen chuparrosas | They look like hummingbirds. |
| que no las puedo ni ver. | I cannot stand them. |

One bola focuses on the neglect of *las buenas costumbres* (proper behavior) and yearns for the good old days when women behaved like women. The author concludes that this evil comportment on the part of women has brought on the wrath of God.

| Las muchachas que hay en la actualidad | Modern-Day Girls |
|---|---|
| Qué capaz que a las muchachas | Today's young women |
| les preocupe hacer el quehacer, | Do not think about housework; |
| andando ellas bien polveadas | They are all well-powdered |
| aunque no hagan de comer. | Even though they don't cook. |
| | |
| Quién se acuerda del metate, | Who remembers the metate, |
| de lavar o de planchar; | Washing dishes or ironing; |
| eso sería un disparate, | That would be unthinkable, |
| se trata hoy de vacilar. | All they want is to have fun. |
| | |
| Por eso Nuestro Señor | That is why Our Lord |
| tal vez nos manda el castigo | Has seen fit to punish us; |
| por causa de las mujeres | It's all the women's fault, |
| que se han subido el vestido. | Because they've shortened their dresses. |

(Guerrero 1924a)

In a corrido from the same era, we learn of the passing of a law that levied taxes on short-haired women in Chicago.

| Contribución a las pelonas | Tax on Bobbed Women |
|---|---|
| Atención pongan, señores, | Attention, gentlemen, |
| de lo que la prensa ha hablado | The press is full of news |
| en motivo de un decreto | Because of a law decreed |
| que en Chicago se ha implantado. | In the city of Chicago. |
| | |
| La mujer que esté pelona | All women with bobbed hair |
| pagará contribución | Will pay a tax, |
| Mexicana o extranjera | Mexican or foreigner |
| sin ninguna distinción | Without distinction. |

(Guerrero 1924a)

The bracero program initiated in the 1940s brought large numbers of Mexican men to the United States. These men viewed their compatriots, the Chicanos and particularly the Chicanas, with a jaundiced eye. Here were men and women who belonged to the same racial stock as they did but whose cultural values and mores were changing. The general tenor of the braceros' songs was more humorous than malicious. In "Natalio Reyes Colás," for example, we encounter a Chicana transforming her bracero boyfriend into "Nat King Cole." However, the pochita in this song proves too acculturated for Nat King Cole Martínez de la Garza (see chapter 6 for the complete text).

In a modern version of a very old corrido retitled "La nueva Zenaida" we hear:

| Hace tiempo que pasó la historia | This story took place some time ago |
|---|---|
| De la ingrata y coqueta Zenaida | When the ingrate and coquettish Zenaida |
| | |
| por un rato que se quedó sola | In just the short time she was alone |
| ya le dio por usar minifalda. | Decided to wear miniskirts. |

In the song "Al cruzar la frontera" (Eladio J. Velarde) a Mexican immigrant expresses his extreme disappointment with his girlfriend, who had a personality change when she crossed the border. The narrative depicts a jilted, heartbroken man who decided to return to Mexico to find peace and quiet and soothe his aching heart. The source of this particular immigrant's displeasure is his girlfriend's newly acquired habits: drinking, chewing gum, painting her fingernails, wearing short skirts, and wearing lipstick—in short, she has become an acculturated, citified woman.

### Al cruzar la frontera

Amigos míos, nomás vengo a decirles
la causa y el motivo de mi eterno dolor,
la vieja ingrata a quien yo amaba tanto
la odio para siempre y maldigo su amor.

De California me vine aquí a esta tierra,
buscando calma, buscando un nuevo amor,
vengo cansado y traigo enferma el alma
por tantas penas y de tanto dolor.

Por una ingrata morena presumida
que no sé como me entró en el corazón,
a causa de ella cambió toda mi vida
por sus palabras, mentiras de pasión.

Cuando pasamos unidos la frontera
a la fortuna nos fuimos a buscar,
ella era buena, mas como era ranchera
yo no pensaba que así me iba a pagar.

Mascaba chicle y se iba de parranda
y ya le olía la boca a puro ron,
mas como dicen que allá las viejas mandan
al poco tiempo por otro me cambió.

Al poco tiempo las uñas se pintaba,
a la rodilla la falda se subió,
a cada rato la boca se pintaba
y hasta un abrigo de chivas se compró.

Ya me despido de todos mis amigos,
ya me separo porque no soy de aquí
tengan cuidado con las mujeres falsas,
que no les pase lo que me pasó a mí.

(*Cancionero Mexicano* 1980:51).


## Upon Crossing the Border

My friends, I've only come to tell you
The cause and the reason for my eternal pain
That old woman whom I loved so much
I hate her forever and I damn her love.

From California I come to this land
Looking for calm, looking for a new love
I am tired and sick at heart
From all the sorrows and all the pain.

Because of an ingrate and proud brunette
Who without my knowing came into my heart
Because of her my whole life changed
Because of her words and her lies of passion.

When we crossed the border together
We went seeking our fortunes
She was good and being a country girl
I never thought she would betray me.

She would chew gum and go out drinking
And her mouth smelled of pure rum
And as they say, there (in the U.S.) the women are boss,
In a short time she traded me for another.

Soon she was painting her fingernails
And her skirt climbed up to her knees
And she was constantly painting her mouth
And she even bought herself a goatskin coat.

I bid farewell to all my friends
I leave you all 'cause I am not from here.
Be careful with all those false women
Don't let what I've been through happen to you.

The theme of drinking and the changing mores is reiterated in the song "Las pobres ilegales" (José Martínez Loza). Here, although the main thrust is to depict the suffering and ill treatment Mexican immigrant women are exposed to in the United States, the changed value system of these women is also brought to the listener's attention.

## Las pobres ilegales

*Cantado:*

Las pobres ilegales
que cruzan la frontera
solteras o casadas
mujeres de mi tierra

Se van ilusionadas

dejando sus cariños
buscando a sus maridos
llorando por sus niños.

Sufriendo humillaciones
algunas tienen suerte
pero otras son burladas
se encuentran con la muerte.

## Poor Illegal Immigrant Women

*Sung:*

Those poor illegal immigrant women
Who cross the border
Single women or married ones
Are all my countrywomen.

They leave their land with dreams

Leaving their loved ones behind
In search of their husbands
Crying for their children.

Suffering all kinds of humiliations
Some do have some luck
But others are deceived
They end up dead.

| | |
|---|---|
| Las que logran quedarse | Those who manage to stay |
| siempre andan espantadas | Are always afraid |
| le temen a la migra | They fear the border patrol |
| están desamparadas. | They don't have any protection at all. |
| | |
| Malditos los granjeros | Those damn farm growers |
| que abusan de mujeres | Who exploit women |
| si no es que las denuncían | If they don't turn them in |
| les pagan lo que quieren. | They pay them what they please. |
| | |
| Las vemos en la pizca | We see them picking cotton |
| o allá en la canería | Or working in the canneries |
| soñando en el regreso | Dreaming about their coming home |
| perdida la alegría. | All their joy is gone. |

| | |
|---|---|
| *Hablado:* | *Spoken:* |
| | |
| A tí mujer solitaria | For you lonely women |
| a tí dedico mi canto | To you I dedicate my song |
| tú que sufres en silencio | You that suffer in silence |
| la pena y el desencanto | Your pain and disillusionment |
| la desilución y el hambre | Your hunger and your broken dreams |
| mujer pobre a tí te canto. | Poor women, I sing to you. |

| | |
|---|---|
| *Cantado:* | *Sung:* |
| | |
| Si acaso se casaron | If they happen to get married |
| tienen que trabajar | They have to work |
| paisanos vividores | High-living countrymen |
| las tienden a explotar. | Tend to exploit them. |
| | |
| Luego andan divorciadas | Then when they get divorced |
| tratando de olvidar | They try to forget |
| bailando en las cantinas | Dancing in the dance halls |
| bebiendo sin parar. | Drinking without end. |
| | |
| Las pobres ilegales | Those poor illegal immigrant women |
| cuando se acabrán | When will they cease to go |
| | |
| se fueron de su patria | They left their country |
| ya no regresarán. | They will never return. |

The song "La emigrada" (Francisco Hernández), on the other hand, bitterly and caustically charges a recently legalized Mexican woman with "putting on airs," with acting "uppity," now that she has obtained her green card.

## La emigrada

Ahora que estás emigrada
te crees muy Americana
a *naide** quieres hablarle
te sientes muy elevada
te crees porque *traís*** papeles

pero no sirven pa' nada.


Cuando vivías en tu pueblo
tenías muchas amistades
ahora no quieres ni hablarles

porque ellos son ilegales
no te acuerdas que pasabas
por entre los matorrales.


Andas volando muy alta
no te vayas a caer.
Crees que porque traís la mica

tienes el mundo a tus pies
el mundo da muchas vueltas
y algún día vas a caer.


Para tener buen trabajo
arreglaste emigración
sigues ganando lo mismo
y con drogas de a montón
Si quieres ir pa' tu rancho
no tienes ni pa'l camión.

*naide = *nadie* (nobody)
**trais = *traes* (you have)

## The Legal Immigrant Woman

Now that you've legalized your status
You think you're all American
You want to talk to no one
You feel you're superior
You're uppity 'cause you've got your
documents
But they're good for nothing.

When you lived in your hometown
You had a lot of friends
Now you don't even want to talk to
them
Because they're illegal aliens.
Now you don't remember how
You crossed over hiding in the bushes.

You're really flying high
Be careful you don't fall down.
You think just 'cause you have your
green card
You've got the world at your feet
The world turns and turns a lot
And one of these days you'll fall
down.

In order to get a good job
You became a legal immigrant
You keep earning the same amount
And you've got a lot of debts.
If you want to visit your village
You don't even have bus fare.


These folk songs offer two images of the principal members of the Mex-ican-American family: the male (most of these songs are written by males) who objects to the woman's behavior and attempts to impose his standards, mainly through criticism and ridicule, upon the Chicana and the Mexicana; and the aggressive and defiant woman. Historically speaking, it is a fact that both the Chicana and the Mexicana cut their hair, wore fashionably short dresses, went out dancing—and also worked out in the fields shoulder to shoulder with men. In this particular instance, women won the battle.

The songs present a very intimate view of the Mexicanos' and Chicanos' concern about the acculturation process of their women, be it in the role of wife, sweetheart, or daughter. Genuine fear regarding disruption of family life is evident in the songs: women are not staying home tending the fire, and men do not like it. But the songs also afford fresh insight into the role of the Mexicana and Chicana in the acculturation process. Many of these songs depict a forward-looking young woman eager to adopt new cultural ways of being and defying the mores and values of her culture. The Mexicano and Chicano are projected as policemen, enforcers of the old. The male image is that of a helpless (albeit angry) spectator who is being left behind the times.

The corrido "Muchachas modernas" exemplifies this state of affairs very succinctly.

| Muchachas modernas | Modern-Day Girls |
|---|---|
| Las muchachas que hay ahora<br>ya no les gusta el trabajo<br>se la pasan en la calle<br>nomás *pa'rriba\** y *pa'bajo.\*\** | Young women today<br>Do not like work any more<br>They are always on the street<br>Cruising up and down. |
| Las muchachas que hay ahora<br>no quieren hacer quehacer<br>pero nomás llega el novio<br>y ni quien las vuelva a ver. | Young women today<br>Do not want to do housework<br>As soon as the boyfriend comes<br>No one can find them. |
| Las muchachas que a la moda<br>se visten con pantalones<br>en su casa ya no ponen<br>ni un jarrito de frijoles. | The girls who follow fashion<br>Wear pants<br>And at home they don't cook<br>Not even a pot of beans. |
| Las muchachas que hay ahora<br>les gusta mucho ir al cine<br>casi ya no traen vestido<br>puro short con su bikini. | Young women today<br>Love to go to the movies<br>They almost don't wear dresses<br>Only shorts and bikinis. |
| Cuando cumplen quince años<br>el regalo quieren bueno<br>le dicen a sus papás<br>me comprás un carro nuevo. | When they are fifteen years old<br>They want an expensive gift<br>They tell their fathers,<br>"Buy me a new car." |
| Las mujeres que hay ahora<br>cuando están recién casadas<br>les dicen a sus maridos<br>me consigues una criada. | Young women today<br>When they are newly wed<br>They tell their husbands,<br>"Get me a servant." |

Ya con ésta me despido
porque no aguanto la risa
pobrecitos de los hombres
que ahora planchan sus camisas.

Now I take my leave
'Cause I am dying from laughter
Pity the poor men
Who now iron their own shirts.

*pa'rriba = *para arriba* (up)
**pa'bajo = *para abajo* (down)

## Acculturation of Mexicanos

As pointed out in chapter 4, the acculturation and assimilation of Mexican males into Anglo America was of great concern to the Mexican-American community. The Mexican culture was valued highly, and loss of some or all aspects of this culture was viewed as a great tragedy. And although women who were assimilating into the Anglo world were the principal targets of barbs and caustic criticism, the Mexican male did not escape unscathed. Still, the 1930s economic crisis and U.S. repatriation programs overode fears of Mexican assimilation into the Anglo community. It was not until the middle 1960s that the fear of cultural genocide reappeared in songs.

Some songs of the sixties, such as "Juan Mojao," by Eulalio González, humorously poke fun at the agringados.

### Juan Mojao

### John Wetback

*Cantado:*

*Sung:*

Y me fui de *mojao**
y a pura lumbre me sentaron.

I went as a wetback
And got grilled by the police.

*Cantado:*

*Sung:*

El monte agarró a Juan Pancho
evitando las veredas
pa' no dejar que sus huellas
le hicieran ellas volver sus pasos
pa' donde ya no quería estar.

Juan Pancho took the back trails
Avoiding the known paths
So as not to leave his footprints
Where he could follow them back
To places he didn't wish to be.

Llevaba Pancho entre ceja y ceja
Frontera Norte poder cruzar.
Su pobre jacal dejaba
y en cuanto más se alejaba
*pos*** menos quería mirarlo
no fuera hacer que el jacal
le viera sus intenciones de no volver
tampoco quiso que se supiera
que iba llorando sin contener.

Pancho had in his mind
To cross the border.
He left his hut
And as he left it
He didn't want to look back
He was afraid his hut
Could read his plans of never returning.
He did not want it known
That he was crying profusely.

| | |
|---|---|
| Al cruzar el Río Grande | Upon crossing the Rio Grande |
| al entrar en U.S.A. | Upon entering the USA, |
| se olvidó hasta de su nombre | He forgot even his name. |
| no Juan Pancho, no more Pancho | Not Juan Pancho, no more Pancho, |
| Johnny Frankie if its O.K. | Johnny Frankie, if it's O.K. |
| | |
| Ya no canta más corridos | He doesn't sing corridos anymore |
| pa' las güeras rock en rol | For the blondies, rock and roll, |
| pantalón de abajo ancho | Bell-bottom pants, |
| plataforma y gran tacón | Platform shoes, stacked heels, |
| *chus* de onda | Stylish shoes, |
| nice zapatos | Great shoes, |
| no hurachis anymore, | No sandals anymore, |
| anymore. | anymore. |
| | |
| *Hablado:* | *Spoken:* |
| | |
| Y de repente que se oye el grito | And suddenly the shout is heard: |
| —¡Ay viene la migra! | "Here comes the INS!" |
| Por papeles *traiba*\*\*\* | For documents he brought |
| mica falsa que | A false border-crossing card |
| un malvado le vendió | That an evil man sold him. |
| y a pies hasta South of the Border | And the INS forced him to walk |
| la migración lo llevó. | All they way south of the border. |
| | |
| Se acabaron *chus de* onda | His stylish shoes are gone |
| ni siquiera sus hurachis | Not even his sandals |
| para alivio de sus pies | Did he have for the comfort of his feet |
| sus pobres pies que quemaron | His poor tired feet that burned |
| una y otra y otra vez. | Over and over again. |

\*mojao = *mojado*
\*\*pos = *pues*
\*\*\*traiba = *traía*

## Acculturation of Mexican Children

In the 1980s concern for another group emerged: Mexican children. In "Jaula de Oro" an immigrant father expresses his chagrin at his status as an undocumented worker which makes him a virtual prisoner in the land of milk and honey. He further mourns the "loss" of his children, who now refuse to speak Spanish, do not identify themselves as Mexicans, and refuse to return to Mexico. A sense of deep sorrow at his "imprisonment" and loss of family pervade these lyrics.

| La jaula de oro | The Golden Cage |
|---|---|
| Aquí estoy establecido | I am established here now |
| en los Estados Unidos | In the United States. |
| diez años pasaron ya | Ten years have gone by |

en que crucé de mojado
papeles no he arreglado
sigo siendo un ilegal.

Tengo mi esposa y mis hijos
que los traje muy chicos
y se han olvidado ya
de mi México querido
del que yo nunca me olvido
y no puedo regresar.

De que me sirve el dinero
si estoy como prisionero
dentro de esta gran nación.
Cuando me acuerdo hasta lloro
que aunque la jaula sea de oro
no deja de ser prisión.

*Hablado:*

Padre: "Escúchame, hijo. ¿Te gustaría
que regresáramos a vivir a México?"
(Father: "Listen, son. Would you like for
us to return to Mexico and live there?")
Young Son: "What are you talking
about, dad? I don't wanna go back to
Mexico. No way, dad!"

*Cantado:*

Mis hijos no hablan conmigo
otro idioma han aprendido
y olvidado el español
Piensan como americanos
niegan que son mexicanos
aunque tengan mi color.

De mi trabajo a mi casa
yo no se lo que me pasa
que aunque soy hombre de hogar
casi no salgo a la calle
pues tengo miedo que me hallen
y me puedan deportar.

De que me sirve el dinero
si estoy como prisionero
dentro de esta gran nación.

Since I crossed as a wetback.
I have not gotten my papers
I am still an illegal alien.

I have here my wife and my children
Whom I brought here very young
And they have forgotten now
About my beloved Mexico
About which I never forget
And I cannot return.

What good is money to me
If I am like a prisoner
Inside this great nation.
When I remember this I weep
For even though the cage is golden
It is still a prison.

*Sung:*

My kids don't talk to me
They've learned another language
And they've forgotten their Spanish.
They think like Americans do
They deny they are Mexicans
Even though they have my skin color-
ing.

From my work to my house
I don't know what's become of me
For though I am a family man
I hardly go out on the street
Because I am afraid they'll find me
And that they will deport me.

What good is money to me
If I am like a prisoner
Inside this great nation.

Cuando me acuerdo hasta lloro
que aunque la jaula sea de oro
no deja de ser prisión.

When I remember this I weep
For even though the cage is golden
It is still a prison.

The theme of second-generation acculturation and inability of father and son to communicate due to language loss is reiterated in other recent immigrant corridos, such as "El deportado," by Aciano Acuña.

## El deportado                           The Deported One

*Spoken:*

"Hello, who is this?"
"Soy yo hijo."
"Hey, Dad, where you calling from?"
"De México."
"I miss you, Dad. When you coming home?"

"Hello, who is this?"
"It's me son."
"Hey, Dad, where you calling from?"
"From México."
"I miss you, Dad. When you coming home?"

*Sung:*

Yo también soy deportado
aunque ya estaba casado
no me quisieron dejar.
Dejé mi esposa y mis hijos
quisiera volver con ellos
pero no puedo curzar.

I am also a deported one
even though I was married
they did not want to let me stay.
I left my wife and my children
I want to return to them
But I cannot cross (the border).

Ayer hablé con mi hijo
y él con tristeza me dijo
¿Cuándo vas a regresar?
Mi hijo no habla el español
Muy apenas me entendió
que no me dejan cruzar.

Yesterday I spoke to my son
And he with sadness asked me,
"When are you coming back?"
My son does not speak Spanish
He barely understood
That I am not allowed to cross.

Cuantos hijos como el mío
se han quedado abandonados
sin mirar a su papá.
Yo todo los días me acuerdo
el mío se ha quedado solo
nada más con su mamá.

How many sons like mine
Have been left abandoned
Without seeing their fathers.
I remember everyday
How mine was left alone
With his mother.

Yo le pido a Dios del cielo
que lo cuide y que lo ayude
también a su madre igual.
Estoy sufriendo por ellos
es terrible lo que siento
me dan ganas de llorar.

I ask God above
To take care of him and help him
And also his mother.
I am suffering because of them
It is terrible what I feel
I feel like crying.

Adios mi esposa querida
a los Estados Unidos
ya no podré regresar.
Ya cuando mi hijo sea grande
Dile que venga a buscarme
si es que me quiere en verdad.

Good-bye, my beloved wife
To the United States
I will not be able to return.
When my son has grown up
Tell him to come and look for me
If he truly loves me.

In this song the ex-immigrant decries the injustice of family separation and the fact that he is losing his children to another culture. Similar concerns are expressed in "El emigrante."

## El emigrante

No porque estoy emigrado
de mi nación me he olvidado
como muchos ya lo han hecho
ya cuando están arreglados
y también a su familia
muchos ya la han olvidado.

A México yo le canto
con mucho gusto y afan
aunque yo esté de este lado
no importa que esté legal
de mi tierra no me olvido
siempre la iré a visitar.

Yo les digo a mis amigos
no olvidemos nuestra tierra
allá fue donde nacimos
no hay que avergonzarnos d'ella
y siempre que recordarla
porque es nuestra tierra bella.

A mis hijos yo les digo
porque ellos aquí han nacido
el inglés tienen que hablarlo
pero por ningún motivo
nuestro idioma el español
nunca lo echen al olvido.

No les miento lo que digo
ni lo digo por capricho
ni tampoco son habladas
yo sé muy bien lo que digo
de mi tierra no me olvido
ni la olvidaré lo juro.

## The Emigrant

Just because I have migrated
I have not forgotten my nation
As so many have done
When they acquire legal documents
And also their families
Many have already forgotten them.

I sing to Mexico
With great joy and eagerness
Even though I am on this other side
I don't care if I am a legal resident
I do not forget my land
I will always go visit it.

I tell my friends
Let us not forget our country
That is where we were born
Let us not be ashamed of it
And always keep it in mind
Because our country is beautiful.

I tell my sons
Because they have been born here
They have to speak English
But no matter what
Our Spanish language
They must never forget.

I do not lie to you
And I do not say this in jest
Or because I like to talk
I know what I am saying
I do not forget my country
Nor will I ever forget it.

In "El hijo olvidado" (Aciano Acuña) the twin concerns of disruption and rejection are clearly delineated.

## El hijo olvidado

Cuando mis padres partieron
con rumbo hacia l'otro lado
Llegaron a California
y otro nuevo hogar formaron
como yo era muy pequeño
en México me dejaron.

Dijeron que volverían
en unos dos o tres años
Pero ese tiempo pasó
y ellos nunca regresaron
allá tuvieron más hijos
de mi pronto se olvidaron.

Un día crucé la Frontera
ya tenía ganas de verlos
mis padres me recibieron
alegres y muy contentos
y al hablar con mis hermanos

fui rechazado por ellos.

Aunque no lo quieran creer
la misma sangre llevamos
pero se afrentan conmigo
porque yo soy un mojado
ellos nacieron aquí
se sienten americanos.

A México me regreso
muy triste y decepcionado
mis padres se quedarán

si un día quieren regresar
yo los estaré esperando.

## The Forgotten Son

When my parents left
Headed for the other side
They arrived in California
And formed a new home.
As I was a very young child
They left me in Mexico.

They said they would return
In two or three years
But that time passed by
And they never came back.
There they had more children
And soon forgot about me.

One day I crossed the border
I wanted to see them.
My parents received me
Joyful and full of happiness
But on speaking to my brothers and
    sisters
I was rejected by them.

Even though you may not believe it
We have the same blood
But they are ashamed of me
Because I am a wetback.
They were born here
They feel American.

I return to Mexico
Very sad and disillusioned.
My parents can remain there (in the
    U.S.)
If ever they want to return
I will be waiting for them.

Many Mexicans feel that Chicanos deny their roots, their "race," and do not want to be identified with Mexico. Of course, many Chicanos in fact feel that Mexico is a foreign country and feel no attachment to it. Some of them have been in the States all their lives. The U.S. school systems do an excellent job of socializing immigrant children into their new society, so it is no wonder that many Chicanos feel no attachment to Mexico. Still, this rejection causes deep pain, anger, and resentment on the part of many Mexican people.

The ballads and songs portray the process of acculturation and assimilation which the Mexican immigrants and their children experience. They are an excellent barometer measuring the feelings on both sides of the border regarding this immigrant experience.

# Death

Sierra Blanca, Texas. Eighteen suspected illegal aliens trapped in a locked, steel-walled boxcar were found dead in stifling 120-degree temperatures Thursday in what authorities called a botched smuggling effort.

*Los Angeles Times,* July 3, 1987

*Thirteen* The story was tragic. Nineteen young men between the ages of twenty and thirty from different parts of Mexico were locked in a foam-insulated, airtight boxcar in the railroad yards of El Paso, Texas, headed north. A spokesman for the U.S. Border Patrol said they apparently were making their way to the Dallas–Fort Worth area. Fate decreed the train was to be sidelined because of mechanical failure. The helpless men inside the boxcar were locked in, without water. Soon the temperature rose to 120–130 degrees. The victims died from the heat.

One man survived to tell the tragic tale. Miguel Tostado-Rodríguez, age twenty-one, recounted how he and two guides tried to pry a hole in the boxcar's floor in order to get some air inside. However, "People started dying little by little, little by little. . . . They started fighting with each other because they were desperate to breathe. They didn't have any water. So they started to get crazy and fight each other."

In spite of this tragedy, the very next day "eleven undocumented aliens were detained on the same Union Pacific freight route." Indeed, on the day the bodies of six young men who died in the boxcar arrived for burial in their hometown in the central state of Aguascalientes, other young men were boarding the train headed north. Commented the brother of one of the victims, "It was hunger that drove them from here" (*Los Angeles Times,* July 13, 1987). And another resident of their hometown summed it up: "Until there is something better to keep them here, people are going to continue raffling their lives."

The tragedy so ignited the imagination of the artistic world that a movie about it, *El vagón de la muerte* (The boxcar of death), was soon filmed, and a song depicting the tragedy of the dead men served as the epilogue. The plot in the movie was changed somewhat; instead of several men the movie has four men, a young boy, and a girl. The six characters are trapped in an airtight boxcar in a railroad yard on the border. As time passes they begin to fight with each other, and eventually three of the men are murdered; the young boy dies of untreated rabies, and the young girl loses her mind and kills the only surviving male. The film ends with the singing of the song "El vagón de la muerte," which narrates the actual event that transpired in July 1987.

## El vagón de la muerte

Fueron varios los braceros
los que encontraron la muerte
todos eran mexicanos
algunos de Aguascalientes
Guanajuato y Zacatecas
Lo dijo un sobreviviente.

Un miércoles abordaron
aquel vagón de la muerte
con la ilusión de ganarse
la vida honradamente
pero la vida perdieron
por culpa de un inconsciente.

El que cerrara la puerta
d'ese* vagón de la muerte
ya debe estar acechando
más víctimas inocentes
sin importarle la pena
que ocasionó a tanta gente.

Esos malditos polleros
no son más que delincuentes
por la ambición del dinero
matan a gente inocente
aprovenchando miseria
de los braceros valientes

Tejas se tiñe de sangre
México viste de luto
a las leyes extranjeras
no les importa el asunto
a ellos les da lo mismo
que sean muchos los difuntos.

Ese fatal accidente
cómo poder olvidarlo
lo dice el sobreviviente
y lo comenta llorando

## The Boxcar of Death

There were quite a few braceros
Who found death
All were Mexican
Some from Aguascalientes
Guanajuato and Zacatecas
That's what one survivor said.

On a Wednesday they boarded
That boxcar of death
With the hope of earning
In an honest way their livelihood
But they lost their lives
Because of an immoral person.

He who closed the door
On that boxcar of death
Must be enticing
More innocent victims
Without caring about grief
He caused so many people.

Those damned smugglers
Are nothing but criminals
Because of their greed for money
They murder innocent people
Taking advantage of the poverty
Of those valiant braceros.

Texas is covered with blood
Mexico is dressed in mourning
And the foreign laws
Do not care about the tragedy
To them it is all the same
That there are many dead.

That fatal accident
How can one forget it
The survivor intones
And he weeps as he tells the story

| | |
|---|---|
| porque miraba impotente | Because he watched helplessly |
| como morían sus paisanos. | As his countrymen died. |

| | |
|---|---|
| Ese primero de julio | That first day of July |
| nos deja cruel amargura | Leaves us a cruel memory |
| no volverán a su casa | The men will not return home |
| ya terminó su aventura | Their adventure has ended |
| sus ilusiones quedaron | Their dreams ended |
| en una fría sepultura. | In a cold grave. |

*d'ese = *de ese* (of that)

The route that leads to a better economic life at times leads to death. Immigrants crossing at any point on the 2,000-mile span dividing Mexico and the United States are cognizant that instead of dollars death may be their recompense. The dangerous border has therefore been conceptualized in metaphoric terms as a "tomb." The song "Yo soy mexicano señores," cited in chapter 8, points out how the border was "tumba de tantos hermanos." The song "La tumba del mojado" (Paulino Vargos) reiterates this metaphor.

| La tumba del mojado | The Wetback's Grave |
|---|---|
| No pude cruzar la raya | I couldn't cross the border |
| se me atravezó el Río Bravo | The Rio Grande got in my way |
| me aprehendieron malamente | They apprehended me wrongly |
| cuando vivía al orto lado | When I lived on the other side |
| los dólares son bonitos | The dollars are very pretty |
| pero yo soy mexicano. | But I am a Mexican. |

| | |
|---|---|
| No tenía tarjeta verde | I did not have a green card |
| cuando trabajé en Lusiana | When I worked in Louisiana |
| en un sotano viví | I lived in a basement |
| porque era espalda mojada | Because I was a wetback |
| tuve que inclinar la frente | I had to bow my head |
| para cobrar la semana. | In order to get my week's pay. |

| | |
|---|---|
| La rosa de Mexicali | The Mexicali rose |
| y la sangre en el Río Bravo | And the blood on the Rio Grande |
| son dos cosas diferentes | Are two different things |
| pero en color son hermanos | But their color makes them brothers |
| y la línea divisoria | And the dividing border line |
| es la tumba del mojado. | Is the wetback's grave. |

| | |
|---|---|
| La cerca de la tortilla | The tortilla curtain |
| es ofensa para el pueblo | Is an offense to the people |
| en México se pasean | In Mexico you see traveling |
| franceses, chinos y griegos | Frenchmen, Chinese, and Greeks |

y algunos americanos
son caciques en los pueblos.

And some Americans
In some towns they are bosses.

The song "Un noble engaño" (Nicolás Ochoa and Paul Sandoval) tells of the death of a fifteen-year-old boy who drowns as he attempts to swim the swollen Río Grande while his brother at his side helplessly watches in horror.

## Un noble engaño

*Cantado:*

Joaquín tenía quince años
Pedro tenía diez y seis
venían pa' Estados Unidos
Salieron de Monterrey
traían grandes ilusiones
de tanto que oían hablar
de llegar a Houston, Texas
y ponerse a trabajar.

A Joaquín se le hizo fácil
el Río Grande cruzar
pero el Río Grande iba lleno
y no lo pudo lograr.
Pedro lloraba el fracaso.
Casi perdió la razón
al ver a su hermano hogarse
en ese río traidor.

Un año cumple mi hermano
que el cielo lo recogió.
Mis pobres padres no saben
que a Houston jamás llegó
yo me hago pasar por él
cuando a mis padres escribo
no les digo la verdad
ellos piensan que está vivo.

*Hablado:*

Después de una larga ausencia
yo regreso dispuesto a contarles todo,
todo lo que
encierro aquí en mi pecho
mi pobre madre llorando me
abrazaba y me besaba
"¡Has vuelto al fin hijo mío!"

## A Noble Deception

*Sung:*

Joaquín was only fifteen
Pedro was sixteen
They were coming to the United States.
They left from Monterrey.
They had great dreams
From hearing so much talk.
They wanted to go to Houston, Texas,
And begin working there.

Joaquín thought it was easy
To cross the Rio Grande.
But the river was full
And he could not make it.
Pedro cried at the failure
He almost went insane
Upon seeing his brother drown
In that treacherous river.

It is one year since my brother
Was called back to heaven.
My poor parents don't know
He never reached Houston.
I assume my brother's name
When I write to my parents.
I don't tell them the truth.
They think he's still alive.

*Spoken:*

After a long absence
I returned ready to tell all,
All that is
Locked up in my heart.
My poor mother crying
Hugged and kissed me.
"You have returned at last, my son!"

| | |
|---|---|
| Y sus lágrimas rodaban. | And her tears did fall. |
| Y al preguntar por Joaquín, | And when she asked for Joaquín |
| una sonrisa fingí. | I forced myself to smile. |
| Tuve que seguir fingiendo | I had to continue to pretend |
| para no verla sufrir. | So as not to see her suffer |

| | |
|---|---|
| *Cantado:* | *Sung:* |
| Yo me hago pasar por él | I pretend I am him |
| cuando a mis padres escribo | When I write to my parents. |
| no les digo la verdad | I do not tell them the truth. |
| ellos piensan que está vivo. | They think he is still alive. |

Death may come from unexpected sources, as in Rafael Buendía's "El contrabando del muerto." The grisly story narrated in this song exposes the cruelty of drug dealers who kill an undocumented worker to fill his stomach with drugs.

## El contrabando del muerto

## The Dead Man's Contraband

| | |
|---|---|
| Qué poco vale la vida | How little life is worth |
| comparada con dinero, | Compared to hard cash! |
| mataron a un emigrante | They killed an immigrant man |
| que se pasó de bracero. | Who crossed over as a bracero. |

| | |
|---|---|
| Urdieron que era un soldado | Their plot had him as a soldier |
| que desertó de la guerra, | Who had deserted from the war. |
| luego le hicieron la autopsia | Then they had an autopsy done |
| para mandarlo a su tierra. | Before sending him home. |

| | |
|---|---|
| Lo cruzaron por la línea | They crossed him through the border |
| para darle sepultura, | In order to bury him. |
| le inventaron un velorio | They invented a wake for him |
| con familiares y viuda. | Even with relatives and a widow. |

| | |
|---|---|
| Dicen que a la medianoche | They say that at midnight |
| lo estaban desenterrando, | They were disinterring him |
| porque llevaba la panza | Because his belly |
| bien llena de contrabando. | Was full of contraband. |

| | |
|---|---|
| La banda de traficantes | The band of smugglers |
| pasó una cosa espantosa, | Were terribly shocked |
| ya no encontraron al muerto | Upon not finding the dead man |
| cuando escarbaron la fosa. | When they dug up the grave. |

| | |
|---|---|
| El diablo se lo robó | The devil stole his body |
| hay quienes dicen que es cierto, | Some ascertain this is true. |

todavía siguen buscando
el contrabando del muerto.

They are still searching
For the contraband of the dead man.

(Vélez 1982:67)

Other immigrants await death in a prison cell, as in "Lamento de un bracero," by Paco Camacho.

## Lamento de un bracero

## A Bracero's Lament

*Cantado:*

*Sung:*

Dentro de una celda oscura
está llorando un bracero
es un ranchero valiente
que lo hicieron prisionero.

Inside a dark cell
Lies a bracero crying.
He is a brave rancher
Who was taken prisoner.

Sentado frente a la reja
soportando el frío invierno
él ya se siente morir
pues se encuentra muy enfermo.

Seated in front of the cell bars,
Feeling the bitter cold,
He is near dying,
He is gravely ill.

Se oye que dice el bracero
—¡O virgencita morena
no quiero morir aquí
quiero morir en mi tierra!

One can hear the bracero saying:
"Oh, my dark virgin!
I do not want to die here.
I want to die in my country!"

*Hablado:*

*Spoken:*

¡Ay mis amigos, cuídense de
esa canija *migrechón!**

My friends, be careful of those
Sneaky immigration officers.

*Cantado:*

*Sung:*

Se acerca a la ventanilla
y contempla las estrellas
se acuerda de sus amigos
de su familia y su tierra.

He walks toward the window
And stares at the stars.
He remembers his friends
His family and his land.

Se oye que dice el bracero
—¡O virgencita morena
no quiero morir aquí
quiero morir en mi tierra!

One can hear the bracero saying:
"Oh my dark virgin!
I don't want to die here.
I want to die in my country!"

*migrechón = immigration

# Epilogue

The saga of the Mexican immigrant has not ended. It continues to develop across the American landscape. Mexican immigration to the United States goes on unabated in the 1990s in spite of the Immigration Reform and Control Act approved by Congress and signed into law by President Reagan in 1986. As immigration expert Wayne A. Cornelius, director of the Center for U.S.-Mexican Studies at the University of California, San Diego, reports,

> the 1986 Immigration Reform and Control Act is not deterring the arrival of new migrants from Mexico and Central America, according to evidence from both sides of the border. The UC San Diego Center for U.S.-Mexican Studies conducted a year of detailed field interviews in three Southern California counties, including 100 employers, more than 420 workers and 150 recently arrived undocumented immigrants. Meanwhile, Immigration and Naturalization Service apprehension statistics and systematic observation of illegal entrants by researchers at El Colegio de la Frontera Norte in Tijuana support our findings. (*Los Angeles Times*, July 3, 1988)

The 1986 immigration law, also referred to as the Simpson-Rodino law, was enacted in part to discourage Mexican immigration. Cornelius explains the reason for its failure:

> Those who delayed migration during 1987 are now coming, having observed that work is still available in the United States—even for new arrivals lacking papers. There have been no mass layoffs of undocumented workers by employers, and no mass roundups and deportations by the INS. These facts are now common knowledge in the communities from which migrants come. (Ibid.)

Enterprising Mexican immigrants have found various methods of circumventing the law. According to one provision, employers are required to ask for identification and legal residency documentation. However, a thriving business in fake documents has surfaced and immigrants can easily buy or even rent such documents. Others easily borrow proper documentation from friends or relatives.

Employer sanctions, it appears, have not been as effective as once thought, given that business establishments need only check for identification and legal documents; they do not need to actually verify their authenticity. Thus undocumented workers with fraudulent identification continue to obtain employment.

The travails and sufferings of the Mexican immigrant worker have not ceased, either. Some continue to die as they try to cross checkpoints in the border area. Other immigrants, though escaping with their lives, find physical hardships as affordable housing dwindles in affluent areas, such as Orange County in southern California, and they are unable to obtain lodgings with their meager earnings. The *Los Angeles Times* (September 23, 1988) reported the plight of two men who are representative of homeless immigrant workers.

> Cesario Bautista and his friend, Ampelio Bautista (no relation), awakened in Capistrano Beach Thursday morning on the cold ground of a wooded field inhabited by snakes, insects and coyotes.
>
> The Mexican immigrants had arrived in Capistrano Beach just two days earlier and managed to find jobs paying $4.25 an hour in a local ceramics factory. But since payday is not until Friday and they came here with only a few dollars to their names, the two men said they have had to sleep under the stars—within view of $250-a-night rooms at the Dana Point Resort. . . .
>
> The two men, both originally from Guadalajara, join anywhere from three dozen to 100 Latin American immigrants who sleep each night under bridges, in fields and even in drainage pipes surrounding the Capistrano Beach business district where they go to look for work each day.

In addition to the physical hardships, Mexican immigrants continue to be the target of racist jokes and jibes. Not long ago a radio station in San Diego aired a song written by disc jockey Randy Miller. Entitled "The Mexican National Anthem," it was sung to the tune of "She'll Be Coming 'Round the Mountain" (*Los Angeles Times*, July 3, 1986).

They'll be coming across the border when they come;
They'll be coming across the border when they come;
They'll be coming across the border, 'cause there is no law and order;
They'll be coming across the border when they come;
They'll be carrying drugs and handguns so they can have some real fun;
They'll be carrying drugs and handguns when they come;
They will not have a green card but they sure know how to run hard;
Well, they will not have a green card when they come.
Now, all they know is Spanish and if you don't they will vanish;
Well, now, all they know is Spanish when they come.

According to the *Los Angeles Times,* the song's lyrics were punctuated with the words *tortillas, Taco Bell, qué pasa,* and *Frito-Lay,* and officials at radio station KS-103 thought the song "provided cute commentary about the problems of illegal immigration and drug trafficking." The Mexican-American community was indignant, and the ditty was pulled off the air after listeners complained of its offensive message.

In spite of physical hardship, psychological humiliation, and tragedy, Mexican immigrants continue to flow into the United States. Until economic conditions improve in Mexico (and other Latin American countries), immigration, both legal and "illegal," will continue to be a fact of life—and corridos and canciones no doubt will continue to record the phenomenon.

# Notes

## Introduction

1. See these works for an in-depth exposition: Vicente T. Mendoza, *El romance español y el corrido mexicano* (Mexico City: Ediciones de la Universidad Nacional Autónoma de México, 1939), and *Lírica narrativa de México* (Mexico City: Instituto de Investigaciones Estéticas, Universidad Nacional Autónoma de México, 1964); Américo Paredes, "The Mexican Corrido: Its Rise and Fall," in *Madstones and Twisters*, ed. Mody C. Boatright (Austin: Texas Folklore Society), 91–105; and Merle Simmons, "The Ancestry of Mexico's Corridos," *Journal of American Folklore* 76:1–15.

## 1. Cowboys and Outlaws

1. For a discussion of this issue, see Américo Paredes, *"With a Pistol in His Hand": A Border Song and Its Hero* (Austin: University of Texas Press, 1978); Arnoldo de León, *They Called Them Greasers: Anglo Attitudes toward Mexicans in Texas, 1821–1900* (Austin: University of Texas Press, 1983); Cecil Robinson, *Mexico and the Hispanic Southwest in American Literature* (Tucson: University of Arizona Press, 1977); and Raymund Paredes, "The Origins of Anti-Mexican Sentiment in the United States," in *New Directions in Chicano Scholarship*, ed. Ricardo Romo and Raymund Paredes (University of California, San Diego, 1978), 139–166, and "The Mexican Image in American Travel Literature," *New Mexico Historical Review* 52 (January 1977): 5–29.

2. Among the literary reworkings from the eighteenth century are Charles E. B. Howe, *Joaquín Murieta de Castillo;* Cincinnatus Hiner Miller, *California* (also known as *Joaquín*); Joseph E. Badger, *Joaquín, the Saddle King* (later redone by the fifteen-cent DeWitt Library as *Joaquín: The Claude Duval of California*, which in turn was published by the Echo Seves as *Joaquín: Or the Marauder of the Mine*); and Marcus A. Stewart, *Rosita: A California Tale*. Versions which appeared in the twentieth century include Charles Park, *A Plaything of the Gods: Life and Adventures of the Celebrated Sonoran Bandit Joaquín Murieta;* Joseph Gollomb, *Master Highwaymen;* Ernest Klette, *The Crimson Trail of Joaquín Murieta;* Walter Noble Burns, *The Robin Hood of El Dorado* (this version was freely adapted into a movie in 1936); and Samuel Anthony Peeples, *The Dream Ends in Fury. La Vida y Hazañas de Joaquín Murrieta (Life and Exploits of Joaquín Murrieta)* appeared in 1953. All this information appears in Ridge 1986:xxxv–xlviii). Margaret Williams, in her unpublished manuscript "Joaquin Murrieta," which is housed at the Huntington Library, provides the following bibliography obtained from Farquhar (1932):

> a. *The Life and Adventures of Joaquín Murieta, the Celebrated California Bandit*, by Yellow Bird (John R. Ridge). San Francisco, 1854.
> b. *Joaquín, the Mountain Robber: Or the Guerrilla of California*. Written for the *California Police Gazette* (chapters 3 and 4 in vol. 1, no. 2, July 16, 1854). San Francisco: Henri St. Clair & Co.

c. *A Dramatic Play Entitled Joaquín Murieta de Castillo, the Celebrated California Bandit.* In five acts. By Charles E. B. Howe. San Francisco: Commercial Book and Job Steam Printing Establishment, 1858.

d. *The Life of Joaquín Murieta, the Brigand Chief of California.* In *California Police Gazette* (vol. 1, nos. 34 to 43, September 3 to November 5, 1859).

e. *The Life of Joaquín Murieta, the Brigand Chief of California: Being a Complete History of His Life, from the Age of Sixteen to the Time of His Capture and Death at the Hands of Capt. Harry Love, in the Year 1853.* San Francisco: Published at the Office of the *California Police Gazette*, 1859.

f. *Joaquín (the Claude Duval of California); or, The Marauder of the Mines. A Romance Founded on Truth.* New York: Robert De Witt, Publisher, 1865.

g. *The Life and Adventures of Joaquín Murieta, the Brigand Chief of California. Killed by Captain Harry Love, in the year 1853. The third edition of this Work, comprising a complete History of the Desperado and his gang of Outlaws, and giving a detailed account of his most prominent act of Murder and Violence, and his Subsequent Capture and Death, together with the shooting and dispersion of his Band.* By the late John R. Ridge. San Francisco: Published by Fredrick MacCrellish and Co., "Alta California" Office, 1871.

h. *La Fiebre de Riquezas, Siete Años en California. Descubrimiento del Oro y Exploración de Sus Inmensos Filones, Historia Dramática en Vista de Datos Auténticos e Interesantes Relaciones de Los Más Célebres Viajeros.* Por Don Julio Nombela. Madrid, 1871.

i. *The Life and Adventures of Joaquín Murieta, the Celebrated California Bandit.* Third Edition. Revised and enlarged by the author, the late John R. Ridge. San Francisco: Fredrick MacCrellish and Co. Publishers, 1874.

j. *Joaquín, The Saddle King. A Romance of Murrieta's First Fight.* By Joseph E. Badger, Jr. New York: Beadle's Dime Library, vol. 12, no. 154, October 5, 1881.

k. *Joaquín, the Terrible. The True History of the Three Bitter Blows that Changed an Honest Man to a Merciless Demon.* By Joseph E. Badger, Jr. New York: Beadle's Dime Library, vol. 13, no. 165, December 21, 1881.

l. *Rosita, a California Tale.* By Marcus A. Stewart. San Jose: Mercury Steam Printing Company, 1882.

m. *El Bandido Chileno. Joaquín Murieta en California.* Por Roberto Hyenne. Traducido del Francés por C. M. Edición Illustrada. Santiago (Chile), 1906.

n. *El Bandido Chileno. Joaquín Murieta en California.* Por Roberto Hyenne. Edición Illustrada. Barcelona (and) México, n.d.

o. *El Caballero Chileno. Bandido en California. Unica y Verdadera Historia de Joaquín Murrieta.* Por el Profesor A. Cigar. Barcelona (España): Biblioteca Hércules, n.d.

p. *Vida y Aventuras del Más Célebre Bandido Sonorense Joaquín Murrieta. Sus Grandes Proezas en California.* 4a Edición. México: Ireneo Paz, 1908.

q. *Vida y Aventuras del Más Célebre Bandido Sonorense Joaquín Murrieta. Sus Grandes Proezas en California.* Quinta Edición. Los Angeles: O. Paz y Cia, 1919.

r. *Life and Adventures of the Celebrated Bandit Joaquín Murieta: His Exploits in the State of California.* Translated from the Spanish of Ireneo Paz by Frances P. Belle. Chicago: Regan Publishing Corporation, 1925.

s. *The History of Joaquín Murieta, the King of California Outlaws Whose Band Ravaged the State in the Early Fifties.* By John R. Ridge. Revised Edition. Hollister, Calif.: Evening Free Lance, 1927.

t. *The Robin Hood of El Dorado. The Saga of Joaquín Murrieta, Famous Outlaw of California's Age of Gold.* By Walter Noble Burns. New York: Coward McCann, Inc., 1932.

Additional citations given: Francis P. Farquhar, *Joaquín Murieta, Brigand Chief of California*, San Francisco: Grabhorn Press, 1932; Ernest Klette, *The Crimson Trail of Joaquín Murieta*, Los Angeles: Wetzell Publishing Company (Mason Library, Pomona College); Joaquín Miller, *Joaquín Miller's Poems*, San Francisco: Whitaker and Ray Company, 1915, vol. 2, 121, "Joaquín Murietta" (Mason Library, Pomona College).

Additional works on Joaquín Murieta include Enrique Bunster, *Chilenos en California* (Santiago, Chile: Editorial del Pacífico, 1972); Dane Coolidge, *Gringo Gold: A Story of Joaquín Murrieta the Bandit* (New York: Dutton, 1939); Joseph Henry Jackson, *Bad Company* (New York: Harcourt Brace, 1939); Frank Forest Latta, *Joaquín Murrieta and His Horse Gangs* (Santa Cruz, Calif.: Bear State Books, 1980): Remi Nadeau, *The Real Joaquín Murieta* (Corona del Mar, Calif.: Trans-Anglo Books, 1974); Samuel Anthony Peoples, *Dream Ends in Fury* (New York: Harper, 1949); Manuel Rojas, *Joaquín Murrieta, El Patrio: El "Far West" del México cercenado* (Mexicali: Baja California Government Offices, 1986); Edwin L. Sabine, *Wild Men of the Wild West* (Ayer Co. Publishers, n.d.); William B. Secrest, *Joaquin: Bloody Bandit of the Mother Lode* (Fresno, Calif.: Saga West, 1967); and William B. Secrest, *The Return of Joaquin* (Fresno, Calif.: Saga West, 1973).

## 2. Working and Traveling on the Railroad

1. See also Immigration Commission, *Reports of the Immigration Commission, Immigrants in Industries* (Washington, D.C.: Government Printing Office, 1911), pt. 25, 3:31 and Oscar Handlin, *Race and Nationality in American Life* (Boston: Little, Brown, 1948), 97–131. Reisler states that "the Dillingham Commisssion chaired by Senator William P. Dillingham of Vermont, was created by the Immigration Act of 1907 in order to postpone action on a literacy test measure." It produced a forty-two-page study of immigrants in the United States detailing the contrast between the "old" and "new" European immigrants (1976:17–18).

2. See also Victor S. Clark, "Mexican Labor in the United States," *Bulletin of the Bureau of Labor* 17 (September 1908): 497.

3. See also Samuel Bryan, "Mexican Immigrants in the United States," *Survey* 28 (September 12, 1912): 728.

4. Consult Ernestine M. Alvarado, "Mexican Immigration to the United States," *Proceedings of the National Conference of Social Work* (1920): 479.

## 6. The Bracero Program

1. *Agüita de arroz:* the phrase implies extreme poverty, since rice water is the cheapest food you can eat.

2. *Catrinas:* fancy, upperclass ladies.

3. *Le da de saz:* doesn't care

4. *Plaza del zacate:* a town square in San Antonio on Commerce Street.

5. *Buscón:* from the Spanish novel *El Buscón,* meaning a picaresque individual, a rogue.

6. *Andubo: anduvo.*

7. *Valle:* the Rio Grande Valley.

8. *Ficha lisa:* without money.

9. The sack used to pick cotton is quite heavy, especially when completely filled with cotton; thus picking cotton makes one bend over and look like a hook.

10. *Fierrada:* hard cash, money.

11. *El hueso:* work.

12. *Güera:* a light-skinned woman.

13. *Yompa:* from the English *jumper.*
14. *Te zumba:* you are very good at it.
15. *Grullos:* silver dollars.

## 8. Border-Crossing Strategies

1. A preliminary draft of this chapter was read at a conference, "La Frontera: Symbiotic Relationships on the U.S.-Mexico Border," held April 20–21, 1984, at Arizona State University, Tempe. I wish to thank Professor Jaime Rodríguez, Director of Mexico-Chicano Focus Research Project, Professor Eloy Rodríguez, Director International Chicanos Studies Center, and the Humanities Research and Travel Committee for their generous grants provided to undertake research on this project. See Paredes 1976, Taylor 1969, Herrera-Sobek 1979), and Gamio 1971.

2. For the present book, I have collected more than 150 immigrant songs.

3. See chap. 6.

4. The term *mojado* was used in a disparaging manner and vividly shows the hostility and low regard the general population had for these hardworking men and women. The Mexican press used the more neutral *espaldas mojadas,* a literal translation from the English, which did not carry the hostility and racial slur which the term *wetback* denoted.

5. This information was gleaned from various interviews conducted in 1982–1984. See Herrera-Sobek 1983.

# Bibliography

## Books and Articles

Arora, Shirley
    1977    *Proverbial Comparisons and Related Expressions in Mexican Spanish.* Berkeley: University of California Press.
Bancroft, Hubert Howe
    1888    *California Pastoral.* San Francisco: History Co.
    1890    *History of California,* vol. 7. San Francisco: History Co.
Bauman, Richard
    1977    *Verbal Art as Performance.* Rowley, Mass.: Newbury House.
Ben-Amos, Dan, and Goldstein, Kenneth, eds.
    1975    *Folklore: Performance and Communication.* The Hague: Mouton.
Boatright, Mody C.
    1946    *Mexican Border Ballads and Other Lore.* Austin: Southern University Press and Texas Folklore Society.
Burns, Walter Nobel
    1932    *The Robin Hood of El Dorado.* New York: Coward McCann.
Calavita, Kitty
    1983    "Employer Sanctions Legislation in the United States: Implications for Immigration Policy." In *America's New Immigration Law: Origins, Rationale and Potential Consequences,* ed. Wayne A. Cornelius and Ricardo Anzaldúa Montoya, 73–81. Center for U.S.-Mexican Studies, University of California, San Diego.
Camarillo, Albert
    1979    *Chicanos in a Changing Society: From Mexican Pueblos to American Barrios in Santa Barbara and Southern California, 1848–1930.* Cambridge, Mass.: Harvard University Press.
Cardoso, Lawrence A.
    1979    "Labor Emigration to the Southwest, 1916–1920: Mexican Attitudes and Policy." In *Mexican Workers in the United States: Historical and Political Perspectives,* ed. George C. Kiser and Martha Wood Kiser, 16–32. Albuquerque: New Mexico University Press.
Cardozo-Freeman, Inez
    1976    "The Corridos of Arnulfo Castillo." *Revista Chicano-Riqueña* 4, no. 4: 129–138.
Carreras de Velasco, Mercedes
    1974    *Los mexicanos que devolvió la crisis, 1929–1932.* Mexico City: Secretaría de Relaciones Exteriores.
Clements, George P.
    1929    "Mexican Immigration and Its Bearing on California's Agriculture." *California Citrograph* 15 (November): 3, 28–31.

Cornelius, Wayne A.
　1983　"Simpson-Mazzoli vs. the Realities of Mexican Immigration." In *America's New Immigration Law: Origins, Rationale, and Potential Consequences*, ed. Wayne A. Cornelius and Ricardo Anzaldúa Montoya, 129–149. Center for U.S.-Mexican Studies, University of California, San Diego.

Craig, Richard B.
　1971　*The Bracero Program: Interest Groups and Foreign Policy*. Austin: University of Texas Press.

Crawford, Remsen
　1930　"The Menace of Mexican Immigration." *Current History* 31 (February): 902–907.

Crow, John A.
　1980　*The Epic of Latin America*. Berkeley: University of California Press.

Del Castillo, Richard Griswold
　1984　*La Familia: Chicano Families in the Urban Southwest 1848 to the Present*. Notre Dame, Ind.: University of Notre Dame Press.

De León, Arnoldo
　1983　*They Called Them Greasers*. Austin: University of Texas Press.

Dobie, J. Frank, ed.
　1969　*Puro Mexicano*. Dallas: Southern Methodist University Press.

Downing, Theodore E.
　1979　"Explaining Migration in Mexico and Elsewhere." In *Migration across Frontiers: Mexico and the United States*. Albany: State University of New York, Institute for Mesoamerican Studies.

Dunne, John Gregory
　1967　*Delano*. New York: Farrar, Straus and Giroux.

Farquhar, Francis P.
　1932　*Joaquín Murieta, Brigand Chief of California*. San Francisco: Grabhorn Press.

Fogel, Walter
　1978　*Mexican Illegal Alien Workers in the United States*. Institute of Industrial Relations, University of California, Los Angeles.

Frantz, Joe B., and Julian Ernest Choate
　1955　*The American Cowboy: The Myth and the Reality*. Norman: University of Oklahoma Press.

Fuchs, Lawrence
　1983　"From Select Commission to Simpson-Mazzoli: The Making of America's New Immigration Law." In *America's New Immigration Law: Origins, Rationale, and Potential Consequences*, ed. Wayne A. Cornelius and Ricardo Anzaldúa Montoya, 43–50. Center for U.S.-Mexican Studies, University of California, San Diego.

Galarza, Ernesto
　1956　*Strangers in Our Fields*. Washington, D.C.: Joint U.S.-Mexican Trade Union Committee.
　1964　*Merchants of Labor: The Mexican Bracero Story*. Santa Barbara, Calif.: McNally and Loftin.

Gamboa, Erasmo
　1990　*Mexican Labor and World War II: Braceros in the Pacific Northwest, 1942–1947*. Austin: University of Texas Press.

Gamio, Manuel
　1971　*Mexican Immigration to the United States: A Study of Human Migration and Adjustment*. New York: Dover.

Giron, Nicole
    1976    *Heraclio Bernal: Bandolero, cacique o precursor de la revolución.* Mexico City: Instituto Nacional de Antropología e Historia, Departamento de Investigaciones Históricas.

Goodwyn, Frank
    1944    "Versos populares de los tejanos de habla española." *Anuario de la Sociedad Folkórica de México,* 5:415–433.

Hancock, Richard H.
    1959    *The Role of the Bracero in the Economic and Cultural Dynamics of Mexico: A Case Study of Chihuahua.* Stanford, Calif.: Hispanic American Society.

Herrera-Sobek, María
    1979    *The Bracero Experience: Elitelore versus Folklore.* Los Angeles: UCLA Latin American Center Publications.
    1980    "Verbal Play in Mexican Immigrant Jokes." *Southwest Folklore Journal* 4:14–22.
    1982    "The Acculturation Process of the Chicana in the Corrido." *De Colores: Journal of Chicano Expression and Thought* 6, nos. 1 and 2: 7–16. Also appears in Proceedings of the Pacific Coast Council of Latin American Studies 9:25–34.
    1983    "Crossing the Border: Three Case Studies of Mexican Immigrant Women in Orange County in the 1980s." In *Second Lives: The Contemporary Immigrant Refugee Experience in Orange County: The Shaping of a Multi-Ethnic Community,* ed. Valerie Smith and Michael Bigelow Dixon, 83–86. Costa Mesa, Calif.: South Coast Repertory, 1983.
    1984a   "Mexican Immigration and Petroleum: A Folklorist's Perspective." *New Scholar* 9:99–110.
    1984b   "The Undocumented Mexicana: Strategies Utilized in Crossing the U.S.-Mexican Border at San Ysidro, California." Manuscript.
    1991    "*Mica, Migra,* and *Coyotes*: Contemporary Issues in Mexican Immigrant Corridos and Canciones." In *Creative Ethnicity: Symbols and Strategies of Contemporary Ethnic Life,* ed. Stephen Stern and John Allan Cicala, 87–104. Logan: Utah State University Press.

Hobsbawn, Eric
    1981    *Bandits.* New York.

Hoffman, Abraham
    1973    "Stimulus to Repatriation: The 1931 Federal Deportation Drive and the Los Angeles Mexican Community." *Pacific Historical Review* 42 (May): 205–19.
    1974    *Unwanted Mexican Americans in the Great Depression: Repatriation Pressures, 1929–1939.* Tucson: University of Arizona Press.

Howe, Charles E. B.
    1858    *Joaquín Murieta de Castillo, the Celebrated California Bandit.* San Francisco: Commercial Book and Job Steam Printing Establishment.

Huerta, Jorge
    1982    *Chicano Theater: Themes and Forms.* Ypsilanti, Mich.: Bilingual Press/ Editorial Bilingüe.

Jones, Robert C.
    1945    *Mexican War Workers in the United States.* Washington, D.C.: Pan-American Union.

Kirstein, Peter N.
    1977    *Anglo over Bracero: A History of the Mexican Worker in the United States from Roosevelt to Nixon.* San Francisco: R and E Research Associates.

Klette, Ernest
N.d.    *The Crimson Trial of Joaquín Murieta.* Wetzell Publishing Co.
Levy, Jacques
1975    *César Chávez: Autobiography of La Causa.* New York: Norton.
Limón, José E.
1983    "Texas-Mexican Popular Music and Dancing: Some Notes on History and Symbolic Process." *Latin American Music Review* 4, no 2: 229–246.
1983    "The Rise, Fall, and 'Revival' of the Mexican-American Corrido: A Review Essay." *Studies in Latin American Popular Culture* 2:202–207.
1986    "Folklore, Social Conflict, and the United States–Mexico Border." In *Handbook of American Folklore,* ed. Richard M. Dorson, 216–222. Bloomington: Indiana University Press.
McLean, Robert N.
1929    "A Dike against Mexicans." *New Republic* (August 14): 334–37.
1932    "The Mexican Return." *Nation* (August 24): 165–166.
McNeil, Brownie
1946    "Corridos of the Mexican Border." In *Mexican Border and Other Lore,* ed. Mody Boatright, 1–34. Austin: Southern University Press and Texas Folklore Society.
McWilliams, Carey
1933    "Getting Rid of the Mexican." *American Mercury* (March 28): 322–324.
Mendoza, Vicente T.
1982    *La canción mexicana: Ensayo de clasificación y antropología.* Mexico City: Fondo de Cultura Económica.
Morales, Patricia
1982    *Indocumentados mexicanos.* Mexico City: Editorial Grijalbo.
Neruda, Pablo
1972    *Splendor and Death of Joaquín Murieta.* Trans. Ben Belitt. New York: Farrar Straus and Giroux.
Oppenheimer, Reuben
1932    "The Deportation Terror." *New Republic* (January 13): 231–234.
Pahissa, Angela Moyano
1987    *México y Estados Unidos: Orígenes de una relación 1819–1861.* Mexico City: Secretaría de Educación Pública.
Paredes, Américo
1966    "The Anglo-American in Mexican Folklore," In *New Voices in American Studies,* ed. Ray Browne, 113–127. Lafayette, Ind. Purdue University Press.
1976    *A Texas-Mexican "Cancionero": Folksongs of the Lower Border:* Urbana: University of Illinois Press.
1978    *"With a Pistol in His Hand": A Border Ballad and Its Hero.* Austin: University of Texas Press.
Paredes, Raymund
1977    "The Mexican Image in American Travel Literature." *New Mexico Historical Review* 52 (January 1977): 5–29.
1978    "The Origins of Anti-Mexican Sentiment in the United States." In *New Directions in Chicano Scholarship,* ed. Ricardo Romo and Raymund Paredes, 139–166. University of California, San Diego.
Peña, Manuel
1985    *The Texas-Mexican Conjunto: History of a Working-Class Music.* Austin: University of Texas Press.

Peón, Máximo
    1966     *Como viven los mexicanos en los Estados Unidos.* Mexico City: B. Costa-
             Amic.
Pitt, Leonard
    1966     *The Decline of the Californios: A Social History of the Spanish-Speaking
             Californians, 1846–1890.* Berkeley: University of California Press.
Radin, Paul
    1973     *The Trickster: A Study in American Indian Mythology.* New York: Schocken
             Books.
Reisler, Mark
    1976     *By the Sweat of Their Brow: Mexican Immigrant Labor in the United States,
             1900–1940.* Westport, Conn.: Greenwood Press.
Reyna, José R.
    1976     "Tejano Music as an Expression of Cultural Nationalism." *Revista Chica-
             no-Riqueña* 4:37–41.
Ridge, John Rollin (Yellow Bird)
    1986     *Joaquín Murieta.* Norman: University of Oklahoma Press.
Rivera, Tomás
    1971     *. . . Y no se lo tragó la tierra / . . . And the Earth Did Not Part.* Berkeley,
             Calif.: Quinto Sol Publications.
Robe, Stanley
    1977     *Hispanic Folktales from New Mexico.* Berkeley: University of California
             Press.
Rojas, Arnold
    1958     *Lore of the California Vaquero.* Fresno, Calif.: Academy Literary Guild.
Rojas, Manuel
    1986     *Joaquín Murrieta: "Patrio".* Mexicali: Gobierno del Estado de Baja Cali-
             fornia.
Romo, Ricardo
    1983     *East Los Angeles: History of a Barrio.* Austin: University of Texas Press,
             1983.
Rosenbaum, Robert J.
    1986     *Mexicano Resistance in the Southwest: The Sacred Right of Self-Preservation.*
             Austin: University of Texas Press.
Ross, Stanley R.
    1984     "Mexican Petroleum Policy and the United States." *New Scholar* 9:249–
             256.
Samora, Julian
    1971     *Los Mojados: The Wetback Story.* Notre Dame, Ind.: University of Notre
             Dame Press.
Simmons, Merle E.
    1953     "Attitudes toward the United States Revealed in Mexican Corridos."
             *Hispania* 361:34–42.
Sonnichsen, Phillip
    1975     "Texas-Mexican Border Music." Vols. 2 and 3 Corridos part 1 and 2,
             Linear Notes. Berkeley, Calif.: Folklyric LP9004.
Taylor, Paul S.
    1969     "Songs of the Mexican Migration." In *Puro Mexicano,* ed. J. Frank Dobie,
             234–237. Dallas: Southern Methodist University Press.
United States Executive Agreement Series 278
    1943     *Temporary Migration of Mexican Agricultural Workers.* Washington, D.C.:
             Government Printing Office.

Valdés, Dennis Nodín
    1988    *Al Norte: Agricultural Workers in the Great Lakes Region, 1917–1970.* Austin: University of Texas Press.
Williams, Margaret
    1935    "Joaquín Murrieta." MS. in Huntington Library, San Marino, Calif.
Zurhorst, Charles
    1973    *The First Cowboys and Those Who Followed.* New York: Abelard-Schuman.

## Major Corrido Collections

Arellano, Anselmo
    1976    *Los pobladores nuevo mexicanos y su poesía 1889–1950.* Albuquerque, N.M.: Pajarito Publications.
Austin, Mary
    1919    "New Mexico Folk Poetry." *El Palacio* 7:146–154.
Bonfil, Alicia O.
    1970    *La literatura cristera.* Mexico City: Instituto Nacional de Antropología e Historia.
    1976    *Corridos de la Rebelión Cristera: La Cristiada.* Vol. 20. Linear Notes, Instituto Nacional de Antropología e Historia, LP MC-0780, INAH-20, Mexico city.
Calleja, Julián
    1951–1967    *Método de guitarra sin maestro.* Mexico City: El Libro Español. Various editions.
Campa, Arthur Leon
    1946    *Spanish Folk-Poetry in New Mexico.* Albuquerque: University of New Mexico Press.
Campos, Armando de María y
    1962    *La revolución mexicana a través de los corridos populares.* 2 vols. Mexico City: Biblioteca Nacional de Estudios Históricos de la Revolución Mexicana.
Campos, Rubén
    1929    *El folklore literario de México.* Mexico City.
    1974    *El folklore literario y musical de México.* Mexico City: Secretaría de Obras y Servicios, Colección Metropolitana.
*Cancionero mexicano.*
    1979–1980.    2 vols. Mexico City: Libro-Mex Editores.
*Canciones de México: 200 joyas de la canción mexicana.*
    N.d.    Guadalajara: Dibujos Musicales "Ambríz."
Castañeda, Daniel
    1943    *El corrido mexicano: Su técnica literaria y musical.* Mexico City: Biblioteca Nacional.
Colín, Mario
    1948    *Corridos de Texcaltitlán.* Toluca: H. Ayuntamiento de Texcaltitlán.
    1952    *Corridos populares del estado de México.* Mexico City.
*Corridos mexicanos*
    1975    Mexico City: Colección Adelita.
    1984    Mexico City: Gómez Hnos. Editores.
De Grial, Hugo
    1977    *Músicos mexicanos.* Mexico City: Editorial Diana.
Dickey, Dan Williams
    1978    *The Kennedy Corridos: A Study of the Ballads of a Mexican-American Hero.* Center for Mexican-American Studies, University of Texas, Austin.

Esparza Sánchez, Cuauhtémoc
    1976     *El corrido zacatecano*. Mexico City: Instituto Nacional de Antropología e
             Historia.
Espinosa, Aurelio Macedonio
    1953     *Romancero de Nuevo Méjico*. Madrid: Consejo Superior de Investigaciones
             Científicas.
Fuentes, Rumel
    1977     *14 corridos chicanos de Rumel*. Mimeographed booklet.
Gamio Manuel
    1971     *Mexican Immigration to the United States: A Study of Human Migration and
             Adjustment*. New York: Dover.
Gómez Maganda, Alejandro
    1970     *Corridos y cantares de la Revolución Mexicana*. Mexico City: Instituto
             Mexicano de Cultura.
González, Jovita
    1930     "Tales and Songs of the Texas-Mexicans." In *Man, Bird and Beast*, ed. J.
             Frank Dobie, 86–116. Austin: Publications of the Texas Folk-lore Soci-
             ety.
Guerrero, Eduardo
    N.d.     Collection of corridos in Biblioteca Nacional de México, Mexico City.
    1924a    *Canciones y corridos populares*. 2 vols. Mexico City: Publicados
             por Eduardo Guerrero. Collection of *hojas sueltas* in Biblioteca Na-
             cional.
    1924b    *Corridos mexicanos*. Collection of *hojas sueltas* in Biblioteca Nacional.
    1931     *Corridos históricos de la revolución mexicana desde 1910 a 1930 y otros
             notables de varias épocas*. Mexico City: Eduardo Guerrero Collection at
             Biblioteca Nacional.
Henestrosa, Andrés
    1977     *Espuma y flor de corridos mexicanos*. Mexico City: Editorial Porrúa.
Hernández, Guillermo
    1978     *Canciones de la Raza: Songs of the Chicano Experience*. Berkeley, Calif.: El
             Fuego de Aztlán.
Herrera Frimont, Celestino
    1934     *Los corridos de la revolución*. Pachuca, Hidalgo: Ediciones del Instituto
             Científico y Literario.
Herrera-Sobek, María
    1979     *The Bracero Experience: Elitelore versus Folklore*. Los Angeles: UCLA Latin
             American Center Publications.
Kuri-Aldana, Mario, and Vicente Mendoza Martínez
    1990     *Cancionero popular mexicano*. 2 vols. Mexico City: Dirección General de
             Culturas Populares.
*Libro de oro de la canción: Canciones populares desde 1850 hasta 1953*
    1952     Ed. Fernando de Aragón. Mexico City. 2d ed. published 1953 by Medi-
             na Hermanos 3d ed. n.d.
*Libro de oro de la poesía mexicana*
    1957     Vol. 2. Mexico City: Libro Mex Editores.
Lucero-White, Aurora Lea
    1953     *Literary Folklore of the Hispanic Southwest*. San Antonio, Tex.: Naylor.
*Mejores corridos mexicanos, Los*
    1972     Mexico City: El Libro Español.
    N.d.     Mexico City: Janibi Editores, Album de oro método de guitarra series no.
             9.

Melgarejo Vivanco, José Luis
   N.d.    *"Juan Pirulero" y otros corridos.* Mexico City: Biblioteca Nacional de México.

Mendoza, Daniel
   1978    *Batallas de la Revolución y sus corridos.* Mexico City: Editorial Porrúa.

Mendoza, Vicente T.
   1939    *El romance español y el corrido mexicano.* Mexico City: Ediciones de la Universidad Nacional Autónoma de México.
   1944    *50 corridos mexicanos.* Mexico City: Ediciones de la Secretaría Pública.
   1954    *El corrido mexicano.* Mexico City: Fondo de Cultura Económica.
   1956    *Panorama de la música tradicional de México.* Mexico City: Imprenta Universitaria.
   1964    *Lírica narrative de México.* Mexico City: Instituto de Investigaciones Estéticas, Universidad Nacional Autónoma de México.
   1976    *El corrido mexicano.* Mexico City: Fondo de Cultura Económica.
   1982    *La canción mexicana: Ensayo de clasificación y antología.* Mexico City: Fondo de Cultura Económica.

Mendoza, Vicente T., and Virginia R. R. de Mendoza
   1986    *Estudio y clasificación de la música tradicional hispánica de Nuevo Mexico.* Mexico City: Universidad Nacional Autónoma de México.

Menéndez Pidal, Ramón
   1939    *Los romances de América y otros estudios.*

Paredes, Américo
   1976    *A Texas-Mexican "Cancionero": Folksongs of the Lower Border.* Urbana: University of Illinois Press.
   1978    *"With a Pistol in His Hand": A Border Ballad and Its Hero.* Austin: University of Texas Press.

Pérez Martinez, Hector
   1935    *Trayectoria de corrido.* Mexico City.
*Poesías patrióticas y folklóricas y los corridos de la revolución.*
   1976    Mexico City: Editores Mexicanos Unidos.

Posada, José Guadalupe
   1977    *Las calaveras vivientes de Posada.* Mexico City: Editorial Cosmos-César Macazaga Ordoño.

Prieto Posada, Margarita
   1944    *Del rabel a la guitarra: El corrido mexicano como un derivado del romance español.* Mexico City.

Romero Flores,
   1979    *Corridos de la revolución mexicana.* Mexico City: Costa-Amic Editores.

Sánchez Juárez, Delfín
   1977    *Poemas y corridos.* Mexico City: Manuel Porrúa.

Serrano Martínez, Celedonio
   1973    *El corrido mexicano no deriva del romance español.* Mexico City: Centro Cultural Guerrerence.

Simmons, Merle
   1957    *The Mexican Corrido as a Source of an Interpretive Study of Modern Mexico (1870–1950).* Bloomington: Indiana University Press.

Stanford, Thomas E.
   1974    *El villiancio y el corrido mexicano.* Mexico City: Instituto Nacional de Antropología e Historia.

Taylor, Paul S.
   1969    "Songs of the Mexican Migration." In *Puro Mexicano,* ed. J. Frank Dobie, 221–245. Dallas: Southern Methodist University Press.

Vázquez Santa Ana, Higinio
    N.d.    *Canciones, cantares y corridos mexicanos.* Mexico City: Ediciones León
            Sánchez.
Vélez, Gilberto, ed.
    1982    *Corridos mexicanos.* Mexico City: Editores Mexicanos

## Songs

"Adiós México querido"
    Molina, Juan José. In Vélez 1982:62.
"Ahi viene la migra"
    *Corridos norteños.* Recorded by Ramón Ayala and Los Bravos de El Norte.
    Freddie Records FR-1318.
"Los alambrados"
    Solís, Antonio Marcos. *Los alambrados.* Recorded by Los Bukis. Mexicana
    Records MM 6625 (1977).
"De los ambiciosos patones"
    Guerrero, 1924b.
"La amnistía"
    Gutiérrez, R. M. Sung by Hermanos Ortiz. Discos Latin Internacional DLI-209-
    A.
"Amor norteño"
    Buendía, Rafael. In *Cancionero mexicano* 1:86.
"De aquellas idas al norte"
    Castillo, Dagoberto. *Corridos norteños.* Sung by Dueto Castillo. Audiomex 093.
"Arriba raza"
    In Vélez 1982:62.
"Los betabeleros"
    In Gamio 1971:86–88.
"La bode fatal"
    Camacho, Paco. In Vélez 1982:65–66.
"La bracera"
    Navarrete, Estevan. Recorded by Los Paisanos del Norte. Anáhuac AN-1048.
"El bracero"
    Buendía, Rafael. *Corazón engrandecido.* Sung by Dueto Frontera. Discos Musart
    T-10762 (1979).
"De bracero a petrolero"
    Díaz, Melesio. Discos CBS Internacional DML-20469 (1980).
"El burro norteño"
    González, Eulalio ("El Piporro"). In Calleja, 66.
"De California te escribo"
    Cantú, José Luz Alamís. Sung by Antonio Aguilar. Discos Musart ED-1729
    (1977).
"Canción del interior"
    In Taylor 1969:231–232.
"2ª Canción del interior"
    In Guerrero 1924b.
"Canto al bracero"
    Méndez, Rubén. In *Cancionero mexicano* 1:189.
"La carita tapada"
    Aladaiz, Oscar Curiel. Sung by Los Reniegos del Norte (de San Luis Río
    Colorado, Sonora). Discos Mayra.

"La chicanita"
  Lara Benavídez, Catarino. Sung by Los Sagitarios. Discos Olympico Records
  05218 (1980).
"Al chicano"
  Zaizar, Juan. In Vélez 1982:68.
"El chicano"
  Zalazar, Juan. *El chicano.* Sung by Dueto América. Caliente CLT 7107.
"Chulas fronteras"
  González, Eulalio ("El Piporro"). *Ajúa con "El Piporro."* Gas Records 4081.
"Ciriaco el mojado"
  Padrón, Gil García. Sung by "La Migra." Mar International Records MILP 133
  (1982).
"Concha la mojada"
  Pesqueda, Ernesto. Discos CBS Internacional DML-20686 (1983).
"Consejos a los norteños"
  In Guerrero 1924a, vol. 1.
"El contrabando del muerto"
  Buendía, Rafael. In Vélez 1982:67.
"Contribución a las pelonas."
  *Canciones y corridos populares.* In Guerrero 1924b.
"Corrido de César Chávez"
  Guerrero, Lalo. *Las voces de los campesinos.* FMSC-1 (1976).
"El corrido de César Chávez"
  García, Francisco, and Pablo and Juanita Saludado *Las voces de los campesinos.*
  FMSC-1 (1976).
"Corrido de inmigración"
  In Guerrero 1931. Also in Taylor 1969.
"Corrido de Joaquín Murieta"
  *Texas-Mexican Border Music,* vol. 2: *Corridos,* pt. 1. Folklyric Records 9004.
"Corrido de Kansas"
  In McNeil 1946:1–34.
"Corrido de la causa"
  García, Francisco, and Pablo and Juanita Saludado *Las voces de los campesinos.*
  FMSC-1 (1976).
"Corrido de la emigración"
  In Taylor, 1969:234–235.
"Corrido de la triste situación"
  Leiva, León. In Guerrero 1931.
"Corrido del campesino"
  Carrera, José Luis. *Corridos y canciones de Aztlán.* Xalman SBSR 102980-B
  (1980).
"El corrido del chicano mexicano"
  Fajardo, Ramón. *Corridos y canciones de Aztlán.* Xalman SBSR 102980-B (1980).
"El corrido del ilegal"
  *Las voces de los campesinos.* Recorded by Francisco García and Pablo and Juanita
  Saludado. FM SC-1.
"Corrido del inmigrante"
  In Vélez 1982:61–62.
"Corrido de los desarraigados"
  Arnulfo Castillo. In Cardozo-Freeman 1976:132.
"Corrido de los mexicanos enganchados" ("La Pensilvania")
  In Campos 1962, vol. 2: 329–330.

"El corrido de los mojados"
    Armenta, Luis. Grever Internacional (1976).
"Corrido del petróleo"
    In Campos 1962, vol. 2: 462–463.
"El corrido del Rancho Sespe"
    Toledo, Don Jesús. *Corridos y canciones de Aztlán*. Xalman SBSR 102980-B
    (1980).
"Corrido de Pennsylvania"
    In Guerrero 1931. Also in Paredes 1976:56–57.
"Corrido de Texas"
    In Taylor 1969:227–228.
"Cruzando el puente"
    Hernández, R. *Cruzando el puente*. Recorded by Los Cadetes de Linares. Ramex
    LP 1014 (1977).
"Al cruzar la frontera"
    Velarde, Eladio J. In *Cancionero mexicano* 1:51.
"Los que cruzaron"
    In *Los mejores corridos mexicanos*, 40.
"La cucaracha mojada"
    Cuéllar, Luis. In Vélez 1982:64.
"Defensa de los norteños"
    In Guerrero 1924a. Also in Taylor 1969:238–240.
"Dejé mi amor allá en el Norte"
    Coronel, Isidro. Sung by Felipe Arriaga. Caytronics CYS 1544 (1979).
"El deportado"
    Acuña, Aciano. *Los grandes corridos*. Sung by Los Terribles del Norte. Freddie
    Records FRC-1534 (1990).
"Los deportados"
    In Taylor 1969:236–237.
"La descriminación"
    Pérez, Juan Manuel, and Leobardo Pérez. *De México a Laredo*. Sung by Dueto
    América. Caliente CLT 7242 (1977).
"Desde México he venido"
    In Paredes 1976:162–163.
"Desde el México de afuera"
    Flores, José Vaca. *Desde México de afuera*. Sung by Las Hermanas Huerta. Discos
    CBS International DBL-20310 (1980).
"Desde Morelia"
    In Vélez 1982:62.
"Despedida! De Karnes City, Texas"
    Roque, V. E. In Carreras de Velasco 1974:111.
"Despedida de los reenganchados"
    In Prieto Posada 1944:109.
"Despedida de un norteño"
    In Taylor 1969:222-224.
"A dos dólares la hora"
    In Vélez 1982:65.
"Dos pasajes"
    In Vélez 1982:65.
"Efectos de la crisis"
    In Taylor 1969:232–233.

"A El Paso"
    Ríos, Mario. In Vélez 1982:63.
"La emigración"
    In Hernández 1978:36–40.
"La emigrada"
    Hernández, Francisco. Discos Arpeggio ARP-1008 (1981).
"El emigrado"
    Abrego, Eugenio. *Alegres de Terán*. Sung by Los Alegres de Terán. Falcón
    Records Series 5000, FLP-5034.
"El emigrante"
    *Los grandes corridos*. Sung by Los Terribles del Norte. Freddie Records (1990).
"De 'El interior' o 'Los enganchados' "
    In Mendoza 1964:38.
"De 'El traque' o de 'El lavaplatos' "
    In Mendoza 1964:376.
"El ferrocarril"
    In Gamio 1971:92–93.
"From a Border Zarzuela"
    In Paredes 1976:166–167.
"Frontera internacional"
    Valencia, Enrique. Sung by Los Tigres del Norte. Discos FAMA FA-1730-B.
"Fronteras del Río Bravo"
    Sánchez Mota, Benjamín. In *Cancionero mexicano* 1:483–484.
"Gana el güero y el pollero"
    Rosales, Magdaleno. In Vélez 1982:64.
"El gringo y el mexicano"
    Salas, Adolfo. *En la plaza Garibaldi*. Sung by Los Tigres del Norte. Discos FAMA
    FA-594 (1980).
"El hijo olvidado"
    Acuña, Aciano. Sung by Los Terribles del Norte. Freddie Records FRC-1534
    (1990).
"Los hijos de Hernández"
    *Gracias! América . . . sin fronteras*. Sung by Los Tigres del Norte. Profono
    Internacional PRC-90499 (1986).
"Los ilegales"
    Gavilán, Pepé. Sung by Los Ilegales. Crusoni Records CS-106-A (1977).
"Los inmigrantes"
    In Gamio 1971:84–86.
"Jacinto Pérez de la O"
    Figueroa, José Manuel. *Son tus perjúmenes mujer*. Recorded by Los Alvarado.
    Pronto PTX 1032 (1978).
"La jaula de oro"
    *Jaula de oro*. Sung by Los Tigres del Norte. Profono Internacional PRC-90408
    (1984).
"Juan Mojao"
    González, Eulalio ("El Piporro"). *A Lo Piporro*. Discos Musart TEDM 10656
    (1977).
"Kiansis I"
    In Paredes 1976:53–54.
"Kiansis II"
    In Paredes 1976:55.
"De 'La maquinita' o de 'El emigrado' "
    In Mendoza 1964:383.

"Lamento de un bracero"
  Camacho, Paco. *Soy inocente*. Recorded by Antonio Aguilar. Discos Musart
  EDM 1700 (1976).
"Llegada de buques americanos a Tampico"
  In Guerrero 1924b.
"Los mandados"
  Lerma, Jorge. Recorded by Vicente Fernández. CBS 8065 (1978).
"Me voy a California"
  Villagómez, A. *Amor*. Sung by Los Coyotes del Río Bravo. A-133.
"Me voy a Texas"
  Villagómez, A. *Amor*. Sung by Los Coyotes del Río Bravo. A-133.
"Me voy de California"
  Flores, Emilio. Sung by Los Rinches del Sur. Discos Arpeggio A-001-B (1978).
"Me voy pa'l Norte"
  Esquivel, Manuel. In *Libro de oro de la canción*, 64. Also sung by Dueto América,
  Caliente CLT 7107.
"Mexicano cien por ciento"
  Luna Records LULP 1083 (1982).
"Los mexicanos que hablan inglés"
  In Paredes 1976:164.
"México americano"
  Fuentes, Rumel. In Fuentes 1977:31–32.
"Mi Micaela"
  De Anda, Guillermo. Profono Internacional 45-79-063. (1981). Also in movie
  *Mojado Power*.
"La migra"
  Fuentes, Rumel. In Fuentes 1977:6.
"El mojado"
  Unzueta, M. *Corridos y canciones de Aztlán*. Xalman SBSR 102980-B (1980).
"El mojado fracasado"
  Torres, Salomón Valenzuela. Recorded by Los Alazanes. Discos Cronos LRCR-
  1093 (1977).
"El mojado remojado"
  De Anda, Guillermo. Profono Internacional 45-79-063 (1981).
"Muchachas modernas"
  *Número ocho*. Sung by Los Tigres del Norte. FAMA-564 (1978).
"Mucho me gusta mi novia"
  In Paredes 1976:167.
"La de la nagua azul"
  In Gamio 1971:90–91.
"Natalio Reyes Colás"
  González, Eulalio. *Lo mejor del Piporro*. Discos Musart DC 787.
"Un noble engaño"
  Ochoa, Nicolás, and Paul Sandoval. Recorded by Los Huracanes del Norte.
  Luna Records LULP-1083 (1982).
"No necesito coyote"
  Zermeño, Jesús. Sung by Los Errantes del Valle. Luna Records L-278-B (1981).
"Los norteños"
  In Guerrero 1924a.
"Los norteños" ("Corrido vacilador")
  Saul, Nomelazo. In Guerrero 1924a.
"La nueva Zenaida"
  *Corridos famosos: Contrabando y traición*. Tex-Mex Records TMLP-7021 (1975).

"La opinión de unas gringas"
    Bermúdez, Bulmaro. Arcano Records DKLI-3459-B (1979).
"Oro verde por oro negro"
    Ollúa, Pedro. Sung by Los Errantes del Valle. Luna Records L-278-A (1981).
"El padre del Charro Vargas"
    In Gamio 1971:94–96.
"Pancho Martínez"
    Rosales, Rigoberto. In Vélez 1982:65–66.
"Los paños colorados"
    In Gamio 1971:89.
"Paso del Norte"
    Morena de ojos negros. Sung by Los Gavilanes del Norte. Discomex LPDM-516.
"La patera (Juana La Patera)"
    Oliva, Magdaleno. Sung by Rosenda Bernal. Odeón MST-24312 (1979).
"El peligro de la intervención americana"
    In Guerrero 1924b.
"Las pelonas vaciladoras"
    In Guerrero 1924a.
"La Pensilvania"
    In Campos 1962:329–330.
"El petróleo (ahora sí)"
    Franco, Enrique. Exitos de 1979. Discos Cronos LP CR1138 (1979).
"Plática entre dos rancheros"
    In Taylor 1969:241–245.
"Las pobres ilegales"
    Loza, José Martínez. Sung by Yolanda del Río. Arcano Records DKLI-5608.
"La pochita"
    Hernández, R. In Calleja 1963:134.
"El pocho"
    González, Eulalio ("El Piporro"). In Ajúa con "El Piporro." Gas Records 4081 (1973).
"Las pollas de California"
    In Guerrero 1924b.
"Por el puente"
    In Vélez 1982:63.
"Las puntadas de Canuto en la pizca de algodón"
    In Goodwyn 1944:416–419.
"Los que cruzaron"
    Cordero, Víctor. In Los mejores corridos mexicanos 1972:40.
"Los que vuelven"
    In Calleja 1973.
"Radios y chicanos 1 and 2"
    In Hernández 1978:30–32.
"Ramón Delgado"
    In Hernández 1978:16–18.
"El rancho donde yo nací"
    In Hernández 1978:20–22.
"Recordando a México"
    Buendía, Rafael. In Corridos mexicanos 1984:67.
"Las redadas"
    Prieto, Juan. Sung by Los Alegres de Terán. Caytronics Cy 8195 (1976).
"Los reenganchos a Kansas"
    In McNeil 1946:11–13.

"Rejuego de las pelonas"
  In Guerrero 1924a.
"El renegado"
  In Gamio 1971:93–94.
"Los repatriados"
  In Calleja 1956:75–76.
"La restrinción del azúcar"
  Ortiz, Bartolo. In Goodwyn 1944:430–433.
"Rumbo al Norte"
  Enciso, J., and A. Gastelum. Fiesta Records FIE-611 (n.d.).
"De sangre mexicana"
  Trujillo, Francisco. Arcano Records DKLI-3459-A (1979).
"Superman es ilegal"
  Lerma, Jorge. *10 Exitos de los Hermanos Ortiz.* Profono Internacional PI 3088 (1982).
"Tanto tienes, tanto vales"
  Botello, Pablo. *Corridos y canciones de Aztlán.* Xalman SBSR 102980-B (1980).
"En estos tiempos modernos"
  In Hernández 1978:30–32.
"Tierras de California"
  Paredes, Pascuala. Peerless M/S 2067 (1978).
"De las tres que vienen ai"
  In Taylor 1969:221–245.
"La tumba del mojado"
  Vargas, Paulino. *Internacional norteños!* Sung by Los Tigres del Norte. Golondrina Estereo LPG 103121.
"Uno más de los mojados"
  Figueroa, José Manuel. *La muerte de un gallero.* Recorded by Antonio Aguilar. Discos Musart ED 1721.
"Vacilada algodonera"
  In Goodwyn 1944:419–422.
"El vagón de la muerte"
  In the movie *El vagón de la muerte.* Mexico City: Eco Films (1987).
"Vamos a cruzar, Julián"
  Valdez Patiño, Juana. In Vélez 1982:63.
"Versos de los betabeleros"
  In Goodwyn 1944:422–423.
"Versos de los enganchados"
  In Goodwyn 1944:423–424.
"Del viaje de la típica de policia a California"
  In Mendoza 1964:396.
"Vida, proceso, y muerte de Aurelio Pompa"
  In Gamio 1971:104–107.
"Vivan los mojados"
  Armenta, Luis. In Vélez 1982:61.
"Voy a cruzar la frontera"
  Villa, J., and J. Maldonado. *El Palomo y El Gorrión.* DLV USA 2003 (1975).
"Ya nos dieron permiso"
  Armenta, Jesús. *Número ocho.* Sung by Los Tigres del Norte. Discos FAMA-564 (1978).
"Yo soy mexicano señores"
  Valdovinos, Juan Manuel. *Corridos y canciones de Aztlán.* Xalman SBSR 102980-B (1980).

# Index

Abrego, Eugenio: composer of corrido, 128–29

Acculturation: Mexican concern over in 1920s, 106–21; Mexican attitudes toward deportees in 1930s, 137; theme of in "Natalio Reyes Colás," 170; of women in corridos, 279–90; of men in corridos, 290–91; of children in corridos, 291–96. *See also* Assimilation; Culture

Acuña, Aciano: composer of corridos, 293–94, 295

"Adiós, México querido" ("Good-bye, My Beloved Mexico"): patriotic love, 257

Agriculture: peasant societies and social banditry, 12; Mexican workers and immigration laws during World War I, 37; Mexican workers during Great Depression, 38, 125–26; Mexican workers during World War II, 38–39, 147–51; corridos and Mexican workers in 1920s, 91–94; social justice movements of 1960s and unions, 177–79; corridos and unions, 180–86

*Agringados:* as pejorative term for Americanized Mexican immigrants, 279

"Ahi viene la migra" ("Here Comes the Border Patrol"): illegal aliens and border patrol, 211–12

*Alambrado:* origins and use of term, xvii

"Los alambrados" ("The Wire Jumpers"): illegal aliens and border-crossing strategies, 198–99

Alamís Cantú, José Luz: composer of corrido, 255–56

Los Alegres de Terán: recording of "El emigrado," 128

Amnesty program: U.S. policy on Mexican immigration, xvii; as political issue for undocumented workers, 250–53

"La amnistia" ("The Amnesty"): undocumented workers and amnesty program, 251–52

"Amor norteño" ("Northern Love"): depiction of "Latin lover," 275

*Annual Report of the Commission-General of Immigration* (1911): railroads and Mexican labor, 35

"De aquellas idas al Norte" ("Those Trips to the North"): theme of brokenhearted bracero, 271–72

Arizona: desert and illegal aliens, 214

Armenta, Jesús: composer of corrido, 252–53

Armenta, Luis: composer of corrido, 196

Assimilation: Mexican-American population in World War II and postwar era, 150. *See also* Acculturation

Atchison, Topeka, and Santa Fe Railroad: employment of Mexican workers, 41

Ballads: image of train as motif in twentieth-century immigrant, 49–50. *See also* Corridos; Folk songs

Bancroft, Hubert Howe: fictionalized accounts of Murieta legend, 21, 25, 26

*Barrios:* growth of in early twentieth century, xx, 89. *See also* Community, Mexican-American

Beet sugar industry: Mexican immigrant labor, 93–94

Bell, Horace: Murieta as revolutionary, 26

Benavídez, Catarino Lana: composer of corrido, 264

Bermúdez, Bulmaro: composer of corrido, 237, 239–40

Bethlehem Steel Company: recruitment of Mexican workers, 94

"La boda fatal" ("The Fatal Wedding"): romantic love and betrayal, 269–70

*Bola:* early form of satirical corrido, 282

Border patrol: advice in corrido on, 135; illegal aliens and conflict with in corridos, 189–90, 206–214. *See also* Immigration and Naturalization Service

Botello, Pablo: composer of corrido, 234–36

"La bracera" ("The Bracera"): marriage and legal resident status, 194–95

"El bracero" ("The Bracero"): illegal aliens and border-crossing strategies, 199–200; economic need as reason for emigration, 236

"De bracero a petrolero" ("From Bracero to Oil Rigger"): petroleum and optimism about future of Mexico, 248–49

Bracero program: World War II and U.S. need for Mexican labor, xvii; information on experience from studies of, 147–51; corridos from 1942–1964 period, 164–74; increased efforts at union organization

*María Herrera-Sobek,* Professor
of Spanish and Portuguese at the University of California, Irvine, is author of *The Mexican Corrido: A
Feminist Analysis, The Bracero Experience: Elitelore versus Folklore, Beyond Stereotypes: The Critical Analysis of
Chicana Literature, Reconstructing a Chicano/a Literary
Heritage: Hispanic Colonial Literature of the Southwest,*
and *Gender and Print Culture: New Perspectives on International Ballad Studies.* She is co-author of *Saga de
México* and *Chicana Creativity and Criticism: Charting
New Frontiers in American Literature,* and is one of
three poets featured in the anthology *Three Times a
Woman.*

A

A'